EDUCATION
FOR LIBERATION

Readings from
An
Ideological Perspective

Edited by

NORMAND R. BERNIER

University of Wisconsin–Milwaukee

and

JACK E. WILLIAMS

University of Wisconsin–Milwaukee

PRENTICE-HALL, INC., Englewood Cliffs, N.J.

Library of Congress Cataloging in Publication Data

BERNIER, NORMAND R comp.
   Education for liberation.

    1. Education—Philosophy.   2. Education—United
States.   3. Education and state—United States.
I. Williams, Jack E., joint comp.   II. Title.
LB7.B47   370.1   72-11989
ISBN 0-13-238956-8
ISBN 0-13-238949-5 (pbk)

© 1973 by Prentice-Hall, Inc.
Englewood Cliffs, New Jersey

Printed in the United States of America

10 9 8 7 6 5 4 3 2 1

Prentice-Hall International, Inc., *London*
Prentice-Hall of Australia, Pty. Ltd., *Sydney*
Prentice-Hall of Canada, Ltd., *Toronto*
Prentice-Hall of India Private Limited, *New Delhi*
Prentice-Hall of Japan, Inc., *Tokyo*

CONTENTS

PREFACE   ix

Introduction
THE IDEOLOGICAL PERSPECTIVE   1

Part I
SCIENTISM   15

Introduction, 15

An Analytical View: A Brief Survey

The Scientific Outlook: Naturalism and Humanism, *Herbert Feigl,* 18

The Creed: Scientific Admonitions

The Intellectual Qualifications of the Good Scientist, A. *Cornelius Benjamin,* 30

Representative Expressions: An Historical Perspective

1. The Principles of Teaching Based on Psychology, *Edward L. Thorndike,* 34
2. Forecast for the Seventies, *Harold G. Shane* and *June Grant Shane,* 42

Pedagogical Model: The Teacher as Behavior Modifier

The Science of Learning and the Art of Teaching, *B. F. Skinner,* 49

Part II
ROMANTICISM   61

Introduction, 61

An Analytical View: A Brief Survey

The Diogenes Style, *Kingley Widmer,* 65

The Creed: Romantic Admonitions

1. Proverbs of Hell, *William Blake,* 74
2. Revolution for the Hell of It, *Abbie Hoffman,* 77

Representative Expressions: An Historical Perspective

1. Emile, *Jean Jacques Rousseau,* 79
2. Education, *Ralph Waldo Emerson,* 82
3. Eyes of Flesh, Eyes of Fire, *Theodore Roszak,* 84

Pedagogical Model: The Teacher as an Artist

Fascination: A Phenomenological Perspective of Independent Learning, *Sidney M. Jourard,* 89

Part III
PURITANISM   101

Introduction, 101

An Analytical View: A Brief Survey

The Moral Athlete, *Ralph Barton Perry,* 105

The Creed: Puritan Admonitions

1. The Revolution of the Saints, *Michael Walzer,* 119
2. British and American Scout Oath (Promise) and Law, 121
3. The Code of the Good American, *Character Education Institution of Washington, D.C.,* 126

Representative Expressions: An Historical Perspective

1. Bonifacius: An Essay upon the Good, *Cotton Mather,* 131
2. The Autobiography, *Benjamin Franklin,* 136
3. Eclectic Fourth Reader, *William Holmes McGuffey, ed.,* 138
4. The Challenge of Facts, *William Graham Sumner,* 145
   The Concentration of Wealth: Its Economic Justification,
   The Independent, 148
   The Abolition of Poverty, *The Independent,* 149
5. Wealth, *Andrew Carnegie,* 149

Pedagogical Model: The Teacher as Moral Exemplar

The Education of Character, *Martin Buber,* 153

Part IV
NATIONALISM   161

Introduction, 161

An Analytical View: A Brief Survey

Ideology and the American Way of Life, *Yehoshua Arieli,* 165

The Creed: National Admonition

    1. The Declaration of Independence, *Thomas Jefferson*, 175
    2. The American's Creed, *William Tyler Page*, 178

Representative Expressions, An Historical Perspective—The Issue of National Cohesion

    1. The Melting Pot Outlook
       a. *J. Hector St. John de Crevecoeur*, 179
       b. *Israel Zangwill*, 181
       c. *The United States Supreme Court*, 181
    2. The Cultural Diversity Outlook
       a. *John Dewey*, 186
       b. *Stokely Carmichael* and *Charles V. Hamilton*, 190

Pedagogical Model: The People as Teacher

    Technical and Social Qualifications of the Ruler-Teacher, *George A. Coe*, 196

Part V
PROGRESSIVISM   201

    Introduction, 201

An Analytical View: A Brief Survey

    The California Progressive and His Rationale: A Study in Middle Class Politics, *George E. Mowry*, 205

The Creed: Progressivist Admonitions

    My Pedagogic Creed, *John Dewey*, 214

Representative Expressions: An Historical Perspective

    1. "New Articles of Faith," *Harold Rugg* and *Ann Schumaker*, 220
    2. Dare the Schools Build a New Social Order?, *George S. Counts*, 227
    3. Report of the National Conference on Life Adjustment Education (Prosser Resolution), 232
    4. Open v. Closed Classrooms, *Mario D. Fantini*, 236

Pedagogical Model: The Teacher as Facilitator

    1. Check Your Inquiry-Teaching Technique, *Mary Sugrue* and *Jo A. Sweeney*, 243
    2. What is Team Teaching?, *J. Lloyd Trump*, 246

Part VI
EDUCATIONISM   253

    Introduction, 253

An Analytical View: A Brief Survey

Faith in Education, *V. T. Thayer* and *Martin Levit,* 258

The Creed: Educationist Admonitions

Code of Ethics, *National Education Association,* 269

Representative Expressions: An Historical Perspective

1. Twelfth Annual Report on Education (1848), 273
2. Theory and Practice of Teaching: Or, The Motives and Methods of Good School-Keeping, *David Page,* 279
3. Cardinal Principles of Secondary Education, 282
4. Industrial Education for the Negro, *Booker T. Washington,* 284
5. The Talented Tenth, *W. E. B. DuBois,* 287
6. Plessy v. Ferguson, *U.S. Supreme Court,* 291
7. Plessy v. Ferguson, *Justice Harlan dissenting,* 297
8. Collective Negotiations and Professionalism, *Donald L. Conrad,* 300

Pedagogical Model: The Teacher as Professional

"Public and Professional Decisions," *Myron Lieberman,* 305

PREFACE

This anthology is presented with some degree of reservation, for the editors are vividly aware that the educational marketplace has been deluged recently by a niagara of books composed of articles dealing with the educational endeavor. Many of these readers offer similar perspectives and often include common articles. Consequently, we did not want to add "just another reader."

The reader deserves a few comments concerning our reasoning in presenting this compilation. First, the collection emerged from our research on an accompanying textbook entitled, *Beyond Beliefs: Ideological Foundations of American Education.* Indeed, some of the articles included served as valuable resources in our development of an ideological approach to analyzing American education. Second, and more importantly, in utilizing the ideological approach to unravel the bases of American education in our Social Foundations of Education courses, we were confronted continuously by students who desired to read materials that *reflected* the ideologies discussed. Our students agreed with us that analyzing the thematic emphases in documents written by ideologists served not only to clarify but also to add spice and sometimes humor to the intellectually demanding task of unraveling ideological structures.

This anthology differs significantly from other books of readings which focus upon the educational enterprise. The subject matter for analysis—ideologies and their influence on education—has not been approached previously in the thematic manner presented here. Indeed, the ideological basis of education has not been explored adequately in the past and needs extensive further research. Because of the peculiar emphasis of this anthology, many of the articles presented have not been included in previous readers concerning American education.

This reader also differs from others in its basic emphasis. In most cases, readers focus upon educational aims or educational issues. In the former case they provide a philosophical—sometimes idealized and ethereal—approach to schooling whereas in the latter case they often reflect the volatile and cynical perspective that accompanies the reaction to a particular crisis. Although these views are valuable, they often fail to add the important link between theory and practice, between ideals and reality.

The ideological perspective furnishes a framework which permits us to examine both theoretical idealized constructs and practical realities. Ideologies bind ideals to realities, theories to practice, cognition to affection, and traditions to aspirations.

In all societies, especially literate ones, belief systems serve as a major social cement. In the United States the ideological matrix labeled Americanism provides a complex belief system which serves to channel thought, perception, and language, and, consequently, the behavior of Americans.

The educational endeavor and the changes which are occurring within schools reflect ideological patterns and adjustments. Understanding schooling practices as well as the nature of educational change requires that individuals acquaint themselves with materials that analyze ideological forces. Ideologies not only influence the nature of schooling but also define the perimeter in which it must operate.

Each section of this collection focuses upon a particular ideological subsystem within the ideological matrix labeled Americanism. The ideological threads analyzed are (I) Scientism, (II) Romanticism, (III) Puritanism, (IV) Nationalism, (V) Progressivism, and (VI) Educationism. In each case we begin our selection with a brief introduction in which we attempt to identify some of the key concepts and themes which characterize the particular ideological subsystem. After each introduction comes an article by a scholar who analyzes some of the ideological emphases to be found in the articles which follow. This article is *about* the ideology and not an expression of it. It should serve as a *porte-cochère* to the articles which follow and which actually *exemplify* and *express* the ideological bent of their writers.

We have attempted to select articles that reflect historical antecedent conditions as well as current realities. These articles are written by ideologists and reflect their commitment to a particular belief system. Our aim is to illustrate diverse ideological emphases and to provide the reader with examples of their expression. We have not attempted to counterbalance supportive articles with conflicting or debunking ones, but it is our hope that the reader will analyze the ideologies critically, noting elements of diversity and congruency. The reader should become cognizant of the fact that each ideology has strengths and weaknesses, humanizing and dehumanizing characteristics.

Each section concludes with the direct educational expression of the ideological thrust analyzed. Thus the focus is upon the perception of the role of the teacher. For Scientism the teacher's role is that of behavior modifier; for Romanticism, that of artist; for Puritanism, that of moral exemplar; for Nationalism, that of patriot; for Progressivism, that of facilitator; and for Educationism, that of professional.

The title of this anthology reflects our intent in compiling these articles. By assisting the reader in unraveling the sometimes mysterious forces which guide the educational enterprise, we hope that it will enhance his ability to challenge outmoded practices and to effectively implement innovation in his teaching and in his school. Liberation implies that individuals understand the forces that effect them and thus can choose to accept, ignore, reject, or nullify them. Understanding ideological pressures ensures that forces which can *determine* individual behavior can be controlled by human beings and thus become merely *influences*. Free men are influenced by their environment, enslaved ones are defined and shackled by it. Ideological forces are chains which can be broken by the ideological explorer. Liberation awaits those who search courageously through the net of ideological threads which forms the social religion of his neighbors. Such an exploration, one may well hope, will enhance his humanness. Before human beings can accept their differences they must first become aware of them. With the understanding and acceptance of ideological pluralism, the road toward intranational concord and international peace is less hazardous and more promising.

Introduction

THE IDEOLOGICAL
PERSPECTIVE

Animals with complex brains require an extended period of dependency upon adults during their infancy. The human being is such a creature. The children of man, unlike most newborn creatures, do not possess the necessary instinctive *savoir-faire* to ensure their survival. They require a social environment and the care of adults for a lengthy period after their birth. Indeed, the human gestation phase can be accurately described as extending beyond birth into infancy, for a newborn child left to fend for himself would soon die. The survival of the human species rests upon man's ability to create and sustain social groupings in which newborn infants can be protected while learning the human ways.

Similarly, human adults throughout man's evolutionary journey would not have overcome the incredible odds against their survival if they had not banded together. Besides providing collective protection against an extremely hostile environment, such unity also ensured that knowledge gained in one generation by some creative individuals could be transmitted to others. Such accumulation of knowledge served as a wellspring for human survival. Synthesizing, storing, and transmitting knowledge have served as the major tools in the human survival kit. Without these socially rooted functions, human beings would have been overcome easily by numerous other animal creatures who possess remarkably well developed instinctive and physiologically specialized mechanisms for survival.

Besides furnishing man with the physical necessities for his protection and survival, his social groupings also provide him with the emotional, aesthetic, and spiritual stimuli needed for his growth and happiness. It is within social settings that *homo sapiens* is humanized. Man's arts, religions, and philosophical propositions gain their relevancy from the fact that he is a social animal. It is through the historical continuity of his groups that man becomes aware of the immortality of his aspirations and deeds.

Although man possesses a gregarious instinct, he also is capable of antisocial behavior. Even though man's individual and social qualities cannot be separated, individuals throughout history have revealed a remarkable ability to withstand the social pressures for conformity and order. Man is capable of anarchical behavior and is not totally predictable.

Because social groupings cannot depend upon man's instincts for their survival—for humans distinguish between existence and living—various mechanisms have been devised to preserve social cohesion and to control human perfidy and irrationality. Some of these techniques of social control have been based upon overt threat and physical oppression; others have elicited love and freely given loyalty. Current research reveals an inordinate interest in the use of chemical agents and genetic manipulation as means of preserving social order. These "solutions," however, are similar to increases in police power and force, for they exemplify a failure of social systems to obtain the freely given loyalty of the individuals who compose them.

Generally, the most central and important community in man's life is the social unit which encompasses his immediate human environment. It is within groups in which individuals have face-to-face contact that they grow from instinctual dependent beings into independent thinking and empathizing persons. Thus an individual's family, clan, gang, commune, or neighborhood have served as the major source of the humanization process. When these social groupings fail to facilitate the expression of human potential, irreparable psychological damage may result. Such face-to-face groupings are often extremely cohesive and serve as the primary object of an individual's loyalty. Larger social groupings which are characterized by cohesiveness either are supported by primary groupings or have neutralized them.

Within primary groupings the love between and among individuals often serves as the major bond or social cement. Social cohesion, however, depends upon the "we-feeling" of a collective identity. Such a community is characterized by clearly defined role expectations within a system of reciprocal relationships and by a belief that the group is an essential part of individual identity and is necessary for survival and happiness. Common and shared experiences serve to increase the interdependence of individuals within such communities.

Man's early history was characterized by simple, cohesive, and homogeneous groupings. The limitations imposed upon human beings by their underdeveloped technical skills necessitated that they group themselves into relatively small social units. Neolithic man, for example, had not developed the skills which could form a technical base to support a large group of individuals. Agricultural skills were simple, and thus the productivity of the land was limited. Thus, neolithic villages rarely if ever exceeded fifty households. Within such a limited social environment, individuals were socialized and acculturated through a process of sharing common experiences. They often developed intense loyalty for their group and for the members of their group. In some cases they viewed "foreigners" as barbarians, or even nonhuman, and participated in diverse forms of collective defense and aggression which in turn enhanced the we-feeling and the sense of interdependence.

In small, isolated, and primitive communities, the shared ways of life far exceeded the specialized interests of occupational or social groupings. Cultural homogeneity served as a major social cement. In such social groupings, education and socialization processes were informal and indistinguishable from the daily life of the people. The neophytes of primitive social systems learned by observing and imitating the behavioral patterns of appropriate elders. The tribal elders, therefore, served as teachers without portfolio. They performed their tasks and fulfilled their role expectations and thus served as exemplars for the children and youth. Learning by the young resulted from the natural focus of their attention rather than from explicit teaching by the adults. Primitive societies, therefore, had teachers but no schools. The social system's rules, norms, and behavioral expectations were taught implicitly and informally. Major cultural assumptions were rarely if ever questioned. As such groups grew in size, cultural homogeneity as well as political hegemony served as the major cement for their unity.

As man's social systems became more complex and extended, formal schooling gradually assumed the task of teaching the cultural universals and alternatives. Although formal schooling did not play any significant part in primitive societies, the rudiments of schooling can be discovered in such social systems. Because specialization requires in-depth analysis, formal curricula were devised through varied apprenticeship systems to prepare specialists in various realms of activity ranging from the art of mumification to the science of princely behavior. Although the cultural universals and alternatives were learned largely through observation, imitation, and performance, fields of specialization were deliberately taught. As civilizations became more complex, the formal educational function was expanded. The ancient Spartans and Israelites, for example, organized formal schooling to train and educate the young according to the dictates of their cultures. The former trained their young to reflect the militaristic and puritanical patterns of their culture, while the latter focused upon historical traditions and a rich religious heritage.

As human beings developed their technical and social skills, they increasingly subdued the physical environment and extended the complexity and size of social systems. Face-to-face contact continued to play a major role in the socialization process, but the socialization that resulted did not always reflect the cultural assumptions of the total society as cultural homogeneity increasingly was replaced by ethnic pluralism. Cultural diffusion, increased occupational specialization, conquest, migration, and socioeconomic differentiation as well as literacy served to decrease cultural similarity. Acculturation and politicization could no longer be left to chance for provincialism and ethnic localism could easily destroy the stability of extended political groupings. For this reason secular educational institutions were developed in order to deliberately socialize and politicize the young and the newly arrived by migration, territorial expansion, or conquest. In extended, complex, multiethnic political groupings, the family and the neighborhood could not be relied upon to fulfill the acculturation process for their emphases were invariably provincial and parochial; thus public formal schooling became a *sine qua non* of national cohesion in such multi-ethnic secular nation-states, and formal educational agencies as well as mass media increasingly were utilized in the process of socializing and politicizing the children and youth.

The emergence of national consciousness in Western Europe in the eighteenth and nineteenth centuries began a struggle between national groupings for control over the lives of individuals. With the breakdown of the primacy of religious identity and the demise of the remnants of the Holy Roman Empire, national provincialism became the major focus of political action.

The age of Nationalism witnessed the emergence of two major types of national grouping which have continued to influence twentieth-century man. Political groupings—that is, nation-states—which are based upon citizenship identity and which in turn are the basis of modernization and secularization, vie with cultural groupings—that is, nationalities —which are rooted to ethnic kinship, for the loyalty of individuals.

The myth of cultural unity in modern nation-states has been effectively perpetuated. In the large multi-ethnic nation-states such as the Soviet Union and the United States, the myth of emerging cultural homogeneity has been rooted to the belief that cultural differences were being moderated and that emerging cultural universals would bind the peoples in the future. In the United States the concept of a "melting pot" has been extensively utilized (though rarely analyzed) to describe a process whereby all ethnic groups divest themselves of their traditional and nonAmerican cultures and eventually melt into the American cauldron to produce a new man—a mongrel labeled an American. Over the course of American history the cauldron has been variously located on the frontier, in the large urban centers and in the public school system.

While generations of Americans basked in the belief that the American cauldron was forming a new man, actual social practices revealed that America was analogous to a tossed salad—a salad in which the Anglo-Saxon cauliflower remained dominant and intact. Segregated schools, for example, were designed to ensure that the major races would not melt into one. Similarly, housing patterns, employment practices, and the socioeconomic class structure all served to inhibit the emergence of cultural homogeneity. Similarly, ghettoism and sectionalism ensured that intranational differences would remain—which, indeed they have done. In the 1960s these carefully preserved differences became major disruptive forces and they continue to cast ominous clouds across the land.

Of course, schools and other socialization agencies served to moderate some of these cultural differences and succeeded partially in ensuring that most Americans learned one of the American English dialects. Similarly, the mass media has served to homogenize the taste of Americans by tempting and taunting them with images of "ideal" types who behave according to Madison Avenue precepts and who wallow in consumption.

Although the call for the preservation of cultural differences is rarely heard in the halls of assimilative agencies of the national and state governments, the fact remains that ethnic pluralism continues to characterize most nation-states and that the past decade reveals an upsurge in the demand for the preservation of cultural pluralism. In one sense this demand appears to be atavistic, for the forces of modernization seem to be leveling cultural differences under the steamroller of technological advancement. Because of the increasing technocratization of modern life brought about by modernization and the secularization, political identification, centralization, and bureaucratization that follow in its wake, cultural differences have become less discernible among the affluent classes in the various technologically advanced nation-states. Despite markedly different cultural antecedents, a Soviet technocrat has more in common with an American technocrat than with a peasant from his own nation-state. Individuals who spend their working hours supporting similar technological robots develop similar perspectives. Indeed, the countervailing political ideologies of the two countries reveal an unmistakable *rapprochement* necessitated by the imperatives of technological advancement.

Even though cultural homogeneity appears to be taking root in large nation-states and between nation-states among peoples in the "middle classes," such a process generally reveals the influence of technological imperatives rather than the deliberate attempts of social agencies to design uniform cultural frameworks. Indeed, the socialization processes that result from technological imperatives often appear to negate overt attempts to politicize individuals according to archaic political ideologies.

Significant cultural differences continue to exist among and within nation-states. The differences, however, reveal themselves when comparing the so-called technologically "underdeveloped" with the technologically "advanced" nation-states and when comparing the poor with the more affluent social classes. The fact that socioeconomic differences reflect ethnic stratification indicates the extent to which antecedent cultural patterns and racial identity were at the basis of the previous social order. Even though such ethnic and cultural stratification increasingly is denounced by enlightened political leaders, the fact remains that cultural pluralism not only has been preserved but has been utilized to pervert the American dream.

The nineteenth and twentieth centuries witnessed a continuous struggle between political and cultural nationalists. While cultural nationalists invariably have sought to win autonomy for their cultural or ethnic group from the overriding political nation-state, political nationalists have struggled to yoke together various cultural strains in a unified political nation-state. Because of numerous factors, not the least of which are the close relationships between modernization and political identity, and military power and citizenry, political communities generally have succeeded in withstanding the secessionist demands of cultural minorities. Thus nation-states such as Northern Ireland, the United States, Nigeria, and the Soviet Union, for example, have withstood the secessionist demands of some of their citizens. Pakistan, however, was unable to preserve its political cohesion when the Bengali nationality declared its political autonomy and established the nation-state labeled Bangladesh.

Because public schools are agencies directly or indirectly responsible to the citizenries which support them financially, they invariably have been assigned the task of acculturating the young. And because acculturation within multi-ethnic nation-states implies selection, schools have focused upon particular cultural elements which reflect the life style of the majority *or* dominant group. Conversely, most private schools, religious and otherwise, as well as nieghborhood ethnic community houses, often have served as agencies for the development of ethnic pluralism despite the fact that their official policy is to support the ideals of the nation-states in which they are situated.

In spite of the popularity of the view that political national groupings should be culturally unified, cultural homogeneity is rarely if ever the basis for national political cohesion. The fear that cultural pluralism will result in the demise of nation-states is largely the result of propaganda generated by homogeneity buffs. Unity need not require similarity. Indeed, diversity is supposedly an implicit source of strength in a democracy.

Rarely have nationalities and citizenries been coterminous. Indeed, in such cohesive communities as Spain and Great Britain, cultural pluralism has flourished or at least persisted for centuries. Such intranational cultural differences often are viewed as quaint relics of the past and as colorful expressions of localism, but they can become the cause of social discontent and political activism when they are utilized as the basis of the socioeconomic class structure. Ethnic and racial pluralism is *not* a cause of political unrest, but narrow-minded and/or vicious individuals who utilize such differences as the basis of a socioeconomic hierarchy invariably succeed in turning these differences into sources of conflict. The problem rests with the perception of the differences and not with the differences themselves.

Of course, ethnicity is often international in design. Nation-states such as North and South Korea, North and South Vietnam, East and West Germany, the United States, and Canada include nationals who can be viewed as culturally tied to more than one nation-state. Their cultural similarities, however, do not serve to overcome the political differences that separate them.

Ethnicity is able to serve as a major social bond in some situations because when people *believe* they share a culture, such a sharing becomes an important fact of life for them. Although most nation-states are not characterized by cultural unity, the *belief* in cultural homogeneity does serve to preserve social cohesion in certain cases. On the other hand, it may serve as a divisive element if the mythic nature of this homogeneity is unveiled by circumstances. Thus in searching for the cement which has preserved the unity and order within modern nation-states, *belief systems* rather than cultural patterns should be analyzed. Indeed, belief systems rather than cultural elements may serve as the major element which preserves unity within political or social organizations composed of ethnically similar peoples. And again the same converse applies: namely, that belief systems may serve to divide peoples who share similar cultural perspectives. In short, belief systems are among the most powerful forces affecting social cohesion either positively or negatively; they can support the cohesion that comes from a common culture and can override cultural differences to create cohesion where there was none, but under different circumstances they can tear asunder cultural bonds and turn ethnic brothers into enemies.

Belief systems, or ideologies, bind the peoples within nation-states and serve to distinguish them from individuals within other nation-states regardless of their particular cultural identity, life style, socioeconomic class, or occupational group.[1] Ideologies, for example, serve to provide citizens suffering from economic deprivation with a view of the world that is similar in many aspects to the views expressed by their wealthy fellow nationals. Thus, most Americans in the United States share relatively similar perspectives about the American Revolutionary War, progress, technological advancement, man's ability to conquer his environment, and the ideals of liberty and equality of opportunity.

National ideological systems are complex and delicate; they can be rent by intranational discord. Despite the fact that ideological systems may be destructive to national unity, the fact remains that massive political systems which are characterized by literacy and modernization depend upon shared belief systems for the preservation of social order.

Ideologies are the social religions of man. They are belief systems which are shared by individuals within a society and which serves to provide them with a "we-feeling" and a sense of participation in the social system. Ideologies create communities of identity and communities of purpose. Because ideologies are based upon perceived social realities and because they emerge from the historical experience of social systems, they do not express the orderly, systematic view of life which characterizes philosophical systems. In addition, ideologies include highly emotive symbolism and complex language patterns that prevent the kind of simplistic analysis that characterizes many "scientific studies."

Inasmuch as ideologies focus primarily upon the social experience of man, they differ from cultures, which encompass the total aspect of man's existence. Ideological systems may extend beyond cultural groupings or they may be encompassed by them. Ideological and cultural communities are two major elements of man's group identification.

Ideologies include ideas, attitudes, beliefs, myths, truths, falsehoods, hopes, justifications, goals, traditions, and symbols. Because they are rooted to the social experience of man they are perpetually changing and cannot be logically ordered. When analyzed they reveal remarkable inconsistencies and often present sets of configurations which are presented as true but which are mutually exclusive.

The language of an individual or group is inextricably interwoven with its ideological systems. In relatively homogeneous communities the problem of communication is minimized by the fact that social experiences are quite similar. In terms of language, members of such com-

---

[1] Of course, some ideologies are not national in design and may serve to bind individuals regardless of national identity. Roman Catholicism and Marxism, for example, are international ideologies which transcend national boundaries. The fact that they have been nationalized, however, reveals the centrality of national ideological perspectives in the twentieth century.

munities seldom distinguish between denotative and connotative factors involved in word usage. In more complex, heterogeneous social systems, howver, such a distinction does exist and is of major significance in the analysis of ideologies. Indeed, an awareness of language complexity is essential for communication in such social contexts. It should be noted, however, that the ability to communicate necessitates understanding, not necessarily agreement.

Different ideologies may share words but not meanings. Adherents to Scientism and Romanticism, for example, both value artist-teachers, yet they strongly disagree about who in fact is an artist teacher. Similarly, Puritans and Romanticists emphasize freedom and individualism, but quarrel vehemently about the meaning of these terms. Disagreements between individuals and/or groups concerning the meaning of words are not "simply a matter of semantics"; nor can they be resolved by resorting to a dictionary. Inasmuch as language represents thought patterns and is inherently colored by ideological systems, an analysis of language must be accompanied by an awareness of ideological differences. For the person who lacks a concern for ideological implications, words remain abstract and vague; ideologies enhance words by giving them meaning and specificity.

Belief systems differ in their complexity and in their flexibility. Flexible and complex ideologies tend to disintegrate because they easily become diffused; conversely, static and simple ideological configurations often cannot withstand the pressures imposed by rapid change and are doomed to be replaced by emerging "relevant" ideologies. Thus ideological systems must remain functionally flexible, and at the same time must retain sufficient cohesiveness to serve as an anchorage for individuals to utilize in their daily lives. A central ideological issue, therefore, is the ability of a belief system to achieve a degree of cohesiveness while presenting a view of reality which can be altered to meet the needs imposed by rapid change.

Ideologies also differ in specificity. Some provide individuals with a comprehensive *Weltanschauung*, a world view, while others serve primarily as a justifying rationale for a particular social movement or political program.

When they are effective, ideological systems present a view of reality which individuals who adhere to them accept as the only valid way of perceiving reality. They force compliance and serve as an internal gyroscope which ensures that individuals within social systems will perceive the world in "acceptable ways." Inasmuch as ideologies often assume a sacred countenance, individuals who deviate from the ideological framework adhered to by their neighbors are liable to be judged as criminal, heretical, or insane. When elevated to this sacrosanct status, ideologies become ends rather than means, and as soon as this happens they are destructive to human life. Although some ideologies are more humane than others (e.g., Progressivism is more humanistic than Racism), all ideologies which have become self-justifying ends support fanatics in their inquisitions and "witch hunts." History sadly reveals that in the name of love and brotherhood human beings have put one another to death.

Ideologies serve as a mechanism to ensure that members of a group will perceive events in a similar fashion. Thus, when ideological systems are working effectively, guidance counselors and policemen are not needed to ensure that most individuals will behave in acceptable fashion. Effective ideological systems provide an anchorage for individual perception, rooting it to the norms which regulate the society. When ideological systems collapse, however, external threat and physical force may be the only effective means to ensure compliance to social norms and rules. The recent ferment in most of the nation-states that have undergone rapid technological change results in the obsolescence of many ideological systems, which in turn results in anomic societies populated by alienated individuals. Ideological systems offer individuals a basis from which to make value choices, but the collapse of a society's ideological anchorage deprives its citizens of a referent for moral choice. Consequently they experience anxiety.

Ideologies may serve as a creative and inspirational force, and it is generally within ideological systems that individuals find the source for their commitment and the guide to their behavior. Serving as a wellspring for human creative energies, ideological systems have inspired such individuals as Jefferson, Beethoven, St. Theresa, Dylan Thomas, Mao Tse-Tung, and Eleanor Roosevelt. Indeed, ideologies are as pervasive as cultures and the deeds performed by human beings, especially in literate societies, cannot be understood except within the context of ideological systems.

The ideological system labeled Americanism contains numerous ideological subsystems or strands. During periods of intranational stability—which are often the result of some real or imagined "foreign threat"—the various ideological subsystems are combined within the national ideological fabric and are not distinguishable one from another. Thus, during the American Revolutionary War, during the era following independence when nation-building was a shared task, and during World War II, the American ideological fabric presented a rather smooth and united surface. National slogans, national heroes, and national ideals combined with a sense of national destiny and served to inspire a belief in Americanism and to cement the society. Such cohesive and integrated ideological patterns characterize most recently emerged nation-states.

Thus the People's Republic of China and Cuba under Castro are characterized by simplistic ideological systems that unite their peoples and that visitors find impressive but often conformist and bland.

National cohesion often rests upon the ever-present slogans which reflect the ideals adhered to by the peoples within a nation-state. During periods of intranational discontent, such as the United States is experiencing as a result of an unpopular war (a war not perceived to be threatening to the average American) and racial inequalities, the national ideology begins to show wear and tear and the various ideological threads increasingly disentangle themselves. During such a period of time individuals are often forced to make ideological choices which previously had not appeared to be significant. Similarly, in large technological societies which have achieved a plateau of nation-building, the ideological fabric undergoes some alterations, especially when rapid technological change further weakens the validity and reliability of the prevailing ideological system. The threads or subsystems which compose it become more apparent and ideological differences are enhanced. Thus fellow nationals are faced with ever-increasing ideological differences as various subnational ideological communities begin to emerge. Such ideological pluralism is often confused with cultural pluralism and emerging ideological subsystems are inaccurately labeled "countercultures," a term which implies more permanent change.

The ideological matrix termed Americanism contains numerous strands. Noteworthy among them are (1) Scientism, (2) Romanticism, (3) Puritanism, (4) Nationalism, (5) Progressivism, and (6) Educationism—the ideologies focused upon in this anthology. These ideological subsystems are not the only belief systems that influence Americans, but they have been singled out for attention here because they have profoundly influenced American life and the nature of emerging educational patterns. They also promise to be the major ideological emphases of the coming decade.

The reader is cautioned to avoid assuming that some of these ideologies are inherently defective and that others are inherently benevolent in their effect. All of them possess qualities which are humanizing and supportive of man's creativity. Similarly, when driven to excess, they are all destructive to individuality and to social order. Although some ideologies within the American belief system are inherently destructive (e.g. racism), the six ideological systems analyzed in this anthology are all capable of enhancing man's human qualities.

The importance of these ideological systems as well as their interrelationships with each other should be emphasized. Scientism, with its emphasis upon the technological control of human life as a means of improving human existence, portends to become increasingly powerful as man improves his ability to alter his own genetic composition and to control his consciousness chemically. As an ideological system, Scientism provides the fundamental elements for an ever-increasing technocratization of society and serves as a powerful force in channeling human perceptions. Consequently, ideologies that emphasize subjectivity and mysticism are being disregarded while Scientism with its focus upon predictability, objectivity, and rational manipulation continues to gain prestige.

Obviously, the future of Scientism is bright. The burgeoning technostructure with its demand for social planning and its promises of increased affluence offers an irresistible avenue for the further popularization of Scientism. Such achievements as human organ transplants and moon landings have been emphasized and widely advertised as irrefutable evidence for the necessity of further expanding the ideological perspective of Scientism.

Because of the bland exigencies imposed by the ideology of Scientism, however, the less methodological individuals within the massive technological system increasingly have asserted their hunger for psychic liberation from the predictable world of objective consciousness. As in all eras when the "rational ordering" of life becomes excessive, a countervailing ideology emerges to challenge Scientism. This countervailing force, Romanticism, has served as a major ideological expression of man's inner drive to assert his individuality and to nullify some of the social controls which channel his behavior.

The terms "Establishment" and "counterculture" have been popularized in the previous decade to refer, respectively to the collective adherents of Scientism and of Romanticism. Although the terms may change, the fact that all social systems reveal the pull and tug between these two ideological antinomies is a reality. In the coming decade, the United States no doubt will witness further developments in the ideological conflict. Schools will be the center of the conflict, for Romanticism is the ideology of the young but the schools have been designed to reflect the ideals of Scientism.

Puritanism, the ideology of transition, has always played a major role in the ideational configuration of Americans. Indeed, with its emphasis upon work, self-reliance, social responsibility, and commitment, it has served as a major force in ensuring that the task of building the "Great Republic" would continue. Although Puritanism invariably declines during periods of affluence and social stability, and thus is waning as an influential ideology, it remains latent in social systems and emerges rapidly whenever individuals and social orders encounter crises and doubts. Certainly it is an ideology worthy of exploration, for its influence is ever present in the educational system.

Progressivism has emerged as an ancillary force of Scientism. Essentially a conservative ideology, it functions to develop a form of social cohesion based upon individual and/or group participation. Despite the fact that Progressivism is not inconsistent with the needs generated by technological systems, it serves to moderate the dehumanizing forces exerted by rigid Puritanism and unleashed Scientism. Both Progressivism and Puritanism have been major ideological influences upon public schooling in America. Where Puritanism emphasizes competitive individualism and the role of the teacher as a moral exemplar, Progressivism focuses upon group cooperation and places the teacher in the role of facilitator. During the past decade Progressivism has reasserted itself in American education. Numerous "recent innovations"—such as the "open classroom," "team teaching," "community schools," and "student-designed curricula"—are experiments that have had their counterpart in previous progressive periods in American education.

Nationalism, of course, is a major ideological strand in the twentieth century. It has served to unite nation-states politically as well as to provide a rationale for unifying ethnic minorities. It is an ideology which presently functions as the core of most ideological systems. Indeed, the fact that most ideological systems are transnational has been obscured as a result of the pervasiveness of Nationalism. A nonnational ideology such as Puritanism, for example, is nationalized whenever it becomes the prime ideology in nations going through revolutionary political upheavals and/or the process of nation-building. Thus in Communist China the virtues associated with Puritanism are promoted as though they were specifically Chinese virtues.

In recent years Nationalism increasingly has taken on cultural dimensions. Although political Nationalism (the ideology that legitimizes and sustains political communities) continues to dominate the world order, romantic Nationalism (the Nationalism that relates to ethnic identity) has increasingly asserted itself through various intranational movements for cultural or political liberation. In the United States, the call for civil rights and cultural rights by ethnic minorities has influenced educational policies, especially in urban centers. To be sure, the public schools continue to function as agencies for the politicization of the children and youth, but their responsibility for preserving the richness of ethnic diversity has been increasingly emphasized.

The final ideology analyzed in this anthology relates to the belief system that sustains and guides the formal educational programs in the United States. Educationism is the ideology which gives credibility and direction to the massive public school system. Adherents of this ideology generally believe that extended formal schooling will provide the country with a politically enlightened citizenry and will serve as a panacea for social ills. In generating the ideological energy behind the expansion of the educational system, Educationism emphasizes the three elements of schooling: professionalism, institutionalism, and formalism.

The reader of this anthology should avoid the temptation to classify himself or others according to the various particular personality types often associated with each of these ideological perspectives. Ideologies are *orientations* for individuals and should be viewed as such. Individuals who are not aware of the influences of ideologies upon their cognitive and affective processes are doomed to be *determined* by them, but those who seek to liberate themselves from the restricted vision imposed by ideological systems may transcend them. Ideologies are like cultures in that they influence and define perimeters for human behavior. They also serve as wellsprings for man's creative expression, and thus can be a source of human fulfillment. Consequently, the future of civilization rests, in part, upon the ability of man to understand the nature of ideological systems rather than to continue being determined by his various social religions. This awareness is essential for liberation, a fundamental requirement for humanness.

Part I

SCIENTISM

Introduction

During the past several centuries the ideology of Scientism has emerged as a dominant force in channeling the perceptions of man and the structure of society. The theoretical constructs of science have been fused with the practical applications of technology to produce a material wealth unsurpassed in the history of mankind. Promising social efficiency and continually increasing prosperity, the ideology of Scientism has assumed a position of significance that diminishes the importance of the classical distinctions between liberalism and conservatism or between capitalism and communism. Indeed, technological achievements have become the standard by which modern man measures progress and judges his relative degree of civilization. Scientism has combined with Nationalism in the process of modernization.

The ideology of Scientism has retained a strong alliance with the business community and the military establishment. In America the competitive nature of capitalism has served to enhance the need for research and development in the area of consumer goods, while international wars, both hot and cold, have served to escalate the demand for further technological achievements.

Since the establishment of Massachusetts Bay Colony in 1630 the acceptance of the ideology of Scientism has grown at a nearly exponential rate. Although the Bay Colony Puritans maintained a firm commitment to biblical scriptures, they developed an activist orientation toward the world and a definite interest in secular endeavors. In fact, some of the leading members of the theocracy were involved in the scientific activities of the Royal Society of England.

Lacking a feudal tradition and an established guild system, America was relatively free to develop an industrial society rapidly. Spurred by the Puritan values of hard work and self-reliance, and by the frontier ethos of practicality and growth, "Yankee ingenuity," as it was termed, rapidly "civilized" the new country.

The extension of formal schooling and the creation of vocational schools and land grant universities further enhanced the growth of Scientism. School children were taught the virtues of science and technology and many were trained for the rapidly expanding industrial order.

During the latter decades of the nineteenth century the American faith in universal education encountered the problems emanating from immigration, urbanization, and industrialization. Scientism promised prestige to the members of a rapidly growing profession and efficiency to the burgeoning number of participants in the educational system. After the turn of the century, psychologists such as Edward L. Thorndike and Alfred Binet developed systems of tests and measurements for determining an individual's intellectual ability and assessing his potential for academic achievement. Individuals could then be selected to meet the needs of the industrial society. During the past two decades, adherents to Scientism, supported by the increasing popularity of logical empiricism and linguistic analysis, have focused upon behavioral analysis and modification. Behavior modification (by means of operant conditioning) demands that teachers operationally define desired behavioral changes and, by utilizing a system of rewards (positive reinforcements), manipulate students toward acceptable behavioral patterns. Recent developments also have focused upon genetic manipulation and the use of chemical agents to control the development and behavior of man.

In the mid 1950s the American educational system received a jolt from the launching of the Russian satellite. Adherents to Scientism such as Hyman Rickover and James Conant received extensive public attention and spurred the nation into making a renewed commitment to science and technology. Scientism promised the American citizens victories in the space and arms races.

During the sixties and seventies, with the continuance of the civil rights movements, the ideology of Scientism gained further influence. Countless programs sponsored by various levels of government create an immense need for research and development, and the government's insistence upon accountability, with its implicit demand for quantifiable data and statistical evaluation, is obviously just what Scientism can deliver best.

In the following articles it will be noted that the ideology of Scientism is founded upon a faith in the order of the universe. Adherents to Scientism believe that this order, whether it is natural or divine, can be discovered and/or rationally determined. Consequently, by using the inductive-deductive methodology of science man can predict and control both his environment and his behavior. Thus man progresses. The reader might also note that the "enemies" of Scientism focus on such factors as human irrationality, superstition, subjectivity, and mysticism.

Adherents to Scientism assert that scientific methodology is objective; that is, by maintaining a strict conformity to the tenets of science, universal consensus can be attained inasmuch as the truths thus arrived at will be empirically verifiable and publically demonstrable. The methods of science, so the proponents proclaim, are value-free and the technological achievements resulting from scientific theory are ethically neutral. In the language of Scientism, science and technology are neither good nor evil: their value depends upon how they are utilized.

In his essay "The Scientific Outlook: Naturalism and Humanism," Herbert Feigl, the well-known philosopher of science, discusses the scientific method. In addition, he provides persuasive arguments to counter various criticisms of Scientism. Rather than viewing Scientism and Humanism as conflicting ideologies, Feigl asserts their necessary compatibility.

The creed of Scientism, expressed in part by Feigl, is further illustrated by A. Cornelius Benjamin in his description of the intellectual qualities of a good scientist. Benjamin's discussion of "the scientific habit of thought" represents a moderate view often ignored or distorted by the more rabid adherents to the ideology of Scientism.

From a historical perspective, the writings of Edward L. Thorndike dating from 1909 are strikingly similar to those of B. F. Skinner written one-half century later. The Thorndike material included here, selected from *The Principles of Teaching*, describes the meaning of education from the perspective of Scientism. His ideas obviously are intellectual antecedants for behavior modification.

"Forecast for the Seventies," by Harold G. Shane and June Grant Shane, serves to illustrate the possible if not necessarily probable logical extension of Scientism into the education of the future. Schooling will be extended into many areas of life and an ever-increasing division of labor and more intense specialization will magnify the necessity of credentials in a society increasingly run on the principles of a meritocracy. The Shanes' optimism about the future is shared, no doubt, by many adherents to Scientism who envision a greater role for themselves in the educational institutions of tomorrow.

In the final article of Part I, B. F. Skinner, the most notable advocate of operant conditioning, describes the role of the teacher as a behavior modifier. Although his forthright proposals to go beyond "freedom and dignity" are quite shocking to romanticists and many humanists, they appear to have gained many ardent supporters. Efficiency, order, and materialistic progress, the promises of Scientism, are rewards people may find extremely difficult to reject.

AN ANALYTICAL VIEW: A Brief Survey

THE SCIENTIFIC OUTLOOK: NATURALISM AND HUMANISM
Herbert Feigl

An Essay on Some Issues of General Education and a Critique of Current Misconceptions Regarding Scientific Method and the Scientific Outlook in Philosophy

The main purpose of this essay is to dispel certain confusions and misunderstandings which still prevent the much-needed constructive synthesis and mutual supplementation of the scientific and humanistic elements in general education. It is my contention that the philosophical foundations of both science and the humanities are widely misconceived; and that the frequently held claim of their basic incompatibilities arises out of philosophical prejudices which, owing to cultural lag, have unfortunately not as yet been completely relegated to oblivion. Science is still identified with an absurd mechanistic reductionism, but this is the caricature of science drawn by representatives of the humanities who are largely ignorant of the nature of modern science and also of the more recent scientific outlook in philosophy. The defenders of the humanities often enough increase the existing tension by holding an equally distorted view of the philosophical basis of the humanities.

The errors committed may well be characterized respectively as *reductive* and *seductive* fallacies. It is claimed that science either ignores (perhaps by its very method cannot help ignoring) or else explains away the most essential human values. Science is here charged with the reductive fallacy. Usually the same group of thinkers maintains also that there are aspects of the human mind, manifest especially in the domains of morality, religion, and the arts, which contain an irreducible spiritual element and for that reason will never be capable of explanation by the

From Herbert Feigl, "The Scientific Outlook: Naturalism and Humanism," *American Quarterly*, I, No. 2 (1949), 138–48. Copyright, 1949, Trustees of the University of Pennsylvania. Reprinted by permission of the editor and the author.

scientific method, no matter how far it advances. I call this fallacy seductive because it is usually committed by those who indulge in what William James called "tender-minded," that is, wishful and sentimental, thinking.

The impasse between seductive thesis and reductive antithesis can be overcome only by a constructive synthesis that retains and develops whatever valid suggestions or emphases we may discover underneath the grandiose verbiage of the first and the harsh austerities of the second. Neither a philosophy of the "Something More" nor a philosophy of the "Nothing But" will do for our time. Only an approach that is resolutely guided by the question "What is what?" will avoid reading mysteries into the facts, as well as refrain from impoverishing them by reduction to something less than experience attests them to be. Such a philosophical outlook, if not yet fully achieved, is fortunately very much in the making.

Especially in the melting pot of American thought, we find that the valuable elements of naturalism and humanism are gradually united in a new integration: the pragmatism of Peirce, James, Dewey, Mead, Otto, Kallen, and Hook; the naturalistic realism of Perry, Holt, R. W. Sellars, Drake, and Santayana; the scientific empiricism of Bridgman, Hull, Tolman, Lundberg, N. Wiener, P. Frank, C. Morris, Northrop, Carnap, Reichenbach, Nagel, and others; the liberal ("American Humanist") wing of Unitarianism. All these trends of thought and many others converge in a broad movement that one may well be tempted to regard as the twentieth-century sequel to the enlightenment of the eighteenth century.

The humanism held in common to a very large extent in these scientifically oriented philosophies is too well known to require an elaborate restatement. Suffice it to say that such human values as freedom and responsibility, rights and obligations, creative and appreciative capacities, are here disengaged from the theological and metaphysical ideologies that have traditionally pervaded their conception. Increasingly adequate and nonreductive analyses have been propounded in the last five or six decades. This reconstruction in philosophy has been and still is in the making. Under the impact of modern science philosophy is abandoning some of its earlier grandiose and overambitious claims in favor of a humbler and more useful function: the clarification of the foundations of knowledge and valuation. I shall now attempt to apply what seem to me to be the most important insights and suggestions of these currents of thought to the issues of general education.

Clearly nothing is more urgent for education today than a social philosophy that will be appropriate and workable in an age of science. Among the various prominent philosophies of education I mention first two currents which may be styled traditionalistic and which have on the whole either ignored the facts of the age of science or have tried (unsuccessfully, I think) to dispute and combat them: Neo-Thomism and Literary Humanism. Reliance on theological or metaphysical presuppositions makes these views incompatible with the modern scientific outlook. More definitely products of the modern scientific attitude are two other schools of thought: Dialectical Materialism, the official philosophy of Soviet Russia, but also fashionable in certain English scientific groups; and, scarcely worthy of being called a philosophy, the attitude of Vocationalism, quite prevalent in American education. The common element of these two views is their exclusive interest in the practical, technological applications of the natural and the social sciences. This, as well as other shortcomings, makes both points of view appear objectionable or at least badly in need of correction or supplementation. A much more acceptable position is that of Scientific Humanism. This view, at least in general outlook, is related to what is known as Progressivism or Reconstructionism in American education: a synthesis of the scientific attitude with an active interest in the whole scale of human values. Education in both the sciences *and* the humanities is the urgent need of our time. But how can these two aims properly be combined? The question reveals an uneasy feeling as to the compatibility of science and humanism.

Misunderstandings of the nature of science are primarily responsible for the appearance of incompatibility here. A proper historical and analytical perspective of the development of the scientific outlook and its distinctive traits as compared with prescientific and nonscientific attitudes helps to show that mankind achieves intellectual adulthood only with the scientific way of thinking.

Our age is still replete with remnants of and regressions to such prescientific thought patterns as magic, animism, mythology, theology, and metaphysics. The outstanding characteristics of modern scientific method are mostly absent or at best only adumbrated in those less mature phases of intellectual growth.

Criteria of the Scientific Method

What, then, are the basic characteristics of the scientific method? The often alleged difficulties of an adequate definition of science seem to me mainly a matter of terminology. We must first distinguish between pure mathematics as an exclusively formal-conceptual discipline, and the factual (or empirical, that is, the natural and the social-cultural) sciences. The certainty, complete exactitude, and necessity of pure mathematics depends precisely on its detachment from empirical fact. Mathematics as applied in the factual sciences merely lends its forms and deductive structures to the contents furnished by experience. But no matter how predominant mathematics may be in the formulations and derivations of empirical facts, factual knowledge cannot attain either the absolute precision or necessity of pure mathematics. The knowledge claimed in the natural and the social sciences is a matter of successive approximations and of increasing degrees of confirmation. Warranted assertibility or probability is all that we can conceivably secure in the sciences that deal with the facts of experience. It is empirical science, thus conceived as an unending quest (its truth-claims to be held only "until further notice"), which is under consideration here. Science in this sense differs only in degree from the knowledge accumulated throughout the ages by sound and common sense.

The aims of science are description, explanation, and prediction. The first aim is basic and indispensable, the second and third (closely related to each other) arise as the most desirable fruits of scientific labors whenever inquiry rises beyond the mere fact-gathering stage. History, often and nowadays quite fashionably declared an art, is scientific to the extent that it ascertains its facts concerning past events by a meticulous scrutiny of present evidence. Causal interpretation of these facts (in history, but similarly also in psychology, sociology, cultural anthropology, and economics) is usually much more difficult than, but in principle not logically different from, causal interpretation (that is, explanation) in the natural sciences. The aims of the pure (empirical) sciences are then essentially the same throughout the whole field. What the scientists are seeking are descriptions, explanations, and predictions which are as adequate and accurate as possible in the given context of research.

The quest for scientific knowledge is therefore regulated by certain standards or criteria which may best be formulated in the form of ideals to be approximated, but perhaps never fully attained. The most important of these regulative ideas are:

1. *Intersubjective Testability.* This is only a more adequate formulation of what is generally meant by the "objectivity" of science. What is here involved is not only the freedom from personal or cultural bias or partiality, but—even more fundamentally—the requirement that the knowledge claims of science be in principle capable of test (confirmation or disconfirmation, at the least indirectly and to some degree) on the part of any person properly equipped with intelligence and the technical devices of observation or experimentation. The term *intersubjective* stresses the social nature of the scientific enterprise. If there be any "truths" that are accessible only to privileged individuals, such as mystics or visionaries —that is, knowledge-claims which by their very nature cannot independently be checked by anyone else—then such "truths" are not of the kind that we seek in the sciences. The criterion of intersubjective testability thus delimits the scientific from the nonscientific activities of man.

Religious ecstasy, the elations of love, the inspiration of the artist, yes, even the flash of insight on the part of a scientific genius are not in themselves scientific activities. All these processes may eventually become subject matter for scientific study. But in themselves they do not validate knowledge-claims. They may, as in the case of the scientific intuition (or empathy in the psychological-cultural field) be instrumental in the generation of knowledge claims. But it is these knowledge-claims which have to be, first formulated in an intersubjectively intelligible (or communicable) manner, and, second, subjected to the appropriate kind of tests in order to ascertain their validity. Beliefs transcending all possible tests by observation, self-observation, experiment, measurement, or statistical analysis are recognized as theological or metaphysical and therefore devoid of the type of meaning that we all associate with the knowledge-claims of common sense or factual science. From the point of view of the scientific outlook in philosophy it may be suggested that the sort of significance with which the in-principle-unconfirmable assertion of transcendent theology and metaphysics impress so many people is largely emotive. The pictorial, emotional, and motivational appeals of language, no matter how indispensable or valuable in the contexts of practical life, art, education, persuasion, and propaganda, must, however, not be confused with the cognitive meanings (purely formal- and/or factual-empirical) that are of the essence of science. Each type of significance has its function, and in most uses of language both are combined or even fused. The only point stressed here is that they must not be *con*fused, that is, mistaken for one another, if we wish to be clear as to what we are about.

2. *Reliability, or a Sufficient Degree of Confirmation.* This second criterion of scientific knowledge enables us to distinguish what is generally called "mere opinion" (or worse still, "superstition") from knowledge (well-substantiated belief). It may be considered as the delimitation of the scientific from the unscientific knowledge-claims. Clearly, in contrast to the first criterion, we face here a distinction of degree. There is no sharp line of demarcation between the well-confirmed laws, theories, or hypotheses of science, and the only poorly substantiated hunches and ideas-on-trial which may ultimately either be included in the corpus of scientific knowledge or else rejected as unconfirmed. Truth-claims which we repudiate as "superstition," and, quite generally, as judgments based upon hasty generalization or weak analogy (if they fulfill the criterion of testability), differ from what we accept as "scientific truth" in the extremely low degree of probability to which they are supported by the available evidence. Astrology or alchemy, for example, are not factually meaningless, but they are considered false to fact in that all available evidence speaks overwhelmingly against them. Modern techniques of experimentation and of statistical analysis are the most powerful tools we have in the

discernment between chance and law and hence the best means of enhancing the reliability of knowledge.

3. *Definiteness and Precision.*   This obvious standard of scientific method requires that the concepts used in the formulation of scientific knowledge-claims be as definitely delimited as possible. On the level of the qualitative-classificatory sciences this amounts to the attempt to reduce all border-zone vagueness to a minimum. On the level of quantitative science the exactitude of the concepts is enormously enhanced through the application of the techniques of measurement. The mensurational devices usually also increase the degree of objectivity. This is especially clear when they are contrasted with purely impressionistic ways of estimating magnitudes. Of course, there is no point in sharpening precision to a higher degree than the problem in hand requires. (You need no razor to cut butter.)

4. *Coherence or Systematic Structure.*   This is what T. H. Huxley had in mind when he defined science as "organized common-sense." Not a mere collection of miscellaneous items of information, but a well-connected account of the facts is what we seek in science. On the descriptive level this results, for example, in systems of classification or division, in diagrams, statistical charts, and the like. On the explanatory levels of science sets of laws, or theoretical assumptions, are utilized. Explanation in science consists in the hypothetico-deductive procedure. The laws, theories, or hypotheses form the premises from which we derive logically, or logico-mathematically, the observed or observable facts. These facts, often belonging to heterogeneous domains, thus become integrated into a coherent, unifying structure. (Theological and metaphysical systems have, frequently enough, ambitiously tried to imitate this feature of science; but even if they succeeded in proceeding *more geometrico,* the important difference from science remains: they either lack testability or else reliability in the senses specified in our previous points.)

5. *Comprehensiveness or Scope of Knowledge.*   This final point in our enumeration of criteria of science also characterizes scientific knowledge as different in degree (often enormously) from common-sense knowledge. Not only through bold and sweeping hypotheses, but especially through the ingenious devices by means of which they are tested, science acquires a reach far beyond the limits of our unaided senses. With telescopes, microscopes, spectroscopes, Geiger Counters, lie detectors, and the thousands of other contrivances of modern science we manage to amplify our senses and thus open up avenues of at least indirect access to the worlds of the very distant, the very large, the extremely small, or the disguised and concealed. The resulting increase in the completeness of our knowledge is, of course, popularly the most impressive feature of

science. It must be kept in mind, however, that the scope thus achieved is a product of hard labor, and not to be confused with the sham complete-ness metaphysicians procure for their world pictures by verbal magic. Instead of presenting a finished account of the world, the genuine scientist keeps his unifying hypotheses open to revision and is always ready to modify or abandon them if evidence should render them doubtful. This self-corrective aspect of science has rightly been stressed as its most im-portant characteristic and must always be kept in mind when we refer to the comprehensiveness or the unification achieved by the scientific account of the universe. It is a sign of one's maturity to be able to live with an unfinished world view.

The foregoing outline of the criteria of science has been set down in a somewhat dogmatic tone. But this was done only for the sake of brevity.[1] The spirit behind it is that of a humble account of what, I think, an im-partial and elaborate study of the history of thought from magic to science would reveal. In any case, these criteria seem unquestionably the guiding ideals of present-day empirical science. They may therefore be used in a definition of science as we understand this term today. It seems rather useless to speculate about just what this term, by a change of meaning, might come to connote in the future.

It should be remembered that the criteria listed characterize the *pure* factual (empirical) sciences. The aims of the *applied* sciences—the tech-nologies, medicine, social and economic planning, and others—are practical control, production, guidance, therapy, reform, and so forth. Responsible activity in the application of science clearly presupposes information which is fairly well substantiated by the methods of the pure sciences. (These re-marks intend to draw merely a logically important distinction. The obvi-ous practical interpretation and important mutual fertilization of the pure and the applied disciplines is of course not denied here.)

Critique of Misconceptions

Having indicated at least in broad outline the nature of scientific method we may now turn to the critique of some of the misconceptions to which it is all too commonly exposed. In what follows, a dozen typical charges against science are stated and answered consecutively.[2]

---

[1] A thorough discussion of the logical, epistemological, methodological, and historical issues connected with the criteria would require a whole book, not just an-other essay.

[2] These charges are not straw men. In more than twenty years of reading, lis-tening, teaching, and argument I have encountered them again and again in Europe and just as frequently in this country. If space permitted and time were less valuable, I could quote many well-known writers in connection with each charge.

Science arises exclusively out of practical and social needs and has its only value in serving them in turn. (Dialectical Materialism and Vocationalism)

While this is important it does not tell the whole story. Science has always also been the pursuit of knowledge, the satisfaction of a deep-rooted curiosity. It should be recognized as one of the cultural values along with art, literature, and music. Better teaching of the sciences and their history can redress the balance. Fuller utilization of results and suggestions from the history and the philosophy of science would give the student a deeper appreciation of the evolution of scientific knowledge and of the scientific point of view. Through proper instruction, the student could be led to rediscover some of the important results of science. The intellectual gratification that comes with a grasp of the order of nature, with the understanding of its processes by means of laws and theories, is one of the most powerful incentives in the pursuit of pure knowledge.

Science cannot furnish a secure basis for human affairs since it is unstable. It changes its views continually. (Traditionalism)

While there is constant evolution, and occasionally a revolution, in the scientific outlook, the charge is a superficial (usually journalistic) exaggeration. The typical progress of science reveals that later views often contain much of the earlier views (to the extent that these have stood the test of repeated examination). The more radical or revolutionary changes usually amount to a revision of the conceptual frame of a scientific discipline. The criticism often also presupposes other sources of certainty which will simply not bear critical scrutiny. The quest for absolute certainty is an immature, if not infantile, trait of thinking. The best knowledge we have can be established only by the method of trial and error. It is of the essence of science to make such knowledge as reliable as is humanly and technically possible.

Science rests on uncritical or uncriticized presuppositions. It validates its outlook by its own standards. It therefore begs the question as regards alternative approaches for settling problems of knowledge and action.

Science has been clarifying and revising its basic assumptions throughout its development. Particularly since the beginning of the modern age and still more intensively since the beginning of our century, an increasing awareness of, and critical attitude toward, the fundamental presuppositions has been most fruitfully applied in the repudiation of dogmatic prejudices and in the articulation of the conceptual frame of scientific method. It can be shown (through logical analysis) that the procedure of science is the only one we are *certain* will yield the results (reliable knowledge, that is, valid explanation and predictions) *if* such results can at all be achieved. Any alleged rival method—theology, meta-physics, mysticism, intuition, dialectics—if it made any contributions at all could not be examined and appraised on any basis other than the usual inductive criteria of science. Generally, it seems that these alleged alter-natives do not even aim primarily at knowledge but, like the arts, at the enrichment of experience. They may therefore more properly be said to be *non*scientific, rather than *un*scientific.

Science distorts the facts of reality. In its Procrustean manner it introduces discontinuities where there is continuity (and vice versa). The abstractions and idealizations used in science can never do justice to the richness and complexities of experience.

Since the task of science is to discover reliable and precise knowl-edge of what happens under what conditions, it always tries to approxi-mate the facts as closely as the problem on hand requires and permits. Both continuity and discontinuity can be formulated mathematically and be given an adequate formulation only with the help of modern mathe-matics.

Science can deal only with the measurable and therefore tends to "explain away" that which it cannot measure.

While measurement is eminently desirable in order to enhance the precision and objectivity of knowledge, it is not indispensable in many branches of science or, at least, on their more qualitative levels of analysis. Science does not explain away the qualities of experience. It aims at, and often succeeds in, making these qualities more predictable.

Science never explains, it merely describes the phenomena of experi-ence. The reality beyond the appearances is also beyond the reach of science.

This is partly a terminological issue and partly a result of the (tradi-tional but most misleading and useless) metaphysical distinction between appearance and reality. In the sense in which the word *explaining* is used in common life, science *does* explain facts—it deduces them from laws or theoretical assumptions. Questions which are in principle incapable of being answered by the scientific method turn out, on closer analysis, not to be questions of knowledge. They are expressions of emotional tensions or of the wish for soothing (or exciting) experience.

Science and the scientific attitude are incompatible with religion and the religious attitude.

If by religion one refers to an explanation of the universe and a derivation of moral norms from theological premises, then indeed there is logical incompatibility with the results, methods, and general outlook of science. But if religion means an attitude of sincere devotion to human values, such as justice, peace, relief from suffering, there is not only no conflict between religion and science but rather a need for mutual supplementation.

Science is responsible for the evils and maladjustments of our civilization. It is creating ever more powerful weapons of destruction. The employment of scientific techniques in the machine age has contributed to the misery, physical and mental, of the multitudes. Moreover, the biological facts of evolution imply the negation of all morality: the law of the jungle.

These are particularly superficial charges. It is the social-political-economic structure of a society that is responsible for these various evils. Scientific knowledge itself is socially and morally neutral. But the manner in which it is applied, whether for the benefit or to the detriment of humanity, depends entirely on ourselves. Scientists are becoming increasingly aware that they, even more than the average citizen, have to work for enlightenment toward the proper use of knowledge. The facts and theories of evolution have been construed in many ways as regards their implications for ethics. Julian Huxley reads them very differently from the way his grandfather Thomas Henry did.[3] It should be easy to see that the forces active on the level of human civilization and intelligent communal life are not completely reducible to those involved in the ruthless struggle for survival.

The ethical neutrality of scientific truth and the ivory tower situation of the pure researcher is apt to generate an attitude of indifference toward the pressing problems of humanity.

Only maladjusted individuals are unable to combine the detachment necessary for the pursuit of truth with an ardent interest in the improvement of the condition of humanity.

Scientific method, while eminently successful in the explanation, prediction, and control of physical phenomena, is distinctly less successful in regard to the facts of organic life and almost altogether hopeless in the mental and social realm. The methods of the physical sciences are essentially mechanistic (if not materialistic) and therefore reductionistic; they cannot do justice to the complex organismic, teleological, and emergent features of life and mind.

"Scientism" as a slogan of criticism and reproach is very fashionable these days. It is true that some scientists and especially some of the popu-

---

[3] Compare Julian Huxley, *Touchstone for Ethics* (Harper, 1947); but see also C. D. Broad, "Review of Julian S. Huxley's Evolutionary Ethics" (*Mind*, 53, 1944), reprinted in H. Feigl and W. Sellars, *Readings in Philosophical Analysis* (Appleton-Century-Crofts, 1949).

larizers of science have indulged in reductive fallacies of various sorts. But the true scientific spirit as exemplified in some of the foremost researchers is free from that impatience and simple-mindedness that tries to finish the unfinished business of science by hasty speculation. Admittedly, there are tremendous problems yet to be solved. On the other hand what method is there but the method of science to solve them? Explanations of the mechanistic type (in *one* sense of the term) have been abandoned even in physics. But mechanistic explanation in the wider sense of a search for law (deterministic or statistical) is still the indispensable procedure of all sciences that have gone beyond the purely classificatory level. Organic wholeness, teleology, and emergence can be understood, if at all, only by causal analysis on the usual empirical basis. Purposiveness and freedom of choice, far from being incompatible with causality, presuppose causal order.

The methods of science can never replace the intuitive insight or empathic understanding of the practical psychologist, psychiatrist, cultural anthropologist, or historian. This claim is made particularly wherever the object of knowledge is the individual, the unique and unrepeatable.

It is only through the scientific method that the validity and reliability of the intuitive approach can be gauged. There is, on this ground, some doubt as to its more exaggerated claims. However, there is nothing in the principles of scientific method that would deny the occasional, or even frequent, efficacy of intuitive judgments based, as they must be, on a rich (but often not articulated) background of experience in the given field. Aside from the mere artistic contemplation of the unique and individual, knowledge, in the proper sense of the word, always means the subsumption of the specific case under general concepts or laws. This holds in the social sciences just as much as in the natural sciences.

Science cannot determine values. Since scientific knowledge can (at best) find out only what is the case, it can, by its very nature, never tell what ought to be.

This final challenge often comes from theology or metaphysics. It usually maintains that questions of aims, goals, and ideals cannot be settled by the methods of science but rather require recourse either to divine revelation, the voice of conscience, or some metaphysical a priori truths. The answer to this in a scientific age would seem to be that a mature mankind should be able to determine its own value standards on the basis of its needs, wants, and the facts of the social condition of man. But it is true that science cannot dictate value standards. It can, as in social psychology, ascertain the actual evaluations of groups and individuals, study their compatibilities and incompatibilities, and recommend (that is *applied* science!) ways and means of harmonizing conflicting evaluations. True enough, in many of the urgent issues that confront us, we do not possess enough scientific knowledge to warrant a course of action. This means that we have to act, as so often in life, on the highest probabilities available even if these probabilities be low in themselves. But such estimates of probabilities will still be made most reliable by the scientific method. Common life experience and wisdom, when freed from its adherence to prescientific thought patterns, is not fundamentally different from scientific knowledge. In both we find the procedure of self-correction, so essentially needed if knowledge is to be a guide for action. There is an important common element in mature thinking (as we find it in science) and mature social action (as we find it in democracy): progress arises out of the peaceful competition of ideas as they are put to intersubjective test. Cooperative planning on the basis of the best and fullest knowledge available is the only path left to an awakened humanity that has embarked on the adventure of science and civilization.

The scientific view of the world that we have characterized and defended against criticisms from various quarters may with historical and terminological justice be called Naturalism.[4] It differs from mechanistic materialism (too often a mere straw man put up by theologians or idealistic metaphysicians) in that it steers clear of reductive fallacies. If uninformed persons insist on viewing science as essentially materialistic and the humanities as essentially idealistic (not to say spiritualistic) the hopes of fruitful collaboration of both fields in education are slim indeed. But science, properly interpreted, is not dependent on any sort of metaphysics. It merely attempts to cover a maximum of facts by a minimum of laws. On the other side, a mature humanism requires no longer a theological or metaphysical frame either. Human nature and human history become progressively understood in the light of advancing science. It is therefore no longer justifiable to speak of science *versus* the humanities. Naturalism *and* humanism should be our maxim in philosophy and in education. A Scientific Humanism emerges as a philosophy holding considerable promise for mankind—*if* mankind will at all succeed in growing up.

---

[4] It should scarcely need mentioning that this meaning of naturalism has only a distant and tenuous relation to the other meaning in which it is applied to a certain type of literature.

THE CREED: Scientific Admonitions

THE INTELLECTUAL QUALIFICATIONS
OF THE GOOD SCIENTIST
A. Cornelius Benjamin

1. Fervent Impartiality

The devotion of the scientist to the pursuit of knowledge is too well recognized to require elaboration here. The scientist, perhaps more honestly than anyone else, can say in the words of A. H. Clough,

> It fortifies my soul to now
> That though I perish truth is so.

The theme of scientific martyrdom runs through history, poem, and story. While the actual cases of individuals who gave their lives for the advancement of science are few (Socrates and Bruno [1] are the best-known examples), we tend to forget how many have shortened their lives by long hours in the laboratory, through accidents suffered in the course of research, through illness contracted in the study of disease, through exposure to hardships and privations while engaged in geographical explorations, and so on. A. E. Housman says that the passion for truth is one of the weakest of human passions. This seems to me to be contradicted by the history of science. The passion for truth may be the *rarest* of human passions, since the number of scientists and scholars is small compared to the total population, but it certainly is not the *weakest*.

This is, however, only one side of the scientific personality. While a strong dedication to truth is essential to science, an uncontrolled enthusiasm can bring about its destruction. An ardent love can be blind in matters of the intellect as well as in human relationships. Extreme devo-

From A. Cornelius Benjamin, *Science, Technology, and Human Values* (Columbia, Missouri: University of Missouri Press, 1965), pp. 161-69. Copyright © 1965 The Curators of the University of Missouri. Reprinted by permission of the University of Missouri Press.

[1] Giordano Bruno, 1548?–1600. Renaissance philosopher and teacher.—ed.

tion to any cause may produce an intellectually warped vision. [Francis] Bacon said that the scientist must never show eyes lustrous with human passion.

2. Imaginative Objectivity

Here the problem of the personality of the scientist is that of reconciling two strong, but often sharply opposed, urges—one, to remain faithful to the facts and to avoid fruitless speculation, and the other, to explain and account for the facts which have been disclosed through observation and experimentation. The proper understanding of science clearly involves recognition of the respective roles of both data and hypotheses.

There are, of course, no ideas without facts and no facts without ideas. [Charles] Darwin said that no one can be a good observer unless he is an active theorizer, but he also said that any fool can generalize and speculate. Bacon spoke of the need for "holding the imagination in leash"—a particularly apt phrase since the scientist commonly feels the "pull" toward centuring an explanation before adequate foundation has been laid in the facts. Buffon [2] said that genius is essentially patience; Tyndall [3] . . . stressed the need for "preparing" the imagination by carefully examining the facts; and Santayana [4] coined the phrase, "chastened imagination."

To be faithful to the facts, yet to see behind the facts—this is the essence of imaginative objectivity.

3. Tolerant Rigidity

Openness of mind is an important attribute of the scientific thinker. New theories—indeed, revolutionary theories—are continually emerging from the background of research. While there is considerable exaggeration in the reply of the physicist who when asked what the latest theory of matter was replied that he could not answer the question since he had not yet seen the morning paper, there is a measure of truth in what he said. What should be the attitude of the scientist toward each new

[2] Georges Louis Leclerc, Comte de Buffon, 1707–1788. French naturalist and author.—ed.

[3] John Tyndall, 1820–1893. British physicist and popularizer of science. He was professor of natural philosophy at Royal Institution.—ed.

[4] George Santayana, 1863–1952. Spanish poet and philosopher, he taught at Harvard University (1889–1912).—ed.

theory which presents itself? Since theories arise through imaginative insight and this method by itself provides no criteria for validation, the scientist can neither accept nor reject a theory until satisfactory confirmation or disconfirmation has been provided. But here is precisely where the difficulty arises. For how conclusive must the confirmation be before a theory is admitted into the body of science and how conclusive must its disconfirmation be before it is discarded? . . . This seems to characterize that openness of mind which the scientist brings to his study.

But a mind can be admittedly too wide open. The scientific discipline is severe and its criteria of validity are high. Both the facts and the methods of science have been won through the sweat and blood of centuries of disciplined effort, and the scientist has a genuine respect for them. Perhaps he is justifiably impatient, therefore, with circle-squarers and makers of perpetual motion machines. Teachers of high school and college mathematics are plagued, I am told, with students who claim to be able to prove that 1 equals 0. Certainly the scientist is not fairly to be charged with having a closed mind when he is unwilling to listen to those who insist that they have made great discoveries but who have never learned the primer of science. A common complaint of scientific quacks is that scientific journals will not publish their manuscripts and established scientists will not listen to their arguments. But being open-minded does not mean being tolerant of all solutions which are offered for scientific problems, or of solutions proposed for problems which are known to be insoluble. Some things which pose as science are just plain wrong and the scientist can hardly be criticized for being intolerant of this sort of thing. One who does not know what has been done in science cannot expect to make contributions to science. Faraday [5] complained that he was continually bothered by novices who had "discovered old facts."

4. Critical Illogicality

The problem of this final attribute of the scientific personality is simple, yet it is a troublesome one. No one, I should suppose, would ever question the importance to a scientist of a knowledge of logic. Science, in fact, *is* logic applied to a certain subject matter. But this is not precisely the issue. The problem is, rather, to determine the role of conscious logical knowledge in the actual procedure of science. To what extent should the scientist think about his logic while he is carrying on his investigations?

[5] Michael Faraday, 1791–1867. English chemist and physicist.—ed.

On the one hand, some knowledge of the rules of thought seems essential. The scientist must know how to draw valid inferences, how to make accurate observations, how to measure and experiment, and he must certainly know something of the subtle way in which prejudice, emotion, superstition, and unconscious philosophies of life creep into scientific investigations and warp scientific conclusions. The scientist who knows something of logic is, therefore, other things being equal, more likely to contribute to good science than his colleague who does not. Without the knowledge he is more prone to error, more easily confused by complex problems, and less able to expound his results convincingly to others.

Logic contributes to thinking, not while it goes on but after it has been completed; logic acts as the critical evaluator which tells us what kinds of error there are and how to guard against them. From this point of view the scientist can hardly know too much logic. In his use of methodological considerations, therefore, the scientist may well think rationally without necessarily destroying spontaneity. Probably no scientist can proceed effectively without a rudimentary knowledge of the distinction between fact and theory, between valid and invalid inference, between experiments which are properly controlled and those which are not. To this extent logic and the reasoning processes are needed in science. But logic does not *make* science; it gives direction to science but cannot be a substitute for it. The good scientist is one who recognizes the merits and limitations of logic; he knows the logic of his procedure but he also knows that there are not any "rules," as Bacon evidently thought there were, by which the mind can extract ideas from nature in much the same way that one can extract juice from an orange. Genius does not obey laws; it makes them.

REPRESENTATIVE EXPRESSIONS:
An Historical Perspective

1. THE PRINCIPLES OF TEACHING
BASED ON PSYCHOLOGY
Edward L. Thorndike

THE TEACHER'S PROBLEM

The Aims, Materials and Methods of Education. The word Education is used with many meanings, but in all its usages it refers to *changes.* No one is educated who stays just as he was. We do not educate anybody if we do nothing that makes any difference or change in anybody. The need of education arises from the fact that *what is* is not what *ought to be.* Because we wish ourselves and others to become different from what we and they now are, we try to educate ourselves and them. In studying education, then, one studies always the existence, nature, causation or value of changes of some sort.

The teacher confronts two questions: "What changes to make?" and "How to make them?" The first question is commonly answered for the teacher by the higher school authorities for whom he or she works. The opinions of the educational leaders in the community decide what the schools shall try to do for their pupils. The program of studies is planned and the work which is to be done grade by grade is carefully outlined. The grammar-school teacher may think that changes in knowledge represented by the ability to read a modern language ought to be made in boys and girls before the high school, but the decision is rarely his; the primary teacher may be obliged to teach arithmetic although her own judgment would postpone giving the knowledge of numbers until the fifth or sixth grade.

What changes should be made in human nature by primary, grammar and high schools and why these and not other changes should be the aim of the schools, are questions usually answered under the heading "Principles of Education." How most efficiently to make such changes

From Edward L. Thorndike, *The Principles of Teaching Based on Psychology* (New York: A. G. Seiler, 1906), pp. 1, 2, 7, 8, 9, 257–60, 264–68.

as educational aims recommend, is a question usually answered under the headings "Principles of Teaching," or "Methods of Teaching," or "Theory and Practice of Teaching," or "Educational Psychology." This [article] will try to answer this latter question,—to give a scientific basis for the art of actual teaching rather than for the selection of aims for the schools as a whole or of the subjects to be taught or of the general result to be gained from any subject. Not the *What* or the *Why* but the *How* is its topic.

.   .   .

PSYCHOLOGY AND THE ART OF TEACHING

The Scientific Basis of Teaching.   The work of teaching is to produce and to prevent changes in human beings; to preserve and increase the desirable qualities of body, intellect and character and to get rid of the undesirable. To thus control human nature, the teacher needs to know it. To change what is into what ought to be, we need to know the laws by which the changes occur. Just as to make a plant grow well the gardener must act in accordance with the laws of botany which concern the growth of plants, or as to make a bridge well the achitect must act in accordance with the facts of mechanics concerning stresses and strains, or as to change disease into health the physician must act in accordance with the laws of physiology and pathology, so to make human beings intelligent and useful and noble the teacher must act in accordance with the laws of the sciences of human nature.

The sciences of biology, especially human physiology and hygiene, give the laws of changes in bodily nature. The science of psychology gives the laws of changes in intellect and character. The teacher studies and learns to apply psychology to teaching for the same reason that the progressive farmer studies and learns to apply botany; the architect, mechanics; or the physician, physiology and pathology.

Stimulus and Response.   Using psychological terms, the art of teaching may be defined as the art of giving and withholding stimuli with the result of producing or preventing certain responses. In this definition the term stimulus is used widely for any event which influences a person,—for a word spoken to him, a look, a sentence which he reads, the air he breathes, etc., etc. The term response is used for any reaction made by him,—a new thought, a feeling of interest, a bodily act, any mental or bodily condition resulting from the stimulus. The aim of the teacher is to produce desirable and prevent undesirable changes in human beings by producing and preventing certain responses. The means at the disposal of the teacher are the stimuli which can be brought to bear upon the pupil,—the teacher's words, gestures and appearance, the condition and appliances of the school room, the books to be used and objects to be seen, and so on through a long list of the things and events which the teacher can control. The responses of the pupil are all the infinite variety of thoughts and feelings and bodily movements occurring in all their possible connections.

The stimuli given by the teacher to arouse and guide the pupil's responses may be classified as:—

A. Stimuli under direct control.

The teacher's movements,[1]—speech, gestures, facial expression, etc.

B. Stimuli under indirect control.

The physical conditions of the school,—air, light, heat, etc.

The material equipment of the school,—books, apparatus, specimens, etc.

The social conditions of the school,—the acts (including spoken words) of the pupils and the spirit which these acts represent.

The general environment,—acts of parents, laws, libraries, etc.

The responses may be classified as:—

A. Physiological responses, such as deeper breathing, sounder sleep, vigorous exercise and the like.

B. Responses of knowledge,[2] such as connecting a sense stimulus with an appropriate percept, abstracting one element from a complex fact or making associations of ideas.

C. Responses of attitude, such as the connection of attention, interest, preference and belief with certain situations.

D. Responses of feeling, such as connecting sympathy, love, hate, etc., with certain situations.

E. Responses of action or of conduct and skill, connecting certain acts or movements with certain mental states.

The Value of Psychology.   If there existed a perfect and complete knowledge of human nature,—a complete science of psychology,—it would tell the effect of every possible stimulus and the cause of every possible response in every possible human being. A teacher could then know just what the result of any act of his would be, could prophesy just what the effect of such and such a page read or punishment given or dress worn

---

[1] The knowledge, love and tact of the teacher are, of course, of the highest importance as forces in teaching but their actual operation is in their expression in words, gestures or acts of some sort.

[2] Knowledge is used here in a broad sense to include sensing objects, analyzing facts, feeling relationships and drawing inferences, as well as memory of facts or associations of ideas.

would be,—just how to get any particular response, of attention to this object, memory of this fact or comprehension of that principle.

. . .

The Scientific Study of Teaching

The efficiency of any profession depends in large measure upon the degree to which it becomes scientific. The profession of teaching will improve (1) in proportion as its members direct their daily work by the scientific spirit and methods, that is by honest, open-minded consideration of facts, by freedom from superstitions, fancies or unverified guesses,[3] and (2) in proportion as the leaders direct their choices of methods by the results of scientific investigation rather than by general opinion.

. . .

TESTING THE RESULTS OF TEACHING

The Importance of Tests. No matter how carefully one tries to follow the right principles of teaching, no matter how ingeniously one selects and how adroitly one arranges stimuli, it is advisable to test the result of one's effort,—to make sure that the knowledge or power or tendency expected has really been acquired. Just as the scientist, though he has made his facts as accurate and his argument as logical as he can, still remains unsatisfied until he verifies his conclusion by testing it with new facts, so the teacher, after planning and executing a piece of work as well as he can, must "verify" his teaching by direct tests of its results and must consider uncertain any result that he cannot thus verify.

Their Difficulty. It is true that some of the most important results of teaching cannot be verified at all by the teacher himself. The permanence of interests, the effect of moral inspiration in childhood on adult behavior and the fortification of the pupil's heart against degrading forces that will assault it years after school is done, are of necessity not subject to full or accurate verification. The results of a teacher's work upon the life of the pupils out of school are also to a large extent inaccessible to adequate observation. Finally certain changes in human intellect and character, such as nobler ideals, new ambitions and stronger powers, are hard to test even within the sphere of school and class-room life. The deeper ideals and ambitions are often cherished in secret and revealed only by some sudden access of intimacy or by unusual events. The

---

[3] The right intellectual attitude is, of course, not the sole factor in good teaching. A good will toward children, philanthropic devotion to the work, the zeal for perfection that animates the true artist or craftsman and the personal qualities which work subtly by the force of imitation are also important.

strength of mental powers is not hard to test but the result is almost always the result of delayed capacity,—of mere inner growth,—as well as of the teacher's efforts; hence, the facts are hard to interpret.

In many cases, however, a teacher may not only hope and believe that a desired result has been obtained; he may know. In many cases he can do more than simply try the best plan he can devise; he can try, test the results, find the failures in them, and, with this new knowledge, devise a remedy. Such actual verification of the success of one's work is possible in the case of changes in knowledge, skill and all definite habits. One should be able to tell absolutely whether Johnny Smith gets ideas or only words when he reads, whether Mary Jones can sew well enough to be worth five dollars a week to a dress-maker, whether Fred Brown does or does not treat his class-mates with more justice than he did three months ago.

Their Value to the Teacher.   Testing the results of one's teaching is useful not only because it gives a basis for improvements in one's methods, but also because it is one chief means of gaining knowledge of the mental content and special capacities of individuals. In applying the principle of apperception a teacher is constantly led to test the results of knowledge previously given as a preliminary to giving more. For the main thing in fitting stimuli to the mental make-up of pupils is not a host of ready-made devices to secure the cooperation of previous experience; it is rather constant readiness in testing for the presence of the essentials, in diagnosing the exact result of previous lessons.

Their Value to the Class.   Testing the results of teaching is useful to the class as well as to the teacher, and to the class directly as well as indirectly through the betterment of future steps in teaching. Any scholar needs to know that he knows as well as to merely know; to be ignorant and know that you are so is far more promising than to be ignorant and not know it. By expression and use new ideas and habits get a double value; boys and girls in a school need to know what progress their efforts have achieved and to guide their efforts by objective facts as well as by their own sense of progress.

It is a common opinion that examining a pupil, finding out "whether he knows his lesson" is the least part of teaching, is something that anyone can do. And it is fashionable amongst many teachers to spend the greater part of their time and still more of their energy in giving children opportunities to learn a great deal rather than in making sure that they learn something. The type of testing that uses the entire recitation simply to make sure that the pupil has studied certain pages of a book and remembered what he has learned is a small part of teaching and can be done by even a poor teacher. But the real verification of the work of teaching, that makes sure of just what the pupil knows and feels, that tests his comprehension and attitude as well as his memory, that prevents waste and prepares the way for better teaching of that pupil in the next topic and better teaching of that topic with the next class, is a most essential part of teaching and is one of the hardest things to do well.

The Principles of Effective Testing.   The principle is indeed easy but its successful, concrete application requires both a high degree of capacity for insight into the facts of child life and thorough training. The principle is simply:—To know whether anyone has a given mental state, see if he can use it,[4] to know whether anyone will make a given response to a certain situation, put him in the situation arranged so that that response and that response alone will produce a certain result and see if that result is produced. The test for both mental states and mental connections is appropriate action.

.   .   .

Summary

Testing the results of teaching and study is for the teacher what verification of theories is to the scientist,—the *sine qua non* of sure progress. It is a chief means to fitting teaching to the previous experience and individual capacities of pupils, and to arousing in them the instinct for achievement and the capacity for self-criticism. The test for knowledge, skill, appreciation and morality is in each case appropriate action. A valid test is one in which the response in question (knowledge or skill or ideal or whatever it may be) and only that response will produce a certain observable result.

Testing the General Results of School Work

The Importance of Tests of Methods.   What the teacher should do with respect to each act of teaching each pupil, the leaders in education should do with respect to the general methods of teaching a subject recommended to all teachers. Expectations of results, even if based on right principles, must be corroborated by actual verification.

As a rule the best present judgment about the efficiency of a method of teaching will rest upon its harmony with the principles derived from the facts of human nature and upon its success or failure as measured by the opinion of those who try it. The best present judgment will not be

---

[4] This is not given as a principle of psychology or logic, but as a rule for teaching. We are not here concerned with an ultimate criterion for the existence of a mental state in a given individual, but with a practical means of being assured that John has a certain concept of the class "dog," that Mary knows what "seven" means and the like.

mistaken very often or very much, but there could be safer tests of the worth of methods. For when a principle derived from the facts of human nature is applied under the peculiar conditions of school life it may need modification; and the opinions of even the best teachers concerning the value of a method may be shortsighted and partial. What is needed is the comparatively sure decision of that superior variety of opinion which is called science.

The Characteristics of Scientific Judgments of Methods. The judgments of science are distinguished from the judgments of opinion by being more impartial, more objective, more precise, more subject to verification by any competent observer, and by being made by those who by their nature and training should be better judges.

Science knows or should know no favorites and cares for nothing in its conclusions but their truth. Opinion is often misled by the "unconscious logic of its hopes and fears," by prepossessions for or against this or that book or method or result. Science pays no heed to anything but the facts which it has already made sure of; it puts nothing in the scales but objective evidence. Opinion trusts its personal impressions, bows to authority and follows the crowd. Anyone's opinion constantly favors the methods he is used to and is suspicious of new ideas except his own; it accepts without verification and rejects without a fair trial. Science seeks precise quantitative measures of facts by which changes and correspondences may be properly weighed; opinion is content to guess at amounts of difference and likeness, to talk in the vague terms of more or less, much and little, to rate a method as better or worse without taking the pains to find out just how much better or worse it is. Science reveals the sources of its evidence and the course of its arguments, so that any properly equipped thinker can verify for himself the facts asserted to be true. Opinion offers itself to be accepted or rejected, but not to be verified or intelligently criticized. Science is the work of minds specialized to search after truth and selected as fit for the work by their equals and superiors in it. Opinion is the occasional thought of those who, though important and capable people, are yet only amateurs in the work of getting truth.

Science would decide between two methods, say of teaching reading, by giving each an adequate trial, by measuring exactly the changes in bodily welfare, knowledge, interests, habits, powers and ideals caused by the two, and by comparing impartially the results in the two cases. It would, for instance, arrange that method A should be tried in ten or twenty cases and method B in ten or twenty other classes of equal ability and advantages taught by equally competent teachers. It would make sure that the two groups of teachers tried equally hard and that the two groups of classes were alike with respect to school-room equipment, the amount of time given to reading and the like. It would measure with precision the accomplishment of each pupil in reading itself, in spelling and writing, in knowledge of facts gained, in appreciation of good literature, in interest in reading, in such habits as might be influenced by the special training of reading, in power to learn new things and so on through the list of all the changes which instruction in reading may produce.

The Prospects of Scientific Investigations of Teaching. Obviously such a scientific basis for the professional work of teaching is in every way desirable. But for many reasons only a beginning has been made. The main reasons are perhaps, first that strictly scientific methods have only lately begun to be used in the case of facts of human activities and second that the complexity of the problems of teaching is so great as to make scientific treatment of them very intricate and laborious. There are a score of competent scientists engaged in the study of physical science for every one that is at work on the problems of social institutions. The task of knowing completely the facts and explanation of the mental and moral development of any one child is comparable to the study of the geology of an entire continent or the chemistry of all the metals.

The infrequency of the effort to investigate questions of teaching in the spirit and by the methods of science and the difficulty of the task itself are, however, no excuse for their neglect. The scientific study of teaching is at least as important as the scientific study of medicine and, though difficult, is in no way impossible. Even the subtle changes in powers, interests and aspirations can be measured; for sooner or later they must be manifested in actual facts. Even the remote influences of teaching on life after school can be known if the investigator has unlimited time and energy. The immediate influence of various sorts of teaching upon the knowledge and habits directly concerned, may be studied scientifically with much less difficulty and with promise of quick returns in knowledge. There should be no need to guess at the value of methods of teaching spelling or beginning reading or Latin grammar.

Such investigations lie beyond the scope of the activities of most teachers. The time, the training, the scientific frame of mind and the zeal which they require can only rarely be at the disposal of the teacher, who has so many other things to learn and to do. To advance scientific knowledge of education is a most worthy occupation for anyone who is able to succeed in it but it is not the duty of all or of many teachers. The burden of making exact measurements of children's attainments, of inquiring deeply into the what and why of the facts of school life and of feeling responsible for the verification or disproof of hypotheses about methods may be assumed voluntarily by the investigator, but it should not be imposed upon an already too busy teacher. Teachers should respect and encourage the labors of science but they should not feel bound to share them. The leaders in thought about education, on the other hand, *should* feel bound to study scientifically the field in which they claim to rank as experts. Since their opinions will be accepted by the profession as a whole, it is their duty to verify each opinion by a test of the results to which it leads.

2. FORECAST FOR THE SEVENTIES
Harold G. Shane and June Grant Shane

During the last five years, there has been a marked increase in long- and short-range speculation regarding possible educational futures that may lie before us in the remaining years of the twentieth century. For the past three years, we have studied approximately 400 published and unpublished articles and books in which such conjectures and projections occur.

These current writings clearly indicate that education and schools, as they exist today, will change drastically during the 1970's and will be modified almost beyond recognition by the end of the century. The paragraphs that follow summarize some of the more important developments that could occur in the next decade and propose some of the new roles in which the teacher is likely to be cast. In conclusion, we give thought to the question: For what kind of world should children who will live most of their lives in the twenty-first century be prepared? Here, then, as many scholars see it, are some of the possible designs of educational futures in the seventies.

Education will reverse its traditional pattern of expenditure. From the beginning, more money has been spent per student in higher education, with secondary education coming in a strong second and elementary education, a poor third. Preschool and kindergarten programs have not even been in the race for funds. But now, major support for early childhood education seems highly probable because of our belated recognition that we have spent literally billions at the upper-age ranges to compensate for what we did not do at the two- to seven-year age levels.

Now priorities for education of the youngest will bring to public education nonschool preschools, minischools, and a preprimary continuum.

From Harold G. Shane and June Grant Shane, "Forecast for the Seventies," *Today's Education*, 58 (January 1969), 29–32. Reprinted by permission of the editor and the authors.

As nonschool preschool programs begin to operate, educators will assume a formal responsibility for children when they reach the age of two. We will work with parents of young children both directly and through educational TV programs for young mothers. And we will offer such services as medical-dental examinations and follow-up, early identification of the handicapped and deprived, attacks on nutritional needs, and—of major importance—early referral to cooperating social agencies for treatment of psychobehavioral problems.

New programs for two-year-olds will involve the coordination of community resources, under school auspices, to equalize educational opportunity for these children before cultural deprivation makes inroads on their social and mental health.

The minischool, as envisioned here, is one that provides a program of carefully designed experiences for the three-year-old—experiences deliberately devised to increase the sensory input from which the children derive their intelligence. Each minischool presumably would enroll six or eight children under a qualified paraprofessional. A professionally prepared childhood environmental specialist would directly supervise clusters of approximately six minischools.

We will probably build these small schools into housing projects, make them part of new schoolhouse construction, or open them in improvised space in convenient buildings.

The preprimary continuum is a new creation intended to replace contemporary kindergartens for the four- and five-year-old. This program presupposes that the young learner will spend from one year to four years preparing himself to perform effectively in a subsequent primary continuum, the segment of education now usually labeled grades one through three. The preprimary interval should sharply reduce the problems of widely varied experience and social adjustment encountered by children who are arbitrarily enrolled in grade one at age six regardless of theri previous cultural environment.

Major environmental mediation for two- to six-year-olds, as described above, will permit schools to abandon the current transitional concept of nongrading. In the coming decade, a seamless primary, middle-school, and secondary continuum of coordinated learning experiences will begin to replace the nongraded programs of the sixties.

Here, progress and the time spent on a given topic will become completely individual matters, as one emergent design for learning serves all ages. The intellectually advantaged child, for instance, might spend only two years in the primary or intermediate continuum, accomplishing what most children would accomplish in three or four years.

In this personalized educational continuum, the question of how to group children will no longer be relevant. The child will simply work with others in ephemeral groupings during whatever time certain shared learning experiences happen to coincide.

Admission age quibbles, too, will become irrelevant after several years of minischool and preprimary experience. There is no need to group children for first grade at the magic age of six, since they would be phased into their primary school year at any time from age four at one extreme to age eight at the other.

Promotion problems will also vanish, since in a continuum of learning there are no specific points at which a student passes or fails; he merely moves ahead at his own pace. Grade cards are likewise destined to disappear: Evaluation of progress will be continuous, and a progress report can be made in a parent conference whenever pupil performance analysis is in order.

The school will provide more learning experiences that parallel or accompany conventional academic content. The creative and enjoyable will begin to vie strongly with the utilitarian and academic dimensions of education. Such paracurricular ventures as educational travel, school camping, informal dramatics (including sociodrama), enlarged intramural sports programs that stress mass participation, and engaging youth in useful service to the community are due to increase in frequency and extent.

Biochemical and psychological mediation of learning is likely to increase. New drama will play on the educational stage as drugs are introduced experimentally to improve in the learner such qualities as personality, concentration, and memory. The application of biochemical research findings, heretofore centered in infra-human subjects, such as fish, could be a source of conspicuous controversy when children become the objects of experimentation.

Enrichment of the school environment in the seventies—especially in the ghetto—to "create" what we now measure as intelligence by improving experimental input also will become more accepted. Few are likely to make an issue of efforts to improve educational opportunities for the deprived child. However, there could be a tinderbox quality to the introduction of mandatory foster homes and "boarding schools" for children between the ages of two and three whose home environment was felt to have a malignant influence. Decisions of the 1970's in these areas could have far-reaching social consequences. Although it is repugnant to permit a child's surroundings to harm him, there is no clear social precedent for removing a child from his home because it lacks the sensory input needed to build normal intelligence and, therefore, in effect condemns him to a lifetime of unskilled labor.

The next decade will see new approaches to "educational disaster areas." Most of America's large cities, and some suburban and rural sections, contain a central core that can only be described in this way. Damage surrounding this core decreases from severe, to extensive, to moderate, to negligible.

Up to now, perhaps, we may have spent too much energy and money on just the worst schools of these central cores. In such neighborhoods, we cannot create a decent educational opportunity until the *total* social setting is rehabilitated. In the early 1970's, we may find it both more efficient and more educationally sound to direct our attention initially to improving those areas and schools where educational damage is moderate to extensive rather than drastic. For such areas, immediate attention may prevent their deteriorating in the near future into severe disaster areas. Once the deterioration in these outer ring schools is reversed, greater educational resources will become available to help us close in on the ghetto schools where damage is severe or total.

It would be unthinkable to ignore the children who live in our worst educational disaster areas until we can mobilize the greater forces needed to bring these schools up to necessary standards of excellence. Therefore, until inner cities regain their socioeconomic and educational health, we often will transport their children to outlying areas. In the next decade, this will involve a rapid buildup of facilities in these areas both in terms of enlarging existing schools and of creating new types of learning environments. Removing children from inner-city problem areas has the added merit of stimulating them through contacts with children from other social groups.

Later in the seventies, the elementary school changes will cause the junior and senior high schools to modify their programs. Their curriculums will presumably become more challenging and interesting. Wider age ranges, increased pupil interchange within and between schools, and individualized programs built around new instructional media will inevitably influence emerging secondary school organization.

In the late 1970's or early 1980's, it is not unlikely that students will graduate from high school with knowledge and social insight equal or superior to that of the person who earned a bachelor's degree in the 1960's.

On entering college, these students will be ready to begin postbacalaureate studies, and our undergraduate college programs *in their present forms* will be unnecessary.

If this seems farfetched, bear in mind that the young person pictured here will have had the benefit of carefully developed learning opportunities in a skillfully mediated milieu since he was two or three years old.

During the next 10 years, business will participate in education to a greater extent. Although many of their activities are neither widely known or generally understood, major corporations are already contracting to tackle pollution, teach marketable skills to the deprived, administer police protection, reclaim slums, and manage civic governments.

John Kenneth Galbraith has noted that the modern corporation already has the power to shape society. Frank Keppel commented recently that the revival of U.S. metropolitan schools depends as much on the action of leaders of finance and commerce as it does on educators. And Hazel Henderson commented last summer in the *Harvard Business Review* that industry's expansion into such areas as housing, education, and dropout training is probably the best way to handle our central needs if suitable performance standards and general specifications are properly controlled.

The growth of a cooperative business-and-education relationship will be of great portent in the seventies as corporations both expand the production activities of the education industry and assume more management and control responsibilities.

The roles and responsibilities of teachers will alter throughout the next decade. Future-think suggests that between 1970 and 1980 a number of new assignments and specialties will materialize if present trends continue.

For one thing, the basic role of the teacher will change noticeably. Ten years hence it should be more accurate to term him a "learning clinician." This title is intended to convey the idea that schools are becoming "clinics" whose purpose is to provide individualized psychosocial "treatment" for the student, thus increasing his value both to himself and to society.

In the school of the future, senior learning clinicians will be responsible for coordinating the services needed for approximately 200 to 300 children. In different instructional units (an evolution of the "team" concept) we will find paraprofessionals, teaching interns, and other learning clinicians with complementary backgrounds. Some will be well-informed in counseling, others in media, engineering, languages, evaluation, systems analysis, simulation, game theory, and individual-need analysis.

But on the whole, the learning clinician will probably not be appreciably more specialized in subject matter disciplines than he was in the 1960's except for being more skilled in using educational technology. He will do more *coordinating* and *directing* of individual inquiry and will engage in less 1968-style group instruction. He will be highly concerned with providing and maintaining an effective environment, skilled in interpersonal transactions, and able to work with persons of different ages and learning styles.

Ten years from now, faculties will include—

Culture analysts, who make use of our growing insights into how a subculture shapes the learning style and behavior of its members.

Media specialists, who tailor-make local educational aids, who evaluate hardware and software and their use, and who are adept in the information sciences of automated-information storage and retrieval, and computer programing.

Information-input specialists, who make a career of keeping faculty and administration aware of implications for education in broad social, economic, and political trends.

Curriculum-input specialists, who from day to day make necessary corrections and additions to memory bank tapes on which individualized instructional materials are stored.

Biochemical therapist/pharmacists, whose services increase as biochemical therapy and memory improvement chemicals are introduced more widely.

Early childhood specialists, who work in the nonschool preschool and minischool programs and in the preprimary continuum.

Developmental specialists, who determine the groups in which children and youth work and who make recommendations regarding ways of improving pupil learning.

Community-contact personnel, who specialize in maintaining good communication, in reducing misunderstanding or abrasions, and in placing into the life of the community the increased contributions that the schools of the 1970's will be making.

As educators turn a speculative eye on the next decade, they must seek to answer a question that most of them have hesitated to face. For what kind of world should we strive to prepare children and youth who will spend most of their lives in the next century? We say this question is crucial because educational policy decisions in the 1970's will not only anticipate tomorrow, they probably will help to *create* it.

Recent publications in the physical, natural, and social sciences suggest emerging changes in society that seem likely to characterize the world of 2000 A.D. A number of future-think writers agree that unless unforeseen catastrophes intervene, such developments as the following are probable:

The individual's personal freedom and responsibility will be greater.

The IQ of the average child will be 125, perhaps 135.

Cultures throughout the world will be more standardized because of the impact of mass media and increased mobility.

Access to more information will carry us toward an international consensus as to what is desirable in family life, art, recreation, education, diet, economic policies, and government.

Cruelty will be more vigorously rejected and methodically eliminated.

Leaders will be those who are the most able, regardless of their racial origins, religious beliefs, family backgrounds, or lack of great wealth.

The worldwide status and influence of the female will greatly increase.

Differences in wealth and ownership between haves and have-nots will narrow.

Through the mediation of trends, society will begin to design or give direction to the future so that the years ahead will better serve human welfare.

The changes described above will open many more doors for educational leadership. During the coming decade, however, education must do more than just lengthen its stride to keep pace with trends and innovations. We must bring social perception and long-range vision to the task of designing and planning schools that can help bring about the best of many possible tomorrows.

PEDAGOGICAL MODEL:
The Teacher as Behavior Modifier

THE SCIENCE OF LEARNING
AND THE ART OF TEACHING
B. F. Skinner

Some promising advances have recently been made in the field of learning. Special techniques have been designed to arrange what are called "contingencies of reinforcement"—the relations which prevail between behavior on the one hand and the consequences of that behavior on the other—with the result that a much more effective control of behavior has been achieved. It has long been argued that an organism learns mainly by producing changes in its environment, but it is only recently that these changes have been carefully manipulated. In traditional devices for the study of learning—in the serial maze, for example, or in the T-maze, the problem box, or the familiar discrimination apparatus—the effects produced by the organism's behavior are left to many fluctuating circumstances. There is many a slip between the turn-to-the-right and the food-cup at the end of the alley. It is not surprising that techniques of this sort have yielded only very rough data from which the uniformities demanded by an experimental science can be extracted only by averaging many cases. In none of this work has the behavior of the individual organism been predicted in more than a statistical sense. The learning processes which are the presumed object of such research are reached only through a series of inferences. Current preoccupation with deductive systems reflects this state of the science.

Recent improvements in the conditions which control behavior in the field of learning are of two principal sorts. The Law of Effect has been taken seriously; we have made sure that effects *do* occur and that they occur under conditions which are optimal for producing the changes called learning. Once we have arranged the particular type of conse-

From B. F. Skinner, "The Science of Learning and the Art of Teaching," *Harvard Educational Review*, XXIV (Spring 1954), 86–97. Copyright © 1954 by President and Fellows of Harvard College. Reprinted by permission.

quence called a reinforcement, our techniques permit us to shape up the behavior of an organism almost at will. It has become a routine exercise to demonstrate this in classes in elementary psychology by conditioning such an organism as a pigeon. Simply by presenting food to a hungry pigeon at the right time, it is possible to shape up three or four well-defined responses in a single demonstration period—such responses as turning around, pacing the floor in the pattern of a figure-8, standing still in a corner of the demonstration apparatus, stretching the neck, or stamping the foot. Extremely complex performances may be reached through successive stages in the shaping process, the contingencies of reinforcement being changed progressively in the direction of the required behavior. The results are often quite dramatic. In such a demonstration one can *see* learning take place. A significant change in behavior is often obvious as the result of a single reinforcement.

A second important advance in technique permits us to maintain behavior in given states of strength for long periods of time. Reinforcements continue to be important, of course, long after an organism has learned *how* to do something, long after it has acquired behavior. They are necessary to maintain the behavior in strength. Of special interest is the effect of various schedules of intermittent reinforcement. Charles B. Ferster and the author are currently preparing an extensive report of a five-year research program, sponsored by the Office of Naval Research, in which most of the important types of schedules have been investigated and in which the effects of schedules in general have been reduced to a few principles. On the theoretical side we now have a fairly good idea of why a given schedule produces its appropriate performance. On the practical side we have learned how to maintain any given level of activity for daily periods limited only by the physical exhaustion of the organism and from day to day without substantial change throughout its life. Many of these effects would be traditionally assigned to the field of motivation, although the principal operation is simply the arrangement of contingencies of reinforcement.

These new methods of shaping behavior and of maintaining it in strength are a great improvement over the traditional practices of professional animal trainers, and it is not surprising that our laboratory results are already being applied to the production of performing animals for commercial purposes. In a more academic environment they have been used for demonstration purposes which extend far beyond an interest in learning as such. For example, it is not too difficult to arrange the complex contingencies which produce many types of social behavior. Competition is exemplified by two pigeons playing a modified game of Ping-Pong. The pigeons drive the ball back and forth across a small table by pecking at it. When the ball gets by one pigeon, the other is reinforced.

The task of constructing such a "social relation" is probably completely out of reach of the traditional animal trainer. It requires a carefully designed program of gradually changing contingencies and the skillful use of schedules to maintain the behavior in strength. Each pigeon is separately prepared for its part in the total performance, and the "social relation" is then arbitrarily constructed. The sequence of events leading up to this stable state are excellent material for the study of the factors important in nonsynthetic social behavior. It is instructive to consider how a similar series of contingencies could arise in the case of the human organism through the evolution of cultural patterns.

Cooperation can also be set up, perhaps more easily than competition. We have trained two pigeons to coordinate their behavior in a cooperative endeavor with a precision which equals that of the most skillful human dancers. In a more serious vein these techniques have permitted us to explore the complexities of the individual organism and to analyze some of the serial or coordinate behaviors involved in attention, problem solving, various types of self-control, and the subsidiary systems of responses within a single organism called "personalities." Some of these are exemplified in what we call multiple schedules of reinforcement. In general a given schedule has an effect upon the rate at which a response is emitted. Changes in the rate from moment to moment show a pattern typical of the schedule. The pattern may be as simple as a constant rate of responding at a given value, it may be a gradually accelerating rate between certain extremes, it may be an abrupt change from not responding at all to a given stable high rate, and so on. It has been shown that the performance characteristic of a given schedule can be brought under the control of a particular stimulus and that different performances can be brought under the control of different stimuli in the same organism. At a recent meeting of the American Psychological Association, Dr. Ferster and the author demonstrated a pigeon whose behavior showed the pattern typical of "fixed-interval" reinforcement in the presence of one stimulus and, alternately, the pattern typical of the very different schedule called "fixed ratio" in the presence of a second stimulus. In the laboratory we have been able to obtain performances appropriate to *nine* different schedules in the presence of appropriate stimuli in random alternation. When Stimulus 1 is present, the pigeon executes the performance appropriate to Schedule 1. When Stimulus 2 is present, the pigeon executes the performance appropriate to Schedule 2. And so on. This result is important because it makes the extrapolation of our laboratory results to daily life much more plausible. We are all constantly shifting from schedule to schedule as our immediate environment changes, but the dynamics of the control exercised by reinforcement remain essentially unchanged.

It is also possible to construct very complex *sequences* of schedules. It is not easy to describe these in a few words, but two or three examples may be mentioned. In one experiment the pigeon generates a performance appropriate to Schedule A where the reinforcement is simply the production of the stimulus characteristic of Schedule B, to which the pigeon then responds appropriately. Under a third stimulus, the bird yields a performance appropriate to Schedule C where the reinforcement in this case is simply the production of the stimulus characteristic of Schedule D, to which the bird then responds appropriately. In a special case, first investigated by L. B. Wyckoff, Jr., the organism responds to one stimulus where the reinforcement consists of the *clarification* of the stimulus controlling another response. The first response becomes, so to speak, an objective form of "paying attention" to the second stimulus. In one important version of this experiment, as yet unpublished, we could say that the pigeon is telling us whether it is "paying attention" to the *shape* of a spot of light or to its *color.*

One of the most dramatic applications of these techniques has recently been made in the Harvard Psychological Laboratories by Floyd Ratliff and Donald S. Blough, who have skillfully used multiple and serial schedules of reinforcement to study complex perceptual processes in the infrahuman organism. They have achieved a sort of psychophysics without verbal instruction. In a recent experiment by Blough, for example, a pigeon draws a detailed dark-adaptation curve showing the characteristic breaks of rod and cone vision. The curve is recorded continuously in a single experimental period and is quite comparable with the curves of human subjects. The pigeon behaves in a way which, in the human case, we would not hesitate to describe by saying that it adjusts a very faint patch of light until it can just be seen.

In all this work, the species of the organism has made surprisingly little difference. It is true that the organisms studied have all been vertebrates, but they still cover a wide range. Comparable results have been obtained with pigeons, rats, dogs, monkeys, human children, and most recently, by the author in collaboration with Ogden R. Lindsley, human psychotic subjects. In spite of great phylogenetic differences, all these organisms show amazingly similar properties of the learning process. It should be emphasized that this has been achieved by analyzing the effects of reinforcement and by designing techniques which manipulate reinforcement with considerable precision. Only in this way can the behavior of the individual organism be brought under such precise control. It is also important to note that through a gradual advance to complex interrelations among responses, the same degree of rigor is being extended to behavior which would usually be assigned to such fields as perception, thinking, and personality dynamics.

From this exciting prospect of an advancing science of learning, it is a great shock to turn to that branch of technology which is most directly concerned with the learning process—education. Let us consider, for example, the teaching of arithmetic in the lower grades. The school is concerned with imparting to the child a large number of responses of a special sort. The responses are all verbal. They consist of speaking and writing certain words, figures, and signs which, to put it roughly, refer to numbers and to arithmetic operations. The first task is to shape up these responses—to get the child to pronounce and to write responses correctly, but the principal task is to bring this behavior under many sorts of stimulus control. This is what happens when the child learns to count, to recite tables, to count while ticking off the items in an assemblage of objects, to respond to spoken or written numbers by saying "odd," "even," "prime," and so on. Over and above this elaborate repertoire of numerical behavior, most of which is often dismissed as the product of rote learning, the teaching of arithmetic looks forward to those complex serial arrangements of responses involved in original mathematical thinking. The child must acquire responses of transposing, clearing fractions, and so on, which modify the order or pattern of the original material so that the response called a solution is eventually made possible

Now, how is this extremely complicated verbal repertoire set up? In the first place, what reinforcements are used? Fifty years ago the answer would have been clear. At that time educational control was still frankly aversive. The child read numbers, copied numbers, memorized tables, and performed operations upon numbers to escape the threat of the birch rod or cane. Some positive reinforcements were perhaps eventually derived from the increased efficiency of the child in the field of arithmetic and in rare cases some automatic reinforcement may have resulted from the sheer manipulation of the medium—from the solution of problems or the discovery of the intricacies of the number system. But for the immediate purposes of education the child acted to avoid or escape punishment. It was part of the reform movement known as progressive education to make the positive consequences more immediately effective, but any one who visits the lower grades of the average school today will observe that a change has been made, not from aversive to positive control, but from one form of aversive stimulation to another. The child at his desk, filling in his workbook, is behaving primarily to escape from the threat of a series of minor aversive events—the teacher's displeasure, the criticism or ridicule of his classmates, an ignominious showing in a competition, low marks, a trip to the office "to be talked to" by the principal, or a word to the parent who may still resort to the birch rod. In this welter of aversive consequences, getting the right answer is in itself an insignificant event, any effect of which is lost amid the anxieties, the boredom, and the aggressions which are the inevitable by-products of aversive control.[1]

Secondly, we have to ask how the contingencies of reinforcement are arranged. When is a numerical operation reinforced as "right"? Eventually, of course, the pupil may be able to check his own answers and achieve some sort of automatic reinforcement, but in the early stages the reinforcement of being right is usually accorded by the teacher. The contingencies she provides are far from optimal. It can easly be demonstrated that, unless explicit mediating behavior has been set up, the lapse of only a few seconds between response and reinforcement destroys most of the effect. In a typical classroom, nevertheless, long periods of time customarily elapse. The teacher may walk up and down the aisle, for example, while the class is working on a sheet of problems, pausing here and there to say right or wrong. Many seconds or minutes intervene between the child's response and the teacher's reinforcement. In many cases—for example, when papers are taken home to be corrected—as much as 24 hours may intervene. It is surprising that this system has any effect whatsoever.

A third notable shortcoming is the lack of a skillful program which moves forward through a series of progressive approximations to the final complex behavior desired. A long series of contingencies is necessary to bring the organism into the possession of mathematical behavior most efficiently. But the teacher is seldom able to reinforce at each step in such a series because she cannot deal with the pupil's responses one at a time. It is usually necessary to reinforce the behavior in blocks of responses—as in correcting a work sheet or page from a workbook. The responses within such a block must not be interrelated. The answer to one problem must not depend upon the answer to another. The number of stages through which one may progressively approach a complex pattern of behavior is therefore small, and the task so much the more difficult. Even the most modern workbook in beginning arithmetic is far from exemplifying an efficient program for shaping up mathematical behavior.

Perhaps the most serious criticism of the current classroom is the relative infrequency of reinforcement. Since the pupil is usually dependent upon the teacher for being right, and since many pupils are usually dependent upon the same teacher, the total number of contingencies which may be arranged during, say, the first four years, is of the order of only a few thousand. But a very rough estimate suggests that efficient mathematical behavior at this level requires something of the order of 25,000 contingencies. We may suppose that even in the brighter student a given contingency must be arranged several times to place the behavior

[1] Skinner, B. F., *Science and Human Behavior*. New York: Macmillan, 1953.

well in hand. The responses to be set up are not simply the various items in tables of addition, subtraction, multiplication, and division; we have also to consider the alternative forms in which each item may be stated. To the learning of such material we should add hundreds of responses concerned with factoring, identifying primes, memorizing series, using short-cut techniques of calculation, constructing and using geometric representations or number forms, and so on. Over and above all this, the whole mathematical repertoire must be brought under the control of concrete problems of considerable variety. Perhaps 50,000 contingencies is a more conservative estimate. In this frame of reference the daily assignment in arithmetic seems pitifully meagre.

The result of all this is, of course, well known. Even our best schools are under criticism for their inefficiency in the teaching of drill subjects such as arithmetic. The condition in the average school is a matter of widespread national concern. Modern children simply do not learn arithmetic quickly or well. Nor is the result simply incompetence. The very subjects in which modern techniques are weakest are those in which failure is most conspicuous, and in the wake of an ever-growing incompetence come the anxieties, uncertainties, and aggressions which in their turn present other problems to the school. Most pupils soon claim the asylum of not being "ready" for arithmetic at a given level or, eventually, of not having a mathematical mind. Such explanations are readily seized upon by defensive teachers and parents. Few pupils ever reach the stage at which automatic reinforcements follow as the natural consequences of mathematical behavior. On the contrary, the figures and symbols of mathematics have become standard emotional stimuli. The glimpse of a column of figures, not to say an algebraic symbol or an integral sign, is likely to set off—not mathematical behavior—but a reaction of anxiety, guilt, or fear.

The teacher is usually no happier about this than the pupil. Denied the opportunity to control via the birch rod, quite at sea as to the mode of operation of the few techniques at her disposal, she spends as little time as possible on drill subjects and eagerly subscribes to philosophies of education which emphasize material of greater inherent interest. A confession of weakness is her extraordinary concern lest the child be taught something unnecessary. The repertoire to be imparted is carefully reduced to an essential minimum. In the field of spelling, for example, a great deal of time and energy has gone into discovering just those words which the young child is going to use, as if it were a crime to waste one's educational power in teaching an unnecessary word. Eventually, weakness of technique emerges in the disguise of a reformulation of the aims of education. Skills are minimized in favor of vague achievements—educating for democracy, educating the whole child, educating for life, and so on. And there the matter ends; for, unfortunately, these philosophies do not in turn suggest improvements in techniques. They offer little or no help in the design of better classroom practices.

There would be no point in urging these objections if improvement were impossible. But the advances which have recently been made in our control of the learning process suggest a thorough revision of classroom practices and, fortunately, they tell us how the revision can be brought about. This is not, of course, the first time that the results of an experimental science have been brought to bear upon the practical problems of education. The modern classroom does not, however, offer much evidence that research in the field of learning has been respected or used. This condition is no doubt partly due to the limitations of earlier research. But it has been encouraged by a too hasty conclusion that the laboratory study of learning is inherently limited because it cannot take into account the realities of the classroom. In the light of our increasing knowledge of the learning process we should, instead, insist upon dealing with those realities and forcing a substantial change in them. Education is perhaps the most important branch of scientific technology. It deeply affects the lives of all of us. We can no longer allow the exigencies of a practical situation to suppress the tremendous improvements which are within reach. The practical situation must be changed.

There are certain questions which have to be answered in turning to the study of any new organism. What behavior is to be set up? What reinforcers are at hand? What responses are available in embarking upon a program of progressive approximation which will lead to the final form of the behavior? How can reinforcements be most efficiently scheduled to maintain the behavior in strength? These questions are all relevant in considering the problem of the child in the lower grades.

In the first place, what reinforcements are available? What does the school have in its possession which will reinforce a child? We may look first to the material to be learned, for it is possible that this will provide considerable automatic reinforcement. Children play for hours with mechanical toys, paints, scissors and paper, noise-makers, puzzles— in short, with almost anything which feeds back significant changes in the environment and is reasonably free of aversive properties. The sheer control of nature is itself reinforcing. This effect is not evident in the modern school because it is masked by the emotional responses generated by aversive control. It is true that automatic reinforcement from the manipulation of the environment is probably only a mild reinforcer and may need to be carefully husbanded, but one of the most striking principles to emerge from recent research is that the *net* amount of reinforcement is of little significance. A very slight reinforcement may be tremendously effective in controlling behavior if it is wisely used.

If the natural reinforcement inherent in the subject matter is not enough, other reinforcers must be employed. Even in school the child is occasionally permitted to do "what he wants to do," and access to reinforcements of many sorts may be made contingent upon the more immediate consequences of the behavior to be established. Those who advocate competition as a useful social motive may wish to use the reinforcements which follow from excelling others, although there is the difficulty that in this case the reinforcement of one child is necessarily aversive to another. Next in order we might place the good will and affection of the teacher, and only when that has failed need we turn to the use of aversive stimulation.

In the second place, how are these reinforcements to be made contingent upon the desired behavior? There are two considerations here —the gradual elaboration of extremely complex patterns of behavior and the maintenance of the behavior in strength at each stage. The whole process of becoming competent in any field must be divided into a very large number of very small steps, and reinforcement must be contingent upon the accomplishment of each step. This solution to the problem of creating a complex repertoire of behavior also solves the problem of maintaining the behavior in strength. We could, of course, resort to the techniques of scheduling already developed in the study of other organisms but in the present state of our knowledge of educational practices, scheduling appears to be most effectively arranged through the design of the material to be learned. By making each successive step as small as possible, the frequency of reinforcement can be raised to a maximum, while the possibly aversive consequences of being wrong are reduced to a minimum. Other ways of designing material would yield other programs of reinforcement. Any supplementary reinforcement would probably have to be scheduled in the more traditional way.

These requirements are not excessive, but they are probably incompatible with the current realities of the classroom. In the experimental study of learning it has been found that the contingencies of reinforcement which are most efficient in controlling the organism cannot be arranged through the personal mediation of the experimenter. An organism is affected by subtle details of contingencies which are beyond the capacity of the human organism to arrange. Mechanical and electrical devices must be used. Mechanical help is also demanded by the sheer number of contingencies which may be used efficiently in a single experimental session. We have recorded many millions of responses from a single organism during thousands of experimental hours. Personal arrangement of the contingencies and personal observation of the results are quite unthinkable. Now, the human organism is, if anything, more sensitive to precise contingencies than the other organisms we have studied. We have every reason to expect, therefore, that the most effective control of human learning will require instrumental aid. The simple fact is that, as a mere reinforcing mechanism, the teacher is out of date. This would be true even if a single teacher devoted all her time to a single child, but her inadequacy is multiplied many-fold when she must serve as a reinforcing device to many children at once. If the teacher is to take advantage of recent advances in the study of learning, she must have the help of mechanical devices.

The technical problem of providing the necessary instrumental aid is not particularly difficult. There are many ways in which the necessary contingencies may be arranged, either mechanically or electrically. An inexpensive device which solves most of the principal problems has already been constructed. It is still in the experimental stage, but a description will suggest the kind of instrument which seems to be required. The device consists of a small box about the size of a small record player. On the top surface is a window through which a question or problem printed on a paper tape may be seen. The child answers the question by moving one or more sliders upon which the digits 0 through 9 are printed. The answer appears in square holes punched in the paper upon which the question is printed. When the answer has been set, the child turns a knob. The operation is as simple as adjusting a television set. If the answer is right, the knob turns freely and can be made to ring a bell or provide some other conditioned reinforcement. If the answer is wrong, the knob will not turn. A counter may be added to tally wrong answers. The knob must then be reversed slightly and a second attempt at a right answer made. (Unlike the flash-card, the device reports a wrong answer without giving the right answer.) When the answer is right, a further turn of the knob engages a clutch which moves the next problem into place in the window. This movement cannot be completed, however, until the sliders have been returned to zero.

The important features of the device are these: Reinforcement for the right answer is immediate. The mere manipulation of the device will probably be reinforcing enough to keep the average pupil at work for a suitable period each day, provided traces of earlier aversive control can be wiped out. A teacher may supervise an entire class at work on such devices at the same time, yet each child may progress at his own rate, completing as many problems as possible within the class period. If forced to be away from school, he may return to pick up where he left off. The gifted child will advance rapidly, but can be kept from getting too far ahead either by being excused from arithmetic for a time or by being given special sets of problems which take him into some of the interesting bypaths of mathematics.

The device makes it possible to present carefully designed material in which one problem can depend upon the answer to the preceding and where, therefore, the most efficient progress to an eventually complex repertoire can be made. Provision has been made for recording the commonest mistakes so that the tapes can be modified as experience dictates. Additional steps can be inserted where pupils tend to have trouble, and ultimately the material will reach a point at which the answers of the average child will almost always be right.

If the material itself proves not to be sufficiently reinforcing, other reinforcers in the possession of the teacher or school may be made contingent upon the operation of the device or upon progress through a series of problems. Supplemental reinforcement would not sacrifice the advantages gained from immediate reinforcement and from the possibility of constructing an optimal series of steps which approach the complex repertoire of mathematical behavior most efficiently.

A similar device in which the sliders carry the letters of the alphabet has been designed to teach spelling. In addition to the advantages which can be gained from precise reinforcement and careful programming, the device will teach reading at the same time. It can also be used to establish the large and important repertoire of verbal relationships encountered in logic and science. In short, it can teach verbal thinking. As to content instruction, the device can be operated as a multiple-choice self-rater.

Some objections to the use of such devices in the classroom can easily be foreseen. The cry will be raised that the child is being treated as a mere animal and that an essentially human intellectual achievement is being analyzed in unduly mechanistic terms. Mathematical behavior is usually regarded, not as a repertoire of responses involving numbers and numerical operations, but as evidences of mathematical ability or the exercise of the power of reason. It is true that the techniques which are emerging from the experimental study of learning are not designed to "develop the mind" or to further some vague "understanding" of mathematical relationships. They are designed, on the contrary, to establish the very behaviors which are taken to be the evidences of such mental states or processes. This is only a special case of the general change which is under way in the interpretation of human affairs. An advancing science continues to offer more and more convincing alternatives to traditional formulations. The behavior in terms of which human thinking must eventually be defined is worth treating in its own right as the substantial goal of education.

Of course the teacher has a more important function than to say right or wrong. The changes proposed would free her for the effective exercise of that function. Marking a set of papers in arithmetic—"Yes, nine and six *are* fifteen; no, nine and seven *are not* eighteen"—is beneath the dignity of any intelligent individual There is more important work to be done—in which the teacher's relations to the pupil cannot be duplicated by a mechanical device. Instrumental help would merely improve these relations. One might say that the main trouble with education in the lower grades today is that the child is obviously not competent and *knows it* and that the teacher is unable to do anything about it and *knows that too.* If the advances which have recently been made in our control of behavior can give the child a genuine competence in reading, writing, spelling, and arithmetic, then the teacher may begin to function, not in lieu of a cheap machine, but through intellectual, cultural, and emotional contacts of that distinctive sort which testify to her status as a human being.

Another possible objection is that mechanized instruction will mean technological unemployment. We need not worry about this until there are enough teachers to go around and until the hours and energy demanded of the teacher are comparable to those in other fields of employment. Mechanical devices will eliminate the more tiresome labors of the teacher but they will not necessarily shorten the time during which she remains in contact with the pupil.

A more practical objection: Can we afford to mechanize our schools? The answer is clearly yes. The device I have just described could be produced as cheaply as a small radio or phonograph. There would need to be far fewer devices than pupils, for they could be used in rotation. But even if we suppose that the instrument eventually found to be most effective would cost several hundred dollars and that large numbers of them would be required, our economy should be able to stand the strain. Once we have accepted the possibility and the necessity of mechanical help in the classroom, the economic problem can easily be surmounted. There is no reason why the school room should be any less mechanized than, for example, the kitchen. A country which annually produces millions of refrigerators, dish-washers, automatic washing-machines, automatic clothes-driers, and automatic garbage disposers can certainly afford the equipment necessary to educate its citizens to high standards of competence in the most effective way.

There is a simple job to be done. The task can be stated in concrete terms. The necessary techniques are known. The equipment needed can easily be provided. Nothing stands in the way but cultural inertia. But what is more characteristic of America than an unwillingness to accept the traditional as inevitable? We are on the threshold of an exciting and revolutionary period, in which the scientific study of man will be put to work in man's best interests. Education must play its part. It must accept the fact that a sweeping revision of educational practices is possible and inevitable. When it has done this, we may look forward with confidence to a school system which is aware of the nature of its tasks, secure in its methods, and generously supported by the informed and effective citizens whom education itself will create.

Part II

ROMANTICISM

Introduction

Romanticism is the ideological system which serves as a counter-vailing force to the ideology labeled Scientism. Because it functions primarily as an anti-ideology, Romanticism differs from time to time and from place to place in accordance with the system which it seeks to neutralize. In a dialectic fashion, it serves as an antithesis to a particular form of Scientism. During the first century A.D. it expressed itself as a religious rebellion against Phariseeism. In the eighteenth century, when the romantic rebellion was directed against the pagan classical tradition and the rationalist philosophical orientation, it emerged as a naturalistic, sometimes religious, movement. Twentieth-century Romanticism, popularly known as the counterculture, has assumed an antitechnological and anti-scientific stance; while remaining secular in design, it reflects a mystical and visionary emphasis. The latter-day rebel is an inverse model of the other-directed, Establishment-oriented bureaucrat who was so avidly ridiculed by sociologists of the mid-century.

Romanticism is the ideology of the rebel. Its focus is upon the liberation of the individual by the neutralization of the social forces which inhibit creativity and spontaneity. Adherents of Romanticism are not revolutionaries for they do not seek the transfer of power. Rather, they attempt to diminish the influence of power wherever it may appear. Historically, however, they have been charged with revolutionary activities and have suffered at the hands of the defenders of the established order who invariably label them revolutionaries. Thus rebels such as Jesus of Nazareth, William Blake, Henry Thoreau, and Lenny Bruce were viewed as political revolutionaries by some of their contemporaries and treated with scorn by the Establishment. Thus rebels in Western nation-states such as Great Britain and the United States often are viewed as Communists or fellow travelers, while in Eastern communist countries and in the Soviet Union they are labeled "bourgeois revisionists."

Even though they resemble revolutionaries in their anti-Establishment stance, rebels do not form lasting bonds with revolutionary leaders. Because they are individualists, they rarely abide by the puritanical goal-oriented expectations or accept the self-denigration which flows from revolutionary logic. In recent years the tenuous *entente* between the romantic rebels in the Students for a Democratic Society and the revolutionary faction known as the Weathermen has collapsed. Similarly, the fraternal relationship between the revolutionary and puritan segment of the Black Panthers and the High Priest of the drug cult, Dr. Timothy Leary, ended when Leary's championship of individualistic psychic liberation was viewed as interfering with the effectiveness of the revolutionary plans of the political Black Panthers.

Believing that liberation is achieved through psychological rather than sociological means, rebels are rarely civil libertarians. Their "kingdoms" lie in the psychic world and they seek liberation by neutralizing the socialization process. Social alienation is their badge of identity and often serves as a symbol of their psychic liberation.

Rebels reject the tendency in highly organized societies to objectify life and to pattern it according to the dictates of reason. They adhere to a belief in the supremacy of subjective consciousness and reject the view that man's reason or his scientific postulates are reliable or valid means of seeking to improve the conditions of existence. They reject the rational or scientific ordering of life and seek to unravel the force which they believe is man's best reliance—the natural instinctive urge that lies submerged because of the oppressive socialization process in "civilized" societies.

Because they believe that nature is good, rebels seek to abolish the influence of institutions. They are vociferous debunkers of the middle classes, which they perceive as the citadels of Scientism and institutionalism. Because they view the middle class as a hypocritical class enslaved by the bland demands imposed upon it by the technocracy, romanticists perpetually ridicule bourgeois ways. Their style of ridicule usually entails behaving in a manner which they believe will shock the middle class (*épater la bourgeoisie*).

Romanticism is expressed in various ways. It generally implies the rejection of the existing social system and social norms. Thus rebels seek various alternative life styles. Some have sought to discover freedom through a return to nature or to man's primitive aboriginal state, while others have devised various utopian schemes; some have formed communes while others have sought refuge in exploring their own identity. Still others have utilized various forms of drugs in the search for psychic enlightenment.

In the following readings which reflect the ideology of Romanticism, recurrent key concepts such as liberation, subjectivity, authenticity, and spontaneity are emphasized. The rejection of the "Establishment way" pervades all of the articles and reflects the centrality of defiance in the ideology of Romanticism.

In his essay entitled "The Diogenes Style," Kingley Widmer provides a scholarly and readable overview of the historical roots of the ideology of defiance. Tracing the secular tradition of Romanticism, he compares the styles of the ancient Greek Cynics and the latter-day Beats. His analysis illustrates vividly that in issues which relate to ideological patterns, the French proverb "the more a thing changes, the more it remains the same" contains an element of truth.

The two creeds utilized here to illustrate the romantic position emphasize the centrality of individuality and psychic liberation to the romantic ideology. William Blake was born in 1757 and died in 1827. He was an anarchist, mystic, visionary, poet, artist, philosopher, and genius. His "Proverbs of Hell" appear in *The Marriage of Heaven and Hell* and reveal his paradoxical view of life as well as his spirit of defiance. The second creed was written by a latter-day spokesman for the ideology of rebellion. Abbie Hoffman does not need an introduction. His rebel behavior and his *enfant terrible* style have been amply documented by the popular media.

Jean-Jacques Rousseau's *Emile* has served as the major theoretical educational expression of the ideology of Romanticism. In the excerpt selected here, Rousseau stresses the essential goodness of man and emphasizes a mode of "natural" education that can best be described as individualized instruction. (Rousseau's influence is reflected in the final essay in this section, in which Sidney Jourard focuses upon the role of the guru in individualized instruction.)

Ralph Waldo Emerson is the father of the American romantic literary spirit. Unlike most romanticists, Emerson, an intellectual transcendentalist, viewed formal education as an avenue for liberation. His emphasis upon the importance of individual genius, however, reveals the romantic distrust of mass education.

In *The Making of the Counter-Culture* Theodore Roszak attempted to identify the major epistemological and stylistic differences between the adherents of the counterculture and the defenders of the Establishment. He emphasized the centrality of the romantic rejection of the belief in objective consciousness. In the selection from his book included here, Roszak illustrates the similarity between the romantic spirit of today and its counterpart in man's primitive societies by focusing upon the style of the tribal shaman.

In the final essay, Sidney Jourard provides an educational model that is consistent with the ideology of Romanticism. His artist-teacher, the guru, is similar to Roszak's shaman for he attempts to purify and liberate the spirit of his students. Because Romanticism is an anti-ideology which rejects institutional life patterns, it rarely finds expression in formal educational settings. But by focusing upon authentic independent learning and its relationship to the role of the guru, Jourard may provide a relevant means of bridging the gap between training and education.

AN ANALYTICAL VIEW: A Brief Survey

THE DIOGENES STYLE
Kingley Widmer

Let us start with a literary gesture that marks the perennial attitude of revolt: "I know thy works, that thou are neither cold nor hot; I would thou wert cold or hot. So then because thou are lukewarm, and neither cold nor hot, I will spew thee out of my mouth." [1] This fragment out of Revelation sets the tone of demand and scorn. While much of life and literature necessarily moves in the realms of the tepid, not the rebellious. If one were to do a systematic history of literary rebels, I suppose some time should be spent on pieces from that old anthology, including those of the first identified literary rebels in the Western traditions—Jeremiah and a few of the other prophets. For our purposes, the most modern of the lot, Jonah, might be to the point because he foreshadows the cosmopolitan wanderers in his comic self-consciousness about being a rebel. More generally, it would be hard to over-value for the rebel tradition the significance of the Judaic prophetic mode, including its condemnation of the ways of power, its exaltation of love and compassion as struggle, its expansive metaphoric forms, and its violent manners of lamentation. (Certainly the voices from the wilderness have had their rebellious place in America, not least because the Protestant evangelical movements transmitted rather more of the prophetic fervor than their parochial values could contain.) Modern literary rebels still refract some of the Old Testament rage and repetition—often the first signs of the rebel posture.[2] But

---

From Kingley Widmer, *The Literary Rebel* (Carbondale, Ill.: Southern Illinois Press, 1965), pp. 3–12. Copyright © 1965. Reprinted with permission of the Southern Illinois Press.

---

[1] My most immediate source for the passage is Dostoevsky; it was a favorite of his (it appears twice in *The Possessed*).

[2] For example, see the traditional stridencies of Allen Ginsberg (*Howl* and *Kaddish*). While I am indebted to some of the literature on the Old Testament prophets, the summary, and probably impertinent, nature of my comments suggests not citing any scholar.

much of the Old Testament prophetic mode of revolt does lack modern relevance. Few moderns, rebels included, have the prophets' faith in an ultimately just cosmos, in the sense of personal dialogue with the Divine, or in the engagement to a special historical mission with a peculiar people. There may, of course, come a day when we will find a unique pertinence to the apocalyptic, rather than the moral, passion of the Judeo-Christian prophecies.

The relevance of the Biblical rebel, even in a post-Christian culture, might simply be assumed. Not so, I suspect, with another important and ancient tradition of the rebel voice. The Cynics of the Greco-Roman world, represented by Diogenes of Sinope and his successors, show major parallels with modern literary rebels which may illuminate some of the peculiarities and purposes of even the most recent literature.[3] Though the Cynic does not reveal certain of the self-conscious and syncretistic modern gestures, he does suggest the archetypal pattern of our literary rebels. One obvious reason for his relevance to these times is that, in contrast to many of the Jewish and Christian prophets, the Cynic was the cosmopolitan individualist in a mixed and sophisticated culture and in urbanized and imperial societies. The followers of Diogenes, then and now, may be the sour fruit in an over-ripe time, announcing that rotten-ness is all. The Cynic program announced most notably a philosophy of failure which also provided a devastating commentary on the fatuous successes of ages of counterfeit. Such rebels are not only disaffiliated from their society and culture but also unaffiliated with any overwhelming religious or revolutionary vision which would create a new society and culture. Thus, the most essential rebel style and attitude, I shall maintain, is just that which reveals rebellion as its central and sustained commitment. Beyond rebellion lies something else, not least the conditions which necessarily produce a new call to rebellion.

While there is considerable variation, historical and individual, in the commitment to rebellion, nonetheless, some generic patterns remain. When, for example, we read the commentaries on Diogenes of Sinope and his followers in Greek and Roman writings, and then read commentaries on contemporary American literary rebels, the arguments seem almost paraphrases of each other.[4] Take the basic image of the literary

---

[3] After previously writing a lengthy discussion of the Beats as analogous to the Cynics—"The Literary Rebel," *Centennial Rev.*, VI (Spring, 1962)—I searched through many books and articles for what then seemed the obvious comparison. The only one I found was by Lewis S. Feur, "Youth in the '60's," *New Leader*, XLIV (March 6, 1961), 18–22. While he notes the basic similarity, he also follows the stock contempt of the liberal ideologue and the usual charges of lack of productivity, political program, normal ambitions, etc.—points I try to answer below.

[4] The general characteristics of the Beat style seem to be public information. For examples, bibliographies and selected commentaries see the various anthologies: *The Beat Generation and the Angry Young Men*, ed. G. Feldman and M. Gartenberg (New York, 1959); *The Beats*, ed. Seymour Krim (New York, 1960); *A Casebook*

rebel that was somewhat misleadingly popularized in the 1950's under the rubrics of an American coterie, the Beat Generation or Beat Movement—now the almost world-wide figure of the Beatnik. It shows a rather aging youth, usually with long hair and a beard, in the uniform of the disinherited, obviously contemptuous of cleanliness and decorum. While the beggar's cloak and wallet of the Cynic have been replaced, as signs of office, by jeans and paperback book, the rest of the lineaments, and the essential gestures, remain much the same. In prodigal appearance, in casual domesticity, and in outraging taste, both Cynic and Beat seem similar in the ways in which they rebelliously affront the pretensions of the society at large to "gracious living." So, too, with the language of Cynic and Beat which, in and out of literature, fuses the vulgar and the intellectual in a striking mélange of vivid colloquialisms and highbrow abstractions that persistently violates formality and geniality. Certainly such speech has intrinsic functions, beyond modishness and group identification. For instance, the yoking of terms of obscenity with those of salvation—a Beat stylization which is also one of the most ancient forms of blasphemy—seems part of a demand that we perceive the incongruities in our ordering of the world. "Forbidden" language, used more or less seriously, serves not only to shock but to re-emphasize natural functions and exalt "common" awareness. Done with skill, curses can provide defiant prayers, obscenity a poetry of outrage. Indeed, a literary rebel whose language does not achieve some such sort of violation in itself is neither very poetic nor very rebellious.

Let us characterize further the archetypal rebel—the shape common to many Cynics, Beats, and others—with particular attention to the Cynics not as an historical phenomena but as a style of defiance. Many of the Diogenes anecdotes, such as that of his carrying a lamp in the daylight because he was looking for a real or honest man, achieved near universal recognition. In being a tragic comment on mankind, yet given a witty

---

on the Beat, ed. Thomas Parkinson (New York, 1961); *Marginal Manners*, ed. F. J. Hoffman (Evanston, 1962). In later sections, but not here, I discuss several writers labeled Beat. For the material on Diogenes and the Cynics I have drawn on the standard sources in translation: *Diogenes Laertius*, trans. R. D. Hicks (2 vols.; London, 1925); *Dio Chrysostom*, trans. J. W. Cahoon (5 vols.; London, 1932); *The Works of the Emperor Julian*, Vol. II, trans. W. C. Wright; *Epictetus*, trans. W. A. Oldfather (2 vols.; London, 1932). See also Farrand Sayre, *The Greek Cynics* (Baltimore, 1948—a considerable improvement over the earlier edition). The half-dozen histories of philosophy that I have consulted have not been very helpful on the aspects of Cynicism that concern us here. See, for example, W. Windelband, *A History of Philosophy*, Vol. I (New York, 1958), 86 ff. Neither are the standard reference works helpful; see, for example, Robert Eisler, "Cynics," in the *Encyclopedia of the Social Sciences* who provides a quasi-Marxist polemic. By far the most useful scholarly study for our purposes is Donald R. Dudley, *A History of Cynicism* (London, 1937) who astutely gives much of the essential information. My interpretations, of course, go beyond his suggestions.

twist and presented with burlesque dramatization, it has the distinctive rebel quality. The same style of didactic verve appeared in Diogenes' dramatic emphasis upon perversely free choice in which he matched his metaphors with direct actions. The reader of "existentialist" literature will be struck by the pertinence of the Cynic's insistence that he was a criminal, a debaser of the official coinage (including the currency of conventional standards), a defender of moral violations such as incest (which were never examined), and an exalter of his role as both actual and internal exile. In his quest for authenticity, Diogenes made what a cultivated society considered both buffoonish and felonious gestures, being intentionally crude and outspoken. The Cynics were noted for their obscenity, in act as well as word, and they reportedly were willing to "be natural" about fornicating and defecating, anywhere. Their notorious "shamelessness" was both part of their lesson and part of a way of life. Many of their self-conscious violations of commercial, bureaucratic and upperclass morals and manners suggest the Cynics as the first to intentionally *épater le bourgeois*. Put in this perspective, we may see such favorite rebel defiance as neither bohemian high-spirits nor part of nineteenth-century class conflict but as a more universal effort to dramatically mock complacent and restricted awareness.

Diogenes had a radical dialectic for every part of his personal life. He went about unkempt, dressed in the uniform of a beggar, slept almost anywhere, scornfully took what food came to hand, refused to work, condemned anxious luxuries but not direct pleasures, and was committed to the simplest sort of life. Even his famed bad manners were as much principle as temperament. "Other dogs bite their enemies, I bite my friends—for their salvation." He was an anarchist when it came to political authorities, a libertarian when it came to social customs, and a cosmopolitan when it came to loyalties ("The only true country is that which is as wide as the universe"). His dog's life, physically mean and rough, intellectually tough and biting, was an outrageous dramatization of radical awareness. Plato reportedly called Diogenes a "Socrates gone mad." But Plato was an authoritarian who refused to recognize tragic absurdity, either by allowing the poets in his republic or in understanding the witty buffoonery of a Diogenes. The Cynic, a better judge than the rational idealist of some parts of human nature, said, "Most men are so nearly mad that a finger's breadth would make the difference."

Diogenes would seem plausibly credited with certain literary traditions—mordant satire of things as they are and a popular dialectic of moral discontent. But the dialectical extremity that he lived may be more important, for he was one of the first to dramatize some rather important values: equality, even with rulers and women; freedom, even from the gods and the economic system; self-sufficiency, even to living a dog's life and masturbating freely; and directness, even in public speech and philosophy. Rather more than Thoreau—one of his descendants—and in the city, he attempted to embody individualistic autarchy and immediacy. His "simplicity" took the form of witty denials of superstitions, conventions, authorities and ideologies. Naturally, part of Diogenes' significance is confined to the peculiar conditions of his time. As a rebel against Athenian education (a usual dissident focus), he battled over the Greek definitions in the various schools of "virtue," "nature," "reason," and so on.[5] The antiquarian interest in Cynicism's role as "hard primitivism" or as a sort of left-wing Stoicism need not concern us here. The historical Cynics also display a naïveté about "rational" argument and "virtue" which can be related to the Sophists and Socrates but which strikes us as quaint and would certainly be antipathetic to most modern rebels who find their "reasons" in the irrational in an over-rationalized world. Similarly, Diogenes literal insistence on doing all "according to nature" hardly appears so clear anymore since various romanticisms and sciences have inevitably complicated our responses, and faith, in the natural orders.

Of more permanent importance are other curious qualities of the Cynics. For instance, they were harsh realists, yet also some of the earliest "utopians" with an exotic dream vision of a world where simplicity and directness reigned: the Island of Para—perhaps the secularization of sacred myths, later desecularized by less rigorous prophets. Then, too, the Cynics have a special claim on our attention in being one of the few groups of teachers (really *unteaching* in the Socratic manner) not subsidized by state, church, commerce or their own hierarchy, and also one of the few groups of teachers not submissive to those powers.

But more important to the modern view is the clear extremity of the Cynics' rebel role. For Diogenes, civilization was to be corrected solely by the individual (that ruled out organizations and politics), in active and iconoclastic confrontation (that ruled out snobs and mystics), in the streets and going institutions (that ruled out esoterics and revolutionaries), and with intense scorn (that ruled out the stupid and bland). We may suppose that the only reason Diogenes was not against bureaucratic authority, mass genteel education-entertainment, the Bomb, etc., was that our technological nihilisms had not yet been invented. Since Diogenes' literary works, apparently outrageous dialogues and burlesque tragedies, have not survived we can see that his greatest creation was a nullifidian style. This philosophical tramp (he usually went south in the winter) and wise buffoon (there must have been some natural appropri-

---

[5] See A. O. Lovejoy and George Boas, *Primitivism and Related Ideas in Antiquity* (Baltimore, 1935). My comments throughout intentionally de-emphasize historical sources and significances of the literary rebels, which is not to deny them but to focus on the permanent qualities of rebellion.

ateness for all the wisecracks fathered on him), set standards for the
perennial rebel's defiance of how most men believe and live.

The many anecdotes told of Diogenes and Alexander—no doubt
apocryphal but quite in accord with the Cynic role—insist on independence and equality. When the King of Kings reputedly stood in front of
Diogenes and asked what favor he could grant, and was told to quit
blocking the sunlight, or when the ruler of the world flatteringly compared himself to Diogenes, and Diogenes sardonically confirmed the
comparison, we see the power of negative thinking. Another series of
anecdotes linked to Diogenes provide a mordant last will and testament
—a form of tragic wit drawn upon by many later rebels, such as Villon
and Corbière, who also used death as the harsh test of conventional values. Diogenes' reputed last wishes have his usual wayward wisdom. One
report is that he asked, in a world deeply responsive to Antigone's fu-
nereal scrupulousness, to be cast in a ditch and thus do the beasts some
good. So much for death, and your pieties, foolish Athenians! Another
report has it that he perversely asked to be buried face down. Dialectical
to the end, he explained that the world of his time would soon be turned
upside down, putting him the right way up. While few historians will
disagree with his prophecy, we should also note a more basic point: the
true rebel may be recognized by his commitment to a sardonically apocalyptic vision. The end of a world—and it is always the end of a world
for mortal man—justifies the scorn and negation, and the resulting strate-
gies of simplification and intense living.

Most of the direct history of the Cynics, extending from Diogenes,
which appears to continue for at least half a dozen centuries, mocks the
conventional successes and anxieties of a period marked by fatuous imperial styles and the pervasive sense of meaninglessness. The Cynics' answer was to demonstrate that life could be based on very little, or on a
lively nothingness. Thus worldly failure was shown as a choice and a
victory—the greatest blasphemy to those in power—and an alternative to
the dubious "necessities" and compulsions. But there is more to this style
of rebellion. The admirably humane Crates, Diogenes' follower, appears
to have been a secular saint—the first of the modern saints without a
god that we know of. He gave up his wealth and lived as a simple and
compassionate wiseman and teacher. He also mocked the official peda-
gogy, wrote parodies of accepted morality, and maintained the tradition
of contempt for inequality and conventional restrictions. Most delightful
of all, Crates made one of the few passionate and equal marriages we
hear of in antiquity. Hipparchia, an attractive girl from a "good family,"
pursued outcast Crates. He honorably tried to dissuade her, finally presenting himself stripped naked in warning that he would provide nothing

but a life of honest beggary. Miraculous woman, she accepted, and thus became the first lady philosopher. Their daughter, as a logical result, is one of the first reported sexually emancipated women. Saintly Cynics father pleasure as well as freedom. And much else, for even with the sketchy known history of the Cynics there is a provocative roll-call: Bion, the preaching tramp with a flair for metaphor and arrogance; Menippus, apparently the creator of a major form of satire; Dio Chrysostom, one of the many examples of the wandering Cynic critics of the Roman emperors; Oenomaus, the polemical atheist; and many others.[6] They testify to the greatest creation of Diogenes: the secular prophet. Not Plato in his coterie, not Aristotle in his academy, not the poets at the games and courts, certainly not the priests and magicians, but the Cynic wandering and arguing in the streets is the true forerunner and antitype of the individualistic "outsider" literary intellectual.

In the similar denunciations applied to such rebels in both classical and contemporary writings they are attacked for being outside civilization. Actually, they are right at the heart of it, not only in creating styles of life and intellectual confrontations but literally. Though unpatriotic, except perhaps to the purlieus of the cultural capitals where most often found, they take ideas with both passion and wit. Loafers, culture-bums, hangers-on, parasites, immoralists? Though more or less cultured, rebels do not primarily function as performers or merchants of the arts, institutional intellectuals, or even in most ordinary senses as producers of art and edification. The rebel refuses subordination to social function in assertion of the freely human. He remains "unemployed"—even when working—or as close to it as he can manage for both defiance and self-definition. As a member of the discontented or true leisure class he spends time around about the arts, but many rebels avow that their interest in the arts is secondary to ways of life and states of feeling. That only few rebels are artistic should have nothing of accusation about it, unless one is a pietist to a petty pseudo-religion of art. Why should the rebel produce much art or edification? His vocation is denial and defiance.

The rebel, of course, busies himself with the *mystique* of rebellion, rather more than with the muses. Outside organizational conventions and the usual rationalized self-interests, he justifies himself with his nagging and arrogant "why not?" Main principles, from Cynics to Beats, seem to be claims for individuality, voluntary poverty, simplicity, spontaneous feeling, ingenuous communication, intense sense experience, and a general heightening of immediate life. These qualities the rebel supports with

[6] The main source here is Dudley, *op. cit.* Prof. Marvin Singleton brought to my attention the importance of Crates' wife and daughter.

considerable invective against official society. The mark-of-the-kind may be that when asked for his identity, the rebel most often defines himself by attacking the nonidentity of the prevailing others.

The official society, in turn, often displays an irritated fascination with the rebel, taking much righteous delight in what it calls his barbarism, crudity, immaturity, sickness, immorality and perversity. Most of our knowledge of the Cynics (as with Christian heretics and later rebels, through the Beats) comes from the perplexed or denouncing reports by the unrebellious. These public apologists insistently attack—perhaps with the morality of envy—the rebel's economic and sexual libertarianism. It is curious also that while official teachers scorn the rebels for their lack of significant productivity and for their corrupting effects, the accusers as a group are most open to those very charges. If there were no rebels, public apologists would have to invent them.

At a common-sense level, the attacks on rebels for economic parasitism and lack of social productivity seem the most irrelevant. Even a meager economy could tolerate the simple needs of a rather considerable number of bearded malcontents. Our ornate modern Western societies could, and do, comfortably support vast numbers of people who fit no simple rational needs for goods and services. The hostility of official rhetoricians (and police, employers, welfare services, etc.) to rebels, of course, has little to do with economics or social utility. Similarly, in societies with varied or changing erotic ways, the rebel's views—usually uncoercive demands for sexual directness—do not require more than a modest tolerance. Since rebels, in obvious fact as well as almost by definition, are small in number, why the insistent fuss about their ways in such things as work and sex? Could it be that which hardly any of the contemners of rebels grant: much of the society despises its meaningless labors and burns against its arbitrary restrictions?

Many of the other charges against rebels, from Cynics to Beats, seem equally curious. For example, the recurrent disgust with the rebel making an exhibition of his failure and maladjustment must be based on the requirement that one be miserable only in standard ways. The argument that the rebel denies "civilized life" often rests on some weird definitions of "civilized" which give primacy to impersonal powers, social anxiety, individual repression, warfare, and similar sorts of "progress." The awesome fear that rebels, unless put down, will encourage vast numbers to throw off work and orderly life is more a condemnation of the society than of the rebels. For real defiance of conventions and their conveniences is usually too arduous for all but a few strong souls, and if vast numbers really seem ready to imitate the rebel mode the social order is about to flip-flop anyway. Surely a surplus of bearded bad poets is more desirable than a surplus of clean-shaven bad policemen, even to pietists of the conventional authorities. The "universalist fallacy"—the argument that goes by way of "What if everyone were a rebel?"—is usually sheer anxiety or fraud.

Some anti-rebel arguments have considerable merit. When rhetoricians of things-as-they-are, for example, attack rebels for being tediously noisy little failures who are not really very rebellious, the contemners are using, and thus justifying, real standards of rebelliousness—and the more candid will learn from them. And the quite true charge that the rebel style attracts a number of the pathetic, the incompetent, the pathological and the fraudulent, provides an admirable discriminatory emphasis even more applicable to the commercial and political and academic styles of life. Equally useful is the persistent anti-rebel contention that the latest manifestation of defiance repeats the same old stuff, not really new or original. Perhaps so, for the first modern literary rebels, the Cynics, may have been an essential part of the first full civilization in our Western traditions, and such rebellion thus remains a positive continuity of civilized tradition. Literary wildmen and arch-bohemians hold as permanent a part in our heritage of response and understanding as the supposedly more honorific roles of humanistic and scientific and political hero types. Though often discussed as mere bellwethers of artistic faddishness, the gropings of the young, and moral and political discontent, the significance of the rebels seems rather greater than the topical issues they raise in the public minded. The rebel's style and distinctive identity remains, and becomes its own justification, an existential choice for meeting the comic incongruities and tragic absurdities.

THE CREED: Romantic Admonitions

1. PROVERBS OF HELL
William Blake

In seed time learn, in harvest teach, in winter enjoy.
Drive your cart and your plow over the bones of the dead.
The road of excess leads to the palace of wisdom.
Prudence is a rich, ugly old maid courted by Incapacity.
He who desires but acts not, breeds pestilence.
The cut worm forgives the plow.
Dip him in the river who loves water.
A fool sees not the same tree that a wise man sees.
He whose face gives no light, shall never become a star.
Eternity is in love with the productions of time.
The busy bee has no time for sorrow.
The hours of folly are measur'd by the clock; but of wisdom, no
    clock can measure.
All wholesom food is caught without a net or a trap.
Bring out number, weight & measure in a year of dearth.
No bird soars too high, if he soars with his own wings.
A dead body revenges not injuries.
The most sublime act is to set another before you.
If the fool would persist in his folly he would become wise.
Folly is the cloke of knavery.
Shame is Pride's cloke.

Prisons are built with stones of Law, Brothels with bricks of
    Religion.
The pride of the peacock is the glory of God.
The lust of the goat is the bounty of God.
The wrath of the lion is the wisdom of God.

From *The Complete Writing of William Blake* edited by Sir Geoffrey Keynes and
published by Oxford University Press, 1967. Selected from "The Marriage of Heaven
and Hell," pp. 150–53.

The nakedness of woman is the work of God.

Excess of sorrow laughs. Excess of joy weeps.

The roaring of lions, the howling of wolves, the raging of the stormy sea, and the destructive sword, are portions of eternity, too great for the eye of man.

The fox condemns the trap, not himself.

Joys impregnate. Sorrows bring forth.

Let man wear the fell of the lion, woman the fleece of the sheep.

The bird a nest, the spider a web, man friendship.

The selfish, smiling fool, & the sullen, frowning fool shall be both thought wise, that they may be a rod.

What is now proved was once only imagin'd.

The rat, the mouse, the fox, the rabbet watch the roots; the lion, the tyger, the horse, the elephant watch the fruits.

The cistern contains: the fountain overflows.

One thought fills immensity.

Always be ready to speak your mind, and a base man will avoid you.

Every thing possible to be believ'd is an image of truth.

The eagle never lost so much time as when he submitted to learn of the crow.

The fox provides for himself, but God provides for the lion.

Think in the morning. Act in the noon. Eat in the evening.
    Sleep in the night.

He who has suffer'd you to impose on him, knows you.

As the plow follows words, so God rewards prayers.

The tygers of wrath are wiser than the horses of instruction.

Expect poison from the standing water.

You never know what is enough unless you know what is more than enough.

Listen to the fool's reproach! it is a kingly title!

The eyes of fire, the nostrils of air, the mouth of water, the beard of earth.

The weak in courage is strong in cunning.

The apple tree never asks the beech how he shall grow; nor the lion, the horse, how he shall take his prey.

The thankful receiver bears a plentiful harvest.

If others had not been foolish, we should be so.

The soul of sweet delight can never be defil'd.

When thou seest an Eagle, thou seest a portion of Genius; lift up thy head!

As the catterpillar chooses the fairest leaves to lay her eggs on, so the priest lays his curse on the fairest joys.

To create a little flower is the labour of ages.
Damn braces: Bless relaxes.
The best wine is the oldest, the best water the newest.
Prayers plow not! Praises reap not!
Joys laugh not! Sorrows weep not!

The head Sublime, the heart Pathos, the genitals Beauty, the hands
& feet Proportion.
As the air to a bird or the sea to a fish, so is contempt to the
contemptible.
The crow wish'd every thing was black, the owl that every thing
was white.
Exuberance is Beauty.
If the lion was advised by the fox, he would be cunning.
Improve[me]nt makes strait roads; but the crooked roads without
Improvement are roads of Genius.
Sooner murder an infant in its cradle than nurse unacted desires.
Where man is not, nature is barren.
Truth can never be told so as to be understood, and not be believ'd.
Enough! or Too much.

The ancient Poets animated all sensible objects with Gods or
Geniuses, calling them by the names and adorning them with
the properties of woods, rivers, mountains, lakes, cities, nations,
and whatever their enlarged & numerous senses could perceive.
And particularly they studied the genius of each city & country,
placing it under its mental deity;
Till a system was formed, which some took advantage of, & enslav'd
the vulgar by attempting to realize or abstract the mental
deities from their objects: thus began Priesthood;
Choosing forms of worship from poetic tales.
And at length they pronounc'd that the Gods had order'd such
things.
Thus men forgot that All deities reside in the human breast.

2. REVOLUTION FOR THE HELL OF IT
Free (Abbie Hoffman)

DIGGER CREED FOR HEAD MEETINGS
MEETINGS ARE
INFORMATION
MEDITATION
EXPERIENCE
FUN
TRUST
REHEARSALS
DRAMA
HORSESHIT
MEETINGS ARE NOT
PUTTING PEOPLE DOWN
Shhhh!   LISTEN AT MEETINGS   Shhhhhh!
LISTEN TO eye movements
LISTEN TO scratching
LISTEN TO your head
LISTEN TO smells
LISTEN TO singing
LISTEN TO touches
LISTEN TO silence
LISTEN TO gestalt vibrations
LISTEN TO a baby born in the sea
LISTEN TO the writing on the wall
DON'T LISTEN TO WORDS
DON'T LISTEN TO WORDS
DON'T LISTEN TO WORDS
meetings are life
surrender to the meeting . . . the meeting is the message
MEETINGS ARE CONFRONTATION —
MEETINGS ARE RELAXATION —
DIG OTHER HEADS —
DIG YOUR HEAD

From Abbie Hoffman, *Revolution for the Hell of It* (N.Y.: The Dial Press, 1968), pp. 16–17. Copyright © 1968 by The Dial Press, Inc. Reprinted by permission of the publisher.

dig disrupters, dig poets, dig peacemakers, dig heads who mumble, dig heads who don't go to meetings, dig heads who fall asleep, dig andy kent, dig clowns, dig street fighters, dig heads who scribble on paper, dig hustlers, dig heads that admit they are wrong, dig heads that know they are right, dig doing, dig changes, dig holy men, DIG HEADS who do everything
AT MEETINGS DIG HEADS WHO DIG MEETINGS
all meetings are the same same same same same same same same same same same same same—DIFFERENT
meetings are rivers   —   don't build dams
    BEWARE OF STRUCTURE FREAKS
    BEWARE OF RULES
    BEWARE OF "AT THE LAST MEETING WE DECIDED . . ."
DON'T GO BACK — THERE WAS NO LAST MEETING
DON'T GO FORWARD — THERE IS NOTHING
meetings are Now   you are the meeting   we are Now
WITHOUT MEETINGS THERE IS NO COMMUNITY
                    COMMUNITY IS UNITY
AVOID GANGBANGS . . . RAPE IDEAS NOT PEOPLE
               MAKE LOVE AT ALL MEETINGS
MEETINGS TAKE A MOMENT—Time is Fantasy—
MEETINGS TAKE FOREVER
             there is no WAY to run a meeting
use meetings to help you DO YOUR THING
Go naked to meetings   —   Go high to meetings
             BE PREPARED
PREPARE BY meditation
PREPARE BY doing
COME PREPARED TO DROP OUT   —   COME PREPARED TO STAY FOREVER
IF YOU ARE NOT PREPARED MEETINGS ARE NOT YOUR THING
            ONLY DO YOUR THING
        mene, mene, tekel, upharsin
(meetings are a pain in the ass)

REPRESENTATIVE EXPRESSIONS:
An Historical Perspective

1. EMILE
Jean Jacques Rousseau

The Meaning of Education

Everything is good as it comes from the hands of the Maker of the world but degenerates once it gets into the hands of man. Man makes one land yield the products of another, disregards differences of climates, elements and seasons, mutilates his dogs and horses, perverts and disfigures everything. Not content to leave anything as nature has made it, he must needs shape man himself to his notions, as he does the trees in his garden.

But under present conditions, human beings would be even worse than they are without this fashioning. A man left entirely to himself from birth would be the most misshapen of creatures. Prejudices, authority, necessity, example, the social institutions in which we are immersed, would crush out nature in him without putting anything in its place. He would fare like a shrub that has grown up by chance in the middle of a road, and got trampled under foot by the passers-by.

Plants are fashioned by cultivation, men by education. We are born feeble and need strength; possessing nothing, we need assistance; beginning without intelligence, we need judgment. All that we lack at birth and need when grown up is given us by education. This education comes to us from nature, from men, or from things. The internal development of our faculties and organs is the education of nature. The use we learn to make of this development is the education of men. What comes to us from our experience of the things that affect us is the education of things. Each of us therefore is fashioned by three kinds of teachers. When their lessons are at variance the pupil is badly edu-

Reprinted with the permission of the publisher from William Boyd (tr. and ed.), *The Emile of Jean Jacques Rousseau* (New York: Teachers College Press, 1962; by arrangement with William Heinemann, Ltd.), pp. 11–15.

cated, and is never at peace with himself. When they coincide and lead to a common goal he goes straight to his mark and lives single-minded. Now, of these three educations the one due to nature is independent of us, and the one from things only depends on us to a limited extent. The education that comes from men is the only one within our control, and even that is doubtful. Who can hope to have the entire direction of the words and deeds of all the people around a child?

It is only by good luck that the goal can be reached. What is this goal? It is nature's own goal. Since the three educations must work together for a perfect result, the one that can be modified determines the course of the other two. But perhaps "nature" is too vague a word. We must try to fix its meaning. Nature, it has been said, is only habit. Is that really so? Are there not habits which are formed under pressure, leaving the original nature unchanged? One example is the habit of plants which have been forced away from the upright direction. When set free, the plant retains the bent forced upon it; but the sap has not changed its first direction and any new growth the plant makes returns to the vertical. It is the same with human inclinations. So long as there is no change in conditions the inclinations due to habits, however unnatural, remain unchanged, but immediately the restraint is removed the habit vanishes and nature reasserts itself.

We are born capable of sensation and from birth are affected in diverse ways by the objects around us. As soon as we become conscious of our sensations we are inclined to seek or to avoid the objects which produce them: at first, because they are agreeable or disagreeable to us, later because we discover that they suit or do not suit us, and ultimately because of the judgments we pass on them by reference to the idea of happiness or perfection we get from reason. These inclinations extend and strengthen with the growth of sensibility and intelligence, but under the pressure of habit they are changed to some extent with our opinions. The inclinations before this change are what I call our nature. In my view everything ought to be in conformity with these original inclinations.

There would be no difficulty if our three educations were merely different. But what is to be done when they are at cross purposes? Consistency is plainly impossible when we seek to educate a man for others, instead of for himself. If we have to combat either nature or society, we must choose between making a man or making a citizen. We cannot make both. There is an inevitable conflict of aims, from which come two opposing forms of education: the one communal and public, the other individual and domestic.

To get a good idea of communal education, read Plato's *Republic*. It is not a political treatise, as those who merely judge books by their titles think. It is the finest treatise on education ever written. Communal education in this sense, however, does not and can not now exist. There are no longer any real fatherlands and therefore no real citizens. The words "fatherland" and "citizen" should be expunged from modern languages.

I do not regard the instruction given in those ridiculous establishments called colleges as "public," any more than the ordinary kind of education. This education makes for two opposite goals and reaches neither. The men it turns out are double-minded, seemingly concerned for others, but really only concerned for themselves. From this contradiction comes the conflict we never cease to experience in ourselves. We are drawn in different directions by nature and by man, and take a midway path that leads us nowhere. In this state of confusion we go through life and end up with our contradictions unsolved, never having been any good to ourselves or to other people.

There remains then domestic education, the education of nature. But how will a man who has been educated entirely for himself get on with other people? If there were any way of combining in a single person the twofold aim, and removing the contradictions of life, a great obstacle to happiness would be removed. But before passing judgment on this kind of man it would be necessary to follow his development and see him fully formed. It would be necessary, in a word, to make the acquaintance of the natural man. This is the subject of our quest in this book.

What can be done to produce this very exceptional person? In point of fact all we have to do is to prevent anything being done. When it is only a matter of sailing against the wind it is enough to tack, but when the sea runs high and you want to stay where you are, you must throw out the anchor.

In the social order where all stations in life are fixed, every one needs to be brought up for his own station. The individual who leaves the place for which he has been trained is useless in any other. In Egypt, where the son was obliged to follow in his father's footsteps, education had at least an assured aim: in our country where social ranks are fixed, but the men in them are constantly changing, nobody knows whether he is doing his son a good or a bad turn when he educates him for his own rank.

In the natural order where all men are equal, manhood is the common vocation. One who is well educated for that will not do badly in the duties that pertain to it. The fact that my pupil is intended for the army, the church or the bar, does not greatly concern me. Before the vocation determined by his parents comes the call of nature to the life of human kind. Life is the business I would have him learn. When he leaves my hands, I admit he will not be a magistrate, or a soldier, or a priest. First and foremost, he will be a man. All that a man must be he will be when the needs arises, as well as anyone else. Whatever the changes of fortune he will always be able to find a place for himself.

2. EDUCATION
Ralph Waldo Emerson

A rule is so easy that it does not need a man to apply it; an automaton, a machine, can be made to keep a school so. It facilitates labor and thought so much that there is always the temptation in large schools to omit the endless task of meeting the wants of each single mind, and to govern by steam. But it is at frightful cost. Our modes of Education aim to expedite, to save labor; to do for masses what cannot be done for masses, what must be done reverently, one by one: say rather, the whole world is needed for the tuition of each pupil. The advantages of this system of emulation and display are so prompt and obvious, it is such a time-saver, it is so energetic on slow and on bad natures, and is of so easy application, needing no sage or poet, but any tutor or schoolmaster in his first term can apply it,—that it is not strange that this calomel of culture should be a popular medicine. On the other hand, total abstinence from this drug, and the adoption of simple discipline and the following of nature, involves at once immense claims on the time, the thoughts, on the life of the teacher. It requires time, use, insight, event, all the great lessons and assistances of God; and only to think of using it implies character and profoundness; to enter on this course of discipline is to be good and great. It is precisely analogous to the difference between the use of corporal punishment and the methods of love. It is so easy to bestow on a bad boy a blow, overpower him, and get obedience without words, that in this world of hurry and distraction, who can wait for the returns of reason and the conquest of self; in the uncertainty too whether that will ever come? And yet the familiar observation of the universal compensations might suggest the fear that so summary a stop of a bad humor was more jeopardous than its continuance.

Now the correction of this quack practice is to import into Educa-

From Ralph Waldo Emerson, "Education," *Lectures and Biographical Sketches* (Boston: Houghton Mifflin and Company, 1883), pp. 150–55. Copyrighted by Edward Waldo Emerson.

tion the wisdom of life. Leave this military hurry and adopt the pace of Nature. Her secret is patience. Do you know how the naturalist learns all the secrets of the forest, of plants, of birds, of beasts, of reptiles, of fishes, of the rivers and the sea? When he goes into the woods the birds fly before him and he finds none; when he goes to the river bank, the fish and the reptile swim away and leave him alone. His secret is patience; he sits down, and sits still; he is a statue; he is a log. These creatures have no value for their time, and he must put as low a rate on his. By dint of obstinate sitting still, reptile, fish, bird and beast, which all wish to return to their haunts, begin to return. He sits still; if they approach, he remains passive as the stone he sits upon. They lose their fear. They have curiosity too about him. By and by the curiosity masters the fear, and they come swimming, creeping and flying towards him; and as he is still immovable, they not only resume their haunts and their ordinary labors and manners, show themselves to him in their workday trim, but also volunteer some degree of advances towards fellowship and good understanding with a biped who behaves so civilly and well. Can you not baffle the impatience and passion of the child by your tranquillity? Can you not wait for him, as Nature and Providence do? Can you not keep for his mind and ways, for his secret, the same curiosity you give to the squirrel, snake, rabbit, and the sheldrake and the deer? He has a secret; wonderful methods in him; he is,—every child,—a new style of man; give him time and opportunity. Talk of Columbus and Newton! I tell you the child just born in yonder hovel is the beginning of a revolution as great as theirs. But you must have the believing and prophetic eye. Have the self-command you wish to inspire. Your teaching and discipline must have the reserve and taciturnity of Nature. Teach them to hold their tongues by holding your own. Say little; do not snarl; do not chide; but govern by the eye. See what they need, and that the right thing is done.

I confess myself utterly at a loss in suggesting particular reforms in our ways of teaching. No discretion that can be lodged with a school-committee, with the overseers or visitors of an academy, of a college, can at all avail to reach these difficulties and perplexities, but they solve themselves when we leave institutions and address individuals. The will, the male power, organizes, imposes its own thought and wish on others, and makes that military eye which controls boys as it controls men; admirable in its results, a fortune to him who has it, and only dangerous when it leads the workman to overvalue and overuse it and precludes him from finer means. Sympathy, the female force,—which they must use who have not the first,—deficient in instant control and the breaking down of resistance, is more subtle and lasting and creative. I advise teachers to cherish mother-wit. I assume that you will keep the grammar, reading, writing and arithmetic in order; 't is easy and of course you will. But smuggle in a little contraband wit, fancy, imagination, thought. If you have a taste which you have suppressed because it is not shared by those about you, tell them that. Set this law up, whatever becomes of the rules of the school: they must not whisper, much less talk; but if one of the young people says a wise thing, greet it, and let all the children clap their hands They shall have no book but school-books in the room; but if one has brought in a Plutarch or Shakespeare or Don Quixote or Goldsmith or any other good book, and understands what he reads, put him at once at the head of the class. Nobody shall be disorderly, or leave his desk without permission, but if a boy runs from his bench, or a girl, because the fire falls, or to check some injury that a little dastard is inflicting behind his desk on some helpless sufferer, take away the medal from the head of the class and give it on the instant to the brave rescuer. If a child happens to show that he knows any fact about astronomy, or plants, or birds, or rocks, or history, that interests him and you, hush all the classes and encourage him to tell it so that all may hear. Then you have made your school-room like the world. Of course you will insist on modesty in the children, and respect to their teachers, but if the boy stops you in your speech, cries out that you are wrong and sets you right, hug him!

To whatsoever upright mind, to whatsoever beating heart I speak, to you it is committed to educate men. By simple living, by an illimitable soul, you inspire, you correct, you instruct, you raise, you embellish all. By your own act you teach the beholder how to do the practicable. According to the depth from which you draw your life, such is the depth not only of your strenuous effort, but of your manners and presence.

3. EYES OF FLESH, EYES OF FIRE
Theodore Roszak

"What," it will be Question'd, "When the Sun rises, do you not see a round disk of fire somewhat like a Guinea?" O no, no, I see an Innumerable company of the Heavenly host crying, "Holy, Holy, is the Lord God Almighty."

WILLIAM BLAKE

From Theodore Roszak, *The Making of a Counter Culture* (N.Y.: Doubleday & Co., Inc., 1968), pp. 239–40, 244–48. Copyright © 1968, 1969 by Theodore Roszak. Reprinted by permission of Doubleday & Company, Inc.

What are we to say of the man who fixes his eye on the sun and does not see the sun, but sees instead a chorus of flaming seraphim announcing the glory of God? Surely we shall have to set him down as mad . . . unless he can coin his queer vision into the legal tender of elegant verse. Then, perhaps, we shall see fit to assign him a special status, a pigeonhole: call him "poet" and allow him to validate his claim to intellectual respectability by way of metaphorical license. Then we can say, "He did not *really* see what he says he saw. No, not at all. He only put it that way to lend color to his speech . . . as poets are in the professional habit of doing. It is a lyrical turn of phrase, you see: just that and nothing more." And doubtless all the best, all the most objective scholarship on the subject would support us in our perfectly sensible interpretation. It would tell us, for example, that the poet Blake, under the influence of Swedenborgian mysticism,[1] developed a style based on esoteric visionary correspondences and was, besides, a notorious, if gifted, eccentric. Etc. Etc.

In such fashion, we confidently discount and denature the visionary experience, and the technocratic order of life rolls on undeterred, obedient to the scientific reality principle. From such militant rationality the technocracy must permit no appeal.

Yet, if there is to be an alternative to the technocracy, there *must* be an appeal from this reductive rationality which objective consciousness dictates. This, so I have argued, is the primary project of our counter culture: to proclaim a new heaven and a new earth so vast, so marvelous that the inordinate claims of technical expertise must of necessity withdraw in the presence of such splendor to a subordinate and marginal status in the lives of men. To create and broadcast such a consciousness of life entails nothing less than the willingness to open ourselves to the visionary imagination on its own demanding terms. We must be prepared to entertain the astonishing claim men like Blake lay before us: that here are eyes which see the world not as commonplace sight or scientific scrutiny sees it, but see it transformed, made lustrous beyond measure, and in seeing the world so, see it as it really is. Instead of rushing to downgrade the rhapsodic reports of our enchanted seers, to interpret them at the lowest and most conventional level, we must be prepared to consider the scandalous possibility that wherever the visionary imagination grows bright, magic, that old antagonist of science, renews itself, transmuting our workaday reality into something bigger, perhaps more frightening, certainly more adventurous than the lesser rationality of objective consciousness can ever countenance.

. . .

[1] Emanuel Swedenborg (1688–1772) a Swedish mystic and philosopher.—ed.

Sorted out into its several surviving traditions, the shaman's craft speaks for itself as a human achievement. But if we look for the creative thrust that once unified these skills and arts, we find the most important thing the shaman has to teach us, which is the meaning of magic in its pristine form: magic not as a repertory of clever stunts, but as a form of experience, a way of addressing the world. Those who still find themselves confronted by something of the unaccountably marvelous in the talents of artists and performers have perhaps been touched by a faint, lingering spark of the ancient shamanistic world view and have, to that extent, glimpsed an alternative reality.

Magic, as the shaman practices it, is a matter of communing with the forces of nature as if they were mindful, intentional presences, as if they possessed a will that requires coaxing, argument, imprecation. When he conjures, divines, or casts spells, the shaman is addressing these presences as one addresses a person, playing the relationship by ear, watching out for the other's moods, passions, attitudes—but always respectful of the other's dignity. For the shaman, the world is a place alive with mighty, invisible personalities; these have their own purposes, which, like those of any person, are apt to be ultimately mysterious. The shaman is on intimate terms with the presences he addresses; he strives to find out their ways and to move with the grain of them. He speaks of them as "you," not "it."

. . . The essence of magic lies in just this sense that man and not-man can stand on communicable terms with one another. The relationship is not that of In-Here impassively observing Out-There, but of man carrying on a personal transaction with forces in his environment which are known to be turbulently, perhaps menacingly alive. The shaman enters into the field of these forces warmly, sensuously; and because he approaches with respect, they welcome him and permit him to strive and bargain with them.

It is not a relationship the presences accept with all comers. Unlike the scientific experiment, which is depersonalized and so should work for anyone who performs it, the magical relationship is available only to those chosen by the presences themselves. The shaman is ordinarily one who discovers his vocation upon being seized up by powers beyond his comprehension. He does not initially train for the position as for a prefabricated office; this is a development that ensues when the shaman's calling becomes routinized into the formal role of the priest. Rather, like the prophets of Israel to whom so much of the primitive tradition clings, the shaman is ambushed by the divine and called forth by surprise. The prophet Amos—protesting significantly in this case to the official temple priest—explains:

I was no prophet, neither was I a prophet's son; but I was an herdsman, and a gatherer of sycamore fruit; And the Lord took me as I followed the flock, and the Lord said unto me, Go, prophesy unto my people Israel. (Amos 7:14–15)

And prophesy he did, with an eloquence that defies explanation in one from so humble an origin.

Communion with the transcendent powers, then, is not a feat that can be achieved by anyone; it is a mystery peculiar to the one elected, and is therefore through and through personal in character. For this reason, the shaman ordinarily becomes one who stands apart from his people—not in a position of institutional authority, but in a position of talented uniqueness. The respect felt for him is the respect many of us still feel for the especially gifted person, the artist or performer whose uncanny influence over us does not lie in any office he holds but in his own manifest skill.

In order to heighten that skill, the shaman devotes himself to a life of severe discipline and solitude. He fasts, he prays, he meditates; he isolates himself in order that he may watch out for such signs as the presences make visible for his education. Above all, he becomes adept in cultivating those exotic states of awareness in which a submerged aspect of his personality seems to free itself from his surface conscious-ness to rove among the hidden powers of the universe. The techniques by which shamans undertake their psychic adventures are many; they may make use of narcotic substances, dizziness, starvation, smoke in-halation, suffocation, hypnotic drum and dance rhythms, or even the holding of one's breath. One recognizes at once in this trance-inducing repertory a number of practices which underlie the many mystical tradi-tions of the world: the practices of oracles, dervishes, yogis, sibyls, prophets, druids, etc.—the whole heritage of mystagoguery toward which the beat-hip wing of our counter culture now gravitates.

By such techniques, the shaman cultivates his rapport with the non-intellective sources of the personality as assiduously as any scientist trains himself to objectivity, a mode of consciousness at the polar ex-treme from that of the shaman. Thus the shaman is able to diffuse his sensibilities through his environment, assimilating himself to the sur-rounding universe. He enters wholly into the grand symbiotic system of nature, letting its currents and nuances flow through him. He may become a keener student of his environment than any scientist. He may be able to taste rain or plague on the wind. He may be able to sense the way the wild herds will move next or how the planting will go in the season to come.

The shaman, then, is one who knows that there is more to be seen of reality than the waking eye sees. Besides our eyes of flesh, there are eyes of fire that burn through the ordinariness of the world and perceive the wonders and terrors beyond. In the superconsciousness of the shaman, nothing is simply a dead object, a stupid creature; rather, all the things of this earth are swayed by sacred meanings. "Primitive man," Martin Buber observes, "is a naive pansacramentalist. Everything is to him full of sacramental substance, everything. Each thing and each function is ever ready to light up into a sacrament for him." [1]

2 Martin Buber, *Hasidism* (New York: Philosophical Library, 1948), p. 133.

PEDAGOGICAL MODEL:
The Teacher as an Artist

FASCINATION: A PHENOMENOLOGICAL PERSPECTIVE OF INDEPENDENT LEARNING
Sidney M. Jourard

The Guru and the Commissar

Every man must learn to speak, move, even experience the world in the ways deemed right and sane where he lives. It is not easy. It takes a long time. The temptation to stray is strong. Commissars stand close to insure that each conforms to his prescribed position and role. Once a man masters the rules of the social game, what then? He plays the games so long as they yield meaningful rewards and the reward of meaning. Ultimately, the game becomes confining, boring, even strangling. The man may then wish to opt out, but he cannot; there are no other games to play. So he may become sick. He will then he patched up by doctors who will pronounce him cured and then send him back into the game. If he seeks new realms of experience, he threatens the sleep of the unawakened. They condemn and invalidate him, so he gives up and becomes "normal." Or else, he seeks a richer experience in private while impersonating a typical person.

Since time immemorial, each society has secretly harbored some *gurus*. These wise men were sought by the sick, sufferers who may have been rich in goods, but poor in spirit. The *guru* taught the seeker to let go his attachments in this world, the better to concentrate on spiritual purification. The ultimate rewards were not wealth, fame, nor power, but rather enlightenment, and liberation, and an enriched, more meaningful experience of oneself and one's world. The *gurus* helped the seekers obtain liberation from entrapment in their culture. Now the society that would not fall must locate and treasure its *gurus*. It must protect

Reprinted with permission of the International Textbook Company (Scranton, Pa.) from "Fascination: A Phenomenological Perspective of Independent Learning" by Sidney M. Jourard in *The Theory and Nature of Independent Learning* (ed. Gerald Gleason). Copyright 1967. Pp. 82–87, 95–101.

them, and not deny seekers access to them. The *gurus* and their ways are not for everyone. *Gurus* cannot be hired, nor bought; they can only be deserved. A society without *gurus* is stagnant and it will perish, as did the dinosaurs, who were unable to change ways to cope with changing conditions.

In America, I think we are experiencing an absence in our midst, an absence of *gurus*. We have many commissars, but no one to lead beyond their ways. The commissars insure that everyone conforms to existing ways, to the image or model of man that is current, that is synonomous with goodness and sanity. Commissars use bribery, guile, and threats of force to get people to follow the prescribed ways—the ways which keep the society and its existing power structure intact. Who are the commissars? Most of our teachers are commissars. So are our parents, our policemen, our psychiatrists, our psychologists, even our neighbors. The radio, T.V., and the press function as commissars. All commissars collude to keep us wanting what we are supposed to want, and doing what we are supposed to do. Conform and be rewarded. Dissent and be damned, or unpopular, which is our current synonym for damnation.

If someone begins to depart from the way of being sane or good, he meets a graduated barrage of pressure aiming to bring him back in line. First the person will experience twinges or onslaughts of guilt and anxiety, if he even thinks of stepping out of line. If this built-in regulation fails, then there is the threat of graduated punishment from without. If the person will not yield to parental or family criticism, rejection or threat, the solid wall of community invalidation will confront him, to threaten exile or imprisonment. If the dissenter (who embodies a protest against ways to live that he cannot live) persists in his dissent, he may finally be condemned as mad, and be banished to a mental hospital where he is shocked, drugged, tranquilized, frozen, or operated upon to get him in line or out of the way.

Valeriy Tarsis, a Russian writer, published a novel . . . called *Ward Seven* (New York: Dutton, 1965). He describes the contemporary situation dissenting intellectuals face in the Soviet Union. Instead of being shot or transported to Siberia, they are regarded as *insane* if they protest against the current regime. They are hospitalized, and then "treated" until they see the folly or the insanity of their ways. And so, the majority of people, young and old, stay in the role in which they have been trained. The commissars win out. In the ultimate victory of the commissars, each man becomes the unchallenged commissar over himself and I think this time is close at hand.

Behavioral scientists help commissars at their tasks. They say "You define your objectives, and we will show you the way, the most efficient way, to implement them." Teachers, parents, and psychiatrists are all informed of those ever new, more effortless, and automatic ways to bring people into line. School curricula are scientifically broken down into units; these are administered in palatable doses by scientifically informed trainers who employ the latest form of programing. Conseling centers, audio-visual aid depots, and a barrage of books and pamphlets are all available to help commissars carry out their assigned tasks of turning pupils off themselves and onto the ways they are supposed to follow. The result is we turn out more graduates from our training institues than has ever been true before in our history, possibly in the history of mankind.

But we are discovering, those of us who graduated from such institutions, that something is missing. The something is *ourselves*. Somewhere along the line, we lost ourselves—our capacity to experience in new modes and qualities. If we are at all sensitive, we notice the absence and we become concerned, and we start to seek ourselves and our lost capacity for experiencing. . . . I hope we find us, but I wouldn't be too sure we will.

Beyond the Tether

We created the problem of independent learning by the way we trained people for the social roles awaiting them in a social structure that resists change. Pedagogues, parents, people in general, invalidated the experiences of learners and shut down their capacity to entertain and pursue wonder and fascination. We created the problem and it haunts us, . . . not because "behavioral sciences have expanded our conception of the human potential by recasting the image of man." No, the problem haunts us, I believe, because we find ourselves at the end of our tether. We are running in circles at its limit. The tether is firmly fixed to a peculiar debasement of a once magnificent image, the American way of life. Originally revolutionary and dynamic in conception, the American way of life is now a design for living in which more and more Americans cannot live without the aid of tranquilizers, and the threat from the ubiquitous commissar. Yet all the time we advertise this way of life abroad, and try to sell it as we sell toilet paper and Buicks with "Hidden Persuaders." . . .

What is independent learning? . . . No authoritative definition which I am aware of has been available, so I invented one to serve the purpose of my exposition. I will look at this phenomenon from the standpoint of the learner. What an observer might call independent learning, learning for oneself, the learner experiences as fascination with some aspect of the world which is envisioned in the mode of possibility. That is to say, in imagination. Independent learning is the embodiment and implementation of imaginative fascination. Some aspect of the world discloses itself to a person. He "flips" from the experiential mode of perception (just looking at the world as it discloses itself to him), to an imaginative consciousness. In that mode, he experiences himself as beckoned, challenged, invited or fascinated by this aspect of the world. The transmutation of this imagined possibility into an actuality then becomes the dominant project of his life. He lives it and he lives for it. The person, in whom fascination has been turned on or awakened, suffers a divine discontent, a magnificent obsession. He will wallow in his obsession, if others leave him alone. He will forget to eat, sleep, play games, socialize, or do anything else until he has brought his image of possibility into actuality or else lie nurturing the wounds from fumbling as he pursues his plan.

Once he has actualized his image of the possible, he may then again show an interest in other kinds of doing and being. But in the midst of his independent learning rampage, he is far from being well-rounded or socially adjusted. In fact, he may depart hugely from current images of how people should be. Indeed, the "turned on" learner needs to be protected from other people. He needs to be protected from self-consciousness, from the need to conform to images, and from distraction. He needs to be protected from serious self-destruction as he contemplates and absorbs himself in the encounter with his fetish. In this case, the fetish is the mystery or the missing skill. When he is thus turned on, no badly written text, no stuttering, boring teacher can be an obstacle or deterrent so long as they embody some of the knowledge that has become the life quest, just then. "The book or the teacher holds something I want just now. I will get it out of him somehow." That seems to express the spirit of what I am saying.

Independent learning defined as I attempted to define it, arises when our present existence has reached an impasse; when our experience has gone stale, when the project of staying the same has lost its meaning, and the person seeks a new interest in life. If he finds one, and he lets himself be addressed by it, he becomes possessed of the divine madness. The burden and dilemma that were his existence have now been thrown off; his existence is now the quest. He is turned on; he will not be diverted; he may appear ruthless if he pursues his quest. He cannot be bored by it, though he may bore others by his talk of it. This state of being, of being involved, of experiencing new possibilities of meaning for one's life, and then being engaged in their fulfillment, this is what I am construing as independent learning. It entails transcending the past, involvements and interests, transcending social pressures; in short it is a matter of detachment and liberation from the momentum and inertia of previous ways of being, behaving, and experiencing.

Now the fascinated question of which I speak, can be evoked in a number of ways. It may occur of itself in someone who is desperate enough; it seems to occur spontaneously in young children before they have been socialized. More commonly, when it does occur, it happens through a relationship between an entrapped person and some other who functions as his *guru* and exemplar. Someone who releases one's imagination, who expands one's consciousness, is someone who offers a "psychedelic" encounter. Indeed, the one functioning as a *guru* may aid the process of liberation from previous attachments by helping the person experience more keenly the degree to which he is trapped. The capacity to become fascinated may be repressed in an overly-trained person. The capacity to re-experience fascination may be impossible until some level of disengagement from usual concerns, ways, and commitments has been reached. Or the one who is to be the *guru* may function as a tempter and seducer. His way of life may evoke envy and/or admiration. His serenity, or his enthusiasm may evoke our curiosity. He may appear to be having more fun, living more fully, experiencing more, or he may disclose images of possibility that attract the attention of the bored, unfulfilled seeker who then becomes fascinated and subsequently experiences his previous involvement as obstacles to his pursuit of new meaning and experience.

Whatever the occasion for being thus turned on, it is this fascinating engagement with an image of possibility that I define as independent learning. We might call it awakening or inspiration, but it is always *intentional;* that is, it is always related to something in the world, it is always awakening to *something,* being inspirited by or for *something,* fascinated with *something.* And it is always embodied; that is, the person lives and acts his experience of awakening. The person who is in this turned on state, which he experiences as different from his usual repetitive experience, should appear different to an observer. In principle, then, we have the possibility of a psychology, a physiology, even an epidemiology and sociology of being turned on. I don't know what we would call it, a "turnology," or something. . . .

Some Factors Which Facilitate Independent Learning

I think that the capacity to become fascinated anew after old fascinations have worn out is abetted by numerous factors, but it is the interpersonal factor that I want to focus upon here. Since each of us is an other to somebody, we can perhaps do something to foster independent learning in the others for whom we are the other. The basic factors in fostering independent learning, including the processes that underlie it and make it emerge as a response to invitation and challenge, are the human responses: challenge, invitation, stimulation of imagination, confirmation, letting be, honest disclosure, and willingness to enter into dialogue. At least these factors seem to me to be relevant.

Confirmation: Martin Buber has said that each man wishes to be confirmed by his fellow and each has the capacity to confirm his fellow. To confirm the other in his being means to stand back and let his being "happen" to you. I invite him to tell me who he is, and I confirm him at each instant of his disclosure as being the one he is: As John, John in despair, John emerged with new goals and values. I view his disclosure with respect; I acknowledge its reality and authenticity.

Confirmation does not mean wishywashy, insincere "permissiveness," because often the most direct confirmation is to take a stand in opposition to the disclosure of the other. The confrontation, the meeting, even in opposition confirms for the other that he is the one that he is. It lets him know that he exists. Confirmation means that I recognize the other person as the author of his acts and his utterances. He is the author. *He* is writing and living his own autobiography. It has not been programed for him. I attribute his acts and utterances to him and to his freedom. I confirm him as a free agent. He chooses his existence and is responsible for it.

The opposite of confirmation is invalidation and disconfirmation. There are many ways to invalidate another person and they all have the net effect of weakening his sense of his own identity and worth, his sense of being a source of experience and action. One can ignore the other. One can pretend he does not exist except as a doll, a thing, a nobody or as just another body. We hear people speaking in this way, "I want fifteen bodies for this job (experiment, class)." One can attribute his actions and utterances to some source other than his free intentionality. One can disconfirm all actions and utterances save those that are compatible with one's concept of the other. For instance, a mother might say, "That wasn't you when you did that. You weren't being yourself." Anything the child says or does which does not fit his mother's expectation of him is "not him." Under a regime of such disconfirmation a person will indeed come to doubt his own existence. He will lose his identity for himself and try to confine his experience and conduct only to that range consistent with his identity for the other. Confirmation is in a sense an act of love. One is acknowledging that other as one who exists in his own peculiar form, with the right to do so.

One recognizes that a concept of someone's being is only that: a concept, and not his being. One recognizes that it is for a person to reveal and define himself for us in *his* way, at *his* pace, thus reinforming and altering our experience and concept of him. It is not only *not* our duty, it is an outright sin to define another's being. Our concept of each other is always out of date. Yet, if another person has a weak sense of his identity for himself, if he is ontologically insecure, he may let us do this, define him, or even ask us to define him. "Tell me who I am, or, how I should be?" When I let the other person be, and confirm him in his being as he discloses it to me, I am creating an ambience in which he can dare to let go of his previous concepts and presentations of himself. They are not binding on him. My suspension of my preconception of his being, invites him to let go while he is in my presence. He can drop these self-presentations, commitments, interests and goals, and explore the possibilities of new ones. Because he said he was interested in something yesterday, doesn't mean that he is committed to it today. He can weaken, regress, enter into himself while with me and feel assured that I am awaiting, perhaps with a hand holding his until he emerges to tell me who he now is. Incidentally, about holding hands: last year I did a study of body contact, of who touches who, where, what are the correlates and so on. Americans are not a very touching people. "Don't touch me. I can't stand being touched." In a research at the University of Florida where there were something like 300 hours of time sampled observations of an elementary school teacher in a classroom with first grade children. Not once did a teacher's hand or part of her body come into contact with any part of the body of any of the children in the classroom. The probabilities against this are fantastic. There is a selective factor at work.

Disclosure: Another factor in the promotion of independent learning is disclosure. Earlier, I said that after a person has abandoned his previous incarnation, his way of presenting himself, after he entered his experiencing and then emerged, *he experiences the world as disclosing new possibilities.* The world is always there, but his way of experiencing it changes. You and I are part of his world, and we have the capacity to disclose ourselves to him even while he is embodied in his usual fixed roles and self-definitions. This is a fascinating thing. A tree, a lamp, a sky, the animal kingdom is always disclosing itself, but we don't always pay attention. People are part of the world and they can disclose their being more vigorously and insistently than a tree can. I can disclose my being with a shout and a roar and a pinch, if it takes that to capture a habit-ridden person's attention. When I am with him I can disclose to him how I experience myself and him. I can enter into dialogue with him. And with each of his utterances or acts, I can respond out of my experience and disclose to him what it is that I am experiencing. If I remain in contact with him consistently in dialogue, I may actually lead him to the edge of going out of his mind and habits, thus clearing the way for the emergence of a new self, new fascination, new experiencing. I ask you to consider dia-

logue; you say something from your being. Let's use jazz combo to illustrate. I blow a phrase on my trumpet and you respond with a passage on
your saxophone. Your response is a reply to me, a question and a challenge. And so I reply again and so it goes until the one of us loses his nerve
and dares not let spontaneous true disclosure out. Dialogue has ended
for a time.

Now switch to dialogue in psychotherapy. The patient says something to me. I reply in honesty. My reply (which is a disclosure of part
of his world to him) evokes experiencing in him, so he utters this. This
evokes a reply from me. We continue in this way until one of us has
tripped off panic in the other and at this point insincerity, role playing
and dissemblance begin. Truth and dialogue have ceased. One of the participants does not wish to be known and he holds back. In dialogue at
its best, the participants remain in contact and let their reciprocal dis-
closures affect one another. If the dialogue occurs in the context of "letting
be" and confirmation, then the weaker of the two may indeed flip into
raw experiencing, find it safe if the other is authentically of good will
and supporting, and emerge in an awakened turned on state. Authentic
disclosure of self then, is a likely factor in the promotion of awakening,
authentication and validation of the other, and in the emergence of independent learning.

More common than dialogue in interpersonal relations is semblance,
role playing, impersonation of the "other" one wishes to seem to the other.
Hence, the other person seldom truly encounters a *person in process*.
Instead he meets the other as one who seems to have taken a pledge of
consistency, as if the other one has pledged to be the same tomorrow as
he was today. He meets a world of people who do not invite him into
new possibilities. If I am in your world and I don't grow and change, then
you are in a world that can obstruct and impede your growth. Now
teacher-trainers are part of a world for somebody: children. In true encounter, there is a collapse of roles and self concepts. No one emerges
from an encounter the same as he entered. My willingness to disclose myself to you, to drop my mask, is a factor in your trusting me and daring,
then, to disclose yourself to me. This disclosure of yourself to me aids the
process of disengaging you from your previous ways of being. When I
disclose myself to you, *I am your world*, and this world discloses new possibilities to you. It evokes new challenges and invitations that may stir
you and revivify your imagination.

Challenging the other's imagination: This is another factor in independent learning. If independent learning is the implementation of fascination with imagined possibilities, then we must concern ourselves with
ways to evoke the imaginative mode of experiencing. We already know
a great deal about perception, the perceptual mode of experiencing, but

imagining, the imaginative conscious, is less fully understood. To imagine means to transcend the here and now, to shut off one's perception for the time, and invent new possibilities that thus far cannot be perceived by anybody. The possibilities exist in the imaginative consciousness of the experiencer and it is for him to "real-ize" these, to make them real, to make them perceptible, to make it possible for him and others to perceive in actuality what before existed only as his image. The free imagination, like freedom itself, is a threat to all status quo. The free imagination appears to make intentional learning, independent learning possible.

The learner, even in a school room, is animated by the image of a future possible being that is not yet attained. The good pedagogue will seek to vivify and intensify this image of what it will be like when one can read, count, or play the piano. Even advertisements in comic books capitalize on this when they say "Can you see yourself as the life of the party? Would you like to be? Then enroll now." The dull child, the one who resists the teacher's efforts to teach, is often the one whose imagination has been turned off because the possible being it could disclose is frightening. Or his world is so threatening he must stay in the mode of perception lest a danger appear and he may not notice it. Imagining is dangerous because it means a cessation of vigilant scanning.

This makes me think of the "intellectual paranoids" in our universities who don't dare turn their imagining loose, who rivet their attention on their last set of words, lest an enemy be near to challenge them. The teacher who turns on the dull pupil, the coach who elicits the magnificent performance from someone of whom it could not have been expected, are people who themselves have an image of the pupils' possibilities, and they are effective in realizing their image. Good leaders who have a vivid image of possibility produce followers in whom this image is awakened, and the followers achieve remarkable feats on their own. The art of challenge needs to be better understood, but it does seem from this sketchy analysis to entail the ability to awaken a sleeping imagination so it can envision fascinating new possibilities of being. It also seems to involve the possibility of becoming fascinated. Good pornographers are able to awaken images of sexual possibilities, even in neurotics who ordinarily repress their sexual imagination. I think teachers who would like to turn students on might learn something from them. A good *guru* is able to awaken the imagination of possibilities in the experience of the seeker. Beyond the awakening of possibility, however, the good *guru* is effective at challenging a person to commit himself to realize the possibility.

Encouragement: It is often a long and discouraging voyage to make an envisioned possibility actual. A friend, parent, teacher, or *guru,* may help the independent learner make his way by offering courage, encouragement, and support in the face of blind alleys, setbacks, and temporary failures. Many people have the capacity to imagine possibilities, even fascinating possibilities, but they stop their pursuit after a failure or two. The helper will offer the support which keeps the seeker seeking and trying. The seeking is what is applauded, not solely the successful attainment. Kazantzakis puts these words into the mouth of Odysseus in *The Odyssey, a modern sequel.* Odysseus says, "Your voyages, O my soul, are my native land." Not the harbor, the *voyaging.* The seeking is what is applauded not solely the successful attainment. This also reminds me of the slogan in Canada when I went to school. We were always told, we had it drummed into us, "It doesn't matter who wins the game, it is how hard and well you play that counts." And we believed it. I believe it to this day. It is an English import. Many people will neither imagine nor try because they cannot be guaranteed visible success.

Conclusion

I am going to conclude now. Where are the *gurus?* People who relate to others in a confirming, authentic, challenging and encouraging way seem to be agents in fostering independent learning in others. Likely, too, they are fascinated people themselves, animated by images of possibility that they are in the process of actualizing. The imitation of admired role models—hero worship, identification—is certainly an influential factor in everyone's development. We should not underrate the importance of this in our deliberations here. Indeed, how admirable, how heroic, how growing, how seeking in fascination are the available *Others* in society just now? Who wants to be like his father, or his mother, or his school teacher?

If the young people of today are any illustration, they seem to be hell-bent on pursuing an image of a possible being that is portrayed for them by the mass media. The image of men who play with Bunnies, and of Bunnies who are playmates to Playboys, seem more to inspire fascination and the desire to learn how to look like one and behave like one than do professors of Introductory Psychology or the teachers of third-grade Social Studies. Now granted those who promote these models are corrupt *gurus.* They do it for cash, but they turn people on and we might well learn something from them. Hitler turned people on, and so did Jesus. I wonder if the "establishment" in society can tolerate *gurus,* or people who function like *gurus.* I wonder if schools, homes, industry, politics, and business will permit people to be turned on to projects of their own choosing.

Independent learners rock the boat. True education, as opposed to training, is by definition *subversive,* and it is at this point that I want to comment about a statement that appears in a booklet entitled *A Guide to Preparation of Programs for Programed Instruction.* In this book it says, "Failure to define the purposes and specific goals is a little like setting out on a long journey without deciding on a destination. It might prove to be an interesting trip, but the traveler could wander for a long time, without getting far from his starting point and without ever reaching the distant places he wanted to visit." Now I rather think that education, as I am defining the term here, and which I am calling subversive, is indeed a failure to define the purpose and specific goals. Training, by contrast, deliberately reduces variance, diminishes freedom in a sense, and lessens autonomy. We cannot ignore the fact that education, as I have defined it, is a political act, or better it is the embodiment of the political stance of the loyal opposition, and sometimes the anarchist or revolutionary. Every society needs its anarchists, its *gurus,* its true educators and teachers, or it will shatter from its own rigidity. Do we have any, do we have enough, and are they honest?

Part III

PURITANISM

Introduction

Throughout the history of American thought few belief systems have been as resolutely acclaimed yet as harshly derided as the ideology of Puritanism. Advocates assert that adherence to such puritan virtues as hard work and self-reliance has created a near perfect society which is certainly worthy of emulation. Puritanism is rigidly moralistic and characterized by a tough-minded realism. Opponents of Puritanism, on the other hand, maintain that the ideology is responsible for the majority of the psychological and socioeconomical problems that the American citizenry has encountered. Both eulogists and critics would agree, however, that the ideology of Puritanism has been a major force in structuring the values and the institutions of American society.

To its most ardent proponents in the country, the ideology of Puritanism is equated with Americanism. Yet the ideology is shared by citizens of many countries throughout the world. American citizens, returning from visits to such countries as the Soviet Union, Cuba, and, more recently, the Peoples' Republic of China, have noted that their governments place a firm emphasis upon work, thrift, mental and moral discipline, and social responsibility. In fact, some Americans, perceiving the United States to be in a state of anarchy and hedonistic decadence, express sympathy for the virtues of these countries and speak somewhat nostalgically about a prior age of American history in which the puritan virtues were more universally shared and exemplified.

Historically, in America, elements of Puritanism have been associated with those individuals who, disenchanted with their situation in England, established the Massachusettes Bay Colony in 1630. The ideology espoused by the theocratic magistrates who founded this colony was typical of the belief systems often found in periods of transition. When traditional and/or predetermined roles no longer provide a structure for human endeavor, the ideology of Puritanism serves to unify its believers while they establish a new social order. With the decline or the overthrow of a feudal aristocracy, for example, Puritanism provides a foundation for the formation of an industrial society.

Although numerous scholars have asserted that Puritanism provided the ideological foundation for capitalism, it should be noted that the ideology also has played a role in the formation of communist states. Mao Tse-Tung's *Red Book*, for example, contains many statements that reflect the ideology of Puritanism. In fact, a major element of the ideology, social responsibility, is certainly more congruent with a government-controlled economy than with one based upon a concept of laissez-faire. After the influence of the concept of community has diminished, however, laissez-faire capitalism may flourish in perfect harmony with Puritanism.

The writings of Benjamin Franklin, extolling the puritan virtues of perseverance, industry, and frugality provided a rationale for the emerging middle class comprised of craftsmen, clerks, and entrepreneurs. In contrast to the earlier radical phase, the Puritanism represented by Franklin was moderate, secular, and democratized. Morality was equated with individual worldly success.

Throughout the latter half of the nineteenth century the ideology of Puritanism was reflected in the *Eclectic Readers* of William Holmes McGuffey and the numerous novels of Horatio Alger in which the puritan virtues were portrayed as prerequisites for the fulfillment of the American Dream. In addition, they were incorporated into the social theories of William Graham Sumner in America and Herbert Spencer in England. Influenced by the writings of Charles Darwin, Sumner and Spencer created a social theory based upon the facts of overpopulation, variation, competitive individualism, and the survival of the fittest. This social theory of natural selection, Social Darwinism, provided the rationale and the legitimacy for the activities of the industrial Barons who led the process that transformed America from an agrarian to an industrialized society.

The twentieth century has witnessed the emergence of an automated, technological society, a society founded upon consumption and leisure rather than production and work. Consequently, many of the elements of Puritanism appear to be outmoded as we increasingly focus upon personal pleasures in a rather relaxed, permissive atmosphere. Yet the ideology remains viable for individuals interested in radical reform, and it continues to provide a system of beliefs for those whose lives are in a state of transition.

The major emphasis of Puritanism has been altered by changing social and economic conditions. Yet the reader will note recurring key concepts. In the first article, the eminent historian Ralph Barton Perry examines the Puritans' paramount concern for morality. Obviously, an overemphatic insistence upon adherence to a rigid moral code would be tyrannical; on the other hand, however, a simplistic moral relativism or a superficial situational ethics can result in apathy and nihilism. This dilemma is astutely delineated by Perry.

In the next essay, the role of the puritan creed as a blueprint for radical politics is outlined by the historian Michael Walzer. Walzer's model can be applied to various revolutionary groups, including Bay Colony Puritans, Bolsheviks, and Maoists. It represents Puritanism in the early phase of revolutionary transition when the creed is highly demanding and rigidly enforced.

The puritan virtues are openly espoused in the Scout Oath and the Code of the Good American. The Boy Scouts were organized at the turn of the twentieth century by Lieutenant General Sir Robert S. S. Baden-Powell. A leader of the Constabulary in South Africa, Baden-Powell found that his troops were not trained properly for survival in their pioneering work. To meet this need he established a rigid moral-physical training program, the concept of which he later utilized when he created the Boy Scouts. The term scoutmaster, in fact, was adopted from a title used in the ranks of the Puritan general Oliver Cromwell.

The Code of the Good America emanated from a nationwide movement for character education. The Code, an obvious equation of Puritanism with Americanism was printed in poster form and distributed to schools throughout the country by the National Education Association in 1946 and 1947.

From an historical perspective, Cotton Mather's "Essay" reflects the Puritan's concern for self-examination and moral exemplarism. Starting from the Puritan assumption of man's inherent sinfulness, Mather focuses upon the importance of proper childrearing. The ravages of the wilderness and the influences of Satan, he warns, await those who go astray.

Many of the writings of Benjamin Franklin were published under pen names. Several early essays, for example, cuttingly satirized the pomposity and irrelevance of Harvard College education and were signed "Silence Dogood," a name adopted from Mather's "Essay." Franklin, emerging from rather humble puritan origins, emphasized practical methods for achieving the success of a self-made man. His programed instruction for the "bold and arduous Project of arriving at moral Perfection" appeared in his *Autobiography*. The puritan virtues are clearly illustrated here, albiet in moderate form, tempered and individualized by the mentality of the Enlightenment. Franklin's "how-to" approach continues to be reiterated in numerous American writings.

Few books have been so universally shared by Americans as the *Eclectic Readers*. Edited by William Holmer McGuffey, the *Readers* were utilized by schools throughout the country for over half a century. The stories were blatantly moralistic, containing maxims that reflected the puritan elements of perseverance, self-reliance, thrift, and industry. By diligently practicing the puritan tenets, the student would be guaranteed success in the eyes of God, and quite possibly would achieve worldly success as measured by material rewards.

The writings of Herbert Spencer and William Graham Sumner reflect the puritan virtues incorporated within a theoretical construct later termed Social Darwinism or "rugged individualism." The selections reprinted here from the essays of Sumner illustrate the Social Darwinists' belief that individuals who maintained the fundamental puritan virtues would be prepared for the "struggle for existence" and prosper because nature worked on the principle of the "survival of the fittest." Natural selection would reject the "misfits" and promote the "fittest." Thus civilization progresses.

Social Darwinism provided the rationale for emerging industrial Barons, as exemplified in the essay by Andrew Carnegie included here. The puritan concept of community reappears here in the emphasis on philanthropy.

In the final essay of this part, the theologian Martin Buber focuses upon morality and character formation as fundamental elements in the concept of true education. Buber expresses the puritan distrust for simply equating intelligence or "book learning" with ethical behavior. To create the good society, puritans believe, educators must begin with the hearts of men. As Buber notes, the best educators are those who teach by example.

AN ANALYTICAL VIEW: A Brief Survey

THE MORAL ATHLETE
Ralph Barton Perry

1

Puritanism proclaimed a supreme good—and insisted on its supremacy. But the moral hierarchy of value did not coincide with the order of natural inclination. The true way of life was not the line of least resistance, but an unnatural spiritual condition to be achieved by discipline, method, and dogged determination. There was need of what George Herbert Palmer has called "the exercise of . . . subordination." [1] It is this phase of puritanism—its moral rigorism—on which I wish now to focus attention. Indulgently judged, the puritan is the exponent of moral zeal and perfectionism. To less sympathetic judges he is a moral virtuoso; a moral martinet; or a sort of moral Hercules of the worst period, disproportionately developed in his moral muscles.

The puritan's moral rigorism, whether just or excessive, sprang from his dualism. There were several dualities in the puritan system of belief. The elect and the damned formed a complete disjunction: every man belonged to the one group or the other, and no man could belong to both. If one was saved, one was totally saved, and if one was damned, one was totally damned—a duality like that which plays so important a part in modern moral judgments, between those who are in jail and those who are out of jail. The Lutheran doctrine of justification by faith implied, or at any rate generated, a further duality between the occurrence and nonoccurrence of a specific religious experience, such as that of conversion or sanctification. The Calvinistic emphasis on the will of God created still another dualism, between acts of obedience and acts of disobedience.

From Ralph Barton Perry, *Puritanism and Democracy* (N. Y.: Harper & Row Publishers, Inc., 1944), pp. 246–68. Copyright 1944 by Ralph Barton Perry. Reprinted by permission of Harper & Row Publishers, Inc.

---

[1] G. P. Adams and W. P. Montague, eds., *Contemporary American Philosophy*, 2 vols., Macmillan, 1930, Vol. I, p. 18.

When this doctrine was combined with the acceptance of the Bible as a codification of the divine will, there resulted a legalistic distinction between wholly right and wholly wrong, according as the act does or does not conform to the rule. If there is a statute forbidding the riding of a bicycle on the sidewalk, the right and the wrong are divided by the edge of the curb.

All of these ideas tended to present moral differences as white and black divided by a sharp line. But although they fostered a cult of strictness, they did not in themselves define a dynamic antithesis. This second form of moral dualism sprang from a motive more deeply rooted both in the Christian tradition and in the universal moral experience—the inner tension, namely, between will and appetite, or, to use Kant's familiar terms, between duty and inclination. Since the better life did not in principle agree with inclination; since it might, therefore, at any particular time require a departure from inclination; and since inclination was a force— it followed that there was need of a moral counterforce by which inclination could, if necessary, be overcome.

2

The puritan's name implies that he was a purist. He had clearly defined standards and he judged himself strictly by them. If his grade was fifty on the scale of a hundred, he did not congratulate himself for rising so high, but condemned himself for falling so short. He recognized that man was by nature sinful, as modern psychology recognizes that man is by nature irrational. Such an acknowledgment of weakness may lead to either of two judgments: one may expect nothing, or one may demand everything. One may say that it is remarkable, considering his corrupt nature, that man is no worse than he is; or one may say, with puritanism, that considering his divine origin and ideal possibilities, it is disgraceful that he is no better. It is this perfectionism which led the puritan to place the generality of mankind so low, and at the same time to exalt the elite of saintliness so high.

The ideal of purity or strictness was, as we have seen, in part an outgrowth of ethical legalism. For the average man in his everyday life the puritan faith translated itself into obedience of God's will as written down plainly in the Bible. Or, if it was not plain, it seemed plain when a certain interpretation of it had become generally accepted. The teachings of the Bible, furthermore, were largely identical with the precepts of the secular conscience. The Bible did not ask impossible things. Some of its teachings, at least, were both plain and within man's power to obey. Within these limits one's righteousness might be absolute: precisely what the rule prescribed, one might perform; precisely what it forbade might be avoided.[2]

Is extreme scrupulousness—adherence to the letter of the precept—an odd and unpleasant vagary of historical puritans and their like, or has it some general ethical validity? There are at least two considerations which support the second alternative.

In the first place, the application of precepts means their crystallization into concrete and largely stereotyped habits. Virtue cannot be practiced until it is converted into specific rules to be complied with literally. It is important, no doubt, that the more general virtue should not be confused with the specific rule, so that the latter may be open to amendment. But when a code is actually operative, the agent is adhering strictly to *some* formula. The cavalier is in this generalized sense not less scrupulous in the details of his courtesy than is the puritan in those of his sabbatarianism.

In the second place, there are virtues that have no virtue save in their strict or literal observance. Such, for example, is the virtue of punctuality. The virtue of this rule lies in its enabling two or more persons to meet in the same place at the same time. It is not observed at all unless it is observed precisely. This is not a case in which one would invoke the spirit rather than the letter of the law. If chronometers were introduced, and hours and minutes reckoned, it would not be felt that the transaction had been degraded. But punctuality is an instance of a large class. All concerted human efforts are engagements, depending on a precise commitment by each party, precisely adhered to. They depend on each party's saying just what he means, on his being understood by the other parties, and on all parties conforming their action to their meaning. If human relations of a more slipshod character are possible, it is because there are "precisionists" somewhere who have pledged and kept their word.

.   .   .

3

The wholehearted love of God implies the eradication of rival affections. Saving, perhaps, its depicting of the horrors of hell, there is no feature of puritanism that has seemed so absurd to posterity as its sumptuary legislation. In England during the Puritan Revolution, and in New England during the theocracy, the puritan church through the

[2] For puritan legalism and casuistry, cf. Edward Dowden, *Puritan and Anglican*, 3d ed., London, 1910, pp. 19–20.

civil authorities prohibited amusements and luxuries that to a later age appear not only innocent but right and reasonable. The inquisitorial eye of the Consistory followed the Genevese citizen "from his cradle to his grave." Even personal adornment was "made an affair of public concernment and welfare." [3] The modern reader dismisses such regulations with amused contempt. But the sumptuary legislation, or so-called blue laws, of the puritan are wholly misunderstood if they are construed as independent judgments of good and evil. They constituted a regimen of abstinence designed to deliver the heart from debasing attachments. They were a social manifestation of what Calvin described as "most diligent efforts to extricate ourselves from these fetters" of the world and the flesh.[4]

The evil of personal adornment, of card-playing, dancing, and similar frivolities, lay not in the deed itself, nor in its immediate consequences, but in the inordinate and disloyal fondness by which it was prompted. Believing that his spiritual progress was a doubtful and hazardous enterprise, beset by many pitfalls, the puritan intended to take no chances. He named as temptations to be resisted and prohibited those practices which in his time and place seemed most conspicuously to represent the contrary of the love of God. He was peculiarly suspicious of the sexual appetite, not only because of its strength, but also because of all the appetites it seems most deeply rooted in the body. At the same time it is of all the appetites the most imaginative, so that it is peculiarly difficult to divide the thought from the deed. The point of puritanism was not to impute the sexual imagination where it did not exist, but to recognize the indivisibility of the imagination from the passion, and to distrust the passion as one of the major rivals of the love of God.

4

The puritan's sharp differences of right and wrong, of election and damnation, of regenerate and unregenerate, of belief and unbelief, reduce, then, to the dynamic opposition between the higher love of God and whatever rival loves may claim or threaten the dominion of the human heart. Piety consisted in fidelity. "I see therefore," said John Winthrop, "I must keepe a better watch over my heart, & keepe my thoughts close to good things, & not suffer a vaine or worldly thought to enter, etc.: least it drawe the heart to delight in it." [5]

[3] Cf. Mark Pattison, *Essays collected and arranged by Henry Nettleship,* 2 vols., Clarendon Press, Oxford, 1889, Vol. II, p. 25.
[4] John Calvin, *Institutes of the Christian Religion,* translated by John Allen, 3 vols., Philadelphia, 1813, Vol. II, p. 184. (Bk. III, Chap. IX, § 2.)
[5] Quoted in E. D. Hanscom, ed., *The Heart of the Puritan,* Macmillan, 1917, p. 252.

In dramatizing the opposition between lower and higher goods, and in insisting that the triumph of the one involves the defeat of the other, the puritans followed the immemorial conscience of man. They affirmed an unwelcome truth about life which all moralists have affirmed, but which does not depend on any authority, pagan or Christian. The puritans because they took it so much to heart have come to symbolize it, but they did not invent it. It expresses the fact that the elements of which a good life is composed offer a certain resistance to the form which goodness imposes on them. The moral life is the making of some harmonious purpose out of impulses each of which is endowed with an independent bias which must be checked if the purpose is to be maintained. The will, representing the purpose, sets a limit to each impulse, and stations a sentinel there with instructions to challenge every trespasser. If the purpose is to be a permanent achievement of character, there must be a judgment that says "No," a power to enforce this judgment, and an impulse which obeys. That the impulse obeys reluctantly is implied in the definition of the situation. The imposed limit blocks the very way which the impulse, if left to itself, is inclined to follow.

In other words, the moral shoe pinches. Let us consider some homely workaday aspect of life. One's general purpose in life requires, let us say, that one shall rise in the morning at six o'clock. This purpose provides for sleep, but sets a limit to it. One is not born, like a wound and set alarm clock, with an impulse to bestir oneself at six o'clock. There are mornings in youth (despite the poetic fiction which associates youth with dawn) in which one is governed by a pure impulse to sleep, *only* to sleep, to sleep *more*, to sleep *on* and *on*. The impulse whispers, "Yet a little sleep, a little slumber, a little folding of the hands to sleep." [6] With this impulse the day's program is in irreconcilable conflict. The program requires that one shall leave that warm, soft bed, dispel that delicious languor, turn from that enticing prospect, and do what of all imaginable things is then and there most repugnant. No method has ever been, nor ever will be, invented by which one can both play one's part in the world and also sleep as much as in one's sleepiest moments one would like to sleep.

Sleep, love, hunger, thirst, have their own primitive, inherent, and independent impulsions, which they never lose. Any moral code whatsoever, even the least and lowliest prudence, must begin by subduing them, and must remain in command. There is the same conflict between the pull of private gain and the requirements of public good, or between a preoccupation with American domestic interests and a duty to mankind at large. Everywhere, on every level, there is an inertia or a momentum of the given interest which for the sake of some larger and more legit-

[6] Prov. 6:10.

imate plan has to be overcome or redirected. This is the plain and unpalatable fact which all experience teaches—the most trite, the most disagreeable, and among the most profound, of all moral truths.

Puritanism is rightly associated with this negative incidence of goodness and piety. That the puritan should have exaggerated an aspect of morality so congenial to his zeal, and so abundantly confirmed by his experience, is not surprising. It is not surprising that in his struggle with human enemies or with the forces of nature he should have supposed that he was "battling for the Lord." It was natural that having taken God's side he should assume that God had taken *his,* and that Satan was on the side of his enemies.

. . .

5

Recognizing this need of a centralized control, the puritan proposed to achieve it by extraordinary and systematic effort. This cult of will power, this use of the will for the purpose of strengthening the will, was motivated in the puritan by anxiety. He was tortured by doubt as to the present state and future prospects of his soul. He was forever telling his eternal fortunes, plucking the petals—"He loves me—he loves me not" —the love in question being that divine love which pronounces the word of doom. There can be no doubt of the anxiety. But was it consistent with the basic tenets of puritan theology? Why should the puritan have been anxious about what he imputed to the irrevocable decision of God? Why should he be so much interested in the condition of his will if he was saved by faith and not by works?

These objections are purely academic. He who puts himself in the position of the puritan will not feel any inconsistency. One is either elected to show forth the mercy of God, or damned to manifest his justice. Would one not, on this assumption, like to know which? Has it ever been observed that the candidate for office is indifferent to the returns on election night, even though he realizes that he is now powerless to influence the outcome? It is not surprising, for example, that Cotton Mather should have lived, as he expressed it, "in the very frequent Practice of *Self-Examination,*" or that he should have looked anxiously for what he called the "Mark of an *effectually called* Person." On a certain day in his forty-third year he set himself with "a more singular and exquisite Measure of Consideration" than usual to enumerate his favorable symptoms—such as sorrow for sin, the impulse to prayer, complete resignation to the will of God, compassion for his personal enemies —and asked himself "whether the Man that can find these *Marks* upon himself, may not conclude himself *mark'd out,* for the City of God."

Mather's attitude was not wholly one of curiosity. He undoubtedly sought by "Fasting . . . Contritions . . . Humiliations . . . Supplications . . . [and] Abasements" to *create* the symptoms as well as to find them. But considering what the symptoms were, there is nothing astonishing in this. Whether one does or does not possess a certain degree of physical strength may be tested by lifting a weight of a certain magnitude. If one applies the test, one tries to lift the weight. If one believes that ability to lift the weight is evidence of perfect health, and inability evidence of mortal disease, one will exert oneself to lift it in order to convince oneself of that which one prefers to believe. So in this case, since "*Idleness* . . . *Listlessness* . . . *Slothfulness* . . . Lukewarmness . . . Formality . . . *Pride* . . . Hardness . . . Wantonness" were symptoms of spiritual death,[7] an anxious person such as Cotton Mather would seek to prove his hold on eternal life by manifesting their opposites. His ability to "correspond to the design of God in calling"[8] him would constitute the much desired evidence of his call.

In other words, the puritan was engaged in a trial of strength. The question "Can I?" was experimentally tested by *trying;* and in proportion as he tried, the answer was likely to be affirmative, as he hoped it would be. The effort was doubly motivated: by curiosity as to the answer, and by desire for a particular answer. To this is to be added the further consideration that when the first signs were favorable, confidence rapidly increased because of the doctrine of integral salvation. And this confidence, in turn, generated an access of strength and further increased the desired probability. This is good psychology. Any logical misgivings that remained were easily quieted by the reflection that while God causes all things by his infinite will, he causes many things through man's will; and if what one calls one's own will is in a deeper view of the matter God's, so much the more reason to have confidence in its power.

6

In order to perfect and prove his spiritual strength the puritan engaged in exercises and went into training, much as a youth now sets out to excel in sport. An American schoolboy whom I knew made up his mind to become a high hurdler; not an ordinary everyday high hurdler, but a supreme high hurdler. He placed on his bureau a photograph of Nurmi, the Finnish long-distance champion. He gazed at this photo-

[7] *Diary of Cotton Mather*, 2 vols., Massachusetts Historical Society Collections, Seventh Series, Vols. VII–VIII, 1911–12, Vol. VII, pp. 511, 510, 22, 15, 11, 28.

[8] John Calvin, *Institutes of the Christian Religion*, Vol. II, p. 155 (Bk. III, Chap. VI, § 2).

graph every morning until there came into his face that grim expression which betokens unconquerable and irresistible resolve. This was his prayer. He abstained from candy and tobacco, and ate and drank only what was convertible into those tissues of the body which are employed in high hurdling. This was his fasting. He arranged his vacations, his friendships, his studies, his hours of sleep, his diversions, in the manner that he believed would increase his speed and endurance. Every day he weighed himself and tested himself. Slowly but steadily he clipped fractions of seconds from his record, with a growing assurance that he was one of the elect.

Now let us consider our great puritan champion, Jonathan Edwards. In early life, just after graduating from Yale at the age of seventeen, he went into training to perfect himself in godliness. For several years he recorded in a diary the course of training which he followed. . . .

It is clear that the young Jonathan Edwards was determined to achieve perfect self-mastery and control through the exercise of his will. He deliberately set his will difficult tasks, as one takes bodily exercise by the use of antagonistic muscles. He made a business of moral virtue, felt his spiritual pulse, took his spiritual weight, and measured his spiritual record.

. . .

It may be objected that the puritan's emphasis on moral discipline was disproportionate to the matter in hand. The American athlete is felt by many to have overdone athletics. He violates, we say, the amateur code, in the spirit if not in the letter. By his intense effort to surpass records or defeat opponents he makes work out of what should be play. He makes it uncomfortable for those who have neither the time nor the inclination to take the game so seriously. Now many people have precisely the same feeling toward the puritan. He takes his game of morality too seriously. He "exaggerates" morality, as some colleges are said to exaggerate football. Others who cannot compete with him, because they have only their odd hours to devote to morality, feel that the pace should be slackened. They are advocates of "morality for all," "intramural" morality, morality of a more sportive and spontaneous sort.

But the force of this plea for the amateur spirit in morality is somewhat weakened by the fact that most of those who utter it believe in being professional *somewhere*. They may be professionals in athletics, and although they think that the puritan's perpetual examination of the state of his soul is in bad taste, they have no hesitation in keeping a similar diary of the state of their muscles. Or they may be men of affairs, and want morality tempered to the tired businessman, who, however, is tired because he is so exceedingly businesslike about his business. These critics also think it morbid to balance one's spiritual account, but feel an irresistible urge to balance their bank accounts. And so with the artist, who is perhaps the most contemptuous critic of the puritan. He objects strongly to moral discipline, but devotes himself with infinite patience to the mastery of his own technique.

So it is evident that it is not so much a question of *whether* one shall be strict, as *where* one shall be strict. One will be strict, presumably, about the more important and central things: the athlete about high hurdles, the businessman about profits, the artist about music, painting, or poetry. The difference is over the question of what is important and central, and on this question the puritan held a view which, it must be admitted, is now somewhat outmoded. He held that morality is all-important and all-central.

There is some point in every man's system of ideas at which his sense of humor gives out. If you are a puritan, you may take other things lightly, but morals are no laughing matter. The puritan held, incredible as it may now seem, that morals are more important than athletics, business, or art. He held that to achieve a controlling will by which to conform one's life to what one conceives to be the way of righteousness is the one thing most profoundly needful. Or rather he held that athletics, business, and art should be judged by conscience, and approved only so far as they form parts of that good life—that orderly and integral life, of the person or of society—which must be founded on virtue. Perhaps he was mistaken in his scale of relative values, but at any rate to drive him from this position would require heavier guns than most of his critics carry.

7

There was no notable discrepancy between the inner and the outer life of the puritan. What he professed to others he also confessed to himself. He was not distinguished among men by a lack of candor. Indeed, as George Gissing has suggested, if "hypocrisy" means cynicism wearing a mask of virtue, then it is quite irrelevant to puritanism.[9] It is pharisaism rather than hypocrisy of which he may more reasonably be accused. Pharisaism does not mean wearing a cloak of righteousness; it means sincerely believing that one is more righteous than one really is. This is a failing that the puritan did, indeed, have difficulty in avoiding. He believed himself to be one of the elect, and that implied a moral eminence which contemporaries or later historians have not always found him to occupy. There seems to be a discrepancy between what he was

[9] Cf. *The Private Papers of Henry Ryecroft*, Modern Library, 1918, pp. 230–39.

and what he claimed to be. But so it seemed to him also, and hence the perpetual reproach and haunting doubts which beset him. The puritan believed himself to be called, but since his election implied an unnatural and unusual state of godliness, he could not always feel sure of himself. He alternated between the "very Top of Felicity" and the lowest depths of moral despair. It was a life of mountains and valleys with great and precipitous differences of altitude. . . .

The puritan may always be convicted of failure as judged by his own standard; and of over-belief in himself as judged by his own attainment. But who cannot? It is impossible to have standards at all without exposing oneself to precisely such accusations. There is no way of being zealous in right-doing without being "self-righteous." To have a standard is to set a goal beyond actuality or even possibility; and yet to seek the goal is impossible unless one has moments of belief in one's power to reach it. There is perhaps no one so self-righteous as the man who is fond of calling other people "hypocrites." He is excessively ready to assume that he has attained his own ideal of sincerity. When standards are applied in action there will always be some concession to circumstance, some use of means by which the purity of the action is corrupted; so that it will be possible for critics (including oneself) to point out a discrepancy between the deed and the creed. A practical Christian, like Cromwell, must adjust his ideal to the context of affairs and use what weapons are at hand. A man can do his best only by confidently seeking (and perpetually missing) an unattainable perfection.

Why, then, is the puritan's self-righteousness so odious? In the first place, because the critic frankly takes the side of Mammon, and recognizes the puritan as his enemy. His criticism is self-defense or counter-attack: "In the mouth of a drunkard he is a puritan who refuseth his cups; in the mouth of a swearer he which feareth an oath; in the mouth of a libertine he who makes any scruple of common sins." [10]

. . .

Everyone will, if forced, avow his allegience to some moral code, acknowledge its logical priority over his appetites, and confess his lapses from strict rectitude. But one dislikes to be perpetually reminded of these things. When a puritan is in the neighborhood, one feels the uncomfortable sense of an accusing presence. It is impossible to go on enjoying oneself frivolously in the midst of such gravity. The puritan is the death's-head at the feast. He cannot be lightly ignored, because his admonition is re-echoed and confirmed by one's own conscience. One knows oneself to be vulnerable. Hence one hurls epithets at the puritan, hoping to

[10] Quoted from an undesignated source by John Brown, *The English Puritans*, 1910, p. 3, courtesy of G. P. Putnam's Sons.

frighten him away; or, if not, then to divert his attention and put him on the defensive by calling attention to his own shortcomings.

8

Whatever the motives of the critic himself, the puritan's moral athleticism is abundantly open to criticism. It is marked by one-sidedness and distortion—by defects of omission so serious as to amount, in moral judgment and practice, to defects of commission. Its most glaring fault is that which has invariably manifested itself in asceticism, which is only another name for moral athleticism. The ascetic treats the will as though it were in fact a sort of muscle, which could be strengthened by a moral daily dozen. He fails to see that there is no will which is not a will to do this or that. In his effort to isolate the will he divests it of content. He creates a false dualism between his will and his concrete inclinations. He does not see that if his ruthless war upon his impulses were successful, he would have destroyed himself altogether; and that it *cannot* succeed, because he can after all do no more than range one part of himself against another. Instead of achieving peace and harmony, therefore, he aggravates the antagonisms which already divide him, and converts into unnatural monsters the appetites with which he is endowed.

Similarly, the puritan in his zeal to forge a highly tempered and sharp-edged will loses sight of the ulterior purpose which such a formidable weapon is designed to serve. Its purpose is to put the appetites in their place, but this implies that they may justly claim a place. It is as much the task of the moral will to make room for the appetites as to confine them to that room. It is true that their unruliness must be broken, but only in order that they may thrive in peace. This positive provision for concrete goods and satisfactions provides the only moral justification for their subordination, as the claim of God to the obedience of his subjects rests on his provident love.

The puritan in his insistence upon the effective control of his supreme principle harps upon it incessantly, when it should be reserved for crucial decisions. Suspicious of all intermediaries, he neglects their indispensable role. Because the love of God speaks with authority, it does not follow that it must speak all the time. With God and conscience forever looking over his shoulder, a man cannot devote himself to any interest, however, innocent, with the absorption which is the condition of its satisfaction. To acknowledge God's authority it is not necessary to run to God with every little problem. It is as though a man should take the Supreme Court as his guide, philosopher, and friend. God and conscience, like the Supreme Court, take no cognizance of the greater part of life. It is their function to determine a general orientation and to define limits. Within these limits subordinate principles—the appetites, prudence, family love, communal loyalties, science, and art—must enjoy autonomy. Without that autonomy they cannot be fruitful of good, and the effect is to create a waste instead of orderly abundance.

The moral will divorced from its natural content, freed from accountability to the human desires which it is designed to serve, proceeds to extravagant lengths. It may lead to a masochistic pleasure of self-denial, or to the hoarding of a personal power which yields no good beyond its own subjective satisfactions.

. . .

Excessively developed, and divorced from all positive goods, the moral will takes pride in its own negating, and flaunts it before the world. Deprived of natural delights, it retaliates by affecting to despise them. Instead of conceding the innocence of natural goods until they are proved guilty, it considers them as presumptively guilty, since they have not proceeded from itself.

. . .

By a curious paradox the rigorism of the puritan evades the most serious difficulties of life. His effort takes the form of a kind of brute strength rather than of skill. The difficulties which he overcomes are forces rather than complexities—forces that can be overcome by a dead heave of the will, and with comparatively little discrimination or understanding. Puritanism *wills* hard rather than thinks hard. Similarly, the puritan's precisionism involves the minimum of intellectual difficulty. The casuistical application of rules, especially of rules that are codified and set down in an authoritative document, is perhaps the simplest form of morality, requiring only a few steps of inference. The rules may go against the grain, and their application may require an overcoming of temptation, it may be difficult to *do* what one ought to do; but to *discover* what one ought to do is comparatively easy.

It is only a small part of morality which can be subserved either by "main strength" or by the direct application of rules. Abstinence, yes; and punctuality. But temperance, wisdom, loyalty, friendship, happiness, justice, benevolence, liberty, peace—these are goods which require something more than overcoming, and something more than purity or scrupulousness. The supreme moral difficulties are similar to the difficulties of art, requiring judgment rather than exactness or power. Strength of will divorced from the art of its judicious application leads to brutality; and rules divorced from the purpose which justifies and interprets them lead to pedantry.

9

If it is fair to exhibit the puritan's defects, it is also fair to remember, here as elsewhere, those opposite defects which he condemned—to remember them is to feel some sympathy with the puritan's excessive reaction. He regarded his opponents much as the youthful athlete of today regards the libertine. The lack of moral control, whether due to infirmity of will or to violence of emotion, translates itself from age to age into different terms.

The puritan of the seventeenth century had the effect of "bracing character in a period of relaxation." He stood for "the lit lamp" and "the loins girt" against the indulgence and improvidence of his times.[11] That he should have specifically attacked drunkenness, sexual looseness and perversion, the brutality of sport, licentiousness at carnivals and feasts, dancing, card-playing, was in some degree a historical accident. These may or may not remain the most conspicuous symptoms of moral weakness. If not, then others have superseded them. There is always a loose living in some sense, a laxity, a shortsightedness, a recklessness of passion, a narrow preoccupation with the immediate satisfaction, an inordinate fondness for physical pleasures. "Self-indulgence" is a term of reproach under any code, since it implies an indifference or resistance to that code as such, whatever code it be. Therefore he who takes arms against puritanism must consider that by so doing he gives aid and comfort to the puritan's enemy, who is in some sense also his own. . . .

In his insistence upon the importance of salvation, the puritan symbolizes the choice of a supreme good and its preference over all other goods. Conceived as a moral athlete, the puritan symbolizes the enthronement of such a pre-eminent good—its control of the appetites, its practical ascendancy over intermediate goods, and its scrupulous regulation of conduct. He represents that inflexible adherence to creed which will always appear as fanaticism or obstinacy to more balanced minds— as the faith of the early Christians appeared to their more cultivated pagan contemporaries. He represents the ruthless subordination of every lesser consideration to the one thing needful. The puritan was single-minded—which is, in effect, to be narrow-minded. He stripped for battle by divesting himself of worldly attachments, he economized his spiritual resources by reducing his appetitive liabilities, he tempered his will in the fire of enthusiasm.

Such an ancestor may properly be worshiped in those recurrent

[11] Edward Dowden, *Puritan and Anglican,* pp. 15–16.

periods of individual and social reform when there is an ominous sound as of surf on the rocks. The puritan, said Stuart Sherman,

> comes aboard, like a good pilot; and while we trim our sails, he takes the wheel and lays our course for a fresh voyage. His message when he leaves us is not, "Henceforth be masterless," but, "Bear thou henceforth the sceptre of thine own control through life and the passion of life." If that message still stirs us as with the sound of a trumpet, and frees and prepares us, not for the junketing of a purposeless vagabondage, but for the ardor and discipline and renunciation of a pilgrimage, we are Puritans.[12]

The puritan sailed his ship in the open seas. Despite his cult of moral vigor, he was not a moral introvert. He did not confine himself within his moral gymnasium, but used his strength out of doors, in the world. He pursued his calling, and he participated in the public life of his time and place. In the wars and revolutions precipitated by the Protestant Reformation he assumed the role of stateman and soldier. From this school of discipline came men who were notable for doing what they soberly and conscientiously resolved to do, despite temptations and obstacles—such men as William the Silent, Admiral Coligny, John Knox, Oliver Cromwell, John Milton, and our New England ancestors. The puritans imprinted on English and American institutions a quality of manly courage, self-reliance, and sobriety. We are still drawing upon the reserves of spiritual vigor which they accumulated.

[12] *The Genius of America*, Scribner, 1923, p. 75.

THE CREED: Puritan Admonitions

1. THE REVOLUTION OF THE SAINTS
Michael Walzer

It is now possible to suggest a model of radical politics based on the history of the English Puritans and developed, at least in part, in their own terms. Such a model may serve to reveal the crucial features of radicalism as a general historical phenomena and to make possible a more systematic comparison of Puritans, Jacobins, and Bolsheviks (and perhaps other groups as well) than has been attempted here.

(1) At a certain point in the transition from one or another form of traditional society (feudal, hierarchical, patriarchal, corporate) to one or another form of modern society, there appears a band of "strangers" who view themselves as chosen men, saints, and who seek a new order and an impersonal, ideological discipline.

(2) These men are marked off from their fellows by an extraordinary self-assurance and daring. The saints not only repudiate the routine procedures and customary beliefs of the old order, but they also cut themselves off from the various kinds of "freedom" (individual mobility, personal extravagance, self-realization, despair, nervousness, vacillation) experienced amidst the decay of tradition. The band of the chosen seeks and wins certainty and self-confidence by rigidly disciplining its members and teaching them to discipline themselves. The saints interpret their ability to endure this discipline as a sign of their virtue and their virtue as a sign of God's grace. Amidst the confusion of the transitional period, they discover in themselves a predestination, a firm and undeviating sense of purpose, an assurance of eventual triumph.

(3) The band of the chosen confronts the existing world as if in war. Its members interpret the strains and tensions of social change in terms of conflict and contention. The saints sense enmity all about them

Reprinted by permission of the publishers from Michael Walzer, *The Revolution of The Saints: A Study in the Origins of Radical Politics,* pp. 317–19. Cambridge, Mass.: Harvard University Press, Copyright, 1965, by the President and Fellows of Harvard College.

and they train and prepare themselves accordingly. They keep watch and continually calculate their chances.

(4) The organization of the chosen suggests the nature of the new order they seek, but also reflects the necessities of the present struggle.

(a) Men join the band by subscribing to a covenant which testifies to their faith. Their new commitment is formal, impersonal, and ideological; it requires that they abandon older loyalties not founded upon opinion and will—loyalties to family, guild, locality, and also to lord and king.

(b) This commitment is voluntary, based upon an act of the will for which men can be trained, but not born. It is not possible to take one's place in the chosen band through any sort of patronage. To be chosen, one must choose.

(c) The commitment and zeal of prospective saints must be tested and proven. Hence it is not easy to choose sainthood and the band of the chosen remains exclusive and small, each of its members highly "talented" in virtue and self-discipline. Even after men have been accepted as saints, they must still demonstrate their godliness on every possible occasion. They are subject to examination and as they could once have been rejected so they can always be purged. The godly tension which the saints maintain is thus in vivid contrast to the apathy of worldlings, secure and at their ease with their customs and traditions.

(d) Within the band of the chosen, all men are equal. Status counts for little. Members are measured by their godliness and by the contributions they can make to the work at hand.

(5) The acting out of sainthood produces a new kind of politics.

(a) The activity of the chosen band is purposive, programmatic, and progressive in the sense that it continually approaches or seeks to approach its goals. This activity may be defined as an organized effort to universalize sainthood, to reconstruct or reform the political or religious worlds according to objective criteria (revealed, predetermined, written), without any regard for the established forms.

(b) The activity of the saints is methodical and systematic. Politics is made into a kind of work, to which the chosen are required to commit themselves for long periods of time. At work they must suppress all purely personal feelings and behave in a disciplined fashion. They must learn to be patient and to concern themselves with detail. Above all, they must work regularly and hard.

(c) The violent attack upon customary procedures sets the saints free to experiment politically. Such experimentation is controlled by its overriding purposes and the right to engage in it is limited to the chosen few who have previously accepted the discipline of the band. It is not a grant of political free-play, but it does open the way to new kinds of activity, both public and secret. The saints are entrepreneurs in politics.

(6) The historical role of the chosen band is twofold. Externally, as it were, the band of the saints is a political movement aiming at social reconstruction. It is the saints who lead the final attack upon the old order and their destructiveness is all the more total because they have a total view of the new world. Internally, godliness and predestination are creative responses to the pains of social change. Discipline is the cure for freedom and "unsettledness." As romantic love strengthens the bonds of the conjugal family, so ideological zeal establishes the unity of the non-familial brethren and makes it possible for men to feel secure outside the traditional system of connections.

One day, however, that security becomes a habit and zeal is no longer a worldly necessity. Then the time of God's people is over. In this world, the last word always belongs to the worldlings and not to the saints. It is a complacent word and it comes when salvation, in all its meanings, is no longer a problem. But the saints have what is more interesting: the first word. They set the stage of history for the new order.

Once that order is established, ordinary men are eager enough to desert the warfare of the Lord for some more moderate pursuit of virtue. Once they feel sufficiently secure as gentlemen and merchants, as country justices and members of Parliament, they happily forego the further privilege of being "instruments." Hardly a moment after their triumph, the saints find themselves alone; they can no longer exploit the common forms of ambition, egotism, and nervousness; they can no longer convince their fellow men that ascetic work and intense repression are necessary. The experience of other revolutionaries has been similar: the history of their success is brief.

2. BRITISH AND AMERICAN SCOUT OATH (PROMISE) AND LAW

British Boy Scouts Association

THE SCOUT'S PROMISE

"On my honour I promise that I will do my best,
1. To do my duty to God and the King,

Boy Scouts of America

THE SCOUT OATH OR PROMISE

"On my honor I will do my best:
1. To do my duty to God and my country, and to obey the Scout Law;

BRITISH

2. To help other people at all times,

3. To obey the Scout Law."

AMERICAN

2. To help other people at all times;

3. To keep myself physically strong, mentally awake, and morally straight."

THE SCOUT LAW [1]

1. A SCOUT'S HONOUR IS TO BE TRUSTED. If a Scout says, "on my honour it is so," that means that it is so, just as if he had taken a most solemn oath.

Similarly, if a Scout Officer says to a Scout, "I trust you on your honor to do this," the Scout is bound to carry out the order to the very best of his ability, and to let nothing interfere with his doing so.

If a Scout were to break his honour by telling a lie, or by not carrying out an order exactly when trusted on his honour to do so, he may be directed to hand over his Scout Badge, and never wear it again. He may also be directed to cease to be a Scout.

2. A SCOUT IS LOYAL TO THE KING, and to his officers, and to his parents, his country, and his employers. He must stick to them through thick and thin against anyone who is their enemy or who even talks badly of them.

3. A SCOUT'S DUTY IS TO BE USEFUL AND TO HELP OTHERS. And

THE SCOUT LAW

1. A SCOUT IS TRUSTWORTHY. A Scout's honor is to be trusted. If he were to violate his honor by telling a lie or by cheating or by not doing exactly a given task, when trusted on his honor, he may be directed to hand over his Scout Badge.

2. A SCOUT IS LOYAL. He is loyal to all to whom loyalty is due; his Scout Leader, his home and parents and country.

3. A SCOUT IS HELPFUL. He must be prepared at any time to

[1] The discussion under each Law of the British Boy Scouts Association is not a part of the Law, as in America, but is an interpretation—one of several that have been made.

BRITISH	AMERICAN

he is to do his duty before any-thing else, even though he gives up his own pleasure, or comfort or safety to do it. When in difficulty to know which of two things to do, he must ask himself, "Which is my duty?" That is, "Which is best for other people?"—and do that one. He must Be Prepared at any time to save life, or to help injured per-sons, and he must try his best to do a good turn to somebody every day.

save life, help injured persons, and share the home duties. He must do at least one good turn to some-body every day.

4. A Scout is a Friend to all, and a Brother to Every Other Scout, no Matter to what Social Class the Other Belongs. Thus if a Scout meets another Scout, even though a stranger to him, he must speak to him, and help him in any way that he can, either to carry out the duty he is then doing, or by giving him food or, as far as possible, anything that he may be in want of. A Scout must never be a Snob. A snob is one who looks down upon another because he is poorer, or who is poor and resents another because he is rich. A Scout accepts another man as he finds him, and makes the best of him.

4. A Scout is Friendly. He is a friend to all and a brother to every other Scout.

"Kim," The Boy Scout, was called by the Indians "Little friend of all the world," and that is the name that every Scout should earn for himself.

5. A Scout is Courteous. That is, he is polite to all—but es-pecially to women and children,

5. A Scout is Courteous. He is polite to all, especially to women, children, old people, and the weak

and old people and invalids, cripples, etc. And he must not take any reward for being helpful or courteous.

6. A SCOUT IS A FRIEND TO ANIMALS. He should save them as far as possible from pain, and should not kill any animal unnecessarily, even if it is only a fly—for it is one of God's creatures. Killing an animal for food or an animal which is harmful is allowable.

7. A SCOUT OBEYS ORDERS of his parents, patrol leader or Scoutmaster without question. Even if he gets an order he does not like he must do as soldiers and sailors do, he must carry it out all the same because it is his duty; and after he has done it he can come and state any reasons against it, but he must carry out the order at once. That is discipline.

8. A SCOUT SMILES AND WHISTLES under all circumstances. When he gets an order he should obey it cheerily and readily, not in a slow, hang-dog sort of way. Scouts never grouse at hardships, nor whine at each other, nor swear when put out, but go on whistling and smiling. When you just miss a train or someone treads on your favorite corn—not that a Scout should have such things as corns—or under any annoying circumstances, you should force yourself to smile at once and then whistle a tune, and you will be all right.

A Scout goes about with a

and helpless. He must not take pay for being helpful or courteous.

6. A SCOUT IS KIND. He is a friend to animals. He will not kill nor hurt any living creature, needlessly, but will strive to save and protect all harmless life.

7. A SCOUT IS OBEDIENT. He obeys his parents, Scoutmaster, patrol leader, and all other duly constituted authorities.

8. A SCOUT IS CHEERFUL. He smiles whenever he can. His obedience to orders is prompt and cheery. He never shirks nor grumbles at hardships.

BRITISH

smile on and whistling. It cheers him and cheers other people, especially in times of danger, for he keeps it up then all the same. (Not in present law.)

The punishment for swearing or using bad language is for each offence a mug of cold water to be poured down the offender's sleeve by the other Scouts. It was the punishment invented by an old British Scout, Captain John Smith, three hundred years ago.

9. A SCOUT IS THRIFTY, that is he saves every penny he can, and puts it into the bank, so that he may have money to keep himself when out of work, and thus not make himself a burden to others; or that he may have money to give away to others when they need it.

10. A SCOUT IS CLEAN IN THOUGHT, WORD, AND DEED, that is, he looks down upon a silly youth who talks dirt, and he does not let himself give way to temptation either to talk it or to think, or do anything dirty. A Scout is pure and clean-minded and manly.

(Note: Added in 1912.)

AMERICAN

9. A SCOUT IS THRIFTY. He does not wantonly destroy property. He works faithfully, wastes nothing, and makes the best use of his opportunities. He saves his money so that he may pay his own way, be generous to those in need, and helpful to worthy objects. He may work for pay but must not receive tips for courtesies or good turns.

10. A SCOUT IS BRAVE. He has the courage to face danger in spite of fear, and to stand up for the right against the coaxing of friends or the jeers or threats of enemies; and defeat does not down him.

11. A SCOUT IS CLEAN. He keeps clean in body and thought, stands for clean speech, clean sport, clean habits, and travels with a clean crowd.

12. A SCOUT IS REVERENT. He is reverent toward God. He is faithful in his religious duties, and respects the convictions of others in matters of custom and religion.

3. THE CODE OF THE GOOD AMERICAN
Character Education Institution of Washington, D. C.

The Code

Citizens who are good Americans try to become strong and useful, worthy of their nation, that our country may become ever greater and better. Therefore, they obey the laws of right living which the best Americans have always obeyed.

[1] THE LAW OF SELFCONTROL

The Good American Controls Himself. Those who best control themselves can best serve their country.

I will control my *tongue,* and will not allow it to speak mean, vulgar, or profane words. I will think before I speak. I will tell the truth and nothing but the truth.

I will control my *temper,* and will not get angry when people or things displease me. Even when indignant against wrong and contradicting falsehood, I will keep my selfcontrol.

I will control my *thoughts,* and will not allow a foolish wish to spoil a wise purpose.

I will control my *actions.* I will be careful and thrifty, and insist on doing right.

I will not ridicule nor defile the character of another; I will keep my selfrespect, and help others to keep theirs.

[2] THE LAW OF GOOD HEALTH

The Good American Tries to Gain and Keep Good Health. The welfare of our country depends upon those who are physically fit for their daily work. Therefore:

I will try to take such food, sleep, and exercise as will keep me always in good health.

I will keep my clothes, my body, and my mind clean.

Reprinted by permission of the Journal of the National Education Association, 1946 & 1947.

I will avoid those habits which would harm me, and will make and never break those habits which will help me.

I will protect the health of others, and guard their safety as well as my own.

I will grow strong and skilful.

[3] THE LAW OF KINDNESS

The Good American Is Kind. In America those who are different must live in the same communities. We are of many different sorts, but we are one great people. Every unkindness hurts the common life; every kindness helps. Therefore:

I will be kind in all my thoughts. I will bear no spites or grudges. I will never despise anybody.

I will be kind in all my speech. I will never gossip nor will I speak unkindly of anyone. Words may wound or heal.

I will be kind in my acts. I will not selfishly insist on having my own way. I will be polite: rude people are not good Americans. I will not make unnecessary trouble for those who work for me, nor forget to be grateful. I will be careful of other people's things. I will do my best to prevent cruelty, and will give help to those in need.

[4] THE LAW OF SPORTSMANSHIP

The Good American Plays Fair. Clean play increases and trains one's strength and courage, and helps one to be more useful to one's country. Sportsmanship helps one to be a gentleman, a lady. Therefore:

I will not cheat, nor will I play for keeps or for money. If I should not play fair, the loser would lose the fun of the game, the winner would lose his selfrespect, and the game itself would become a mean and often cruel business.

I will treat my opponents with courtesy, and trust them if they deserve it. I will be friendly.

If I play in a group game, I will play not for my own glory, but for the success of my team and the fun of the game.

I will be a good loser or a generous winner.

And in my work as well as in my play, I will be sportsmanlike—generous, fair, honorable.

[5] THE LAW OF SELFRELIANCE

The Good American Is Selfreliant. Selfconceit is silly, but self-reliance is necessary to citizens who would be strong and useful.

I will gladly listen to the advice of older and wiser people; I will reverence the wishes of those who love and care for me, and who know life and me better than I. I will develop independence and wisdom to think for myself, choose for myself, act for myself, according to what seems right and fair and wise.

I will not be afraid of being laughed at when I am right. I will not be afraid of doing right when the crowd does wrong.

When in danger, trouble, or pain, I will be brave. A coward does not make a good American.

[6] The Law of Duty

The Good American Does His Duty. The shirker and the willing idler live upon others, and burden fellow-citizens with work unfairly. They do not do their share, for their country's good.

I will try to find out what my duty is as a good American, and my duty I will do, whether it is easy or hard. What it is my duty to do I can do.

[7] The Law of Reliability

The Good American is Reliable. Our country grows great and good as her citizens are able more fully to trust each other. Therefore:

I will be honest, in word and in act. I will not lie, sneak, or pretend.

I will not do wrong in the hope of not being found out. I cannot hide the truth from myself and cannot often hide it from others. Nor will I injure the property of others.

I will not take without permission what does not belong to me. A thief is a menace to me and others.

I will do promptly what I have promised to do. If I have made a foolish promise, I will at once confess my mistake, and I will try to make good any harm which my mistake may have caused. I will so speak and act that people will find it easier to trust each other.

[8] The Law of Truth

The Good American Is True. I will be slow to believe suspicions lest I do injustice; I will avoid hasty opinions lest I be mistaken as to facts.

I will stand by the truth regardless of my likes and dislikes, and scorn the temptation to lie for myself or friends; nor will I keep the truth from those who have a right to it.

I will hunt for proof, and be accurate as to what I see and hear; I will learn to think, that I may discover new truth.

[9] THE LAW OF GOOD WORKMANSHIP

The Good American Tries to Do the Right Thing in the Right Way.
The welfare of our country depends upon those who have learned to do
in the right way the work that makes civilization possible. Therefore:

I will get the best possible education, and learn all that I can as a
preparation for the time when I am grown up and at my life work. I will
invent and make things better if I can.

I will take real interest in work, and will not be satisfied to do slipshod, lazy, and merely passable work. I will form the habit of good
work and keep alert; mistakes and blunders cause hardships, sometimes
disaster, and spoil success.

I will make the right thing in the right way to give it value and
beauty, even when no one else sees or praises me. But when I have done
my best, I will not envy those who have done better, or have received
larger reward. Envy spoils the work and the worker.

[10] THE LAW OF TEAMWORK

*The Good American Works in Friendly Cooperation with Fellow-
Workers.* One alone could not build a city or a great railroad. One alone
would find it hard to build a bridge. That I may have bread, people have
made plows and threshers, have built mills and mined coal, made stoves
and kept stores. As we learn better how to work together, the welfare of
our country is advanced.

In whatever work I do with others, I will do my part and encourage
others to do their part, promptly, quickly.

I will help to keep in order the things which we use in our work.
When things are out of place, they are often in the way, and sometimes
they are hard to find.

In all my work with others, I will be cheerful. Cheerlessness de-
presses all the workers and injures all the work.

When I have received money for my work, I will be neither a miser
nor a spendthrift. I will save or spend as one of the friendly workers of
America.

[11] THE LAW OF LOYALTY

The Good American Is Loyal. If our America is to become ever
greater and better, her citizens must be loyal, devotedly faithful in every
relation of life; full of courage and regardful of their honor.

I will be loyal to my family. In loyalty I will glady obey my parents or those who are in their place, and show them gratitude. I will do my best to help each member of my family to strength and usefulness.

I will be loyal to my school. In loyalty I will obey and help other pupils to obey those rules which further the good of all.

I will be loyal to my town, my state, my country. In loyalty I will respect and help others to respect their laws and their courts of justice.

I will be loyal to humanity and civilization. In loyalty I will do my best to help the friendly relations of our country with every other country, and to give to everyone in every land the best possible chance. I will seek truth and wisdom; I will work, and achieve if I can, some good for the civilization into which I have been born.

If I try simply to be loyal to my family, I may be disloyal to my school. If I try simply to be loyal to my school, I may be disloyal to my town, my state, and my country. If I try simply to be loyal to my town, state and country, I may be disloyal to humanity. I will try above all things else to be loyal to humanity; then I shall surely be loyal to my country, my state, and my town, to my school, and to my family. And this loyalty to humanity will keep me faithful to civilization.

He who obeys the law of loyalty obeys all of the other ten laws of the Good American.

Loyalty is *the willing and practical and thorogoing devotion of a person to a cause.* A man is loyal when, first he has some *cause* to which he is loyal; when, secondly, he *willingly* and *thoroly* devotes himself to this cause; and when, thirdly, he expresses his devotion in some *sustained and practical way,* by acting steadily in the service of his cause.—From *The Philosophy of Loyalty* by Josiah Royce. Macmillan Company. New York, 1909. Pages 16–17.

REPRESENTATIVE EXPRESSIONS:
An Historical Perspective

1. BONIFACIUS: AN ESSAY UPON THE GOOD
Cotton Mather

Relative to Home and Neighborhood

Parents, Oh! how much ought you to be continually *devising,* and even *travailing,* for the *good* of your *children.* Often *devise:* how to make them *wise children;* how to carry on a desirable *education* for them; an *education* that shall render them desirable; how to render them lovely, and polite creatures, and *serviceable* in their generation. Often *devise,* how to enrich their minds with valuable *knowledge;* how to instill generous, and gracious, and heavenly *principles* into their minds; how to restrain and rescue them from the *paths of the Destroyer,* and fortify them against their *special temptations.* There is a world of *good,* that you have to do for them. You are without *bowels,* Oh! be not such *monsters!* if you are not in a continual agony to do for them all the *good* that ever you can. It was no mistake of *Pacatus Drepanius* in his panegyric to *Theodosius: Instituente natura plus fere filios quam nosmetipsos diligimus.*[1]

. . .

XI. "As soon as we can, we'll get up to yet *higher principles.* I will often tell the *children,* what cause they have to *love* a glorious CHRIST, who has *died* for them. And, how much He will be *well-pleased* with their *well-doing.* And, what a noble thing, 'tis to follow His *example;* which *example* I will describe unto them. I will often tell them, that the *eye of God* is upon them; the great GOD knows all they do, and hears all they speak. I will often tell them, that there will be a time, when they must

[1] Nature teaches us to love our children as ourselves.

appear before the *Judgment-Seat* of the holy LORD; and they must *now* do nothing, that may *then* be a grief and shame unto them. I will set before them, the delights of that *Heaven* that is prepared for pious children; and the torments of that *Hell* that is prepared of old, for naughty ones. I will inform them, of the *good offices* which the *good angels* do for *little ones* that have the fear of God, and are afraid of sin. And, how the *devils* tempt them to do ill things; how they hearken to the *devils*, and are like *them*, when they do such things; and what mischiefs the *devils* may get leave to do them in this world, and what a sad thing 'twill be, to be among the *devils* in the *Place of Dragons*. I will cry to God, that He *will make them feel the power of these principles.*

XII. "When the *children* are of a fit age for it, I will sometimes *closet* them; have them with me *alone;* talk with them about the state of their souls; their *experiences*, their *proficiencies*, their *tempations;* obtain their declared consent unto every stroke in the *Covenant of Grace;* and then pray with them, and weep unto the Lord for His *grace*, to be bestowed upon them, and make them witnesses of the agony with which I am *travailing* to see the image of CHRIST formed in them. Certainly, they'll never forget such actions!

XIII. "I would be very watchful and cautious, about the *companions* of my *children*. I will be very inquisitive, what *company* they keep; if they are in hazard of being ensnared by any *vicious company*, I will earnestly pull them out of it, as *brands out of the burning*. I will find out, and procure, *laudable companions* for them.

. . .

XVI. "When the *children* are in any *trouble*, as, if they be *sick*, or *pained*, I will take advantage therefrom, to set before them the evil of *sin*, which brings all our *trouble;* and how fearful a thing it will be to be cast among the *damned* who are in easeless and endless *trouble*. I will set before them the benefit of an interest in a CHRIST, by which their *trouble* will be sanctified unto them, and they will be prepared for *death*, and for fullness of joy in an happy eternity after *death*.

XVII. "I incline, that among all the points of a polite education which I would endeavor for my *children*, they may each of them, the *daughters* as well as the *sons*, have so much insight into some *skill*, which lies in the way of *gain* (the *limners'*, or the *scriveners'*, or the *apothecaries'*, or some other *mystery*, to which their own inclination may most carry them) that they may be able to subsist themselves, and get something of a livelihood, in case the Providence of God should bring them into necessities. Why not they as well as *Paul the Tent-Maker!* The *children* of the best fashion, may have occasion to bless the parents, that make such a provision for them! The Jews have a saying; 'tis worth my remembering it: *Quicunque filium suum non docet opificium, perinde est' ac si eum doceret latrocinium.*[2]

Certainly, there are many ways, wherein *servants* may be *blessings.* Let your *studies* with your continual *prayers* for the welfare of the *families* to which you belong, and the *example* of your sober carriage, render you such. If you will remember but *four words,* and endeavor all that is comprised in them, OBEDIENCE, HONESTY, INDUSTRY, and PIETY, you will be the *blessings* and the *Josephs* of the families to which you belong. Let those four heads be distinctly and frequently thought upon. And go cheerfully through all you have to do, upon this consideration: *that it is an obedience to Heaven, and from thence will have a recompense.* It was the observation even of a pagan, *that a master may receive a benefit from a servant.* And, *Quod fit affectu amici, desinit esse ministerium.*[3] It is a *friendship* rather than a *service, young man,* if it be with the affection of a *friend,* that you do what you do for your *master.* Yea, even the *maid-servants* in the house, may do an unknown *service* to it, by instructing the *infants* and instilling the *lessons of goodness* into them. So, by *Bilhah,* and *Zilpah,* may children be *born again;* the *mistresses* may by the *travail* of their *maid-servants,* have *children,* brought into the Kingdom of God.

Schoolmasters

§15. From the Tribe of *Levi,* we will pass with our PROPOSALS to the Tribe of *Simeon:* from which latter *tribe,* there has been a frequent *ascent* into the former; as well as a step now and then from the former to the latter. The SCHOOLMASTER has manifold *opportunities* to *do good.* God make him sensible of his *obligations!* We read, *The little ones have their angels.* It is an *hard* work to keep a *school.* But it is a *good* work; and it may be so done, as to be in some sort like the *work of angels.* The *tutors* of the children, may be like their *tutelar angels. Melchior Adam* did well to call it, *Molestissimam, sed Deo longe gratissimam functionem.*[4]

Tutors, will you not look upon the *children* under your wing as committed unto you, by the glorious LORD, with a charge of this importance: *Take them, and bring them up for me, and I will pay you your wages!* Every time any new children come under your tuition why should you not think: "Here, my Glorious Lord sends me another object, on which I may do something, that He may be served in the world!"

---

[2] He who does not teach his son a craft, teaches him theft.

[3] What is done with the affection of a friend is no longer the act of a mere servant.

[4] A most troublesome office, but most pleasing to God.

O *suffer little children to come unto* you, and consider, what you may do, that *of such may be the Kingdom of Heaven!*

Sirs, let it be a great intention with you, *to instil documents of piety into the children.* Esteem it, your and their great interest, that they should so *know the Holy Scriptures as to be made wise unto salvation,* and *know the Saviour, whom to know is life eternal.* Oh! take all occasions to drop some *honey out of the rock* upon them! Happy the *children,* and as happy the *master,* where they who make the Relation of their conversion to serious piety, may say, "There was a schoolmaster that brought us to CHRIST!" You have been told: "Certainly, 'tis a nobler work, to make the little ones know their *Saviour,* than to know their *letters.* The lessons of *Jesus* are nobler things than the lessons of *Cato.* A sanctifying *transformation* of their souls, were a nobler thing, than merely to construe *Ovid's Metamorphosis.* He was a good *Schoolmaster,* of whom there was this testimony given.

> Young *Austin* wept, when he saw *Dido* dead;
> Though not a tear for a *dead soul* he had.
> Our Master would not let us be so vain,
> But us from *Virgil* did to *David* train.
> *Textor's* epistles would not *clothe* our souls;
> *Paul's* too we learnt; we *went to school at Paul's.*"

CATECHIZING; that should be a *frequent,* and at least, a *weekly,* exercise of the *school.* And in the most *edifying,* and *applicatory* and *admonitory* manner carried on. "In some reformed places (we are told) the Magistrate countenances none to keep a *school,* but what appears with a *testimonial* of their *ability,* and their *disposition* particularly (*Aptitudinis ad munus illud imprimis puerorum catechisationem*) for the work of *religious catechizing.*"

Dr. *Reynolds,* in a funeral sermon on an eminent *schoolmaster* has a passage worthy to be written in letters of gold. "If *grammar schools* have *holy* and *learned* men set over them, not only the *brains,* but also the *souls* of the children might be there enriched, and the work of *learning* and of *grace* too, be betimes wrought in them." In order to this, 'tis to be proposed, that you would not only *pray* with your scholars every day, but also take occasion from the *public sermons,* and from *remarkable occurrences* of Providence in your neighborhood, often to inculcate the *lessons of piety* upon the children.

Tutors in the *College,* may do well successively to treat each of their *pupils* alone, with all possible solemnity and affection, about their *interior state;* show them how to repent of *sin,* and believe on *Christ;* and bring them to express *resolutions* of *serious piety.* Sirs, you may do a thousand things, to render your *pupils orthodox* in their principles, *regular* in their practices, *qualified* for services!

I have read this experiment of one who had *pupils* under his charge: "He made it his custom, that in every *recitation*, he would, from something or other occurring in it, *make an occasion*, to let fall some *sentence*, which had a tendency to promote the *fear of God* in their hearts; which thing sometimes did indeed put him to more than a little study; but the good effect sufficiently recompensed it."

. . . "I pray God, put it in the hearts of a wise Parliament, to *purge our schools;* that instead of learning vain fictions, and filthy stories, they may be acquainted with the Word of God, and with books containing grave sayings, and things that may make them truly wise and useful in the world": I suppose, there will be little notice taken of such *proposals:* I had as good never mention them; 'tis with *despair,* that I make mention of them.

Among the *occasions* to be taken for instilling of *piety* into the *scholars,* there is one peculiarly at the *writing schools.* And inveterate sinner I have read of, converted unto serious piety, by accidentally seeing that *sentence* of *Austin* written in a window: "He that hath promised pardon to the penitent sinner, has not promised repentance to the presumptuous one." Who can tell what good may be done to the young scholar, by a *sentence* in a *copybook?* Let their *copies* be of *sentences* worthy to be *had in everlasting remembrance;* of *sentences,* that shall have the brightest *maxims of wisdom* in them; worthy to be written on the *fleshy tables* of their hearts; to be graven with the *point of a diamond* there. This may do two executions *with one stone:* God has blessed this unto many *scholars,* it has done them good all their days.

. . .

I will add this: To carry on the *discipline of the school,* with rewards, as well as *punishments,* is most certainly very *advisable,* very *preferable.* There may be invented many ways of *rewarding,* the *diligent* and the *laudable:* and—*ad palmae cursurus honores*[5]—a child of any ingenuity, under the *expectations* and *encouragements* of being *rewarded,* will do to the uttermost. You have an honor for *Quintilian.* I pray, hear *Quintilian: Cavendum a plagis, sed potius laude, aut aliorum praelatione, urgendus est puer.*[6] If a fault must be *punished,* let *instruction,* both unto the *delinquent* and unto the *spectator,* accompany the *correction.* Let the *odious nature* of the *sin,* that has enforced the *correction,* be declared; and let nothing be done in a *passion;* all be done with all the evidence of *compassion* that may be.

[5] Running after the honors of victory.
[6] The boy must be encouraged by praise rather than frightened of flogging.

2. THE AUTOBIOGRAPHY
Benjamin Franklin

It was about this time I conceiv'd the bold and arduous project of arriving at moral perfection. I wish'd to live without committing any fault at any time; I would conquer all that either natural inclination, custom, or company might lead me into. As I knew, or thought I knew, what was right and wrong, I did not see why I might not always do the one and avoid the other. But I soon found I had undertaken a task of more difficulty than I had imagined. While my care was employ'd in guarding against one fault, I was often surprised by another; habit took the advantage of inattention; inclination was sometimes too strong for reason. I concluded, at length, that the mere speculative conviction that it was our interest to be completely virtuous, was not sufficient to prevent our slipping; and that the contrary habits must be broken, and good ones acquired and established, before we can have any dependence on a steady, uniform rectitude of conduct. For this purpose I therefore contrived the following method.

. . . I included under thirteen names of virtues all that at that time occur'd to me as necessary or desirable, and annexed to each a short precept, which fully express'd the extent I gave to its meaning.

These names of virtues, with their precepts, were:

1. TEMPERANCE.

Eat not to dullness; drink not to elevation.

2. SILENCE.

Speak not but what may benefit others or yourself; avoid trifling conversation.

3. ORDER.

Let all your things have their places; let each part of your business have its time.

From Benjamin Franklin, *The Autobiography,* edited by Julian W. Abernethy (New York: Charles E. Merrill Co., 1918), pp. 92–96.

4. RESOLUTION.

Resolve to perform what you ought; perform without fail what you resolve.

5. FRUGALITY.

Make no expense but to do good to others or yourself; *i.e.,* waste nothing.

6. INDUSTRY.

Lose no time; be always employ'd in something useful; cut off all unnecessary actions.

7. SINCERITY.

Use no hurtful deceit; think innocently and justly, and, if you speak, speak accordingly.

8. JUSTICE.

Wrong none by doing injuries, or omitting the benefits that are your duty.

9. MODERATION.

Avoid extreams; forbear resenting injuries so much as you think they deserve.

10. CLEANLINESS.

Tolerate no uncleanliness in body, cloaths, or habitation.

11. TRANQUILLITY.

Be not disturbed at trifles, or at accidents common or unavoidable.

12. CHASTITY.

Rarely use venery but for health or offspring, never to dulness, weakness, or the injury of your own or another's peace or reputation.

13. HUMILITY.

Imitate Jesus and Socrates.

My intention being to acquire the *habitude* of all these virtues, I judg'd it would be well not to distract my attention by attempting the whole at once, but to fix it on one of them at a time; and, when I should be master of that, then to proceed to another, and so on, till I should have gone thro' the thirteen; and, as the previous acquisition of some might facilitate the acquisition of certain others, I arrang'd them with that view, as they stand above. Temperance first, as it tends to procure that coolness and clearness of head, which is so necessary where constant vigilance was to be kept up, and guard maintained against the unremitting attraction of ancient habits, and the force of perpetual temptations. This being acquir'd and establish'd, Silence would be more easy; and my desire being to gain knowledge at the same time that I improv'd in virtue, and considering that in conversation it was obtain'd rather by the use of the ears than of the tongue, and therefore wishing to break a habit I was getting into of prattling, punning, and joking, which only made me acceptable to trifling company, I gave *Silence* the second place.

Form of the pages.

TEMPERANCE.						
EAT NOT TO DULNESS; DRINK NOT TO ELEVATION						
	S.	M.	T.	W.	T.	F.	S.
---	---	---	---	---	---	---	---
T.							
S.	✿	✿		✿		✿	
O.	✿ ✿	✿	✿		✿	✿	✿
R.			✿			✿	
F.		✿			✿		
I.			✿				
S.							
J.							
M.							
C.							
T.							
C.							
H.							

This and the next, *Order,* I expected would allow me more time for attending to my project and my studies. *Resolution,* once become habitual, would keep me firm in my endeavors to obtain all the subsequent virtues; *Frugality* and Industry freeing me from my remaining debt, and producing affluence and independence, would make more easy the practice of Sincerity and Justice, etc., etc. Conceiving then, that, agreeably to the advice of Pythagoras in his Golden Verses, daily examination would be necessary, I contrived the [preceding] method for conducting that examination.

3. ECLECTIC FOURTH READER
William Holmes McGuffey, ed.

II. Try, Try Again.

    1. 'Tis a lesson you should heed,
        Try, try again;
    If at first you don't succeed,
    Try, try again;
    Then your courage should appear,
    For, if you will persevere,
    You will conquer, never fear;
        Try, try again.

    2. Once or twice though you should fail,
        Try, try again;
    If you would at last prevail,
        Try, try again;
    If we strive, 'tis no disgrace
    Though we do not win the race;
    What should you do in the case?
        Try, try again.

    3. If you find your task is hard,
        Try, try again;

From William Holmes McGuffey, ed., *Eclectic Fourth Reader* (New York-Cincinnati-Chicago American Book Company: Van Antwerp, Bragg & Co., 1879), pp. 28–29, 35–38, 38–39, 47, 64–67, 74–77, 113–15.

Time will bring you your reward,
 Try, try again.
All that other folks can do,
Why, with patience, should not you?
Only keep this rule in view:
 Try, try again.

DEFINITIONS.—1. Cour'age, *resolution.* Con'quer, *gain the victory.*
2. Pre-vail', *overcome.* Dis-graçe', *shame.* Win, *gain, obtain.* 3. Reward', *any thing given in return for good or bad conduct.* Pa'-tiençe,
constancy in labor.

EXERCISES.—What does the mark before " 'Tis" mean? What is it
called? What point is used after the word "case" in the second verse?
Why?

. . .

VII. Lazy Ned.

1. " 'Tis royal fun," cried lazy Ned,
 "To coast upon my fine, new sled,
  And beat the other boys;
 But then, I can not bear to climb
 The tiresome hill, for every time
  It more and more annoys."

2. So, while his school-mates glided by,
 And gladly tugged up hill, to try
  Another merry race,
 Too indolent to share their plays,
 Ned was compelled to stand and gaze,
  While shivering in his place.

3. Thus, he would never take the pains
 To seek the prize that labor gains,
  Until the time had passed;
 For, all his life, he dreaded still
 The silly bugbear of *up hill,*
  And died a dunce at last.

DEFINITIONS.—1. Roy'al, *excellent, noble.* Coast, *to slide.* Annoys', *troubles.* 2. In'do-lent, *lazy.* 3. Prize, *a reward.* Bug'-beâr, *something frightful.* Dunçe, *a silly fellow.*

EXERCISES.—What did Ned like? What did he not like?

XXI. Waste Not, Want Not.

1. *Mr. Jones.* Boys, if you have nothing to do, will you unpack these parcels for me?

2. The two parcels were exactly alike, both of them well tied up with good whip-cord. Ben took his parcel to the table, and began to examine the knot, and then to untie it.

3. John took the other parcel, and tried first at one corner, and then at the other, to pull off the string. But the cord had been too well secured, and he only drew the knots tighter.

4. *John.* I wish these people would not tie up their parcels so tightly, as if they were never to be undone. Why, Ben, how did you get yours undone? What is in your parcel? I wonder what is in mine! I wish I could get the string off. I will cut it.

5. *Ben.* Oh, no, do not cut it, John! Look, what a nice cord this is, and yours is the same. It is a pity to cut it.

6. *John.* Pooh! what signifies a bit of pack-thread?

7. *Ben.* It is whip-cord.

8. *John.* Well, whip-cord then! what signifies a bit of whip-cord? You can get a piece of whip-cord twice as long as that for three cents; and who cares for three cents? Not I, for one. So, here it goes.

9. So he took out his knife, and cut it in several places.

10. *Mr. Jones.* Well, my boys, have you undone the parcels for me?

11. *John.* Yes, sir; here is the parcel.

12. *Ben.* And here is my parcel, father, and here is also the string.

13. *Mr. Jones.* You may keep the string, Ben.

14. *Ben.* Thank you, sir. What excellent whip-cord it is!

15. *Mr. Jones.* And you, John, may keep your string, too, if it will be of any use to you.

16. *John.* It will be of no use to me, thank you, sir.

17. *Mr. Jones.* No, I am afraid not, if this is it.

18. A few weeks after this, Mr. Jones gave each of his sons a new top.

19. *John.* How is this, Ben? These tops have no strings. What shall we do for strings?

20. *Ben.* I have a string that will do very well for mine. And he pulled it out of his pocket.

21. *John.* Why, if that is not the whip-cord! I wish I had saved mine.

22. A few days afterward, there was a shooting-match, with bows and arrows, among the lads. The prize was a fine bow and arrows, to be given to the best marksman. "Come, come," said Master Sharp, "I am within one inch of the mark. I should like to see who will go nearer."

23. John drew his bow, and shot. The arrow struck within a quarter of an inch of Master Sharp's. "Shoot away," said Sharp; "but you must understand the rules. We settled them before you came. You are to have three shots with your own arrows. Nobody is to borrow or lend. So shoot away."

24. John seized his second arrow; "If I have any luck," said he;—but just as he pronounced the word "luck," the string broke, and the arrow fell from his hands.

25. *Master Sharp.* There! It is all over with you.

26. *Ben.* Here is my bow for him, and welcome.

27. *Master Sharp.* No, no, sir; that is not fair. Did you not hear the rules? There is to be no lending.

28. It was now Ben's turn to make his trial. His first arrow missed the mark; the second was exactly as near as John's first. Before venturing the last arrow, Ben very prudently examined the string of his bow; and, as he pulled it to try its strength, it snapped.

29. Master Sharp clapped his hands and danced for joy. But his dancing suddenly ceased, when careful Ben drew out of his pocket an excellent piece of cord, and began to tie it to the bow.

30. "The everlasting whip-cord, I declare!" cried John. "Yes," said Ben, "I put it in my pocket today, because I thought I might want it."

31. Ben's last arrow won the prize; and when the bow and arrows were handed to him, John said, "How valuable that whip-cord has been to you, Ben. I'll take care how I waste any thing, hereafter."

DEFINITIONS.—2. Ex-am'ine, *to look at carefully.* 6. Sig'ni-fies, *to be important.* 22. Märks'man, *one who shoots well.* 28. Pru'dent-ly, *with proper caution.* 29. Ceased, *stopped.* 30. Ev-er-last'ing, *lasting always.*

EXERCISES.—What is this lesson designed to teach? Which of the boys preserved his whip-cord? What good did it do him? What did the other boy do with his? What was the consequence? What did he learn from it?

.   .   .

XII. Where There Is a Will There Is a Way.

1. Henry Bond was about ten years old when his father died. His mother found it difficult to provide for the support of a large family, thus left entirely in her care. By good management, however, she contrived to do so, and also to send Henry, the oldest, to school, and to supply him, for the most part, with such books as he needed.

2. At one time, however, Henry wanted a grammar, in order to join a class in that study, and his mother could not furnish him with the

money to buy it. He was very much troubled about it, and went to bed with a heavy heart, thinking what could be done.

3. On waking in the morning, he found that a deep snow had fallen, and the cold wind was blowing furiously. "Ah," said he, "it is an ill wind that blows nobody good."

4. He rose, ran to the house of a neighbor, and offered his service to clear a path around his premises. The offer was accepted. Having completed this work, and received his pay, he went to another place for the same purpose, and then to another, until he had earned enough to buy a grammar.

5. When school commenced, Henry was in his seat, the happiest boy there, ready to begin the lesson in his new book.

6. From that time, Henry was always the first in all his classes. He knew no such word as fail, but always succeeded in all he attempted. Having the will, he always found the way.

> DEFINITIONS.—1. Mán′age-ment, *manner of directing things.* 2. Fûr′nish, *to supply.* 3. Fu′ri-ous-ly, *violently.* 4. Serv′içe, *labor.* Prem′-i-ses, *grounds around a house.*

. . .

XL. Advantages of Industry.

1. I gave you, in the last lesson, the history of George Jones, an idle boy, and showed you the consequences of his idleness. I shall now give you the history of Charles Bullard, a classmate of George. Charles was about the same age as George, and did not possess superior talents. Indeed, I doubt whether he was equal to him in natural powers of mind.

2. But Charles was a hard student. When quite young, he was always careful and diligent in school. Sometimes, when there was a very hard lesson, instead of going out to play during recess, he would stay in to study. He had resolved that his first object should be to get his lessons well, and then he could play with a good conscience. He loved play as well as any body, and was one of the best players on the ground. I hardly ever saw any boy catch a ball better than he could. When playing any game, every one was glad to get Charles on his side.

3. I have said that Charles would sometimes stay in at recess. This, however, was very seldom; it was only when the lessons were very hard indeed. Generally, he was among the first on the play-ground, and he was also among the first to go into school when called. Hard study gave him a relish for play, and play again gave him a relish for hard study; so he was happy both in school and out. The preceptor could not help liking

him, for he always had his lessons well committed, and never gave him any trouble.

4. When he went to enter college, the preceptor gave him a good recommendation. He was able to answer all the questions which were put to him when he was examined. He had studied so well when he was in the academy, and was so thoroughly prepared for college, that he found it very easy to keep up with his class, and had much time for reading interesting books.

5. But he would always get his lesson well before he did any thing else, and would review it just before recitation. When called upon to recite, he rose tranquil and happy, and very seldom made mistakes. The officers of the college had a high opinion of him, and he was respected by all the students.

6. There was, in the college, a society made up of all the best scholars. Charles was chosen a member of that society. It was the custom to choose some one of the society to deliver a public address every year. This honor was conferred on Charles; and he had studied so diligently, and read so much, that he delivered an address which was very interesting to all who heard it.

7. At last he graduated, as it is called; that is, he finished his collegiate course, and received his degree. It was known by all that he was a good scholar, and by all that he was respected. His father and mother, brothers and sisters, came on the commencement day to hear him speak.

8. They all felt gratified, and loved Charles more than ever. Many situations of usefulness and profit were opened to him; for Charles was now an intelligent man, and universally respected. He is still a useful and a happy man. He has a cheerful home, and is esteemed by all who know him.

9. Such are the rewards of industry. How strange it is that any person should be willing to live in idleness, when it will certainly make him unhappy! The idle boy is almost invariably poor and miserable; the industrious boy is happy and prosperous.

10. But perhaps some child who reads this, asks, "Does God notice little children in school?" He certainly does. And if you are not diligent in the improvement of your time, it is one of the surest evidences that your heart is not right with God. You are placed in this world to improve your time. In youth you must be preparing for future usefulness. And if you do not improve the advantages you enjoy, you sin against your Maker.

> With books, or work, or healthful play,
>   Let your first years be passed;
> That you may give, for every day,
>   Some good account, at last.

DEFINITIONS.—1. His'to-ry, *a description or a narration of events.*
2. Con'scien̦ce, *our own knowledge of right and wrong.* Game, *play,
sport.* 3. Com-mit'ted, *fixed in mind.* 4. Rec-om-men-da'tion, *what is
said in praise of any one.* 5. Re-view', *to examine again.* Tran'quil,
quiet, calm. 6. Con-ferred', *given to or bestowed upon any one.* 7.
Grad'u-at-ed, *received a degree from a college.* Com-men̦ce'ment, *the
day when students receive their degree.* 8. U-ni-vers'al-ly, *by all, without exception.* 9. In-va'ri-a-bly, *always, uniformly.* 10. Ev'i-den-̦ces,
proofs. Ad-van'ta-ges, *opportunities for improvement.*

EXERCISES.—What was the character of George Jones? Of Charles
Bullard? How did George appear in the class at school? How did he
behave at recess? How did Charles differ from him in these respects?
Relate what happened when George went to college. What became of
him? Did Charles succeed at college? Which of them do you think
more worthy of imitation? What is said of the idle? What is said of the
industrious? Who watches all our actions wherever we may be? For
what are we placed in this world? Should you not then be diligent in
your studies?

4. THE CHALLENGE OF FACTS
William Graham Sumner

The truth is that the social order is fixed by laws of nature precisely
analogous to those of the physical order.

. . .

The constant tendency of population to outstrip the means of subsistence is the force which has distributed population over the world,
and produced all advance in civilization. To this day the two means of
escape for an overpopulated country are emigration and an advance in
the arts. The former wins more land for the same people; the latter makes
the same land support more persons. If, however, either of these means
opens a chance for an increase of population, it is evident that the advantage so won may be speedily exhausted if the increase takes place.
The social difficulty has only undergone a temporary amelioration, and
when the conditions of pressure and competition are renewed, misery
and poverty reappear. The victims of them are those who have inherited
disease and depraved appetites, or have been brought up in vice and
ignorance, or have themselves yielded to vice, extravagance, idleness,

Reprinted from *The Challenge of Facts and Other Essays,* by William Graham
Sumner, ed. by Albert Galloway Keller. New Haven, Yale University Press, 1914,
pp. 93–94, 95–98.

and imprudence. In the last analysis, therefore, we come back to vice, in its original and hereditary forms, as the correlative of misery and poverty.

The condition for the complete and regular action of the force of competition is liberty. Liberty means the security given to each man that, if he employs his energies to sustain the struggle on behalf of himself and those he cares for, he shall dispose of the product exclusively as he chooses. It is impossible to know whence any definition or criterion of justice can be derived, if it is not deduced from this view of things; or if it is not the definition of justice that each shall enjoy the fruit of his own labor and self-denial, and of injustice that the idle and the industrious, the self-indulgent and the self-denying, shall share equally in the product. Aside from the *a priori* speculations of philosophers who have tried to make equality an essential element in justice, the human race has recognized, from the earliest times, the above conception of justice as the true one, and has founded upon it the right of property. The right of property, with marriage and the family, gives the right of bequest.

. . .

Private property, also, which we have seen to be a feature of society organized in accordance with the natural conditions of the struggle for existence produces inequalities between men. The struggle for existence is aimed against nature. It is from her niggardly hand that we have to wrest the satisfactions for our needs, but our fellow-men are our competitors for the meager supply. Competition, therefore, is a law of nature. Nature is entirely neutral; she submits to him who most energetically and resolutely assails her. She grants her rewards to the fittest, therefore, without regard to other considerations of any kind. If, then, there be liberty, men get from her just in proportion to their works, and their having and enjoying are just in proportion to their being and their doing. Such is the system of nature. If we do not like it, and if we try to amend it, there is only one way in which we can do it. We can take from the better and give to the worse. We can deflect the penalties of those who have done ill and throw them on those who have done better. We can take the rewards from those who have done better and give them to those who have done worse. We shall thus lessen the inequalities. We shall favor the survival of the unfittest, and we shall accomplish this by destroying liberty. Let it be understood that we cannot go outside of this alternative: liberty, inequality, survival of the fittest; not-liberty, equality, survival of the unfittest. The former carries society forward and favors all its best members; the latter carries society downwards and favors all its worst members.

. . .

It is impossible that the man with capital and the man without capital should be equal. To affirm that they are equal would be to say that a man who has no tool can get as much food out of the ground as the man who has a spade or a plough; or that the man who has no weapon can defend himself as well against hostile beasts or hostile men as the man who has a weapon. If that were so, none of us would work any more. We work and deny ourselves to get capital just because, other things being equal, the man who has it is superior, for attaining all the ends of life, to the man who has it not. Considering the eagerness with which we all seek capital and the estimate we put upon it, either in cherishing it if we have it, or envying others who have it while we have it not, it is very strange what platitudes pass current about it in our society so soon as we begin to generalize about it. If our young people really believed some of the teachings they hear, it would not be amiss to preach them a sermon once in a while to reassure them, setting forth that it is not wicked to be rich, nay even, that it is not wicked to be richer than your neighbor.

It follows from what we have observed that it is the utmost folly to denounce capital. To do so is to undermine civilization, for capital is the first requisite of every social gain, educational, ecclesiastical, political, æsthetic, or other.

It must also be noticed that the popular antithesis between persons and capital is very fallacious. Every law or institution which protects persons at the expense of capital makes it easier for persons to live and to increase the number of consumers of capital while lowering all the motives to prudence and frugality by which capital is created. Hence every such law or institution tends to produce a large population, sunk in misery. All poor laws and all eleemosynary institutions and expenditures have this tendency. On the contrary, all laws and institutions which give security to capital against the interests of other persons than its owners, restrict numbers while preserving the means of subsistence. Hence every such law or institution tends to produce a small society on a high stage of comfort and well-being. It follows that the antithesis commonly thought to exist between the protection of persons and the protection of property is in reality only an antithesis between numbers and quality.

THE CONCENTRATION OF WEALTH:
ITS ECONOMIC JUSTIFICATION
The Independent

No man can acquire a million without helping a million men to increase their little fortunes all the way down through all the social grades. In some points of view it is an error that we fix our attention so much upon the very rich and overlook the prosperous mass, but the compensating advantage is that the great successes stimulate emulation the most powerfully.

What matters it then that some millionaires are idle, or silly, or vulgar; that their ideas are sometimes futile and their plans grotesque, when they turn aside from money-making? How do they differ in this from any other class? The millionaires are a product of natural selection, acting on the whole body of men to pick out those who can meet the requirement of certain work to be done. In this respect they are just like the great statesmen, or scientific men, or military men. It is because they are thus selected that wealth—both their own and that intrusted to them—aggregates under their hands. Let one of them make a mistake and see how quickly the concentration gives way to dispersion. They may fairly be regarded as the naturally selected agents of society for certain work. They get high wages and live in luxury, but the bargain is a good one for society. There is the intensest competition for their place and occupation. This assures us that all who are competent for this function will be employed in it, so that the cost of it will be reduced to the lowest terms; and furthermore that the competitors will study the proper conduct to be observed in their occupation. This will bring discipline and the correction of arrogance and masterfulness.

Reprinted from *The Independent*, April–June 1902, in *The Challenge of Facts and Other Essays* by William Graham Sumner, ed. by Albert Galloway Keller. New Haven: Yale University Press, 1914, pp. 171–72.

THE ABOLITION OF POVERTY
The Independent

There is a sense in which it may be said that it is easy to provide a precept for the abolition of poverty. Let every man be sober, industrious, prudent, and wise, and bring up his children to be so likewise, and poverty will be abolished in a few generations.

Reprinted from *The Independent*, August 25, 1887, in *Earth-Hunger and Other Essays* by William Graham Sumner, ed. by Albert Galloway Keller. New Haven: Yale University Press, 1913, p. 230.

5. WEALTH
Andrew Carnegie

The problem of our age is the proper administration of wealth, so that the ties of brotherhood may still bind together the rich and poor in harmonious relationship. . . . The contrast between the palace of the millionaire and the cottage of the laborer with us to-day measures the change which has come with civilization.

This change, however, is not to be deplored, but welcomed as highly beneficial. It is well, nay, essential for the progress of the race. . . . The price which society pays for the law of competition, like the price it pays for cheap comforts and luxuries, is also great; but the advantages of this law are also greater still, for it is to this law that we owe our wonderful material development, which brings improved conditions in its train. But, whether the law be benign or not, we must say of it, as we say of the change in the conditions of men to which we have referred: It is here; we cannot evade it; no substitutes for it have been found; and while the law may be sometimes hard for the individual, it is best for the race, because it insures the survival of the fittest in every department. We accept and welcome, therefore, as conditions to which we must accommodate

From Andrew Carnegie, "Wealth," *North American Review,* 148 (June, 1889), 653–64.

ourselves, great inequality of environment, the concentration of business, industrial and commercial, in the hands of a few, and the law of competition between these, as being not only beneficial, but essential for the future progress of the race. Having accepted these, it follows that there must be great scope for the exercise of special ability in the merchant and in the manufacturer who has to conduct affairs upon a great scale. That this talent for organization and management is rare among men is proved by the fact that it invariably secures for its possessor enormous rewards, no matter where or under what laws or conditions. The experienced in affairs always rate the MAN whose services can be obtained as a partner as not only the first consideration, but such as to render the question of his capital scarcely worth considering, for such men soon create capital; while, without the special talent required, capital soon takes wings. Such men become interested in firms or corporations using millions; and estimating only simple interest to be made upon the capital invested, it is inevitable that their income must exceed their expenditures, and that they must accumulate wealth. Nor is there any middle ground which such men can occupy, because the great manufacturing or commercial concern which does not earn at least interest upon its capital soon becomes bankrupt. It must either go forward or fall behind: to stand still is impossible. It is a condition essential for its successful operation that it should be thus far profitable, and even that, in addition to interest in capital, it should make profit. It is a law, as certain as any of the others named, that men possessed of this peculiar talent for affairs, under the free play of economic forces, must, of necessity, soon be in receipt of more revenue than can be judiciously expended upon themselves; and this law is as beneficial for the race as the others.

Objections to the foundations upon which society is based are not in order, because the condition of the race is better with these than it has been with any others which have been tried. Of the effects of any new substitutes proposed we cannot be sure. The Socialist or Anarchist who seeks to overturn present conditions is to be regarded as attacking the foundation upon which civilization itself rests. for civilization took its start from the day that the capable, industrious workman said to his incompetent and lazy fellow, "If thou dost not sow, thou shalt not reap," and thus ended primitive Communism by separating the drones from the bees. One who studies this subject will soon be brought face to face with the conclusion that upon the sacredness of property civilization itself depends—the right of the laborer to his hundred dollars in the savings bank, and equally the legal right of the millionaire to his millions. To those who propose to substitute Communism for this intense Individualism the answer, therefore, is: The race has tried that. All progress from that barbarous day to the present time has resulted from its displacement. Not evil, but good, has come to the race from the accumulation of wealth by those who have the ability and energy that produce it. . . . It is criminal to waste our energies in endeavoring to uproot, when all we can profitably or possibly accomplish is to bend the universal tree of humanity a little in the direction most favorable to the production of good fruit under existing circumstances. We might as well urge the destruction of the highest existing type of man because he failed to reach our ideal as to favor the destruction of Individualism, Private Property, the Law of Accumulation of Wealth, and the Law of Competition; for these are the highest results of human experience, the soil in which society so far has produced the best fruit. Unequally or unjustly, perhaps, as these laws sometimes operate, and imperfect as they appear to the Idealist, they are, nevertheless, like the highest type of man, the best and most valuable of all that humanity has yet accomplished.

. . .

This, then, is held to be the duty of the man of Wealth: First, to set an example of modest, unostentatious living, shunning display or extravagance; to provide moderately for the legitimate wants of those dependent upon him; and after doing so to consider all surplus revenues which come to him as trust funds, which he is called upon to administer, and strictly bound as a matter of duty to administer in the manner which, in his judgment, is best calculated to produce the most beneficial results for the community—the man of wealth thus becoming the mere agent and trustee for his poorer brethren, bringing to their service his superior wisdom, experience, and ability to administer, doing for them better than they would or could do for themselves.

. . .

The best uses to which surplus wealth can be put have already been indicated. Those who would administer wisely must, indeed, be wise, for one of the serious obstacles to the improvement of our race is indiscriminate charity. It were better for mankind that the millions of the rich were thrown into the sea than so spent as to encourage the slothful, the drunken, the unworthy. Of every thousand dollars spent in so called charity today, it is probable that $950 is unwisely spent; so spent, indeed, as to produce the very evils which it proposes to mitigate or cure. A well-known writer of philosophic books admitted the other day that he had given a quarter of a dollar to a man who approached him as he was coming to visit the house of his friend. He knew nothing of the habits of this beggar; knew not the use that would be made of this money, although he had every reason to suspect that it would be spent improperly. This man professed to be a disciple of Herbert Spencer; yet the quarter-dollar given that night will probably work more injury than all the money which its thoughtless donor will ever be able to give in true charity will do good. He only gratified his own feelings, saved himself from annoyance,—and this was probably one of the most selfish and very worst actions of his life, for in all respects he is most worthy.

In bestowing charity, the main consideration should be to help those who will help themselves; to provide part of the means by which those who desire to improve may do so; to give those who desire to rise the aids by which they may rise; to assist, but rarely or never to do all. Neither the individual nor the race is improved by alms-giving. Those worthy of assistance, except in rare cases, seldom require assistance. The really valuable men of the race never do, except in cases of accident or sudden change. Every one has, of course, cases of individuals brought to his own knowledge where temporary assistance can do genuine good, and these he will not overlook. But the amount which can be wisely given by the individual for individuals is necessarily limited by his lack of knowledge of the circumstances connected with each. He is the only true reformer who is as careful and as anxious not to aid the unworthy as he is to aid the worthy, and, perhaps, even more so, for in alms-giving more injury is probably done by rewarding vice than by relieving virtue.

.   .   .

Thus is the problem of Rich and Poor to be solved. The laws of accumulation will be left free; the laws of distribution free. Individualism will continue, but the millionaire will be but a trustee for the poor; intrusted for a season with a great part of the increased wealth of the community, but administering it for the community far better than it could or would have done for itself. . . .

Such, in my opinion, is the true Gospel concerning Wealth, obedience to which is destined some day to solve the problem of the Rich and the Poor, and to bring "Peace on earth, among men Good-Will."

PEDAGOGICAL MODEL:
The Teacher as Moral Exemplar

THE EDUCATION OF CHARACTER
Martin Buber

Education worthy of the name is essentially education of character. For the genuine educator does not merely consider individual functions of his pupil, as one intending to teach him only to know or be capable of certain definite things; but his concern is always the person as a whole, both in the actuality in which he lives before you now and in his possibilities, what he can become. But in this way, as a whole in reality and potentiality, a man can be conceived either as personality, that is, as a unique spiritual-physical form with all the forces dormant in it, or as character, that is, as the link between what this individual is and the sequence of his actions and attitudes. Between these two modes of conceiving the pupil in his wholeness there is a fundamental difference. Personality is something which in its growth remains essentially outside the influence of the educator; but to assist in the moulding of character is his greatest task. Personality is a completion, only character is a task. One may cultivate and enhance personality, but in education one can and one must aim at character.

However—as I would like to point out straightaway—it is advisable not to over-estimate what the educator can even at best do to develop character. In this more than in any other branch of the science of teaching it is important to realize, at the very beginning of the discussion, the fundamental limits to conscious influence, even before asking what character is and how it is to be brought about.

If I have to teach algebra I can expect to succeed in giving my pupils an idea of quadratic equations with two unknown quantities. Even the slowest-witted child will understand it so well that he will amuse himself by solving equations at night when he cannot fall asleep. And even one with the most sluggish memory will not forget, in his old

From Martin Buber, *Between Man and Man* (New York: The Macmillan Company, 1965), pp. 104–108, 113–17. Copyright © 1965 by The Macmillan Company. Reprinted with permission of The Macmillan Company.

age, how to play with x and y. But if I am concerned with the education of character, everything becomes problematic. I try to explain to my pupils that envy is despicable, and at once I feel the secret resistance of those who are poorer than their comrades. I try to explain that it is wicked to bully the weak, and at once I see a suppressed smile on the lips of the strong. I try to explain that lying destroys life, and something frightful happens: the worst habitual liar of the class produces a brilliant essay on the destructive power of lying. I have made the fatal mistake of *giving instruction* in ethics, and what I said is accepted as current coin of knowledge; nothing of it is transformed into character-building substance.

But tht difficulty lies still deeper. In all teaching of a subject I can announce my intention of teaching as openly as I please, and this does not interfere with the results. After all, pupils do want, for the most part, to learn something, even if not overmuch, so that a tacit agreement becomes possible. But as soon as my pupils notice that I want to educate their characters, I am resisted precisely by those who show most signs of genuine independent character: they will not let themselves be educated, or rather, they do not like the idea that somebody wants to educate them. And those, too, who are seriously labouring over the question of good and evil, rebel when one dictates to them, as though it were some long established truth, what is good and what is bad; and they rebel just because they have experienced over and over again how hard it is to find the right way. Does it follow that one should keep silent about one's intention of educating character, and act by ruse and subterfuge? No; I have just said that the difficulty lies deeper. It is not enough to see that education of character is not introduced into a lesson in class; neither may one conceal it in cleverly arranged intervals. Education cannot tolerate such politic action. Even if the pupil does not notice the hidden motive it will have its negative effect on the actions of the teacher himself by depriving him of the directness which is his strength. Only in his whole being, in all his spontaneity can the educator truly affect the whole being of his pupil. For educating characters you do not need a moral genius, but you do need a man who is wholly alive and able to communicate himself directly to his fellow beings. His aliveness streams out to them and affects them most strongly and purely when he has no thought of affecting them.

The Greek word character means *impression.* The special link between man's being and his appearance, the special connexion between the unity of what he is and the sequence of his actions and attitudes is impressed on his still plastic substance. Who does the impressing? Everything does: nature and the social context, the house and the street, language and custom, the world of history and the world of daily news in the form of rumour, of broadcast and newspaper, music and technical science, play and dream—everything together. Many of these factors exert their influence by stimulating agreement, imitation, desire, effort; others by arousing questions, doubts, dislike, resistance. Character is formed by the interpenetration of all those multifarious, opposing influences. And yet, among this infinity of form-giving forces the educator is only one element among innumerable others, but distinct from them all by his *will* to take part in the stamping of character and by his *consciousness* that he represents in the eyes of the growing person a certain *selection* of what is, the selection of what is "right" of what *should* be. It is in this will and this consciousness that his vocation as an educator finds its fundamental expression. From this the genuine educator gains two things: first, humility, the feeling of being only one element amidst the fullness of life, only one single existence in the midst of all the tremendous inrush of reality on the pupil; but secondly, self-awareness, the feeling of being therein the only existence that *wants* to affect the whole person, and thus the feeling of responsibility for the selection of reality which he represents to the pupil. And a third thing emerges from all this, the recognition that in this realm of the education of character, of wholeness, there is only *one* access to the pupil: his *confidence*. For the adolescent who is frightened and disappointed by an unreliable world, confidence means the liberating insight that there is human truth, the truth of human existence. When the pupil's confidence has been won his resistance against being educated gives way to a singular happening: he accepts the educator as a person. He feels he may trust this man, that this man is not making a business out of him, but is taking part in his life, accepting him before desiring to influence him. And so he learns to *ask*.

The teacher who is for the first time approached by a boy with somewhat defiant bearing, but with trembling hands, visibly opened-up and fired by a daring hope, who asks him what is the right thing in a certain situation—for instance, whether in learning that a friend has betrayed a secret entrusted to him one should call him to account or be content with entrusting no more secrets to him—the teacher to whom this happens realizes that this is the moment to make the first conscious step towards education of character; he has to answer, to answer under a responsibility, to give an answer which will probably lead beyond the alternatives of the question by showing a third possibility which is the right one. To dictate what is good and evil in general is not his business. His business is to answer a concrete question, to answer what is right and wrong in a given situation. This, as I have said, can only happen in an atmosphere of confidence. Confidence, of course, is not won by the strenuous endeavour to win it, but by direct and ingenuous participation in the life of the people one is dealing with—in this case in the life of one's pupils—and by assuming the responsibility which arises from such participation. It is not the educational intention but it is the meeting which is educationally fruitful. A soul suffering from the contradictions of the world of human society, and of its own physical existence, approaches me with a question. By trying to answer it to the best of my knowledge and conscience I help it to become a character that actively overcomes the contradictions.

If this is the teacher's standpoint towards his pupil, taking part in his life and conscious of responsibility, then everything that passes between them can, without any deliberate or politic intention, open a way to the education of character: lessons and games, a conversation about quarrels in the class, or about the problems of a world-war. Only, the teacher must not forget the limits of education; even when he enjoys confidence he cannot always expect agreement. Confidence implies a break-through from reserve, the bursting of the bonds which imprison an unquiet heart. But it does not imply unconditional agreement. The teacher must never forget that conflicts too, if only they are decided in a healthy atmosphere, have an educational value. A conflict with a pupil is the supreme test for the educator. He must use his own insight wholeheartedly; he must not blunt the piercing impact of his knowledge, but he must at the same time have in readiness the healing ointment for the heart pierced by it. Not for a moment may he conduct a dialectical manœuvre instead of the real battle for truth. But if he is the victor he has to help the vanquished to endure defeat; and if he cannot conquer the self-willed soul that faces him (for victories over souls are not so easily won), then he has to find the word of love which alone can help to overcome so difficult a situation.

. . .

The educator's task can certainly not consist in educating great characters. He cannot select his pupils, but year by year the world, such as it is, is sent in the form of a school class to meet him on his life's way as his destiny; and in this destiny lies the very meaning of his life's work. He has to introduce discipline and order, he has to establish a law, and he can only strive and hope for the result that discipline and order will become more and more inward and autonomous, and that at last the law will be written in the heart of his pupils. But his real goal which, once he has well recognized it and well remembers it, will influence all his work, is the great character.

The great character can be conceived neither as a system of maxims nor as a system of habits. It is peculiar to him to act from the whole of his substance. That is, it is peculiar to him to react in accordance with the uniqueness of every situation which challenges him as an active person. Of course there are all sorts of similarities in different situations; one can construct types of situations, one can always find to what section the particular situation belongs, and draw what is appropriate from the hoard of established maxims and habits, apply the appropriate maxim, bring into operation the appropriate habit. But what is untypical in the particular situation remains unnoticed and unanswered. To me that seems the same as if, having ascertained the sex of a new-born child, one were immediately to establish its type as well, and put all the children of one type into a common cradle on which not the individual name but the name of the type was inscribed. In spite of all similarities every living situation has, like a new-born child, a new face, that has never been before and will never come again. It demands of you a reaction which cannot be prepared beforehand. It demands nothing of what is past. It demands presence, responsibility; it demands you. I call a great character one who by his actions and attitudes satisfies the claim of situations out of deep readiness to respond with his whole life, and in such a way that the sum of his actions and attitudes expresses at the same time the unity of his being in its willingness to accept responsibility. As his being is unity, the unity of accepted responsibility, his active life, too, coheres into unity. And one might perhaps say that for him there rises a unity out of the situations he has responded to in responsibility, the indefinable unity of a moral destiny.

All this does not mean that the great character is beyond the acceptance of norms. No responsible person remains a stranger to norms. But the command inherent in a genuine norm never becomes a maxim and the fulfillment of it never a habit. Any command that a great character takes to himself in the course of his development does not act in him as part of his consciousness or as material for building up his exercises, but remains latent in a basic layer of his substance until it reveals itself to him in a concrete way. What it has to tell him is revealed whenever a situation arises which demands of him a solution of which till then he had perhaps no idea. Even the most universal norm will at times be recognized only in a very special situation. I know of a man whose heart was struck by the lightning flash of "Thou shalt not steal" in the very moment when he was moved by a very different desire from that of stealing, and whose heart was so struck by it that he not only abandoned doing what he wanted to do, but with the whole force of his passion did the very opposite. Good and evil are not each other's opposites like right and left. The evil approaches us as a whirlwind, the good as a direction. There is a direction, a "yes," a command, hidden even in a prohibition, which is revealed to us in moments like these. In moments like these the command addresses us really in the second person, and the Thou in it is no one else but one's own self. Maxims command only the third person, the each and the none.

One can say that it is the unconditional nature of the address which distinguishes the command from the maxim. In an age which has become deaf to unconditioned address we cannot overcome the dilemma of the education of character from that angle. But insight into the structure of great character can help us to overcome it.

Of course, it may be asked whether the educator should really start "from above," whether, in fixing his goal, the hope of finding a great character, who is bound to be the exception, should be his starting-point; for in his methods of educating character he will always have to take into consideration the others, the many. To this I reply that the educator would not have the right to do so if a method inapplicable to these others were to result. In fact, however, his very insight into the structure of a great character helps him to find the way by which alone (as I have indicated) he can begin to influence also the victims of the collective Moloch,[1] pointing out to them the sphere in which they themselves suffer—namely, their relation to their own selves. From this sphere he must elicit the values which he can make credible and desirable to his pupils. That is what insight into the structure of a great character helps him to do.

A section of the young is beginning to feel today that, because of their absorption by the collective, something important and irreplaceable is lost to them—personal responsibility for life and the world. These young people, it is true, do not yet realize that their blind devotion to the collective, e.g., to a party, was not a genuine act of their personal life; they do not realize that it sprang, rather, from the fear of being left, in this age of confusion, to rely on themselves, on a self which no longer receives its direction from eternal values. Thus they do not yet realize that their devotion was fed on the unconscious desire to have responsibility removed from them by an authority in which they believe or want to believe. They do not yet realize that this devotion was an escape. I repeat, the young people I am speaking of do not yet realize this. But they are beginning to notice that he who no longer, with his whole being, decides what he does or does not, and assumes responsibility for it, becomes sterile in soul. And a sterile soul soon ceases to be a soul.

This is where the educator can begin and should begin. He can help the feeling that something is lacking to grow into the clarity of consciousness and into the force of desire. He can awaken in young people the courage to shoulder life again. He can bring before his pupils the image of a great character who denies no answer to life and the world, but accepts responsibility for everything essential that he meets. He can show his pupils this image without the fear that those among them who most of all need discipline and order will drift into a craving for aimless freedom: on the contrary, he can teach them in this way to recognize that discipline and order too are starting-points on the way towards self-responsibility. He can show that even the great character is not born perfect, that the unity of his being has first to mature before expressing itself

[1] Moloch, a Semitic deity worshipped through the sacrifice of children.

in the sequence of his actions and attitudes. But unity itself, unity of the person, unity of the lived life, has to be emphasized again and again. The confusing contradictions cannot be remedied by the collectives, not one of which knows the taste of genuine unity and which if left to themselves would end up, like the scorpions imprisoned in a box, in the witty fable, by devouring one another. This mass of contradictions can be met and conquered only by the rebirth of personal unity, unity of being, unity of life, unity of action—unity of being, life and action together. This does not mean a static unity of the uniform, but the great dynamic unity of the multiform in which multiformity is formed into unity of character. Today the great characters are still "enemies of the people," they who love their society, yet wish not only to preserve it but to raise it to a higher level. To-morrow they will be the architects of a new unity of mankind. It is the longing for personal unity, from which must be born a unity of mankind, which the educator should lay hold of and strengthen in his pupils. Faith in this unity and the will to achieve it is not a "return" to individualism, but a step beyond all the dividedness of individualism and collectivism. A great and full relation between man and man can only exist between unified and responsible persons. That is why it is much more rarely found in the totalitarian collective than in any historically earlier form of society; much more rarely also in the authoritarian party than in any earlier form of free association. Genuine education of character is genuine education for community.

In a generation which has had this kind of upbringing the desire will also be kindled to behold again the eternal values, to hear again the language of the eternal norm. He who knows inner unity, the innermost life of which is mystery, learns to honour the mystery in all its forms. In an understandable reaction against the former domination of a false, fictitious mystery, the present generations are obsessed with the desire to rob life of all its mystery. The fictitious mystery will disappear, the genuine one will rise again. A generation which honours the mystery in all its forms will no longer be deserted by eternity. Its light seems darkened only because the eye suffers from a cataract; the receiver has been turned off, but the resounding ether has not ceased to vibrate. To-day, indeed, in the hour of upheaval, the eternal is sifted from the pseudo-eternal. That which flashed into the primal radiance and blurred the primal sound will be extinguished and silenced, for it has failed before the horror of the new confusion and the questioning soul has unmasked its futility. Nothing remains but what rises above the abyss of to-day's monstrous problems, as above every abyss of every time: the wing-beat of the spirit and the creative word. But he who can see and hear out of unity will also behold and discern again what can be beheld and discerned eternally. The educator who helps to bring man to his own unity will help to put him again face to face with God.

Part IV

NATIONALISM

Introduction

Nationalism is the ideological system which is rooted to the belief that national groupings, citizenries, and/or nationalities should serve as the major terminal communities in which individuals group themselves. Because of the pervasiveness of Nationalism during the twentieth century, most ideological systems, including all those systems selected for analysis in this anthology, assume national configurations.

Within recent years, especially in modern nation-states, numerous voices have been raised in protest against political systems. Because of the confusion generated by the misuse of political terminology, such dissatisfaction has generally been directed against the concept of Nationalism—a term which has been "robbed" by political extremists. Thus, the term Nationalism often, somewhat unjustifiably, is used as a pejorative label for extremist viewpoints. Most critics of Nationalism, however, unwittingly reveal their own adherence to one form or another of Nationalism.

Nationalism is an ideology which is based upon the conviction that a national grouping of individuals should serve as the final authority in political decision making. The roots of Nationalism are essentially democratic for they affirm the right of a people to determine their destiny. Thus, Nationalism stands in contrast to *étatism*, the belief that the state or its representatives possess the final authority in matters of political and cultural life. Nationalism, of course, has been utilized to sustain totalitarian regimes. This distortion, however, usually is accompanied by the myth of popular sovereignty.

Nationalism should not be viewed as an extreme form of patriotism, which is, quite simply, an emotional condition characterized by love and freely given loyalty. The type of superpatriotism so rightly scorned is based not on Nationalism but on Ultranationalism and is just a form of chauvinism.

Two major forms of national groupings serve as the basis for the expression of Nationalism—nation-states and nationalities. The former are political communities and the latter cultural communities. Although they are sometimes assumed to be coterminous, they often function as conflicting communities of identity and are the cause of violent political upheavals. While some cultural communities (nationalities) seek to preserve their ethnic identity and to achieve some degree of political autonomy, nation-states utilize national institutions to moderate ethnic differences in order to achieve homogeneity within the political community. Thus Nationalism may serve as a rationale for a separatist movement or as a justification for defeating or crushing an ethnic minority. Pakistanis who fought to preserve the political unity of East and West Pakistan, for example, were fighting in the cause of Nationalism, but those who fought against them in the hopes of establishing an independent nation-state, Bangladesh, were also nationalists. When secessionist demands serve as the basis of a successful revolution, they become the legitimizing rationale for the existence of nation-states. Successful secessionists are national liberators and the fathers of their countries, whereas unsuccessful revolutionaries are viewed as adherents of sectionalism and are dishonored and executed as traitors.

Among the essential ingredients of a national ideology are the principle of national self-determination, a perceived basis for national existence, and a national identity. The principle of national self-determination serves as the central rationale for the existence of a particular national grouping. Nation-states such as France and Germany have been declared to be indivisible social systems because of the shared cultural identity of their citizens. The United States, however, traces its existence to the political "natural right" to be free.

The perceived bases of national groupings also serve as an argument for the legitimacy of their existence as a nation-state and as a justification for their actions. Diverse bases have been forwarded, ranging in kind from something as grandiose as a divinely ordained mission to something as elementary as a shared language. Past history, a shared land mass, a common descent, and utopian dreams also have been forwarded as the bases of a national group's existence, as have such absurd and hideous doctrines as belief in racial purity.

National ideological systems also include beliefs concerning national identity. The issue of national identity is especially critical in nation-states which are characterized by cultural pluralism. When erroneous racial, religious, or cultural identities are forwarded to describe the peoples of a nation-state, the result may be fatal to national existence. For example, the effect of misguided and misinformed attempts to describe the American type by using terms such as "God-fearing," "Anglo-Saxon," and "Caucasian" can only be divisive rather than constructive.

The articles in this section were selected to reflect the critical American struggle to define its national base and to describe its national character. In the brief survey of American Nationalism by Yehoshua Arieli, the reader will note the importance attributed to political *credenda* in defining the American character. Arieli's major theme rests upon his view that the concept "individualism" serves as the core of America's national ideological identity.

In the two creeds presented to illustrate national convictions, the three concepts of "legitimacy," "loyalty," and "unity" are prominently featured. The Declaration of Independence serves as a major document illustrating the revolutionary belief that a people who view themselves as a people have the right to declare their autonomy. The American's Creed illustrates the national belief that political national communities are indivisible—a concept which sometimes rubs against the national views implied in the Declaration of Independence.

In the section labeled "Representative Expressions," various views concerning the nature of American identity and the assimilative process are explored. The two major assimilative models, generally labeled "the melting pot" and "cultural pluralism," are examined in the selections included here.

The "melting pot" model is the most popular view of assimilation in the United States. Despite the popularity of this theory of the assimilative process, in actual practice assimilation in America rarely worked in the way suggested by the model. In most cases the theory was utilized to justify the hope that immigrants would "melt away" their inherited cultures and assume a countenance similar to that of the earliest immigrants. Products of the "melting pot" were vaguely imagined to be a "fuzzy replica of an Englishman."

The question of America's identity was posed by a French immigrant Hector St. John de Crevecoeur on the eve of the American Revolution. His question as well as his faith that the American experience would melt imported differences have been utilized continuously to explore America's identity. His view was reflected much later in the writings of an American historian Frederick Jackson Turner, who posited the thesis that the American frontier served as the cauldron which produced the American type.

The brief passage from Israel Zangwill, the popularizer of the phrase "melting pot," is drawn from his play, *The Melting Pot*, which was first performed in 1908. The words are spoken by the play's hero, David Quixano, a Russian Jewish immigrant aspiring to be a great composer. Subsequently, the author, a fervent Zionist, rejected his "melting pot" construct and declared that cultural identity was unchangeable.

The final selection in the Melting Pot Outlook is the Supreme Court decision ordering the end of segregated schools. Representing the first major federal decision to implement the melting pot construct of assimilation, it was forwarded just as another major assimilation model was emerging into popularity. This model, based on the principle of cultural pluralism, has become an essential element in ethnic demands.

John Dewey, in a relatively obscure speech to the General Assembly of the National Education Association, forwarded a moderate view of cultural pluralism. He accepted pluralism as a fact of life but rejected the view that cultural pluralism should be preserved within enclaves of ethnic identity. Revealing an understanding of the problems generated by ethnic diversity, Dewey in this speech and in his other writings provides a thoughtful defense of cultural pluralism. His moderate view differs significantly from the convincing arguments presented by latter-day advocates of cultural pluralism.

Stokely Carmichael and Charles V. Hamilton's book *Black Power* represents the logical consequence of the theory of cultural pluralism. Reflecting a sensitivity to the relationship between racial identity and individual self-acceptance, the authors in the selection included here urge the black man to assume control over his own destiny and to redefine himself according to his own design.

In the final selection, George A. Coe approaches the issue of citizenship and education. Beginning with the assumption that the people are the rulers, Coe illustrates the indivisible link between the school, the teacher, and the needs of the local and national society. His essay should alert the reader to the role of the teacher as an agent of the people. Such a role does not always fit comfortably with the demands of individuality and political autonomy, as is clear when a teacher faces the dilemma created when community dictates contradict his or her own personal beliefs and moral code.

AN ANALYTICAL VIEW: A Brief Survey

IDEOLOGY AND THE AMERICAN WAY OF LIFE
Yehoshua Arieli

The American Ideology: The Problem Stated

The phenomenon of basic conformity in a free and democratic society, where no real attempt has ever been made to suppress thought or impose opinion by governmental coercion or indoctrination, poses a problem.

In England, Switzerland, and the Scandinavian countries, all of which achieved similar institutional stability and uniformity of outlook, the shock of political and ideological tensions has been absorbed by the vitality of inherited patterns of life and a strong consciousness of national community and unity. These democracies were not troubled, as was the United States, by the social mobility and uprootedness which provide the ideal breeding-ground for ideologies. Ethnic and cultural homogeneity, a common historical tradition, the primary conditions for the consciousness of national unity and community, were conspicuously lacking in American society. And yet an awareness of common purpose and behavior emerged to astonish and puzzle foreign observers. None of them defined more lucidly the problem than Alexis de Tocqueville: "Picture to yourself . . . if you can," he wrote to a friend, "a society which comprises all the nations of the world . . . people differing from one another in language, in beliefs, in opinions; in a word a society possessing no roots, no memories, no prejudices, no routine, no common ideas, no national character, yet with a happiness a hundred times greater than our own. . . . This, then, is our starting point! What is the connecting link between these so different elements? How are they welded into one

From Yehoshua Arieli, *Individualism and Nationalism in American Ideology* (Cambridge, Mass.: Harvard University Press, 1964), pp. 17–25, 27–28. Copyright © 1964 by the President and Fellows of Harvard College. Reprinted by permission of the publishers. Footnotes have been renumbered.

people?" [1] The same question recurred in *De la Démocratie en Amérique.*
How did it happen that in the United States, to which the inhabitants
had only recently immigrated, where the instinctive love of country scarcely
existed, that everyone took as zealous an interest in the affairs of the state
as if they were his own? [2]

The answer could come only through analysis of ideology. More
than any of his contemporaries, Tocqueville was aware of the immense
importance of ideologies in the creation of modern group cohesion and
in the formation of political and social mass movements. He was probably
the first to come to history with a "semantic approach"—that is, to study
"the function which makes the spoken and written word an important
element in the nexus of historical happenings." [3] The chapters in which
he dealt with the emergence of general ideas in democratic societies were
the first mature treatments of the "sociology of knowledge." [4] Since society could "exist only when a great number of men consider a great number of things under the same aspect, when they hold the same opinions
upon many subjects, and when the same occurrences suggest the same
thoughts and impressions to their minds," and since American society
lacked a natural community of tradition, then its cohesion had to be the
product of a community of values, beliefs, and ideas which replaced those
created by tradition and homogeneity.[5]

Democracy, Tocqueville asserted, was the generating principle of
American cohesion. It gave unity to the nation, animated and stabilized
institutions, and controlled habits, feelings, and outlook. "What strikes me
is that the immense majority of spirits join together in certain *common
opinions,*" he noted just a few months after his arrival in the United
States.[6] In America all the laws originated, so to speak, in the same
thought: all society rested on a single principle.[7]

It was, then, the correspondence between the values embodied in
the social structure and those of its ideology that created a consciousness

[1] Quoted by Jacob P. Mayer, *Prophet of the Mass Age; A Study of Alexis de Tocqueville* (London, 1939), p. 30.

[2] Alexis de Tocqueville, *Democracy in America,* ed. Phillips Bradley (New York, 1945), I, 243. See also Tocqueville's diary quoted by G. W. Pierson, *Tocqueville and Beaumont in America* (New York, 1938), p. 114.

[3] Richard Koebner, "Semantics and Historiography," *The Cambridge Journal,* 7:132 (1953).

[4] See Tocqueville, *Democracy in America,* especially "Why The Americans Show More Aptitude And Taste For General Ideas Than Their Forefathers, the En-glish," II, 13ff; "The Philosophical Method of the Americans," II, 3ff; "How The American Democracy Has Modified The English Language," II, 64ff; and on indi-vidualism, II, 98ff.

[5] Tocqueville, *Democracy in America,* I, 392.

[6] See letter to L. de Kergolay, June 29, 1831, as quoted by Pierson, *Tocqueville and Beaumont,* p. 152.

[7] *Ibid.,* p. 693.

of national unity.[8] This thesis actually contained a statement which rarely has been made explicit. Democracy represented in America at one and the same time the principles of national, social, and political organization; national consciousness thus referred also to social and political ideals. The originality of this interpretation consisted in the functional relationship Tocqueville established between the political, social, and national spheres of action and orientation, a relationship determined by the social principle or by democracy as equality of condition.[9] His thesis was that social and political ideals and values determined American national consciousness.

Certain phenomena uniquely American confirmed this view. The expression, "the American way of life," assumed that a certain social-behavior pattern and value system was peculiarly American, though transferable to other nations and not limited by ethnic, racial, or historical group characteristics. Moreover, certain social ideologies were considered American while others were subversive and un-American. Individualism, humanitarian democracy, and "the free enterprise system" were among the former while all socialistic movements and ideologies were among the latter. The character of these social ideologies was different from those which claimed national significance in other countries. The claim of the American ideologies derived not from their compatibility with the nation's aspirations but from their absolute validity in the eyes of the American people. Democracy and liberty, "the American way of life," "the system of individualism," or "the free enterprise system" conveyed a message of universal truth, based upon a total world view. That truth was not subject to the narrow interest of the nation but rather modified the concept and structure of nationalism to its own standards.

The strength of American nationalism thus depended on its nonparochial and universal significance. The peculiar functional relationship between social ideology and national loyalty explained the absence of a strong socialist movement in the United States, the comparative ease with

[8] Tocqueville, *Democracy in America*, I, 244. In speaking of the unity of opinions and states, he notes "the observer . . . will readily discover that their inhabitants, though divided into twenty-four distinct sovereignties, still constitute a single people . . . ," *ibid.*, pp. 392–94.

[9] Though Tocqueville has been generally recognized as one of the earliest and greatest sociological historians, many have been puzzled by his equivocal use of the concept and term "democracy." See Pierson, *Tocqueville and Beaumont*, pp. 7, 165. Pierson, though realizing the sociological approach of Tocqueville, failed to grasp Tocqueville's idea that "democracy" in America referred to a new social system whose unifying principle was democracy. The suggestion that the title of Tocqueville's book should have been "Concerning Equality in America" (Pierson, *Tocqueville and Beaumont*, pp. 7, 158n, 165) does not express the author's concept of the total determination of American life through its social system. See Mayer, *Prophet of the Mass Age;* Bernhard Fabian, *Alexis de Tocqueville's Amerikabild* (Heidelberg, 1957); Albert Salomon, "Tocqueville, Moralist and Sociologist," *Social Research*, 2:420–22 (1935).

which radical or nonconformist thought because suspect, and the leadership assumed by the United States in the struggle with world communism. Like socialists and communists, Americans believed that their social system was universally applicable to all mankind.

This position was unique in the contemporary world. Socialism, communism, and humanitarian liberalism never identified themselves with the interest of any particular nation; their sphere of action transcended national boundaries and interests, although communism under certain conditions furthered nationalistic movements as a means toward an end. A clearcut division between social, political, and national ideas has sometimes permitted greater political realism and sometimes led to a dangerous collision of competing loyalties. But in countries other than the United States, such a division also encouraged the free ideological development of competing claims inside the political framework of the country without threatening the stability of society. A multi-ideological development in most countries of the Western world stimulated understanding of social and political systems differing from their own. The identification of an ideological attitude with America's national interests and aspirations has, on the other hand, made for a strangely unrealistic attitude toward the world at large and toward its own basic problems.

The Structure of the American Ideology: A Preliminary Answer

Patterns of national identification have been achieved in several ways. One involved the imposition of a social philosophy on society by the state, as in the countries under totalitarian communist rule, and the creation of uniformity through the concept of a new social world order. National traditions and loyalties were destroyed and the loyalty and identification with the state achieved through the idea of a universally valid order of human life, sanctified by a scheme of ultimate salvation and redemption.

A similar integration was the product of totalitarian nationalism which imposed uniformity of belief through the idea of the fundamental organic unity and identity of the nation in which all social activities were coordinated and subordinated to the optimal functioning of the group. Totalitarian nationalism created a philosophy of social cooperation and tended toward the concept of the corporate state in which the position of the individual was defined by its function in the whole.[10]

Another type of national identification was achieved through the

[10] Benito Mussolini, "La Dottrina del Fascismo," *Scritti e Discorsi* (Milan, 1934), VIII, 67–96, and "Forza E Consenso," III, 77–79; see also Elie Halévy, *The World Crisis of 1914–1918* (Oxford, 1930), Lecture I.

concept of citizenship. The feeling of national unity resulted from a long-established community of life, traditions, and institutions more than from a unitary ideology. The consciousness of national community did not lead toward conformity and ideological identification. It rather became an elastic framework for diversity of opinion and political orientation, kept in check through the consciousness of the common bonds of a national tradition. To the degree that ideals of citizenship and of political rights became part of the institutional framework, the feeling of national identification increased in strength without threatening the autonomy and variety of individual and group expression. Such has been the development in states which gave birth to liberalism.[11]

The structure of the American national consciousness did not correspond to any one of these types. Instead, the major characteristics of each of them were blended into a new variety. In the United States, national consciousness was shaped by social and political values which claimed universal validity and which were nevertheless the American way of life. Unlike other Western nations, America claimed to possess a "social system" fundamentally opposed to and a real alternative to socialism and communism, with which it competed by claiming to represent the way to ultimate progress and true social happiness.

The claim to represent the real alternative to socialism was expressed in the development of the concept of individualism in the nineteenth and twentieth centuries. This concept, formed from the beginning as the ideological antithesis to socialism, pervaded almost all American politically significant thought in the late nineteenth and early twentieth centuries. Nor did this attitude materially change, though the term "individualism" fell into at least temporary "disgrace" with the great depression and the New Deal. In its stead other terms like "free enterprise system," the philosophy of "a free society," took up the same burden and claimed the same universal significance. The McCarthy years, like the "Red panic" of the 1920's, the frequent denunciations of governmental participation in the national life as "creeping socialism," and the ideological nature of America's opposition to Russia and China, all indicated the identification of the nation with a social philosophy.

And yet, in contrast to socialism and communism, this social ideology was, in addition, an ideology of nationalism. The "American way of life" was also a pattern of national behavior, beliefs, and values; and its social ideology actually described and rationalized the general system of social relations existing in American society.

From this point of view the American ideology resembled other highly developed ideologies of nationalism. The American people devel-

[11] On the spontaneous conformity of the Englishmen see Adolf Löwe, *The Price of Liberty* (London, 1937), pp. 13–25.

oped a strong sense of natonal mission and destiny, and their aggressive nationalism expanded the territory of the United States from the Atlantic to the Pacific.[12] No other Western democracy so frequently applied loyalty tests or made ideological conformity the criterion of patriotism. The sense of national pride and the feeling of uniqueness were commented upon by almost all observers. "Not only are the Anglo-Americans united by these common opinions," observed Tocqueville, "but they are separated from all other nations by a feeling of pride. For the last fifty years no pains have been spared to convince the inhabitants of the United States that they are the only religious, enlightened, and free people . . . hence they conceive a high opinion of their superiority and are not very remote from believing themselves to be a distinct species of mankind." [13]

American nationalism rested on assumptions fundamentally different from those of other nations.[14] The American people were not a folk-nation or a federation of nations. They lacked ethnic, religious, or cultural unity, and all those traits which a common history impressed upon territorial societies. This nation established its identity in patterns of political and social organization and in the benefits and powers deriving from its territory and its state. Citizenship was the only criterion which made the individual a member of the national community: and national loyalty meant loyalty to the Constitution. The formative force of American national unity has been, then, the idea of citizenship; through this concept the integration of state and society into a nation has been achieved.

The identification of the people with the state as citizens has meant participation in political power and the enjoyment of order and security, of civil rights and communal benefits. National identification has meant

[12] See Tocqueville, *Democracy in America*, I, 244; John Robert Godley, *Letters from America* (London, 1844), I, 19; see also James Fenimore Cooper, *Notions of the Americans* (Philadelphia, 1832), II, 108–9; also James Fenimore Cooper, *Gleanings in Europe* (New York, 1928–30), II, 316–17; also [Calvin Colton], *The Americans. By an American in London* (London, 1833), pp. 14–15; Gustav H. Blanke, *Amerikanischer Geist: Begriffs-und wortgeschichtliche Untersuchungen* (Meisenheim am Glan, Hain, 1956), pp. 18–24, 24–29, 29–33, on the concepts of Americans, American literature and American national unity, and pp. 41–42 on the "American System." See also Merle E. Curti, *The Roots of American Loyalty* (New York, 1946); on early nationalism in literature see *Cambridge History of American Literature*, ed. W. P. Trent, *et al.* (New York, 1917–21), I, 168–89; Benjamin T. Spencer, *The Quest for Nationality: an American Literary Campaign* (Syracuse, 1957); Edward H. Reisner, *Nationalism and Education since 1789* (New York, 1922); see also Albert K. Weinberg, *Manifest Destiny; a Study in Nationalist Expansionism in American History* (Baltimore, 1935).

[13] Tocqueville, *Democracy in America*, I, 393–94.

[14] See Friedrich O. Hertz, *Nationality in History and Politics* (London, 1951), p. 21; also Carlton J. H. Hayes, *Essays on Nationalism* (New York, 1928), pp. 86–90, 109–14, 119–23.

the will-to-power and prestige of the in-group in relation to the out-groups of other nations. The group feeling was created by the dividing wall of separate statehood, through the possession of sovereignty.

The strength of this nationalism rested upon the inevitable tension among closed systems of power, which forced the society inside each system to identify its welfare with the state. Its weakness stemmed from the struggle of the different sub-groups of the political society to use the state for the increase of their own power. Unless this nationalism is supported by a consciousness of intrinsic group unity, by a capacity to find areas of identification through which a community of purpose and belonging is created, nationalism may and has in American history become a disruptive rather than a unifying force. It is the character of this positive force of cohesion, of its national consciousness, and its concept of national unity which represents in America a unique configuration.

The singularity of this configuration lies in the fact that it refers exclusively to patterns of social and political values and to norms of thought and behavior and not to natural or historic factors of national unity and cohesion. Yet, the adoption of social and political values and norms as a framework for national identification is possible only if these values are based on some source of apparent ultimate truth or authority which confers on them the character of absolute validity—if they can claim universality. Universal citizenship implies always the incorporation of rationalistic and universal values into the national ideology. But in no other nation have these values become the exclusive connotation of nationality or the exclusive framework of national identification. On the contrary, having arisen in homogeneous societies whose national character has been welded by common historical experience, the nation was taken for granted, and the pattern of rational and universal values referred to the structure of the state and not to the identity of the nation.

In America, on the other hand, the same system of norms and values which justified the establishment of a new political structure, the republic, and brought about the victory of the concept of a citizen-state also brought about the establishment of national independence, the creation of a new nation. *This coincidence of the political and the national Revolution through the application of the same set of principles is the fundamental datum of American nationality and of the structure of its consciousness.*

The revolutionary separation from the mother country involved a radical break with its own past, the transformation of English subjects into American citizens and of the rights of Englishmen into the rights of nature. The very strongly developed consciousness of English national traditions and rights, of the continuity of history and belonging, had to be reinterpreted in new terms which replaced the traditional element by concepts taken from the natural-rights philosophy. The fact that the American nation was created by a revolutionary separation from the mother country brought about the adoption of rationalistic values and norms not only as the basis of an independent statehood, but as a definition of the nature of the new nation. Universal values and modes of thought which had served the British colonists in the struggle against England enabled them to interpret their own pattern of institutions and traditions in new terms. The interpretation of American nationality in terms of universally valid social and political ideals explains and maintains at one and the same time the character of the American nation as state-nation or citizen-nation. It is the paradoxical nature of its nationalism, its universalism, which has created the nation, welded the union, and given American nationalism its missionary and salvationist character. The same fact also explains the fixation of ideological patterns and the uniformity of its ideological developments.

If the unity of a nation is based on contrived grounds, on a conscious pattern of concepts and values, the state, society, and the individual will endeavor to maintain this unity under all conditions as the basis of social and political stability. In societies in which the principle of unity is a natural or a given datum, a variety of ideologies may compete with each other. But in a nation in which social and national cohesion is based on an ideological proposition, diversity can develop only within the framework of its ideological premises.

This interpretation of the American national consciousness has been challenged on the grounds that the American Revolution, unlike the French, hardly altered institutional and social patterns. Independence only changed the superstructure of society, or rather represented a final step in the process of a maturing nation. National character was thus a product of history, environment, and ethnic homogeneity, to which ideological premises or assumptions were irrelevant. This was the actual view of many of the conservative leaders of the Revolutionary generation and was to a certain degree shared by all of them. Washington's Farewell Address appealed to the sentiment of national unity by invoking tradition as well as principle: "The name of American, which belongs to you in your national capacity, must always exalt the just pride of patriotism more than any appellation derived from local discriminations. With slight shades of difference, you have the same religion, manners, habits and political principles. You have in a common cause fought and triumphed together. The independence and liberty you possess are the work of joint councils and joint efforts, of common dangers, sufferings, and successes." [15]

15 H. S. Commager, ed., *Documents of American History* (New York, 1948), I, 170; see also Friedrich von Gentz, *The American and French Revolutions Compared* (Chicago [1955]). The classical expression of this view is given by John Adams: see "Defence of the Constitutions" and John Quincy Adams, *Letters of Publicola*.

Like their prototype and spiritual progenitors, the English Whigs, American Federalists and Whigs attempted to harmonize their own revolutionary inheritance with their tradition and to interpret the republican principles of American society and government as principles inherent in the national character and genius of its inhabitants and their religious heritage of liberty. This sentiment was particularly strong in New England and seemed to the young Tocqueville the ruling sentiment of this region.[16]

.   .   .

All Thirteen Colonies had developed institutional, social, and cultural patterns of life which created the basic conditions for independence and a national consciousness, and this pattern undoubtedly continued without radical change after the Revolution. Nor can it be doubted that a feeling of patriotism and of historical distinctiveness had arisen before the Revolution. For only when a society has become aware of its own corporate existence does it attempt to integrate the state with itself by the notion of nationality. Yet a political consciousness and a strongly homogeneous pattern of social life did not evolve within the American framework before 1765, but rather in the framework of each colony. The new national consciousness was the result of the contest between the colonies and the mother country and, finally, of the Revolution, and this consciousness was built upon the language and concepts of the natural-rights philosophy. Moreover, the establishment of the several states on the same grounds involved a radicalization of thought which brought about a change in all institutional patterns and in the structure of American society itself.

It has also been argued that the formative, historical elite group was ethnically homogeneous, of Anglo-American origin, and that the national pattern evolved in American society was its own pattern of life.[17] This pattern has been threatened, it is contended, by the deracination of American society, by the influx of other ethnic groups which have in the very act of accepting this way of life endangered its survival. Nativism from the beginning of the nineteenth century to our own times expresses the tension created by two competing types of national consciousness, the first universalistic in outlook, the second based on an awareness of belonging to a national organic community whose values are to a certain degree not transferable and whose aim is to determine the character of the nation and the activities of the state according to its own ideals. The interplay between these two tendencies has determined to a large degree the structure and course of American nationalism.

Yet, whatever the impact of universal concepts on the American

[16] See Pierson, *Tocqueville and Beaumont*, pp. 370–71.

[17] This is the whole tenor of Rossiter's *Seedtime of the Republic;* see especially p. 301.

historical experience, the conservative and nativistic interpreters of American history, no less than their opponents, concede that American nationality has to be defined, at least to some degree, by reference to certain political and social concepts; that it is a way of life and an attitude which somehow represents ultimate social values.[18]

[18] Tocqueville, *Democracy in America*, I, 47.

THE CREED: National Admonitions

1. THE DECLARATION OF INDEPENDENCE
Thomas Jefferson

When in the Course of human events, it becomes necessary for one people to dissolve the political bands which have connected them with another, and to assume among the powers of the earth, the separate and equal station to which the Laws of Nature and of Nature's God entitle them, a decent respect to the opinions of mankind requires that they should declare the causes which impel them to the separation. We hold these truths to be self-evident, that all men are created equal, that they are endowed by their Creator with certain unalienable Rights, that among these are Life, Liberty and the pursuit of Happiness. That to secure these rights, Governments are instituted among Men, deriving their just powers from the consent of the governed, That whenever any Form of Government becomes destructive of these ends it is the Right of the People to alter or to abolish it, and to institute new Government, laying its foundation on such principles and organizing its powers in such form, as to them shall seem most likely to effect their Safety and Happiness. Prudence, indeed, will dictate that Governments long established should not be changed for light and transient causes; and accordingly all experience hath shewn, that mankind are more disposed to suffer, while evils are sufferable, than to right themselves by abolishing the forms to which they are accustomed. But when a long train of abuses and usurpations, pursuing invariably the same Object evince a design to reduce them under absolute Despotism, it is their right, it is their duty, to throw off such Government, and to provide new Guards for their future security. Such has been the patient sufferance of these Colonies; and such is now the necessity which constrains them to alter their former Systems of Government. The history of the present King of Great Britain is a history of repeated injuries and usurpations, all having in direct object the establishment of an absolute Tyranny over these States. To prove this, let Facts be submitted to a candid world. He has refused his Assent to Laws, the most wholesome and necessary for the public good. He has forbidden his Governors to pass Laws of immediate and pressing importance, unless suspended in their operation till his Assent should be obtained; and when so suspended, he has utterly neglected to attend to them. He has refused to pass other Laws for the accommodation of large districts of people, unless those people would relinquish the right of Representation in the Legislature, a right inestimable to them and formidable to tyrants only. He has called together legislative bodies at places unusual, uncomfortable, and distant from the depository of their public Records, for the sole purpose of fatiguing them into compliance with his measures. He has dissolved Representative Houses repeatedly, for opposing with manly firmness his invasions on the rights of the people. He has refused for a long time, after such dissolutions, to cause others to be elected; whereby the Legislative powers, incapable of Annihilation, have returned to the People at large for their exercise; the State remaining in the mean time exposed to all the dangers of invasion from without, and convulsions within. He has endeavoured to prevent the population of these States; for that purpose obstructing the Laws for Naturalization of Foreigners; refusing to pass others to encourage their migrations hither, and raising the conditions of new Appropriations of Lands. He has obstructed the Administration of Justice, by refusing his Assent to Laws for establishing Judiciary powers. He has made Judges dependent on his Will alone, for the tenure of their offices, and the amount and payment of their salaries. He has erected a multitude of New Offices, and sent hither swarms of Officers to harass our people, and eat out their substance. He has kept among us, in times of peace, standing Armies without the Consent of our legislatures. He has affected to render the Military independent of and superior to the Civil power. He has combined with others to subject us to a jurisdiction foreign to our constitution, and unacknowledged by our laws; giving his Assent to their Acts of pretended Legislation: For Quartering large bodies of armed troops among us: For protecting them, by a mock Trial, from punishment for any Murders which they should commit on the Inhabitants of these States: For cutting off our Trade with all parts of the world: For imposing Taxes on us without our Consent: For depriving us in many cases of the benefits of Trial by Jury: For transporting us beyond Seas to be tried for pretended offences: For abolishing the free System of English Laws in a neighbouring Province, establishing therein an Arbitrary government, and enlarging its Boundaries so as to render it at once an example and fit instrument for introducing the same absolute rule into these Colonies: For taking away our Charters, abolishing our most valuable Laws, and altering fundamentally the Forms of our Governments: For suspending our own Legislatures, and declaring themselves invested with power to legislate for us in all cases whatsoever. He has abdicated Government here, by declaring us out of his Protection and waging War against us. He has plundered our seas, ravaged our Coasts, burnt our towns, and destroyed the Lives of our people. He is at this time transporting large Armies of foreign Mercenaries to compleat the works of death, desolation and tyranny, already begun with circumstances of Cruelty & perfidy scarcely paralleled in the most barbarous ages, and totally unworthy of the Head of a civilized nation. He has constrained our fellow Citizens taken Captive on the high Seas to bear Arms against their Country, to become the executioners of their friends and Brethren, or to fall themselves by their Hands. He has excited domestic insurrections amongst us, and has endeavoured to bring on the inhabitants of our frontiers, the merciless Indian Savages, whose known rule of warfare, is an undistinguished destruction of all ages, sexes and conditions. In every stage of these Oppressions We have Petitioned for Redress in the most humble terms: Our repeated Petitions have been answered only by repeated injury. A Prince, whose character is thus marked by every act which may define a Tyrant, is unfit to be the ruler of a free people. Nor have We been wanting in attentions to our British brethren. We have warned them from time to time of attempts by their legislature to extend an unwarrantable jurisdiction over us. We have reminded them of the circumstances of our emigration and settlement here. We have appealed to their native justice and magnanimity, and we have conjured them by the ties of our common kindred to disavow these usurpations, which, would inevitably interrupt our connections and correspondence. They too have been deaf to the voice of justice and of consanguinity. We must, therefore, acquiesce in the necessity, which denounces our Separation, and hold them, as we hold the rest of mankind, Enemies in War, in Peace Friends.

We, therefore, the Representatives of the united States of America, in General Congress, Assembled, appealing to the Supreme Judge of the world for the rectitude of our intentions, do, in the Name, and by Authority of the good People of these Colonies, solemnly publish and declare, That these United Colonies are, and of Right ought to be Free and Independent States; that they are Absolved from all Allegiance to the British Crown, and that all political connection between them and the State of Great Britain, is and ought to be totally dissolved; and that as Free and Independent States, they have full Power to levy War, conclude Peace, contract Alliances, establish Commerce, and to do all other Acts and Things which Independent States may of right do. And for the support of this Declaration, with a firm reliance on the protection of divine Providence, we mutually pledge to each other our Lives, our Fortunes and our sacred Honor.

2. THE AMERICAN'S CREED
William Tyler Page

I believe in the United States of America as a government of the people, by the people, for the people; whose just powers are derived from the consent of the governed; a democracy in a republic; a sovereign Nation of many sovereign States; a perfect union, one and inseparable; established upon those principles of freedom, equality, justice, and humanity for which American patriots sacrificed their lives and fortunes.

I therefore believe it is my duty to my country to love it; to support its Constitution; to obey its laws; to respect its flag; and to defend it against all enemies.

REPRESENTATIVE EXPRESSIONS:
An Historical Perspective—
The Issue of National Cohesion

1. THE MELTING POT OUTLOOK
a. J. Hector St. John de Crevecoeur

In this great American asylum, the poor of Europe have by some means met together, and in consequence of various causes; to what purpose should they ask one another what countrymen they are? Alas, two thirds of them had no country. Can a wretch who wanders about, who works and starves, whose life is a continual scene of sore affliction or pinching penury—can that man call England or any other kingdom his country? A country that had no bread for him, whose fields procured him no harvest, who met with nothing but the frowns of the rich, the severity of the laws, with jails and punishments; who owned not a single foot of the extensive surface of this planet? No! Urged by a variety of motives, here they came. Everything has tended to regenerate them; new laws, a new mode of living, a new social system; here they are become men: in Europe they were as so many useless plants, wanting vegetative mould, and refreshing showers; they withered, and were mowed down by want, hunger, and war; but now, by the power of transplantation, like all other plants they have taken root and flourished! Formerly they were not numbered in any civil lists of their country, except in those of the poor; here they rank as citizens. By what invisible power hath this surprising metamorphosis been performed? By that of the laws and that of their industry. The laws, the indulgent laws, protect them as they arrive, stamping on them the symbol of adoption; they receive ample rewards for their labours; these accumulated rewards procure them lands; those lands confer on them the title of freemen, and to that title every benefit is affixed which men can possibly require. This is the great operation daily performed by our laws. From whence proceed these laws? From our government. Whence the government? It is derived from the original genius and strong desire of the people ratified and confirmed by the crown. This is the great chain which links us all, this is

From J. Hector St. John de Crevecoeur, *Letters from An American Farmer* ed. by Warren Barton Blake (New York: E. P. Dutton & Company, n.d.), pp. 41–44.

the picture which every province exhibits, Nova Scotia excepted. There
the crown has done all; either there were no people who had genius or
it was not much attended to: the consequence is, that the province is
very thinly inhabited indeed; the power of the crown in conjunction
with the musketos has prevented men from settling there. Yet some parts
of it flourished once, and it contained a mild harmless set of people. But
for the fault of a few leaders, the whole were banished. The greatest
political error the crown ever committed in America, was to cut off men
from a country which wanted nothing but men!

What attachment can a poor European emigrant have for a country
where he had nothing? The knowledge of the language, the love of a
few kindred as poor as himself, were the only cords that tied him: his
country is now that which gives him his land, bread, protection, and
consequences: *Ubi panis ibi patria* is the motto of all emigrants. What,
then, is the American, this new man? He is either an European or the
descendant of an European; hence that strange mixture of blood, which
you will find in no other country. I could point out to you a family whose
grandfather was an Englishman, whose wife was Dutch, whose son
married a French woman, and whose present four sons have now four
wives of different nations. *He* is an American, who, leaving behind him
all his ancient prejudices and manners, receives new ones from the new
mode of life he has embraced, the new government he obeys, and the
new rank he holds. He becomes an American by being received in the
broad lap of our great *Alma Mater*. Here individuals of all nations are
melted into a new race of men, whose labours and posterity will one
day cause great changes in the world. Americans are the western pilgrims,
who are carrying along with them that great mass of arts, sciences,
vigour, and industry which began long since in the East; they will finish
the great circle. The Americans were once scattered all over Europe;
here they are incorporated into one of the finest systems of population
which was ever appeared, and which will hereafter become distinct by
the power of the different climates they inhabit. The American ought
therefore to love this country much better than that wherein either he or
his forefathers were born. Here the rewards of his industry follow with
equal steps the progress of his labour; his labour is founded on the basis
of nature, self-interest; can it want a stronger allurement? Wives and
children, who before in vain demanded of him a morsel of bread, now,
fat and frolicsome, gladly help their father to clear those fields whence
exuberant crops are to arise to feed and to clothe them all; without any
part being claimed, either by a despotic prince, a rich abbot, or a mighty
lord. Here religion demands but little of him; a small voluntary salary
to the minister, and gratitude to God; can he refuse these? The American
is a new man, who acts upon new principles; he must therefore enter-

tain new ideas, and form new opinions. From involuntary idleness, servile dependence, penury, and useless labour, he has passed to toils of a very different nature, rewarded by ample subsistence. This is an American.

b. Israel Zangwill

Not undertsand that America is God's Crucible, the great Melting-Pot where all the races of Europe are melting and re-forming! Here you stand, good folk, think I, when I see them at Ellis Island, here you stand in your fifty groups, with your fifty languages and histories, and your fifty blood hatreds and rivalries. But you won't be long like that, brothers, for these are the fires of God you've come to—these are the fires of God. A fig for your feuds and vendettas! Germans and Frenchmen, Irishmen and Englishmen, Jews and Russians—into the Crucible with you all! God is making the American . . . the real American has not yet arrived. He is only in the Crucible, I tell you—he will be the fusion of all races, perhaps the coming superman. There she lies, the great Melting Pot—listen! Can't you hear the roaring and the bubbling? There gapes her mouth— the harbour where a thousand mammoth feeders come from the ends of the world to pour in their human freight. Ah, what a stirring and a seething! Celt and Latin, Slav and Teuton, Greek and Syrian,—black and yellow—Yes, East and West, and North and South, the palm and the pine, the pole and the equator, the crescent and the cross—how the great Alchemist melts and fuses them with his purging flame! Here shall they all unite to build the Republic of Man and the Kingdom of God. Ah, Vera, what is the glory of Rome and Jerusalem where all nations and races come to worship and look back, compared with the glory of America, where all races and nations come to labour and look forward! Peace, peace, to all ye unborn millions, fated to fill this giant continent—the God of our *children* give you Peace.

c. The United States Supreme Court

Mr. Chief Justice Warren delivered the opinion of the Court.

These cases come to us from the States of Kansas, South Carolina, Virginia, and Delaware. They are premised on different facts and dif-

From Israel Zangwill, *The Melting Pot* (New York: The Macmillan Company, 1938), pp. 33, 34, 184, 185. Copyright 1909.

ferent local conditions, but a common legal question justifies their consideration together in this consolidated opinion.*

In each of the cases, minors of the Negro race, through their legal representatives, seek the aid of the courts in obtaining admission to the public schools of their community on a nonsegregated basis. In each instance, they had been denied admission to school attended by white children under laws requiring or permitting segregation according to race. This segregation was alleged to deprive the plaintiffs of the equal protection of the laws under the Fourteenth Amendment. In each of the cases other than the Delaware case, a three-judge federal district court denied relief to the plaintiffs on the so-called "separate but equal" doctrine announced by this Court in *Plessy* v. *Ferguson*, 163 U.S. 537. Under that doctrine, equality of treatment is accorded when the races are provided substantially equal facilities, even though these facilities be separate. In the Delaware case, the Supreme Court of Delaware adhered to that doctrine, but ordered that the plaintiffs be admitted to the white schools because of their superiority to the Negro schools.

The plaintiffs contend that segregated public schools are not "equal" and cannot be made "equal," and that hence they are deprived of the equal protection of the laws. Because of the obvious importance of the question presented, the Court took jurisdiction. Argument was heard in the 1952 Term, and reargument was heard this Term on certain questions propounded by the Court.

Reargument was largely devoted to the circumstances surrounding the adoption of the Fourteenth Amendment in 1868. It covered exhaustively consideration of the Amendment in Congress, ratification by the states, then existing practices in racial segregation, and the views of proponents and opponents of the Amendment. This discussion and our own investigation convince us that, although these sources cast some light, it is not enough to resolve the problem with which we are faced. At best, they are inconclusive. The most avid proponents of the post-War Amendments undoubtedly intended them to remove all legal distinctions among "all persons born or naturalized in the United States." Their opponents, just as certainly, were antagonistic to both the letter and the spirit of the Amendments and wished them to have the most limited effect. What others in Congress and the state legislatures had in mind cannot be determined with any degree of certainty.

An additional reason for the inconclusive nature of the Amendment's history, with respect to segregated schools, is the status of public education at that time. In the South, the movement toward free common schools, supported by general taxation, had not yet taken hold.

* Brown *v*. Board of Education of Topeka, 347 U.S. 483 (1954).

Education of white children was largely in the hands of private groups. Education of Negroes was almost nonexistent, and practically all of the race were illiterate. In fact, any education of Negroes was forbidden by law in some states. Today, in contrast, many Negroes have achieved outstanding success in the arts and sciences as well as in the business and professional world. It is true that public school education at the time of the Amendment had advanced further in the North, but the effect of the Amendment on Northern States was generally ignored in the congressional debates. Even in the North, the conditions of public education did not approximate those existing today. The curriculum was usually rudimentary; ungraded schools were common in rural areas; the school term was but three months a year in many states; and compulsory school attendance was virtually unknown. As a consequence, it is not surprising that there should be so little in the history of the Fourteenth Amendment relating to its intended effect on public education.

In the first cases in this Court construing the Fourteenth Amendment, decided shortly after its adoption, the Court interpreted it as proscribing all state-imposed discriminations against the Negro race. The doctrine of "separate but equal" did not make its appearance in this Court until 1896 in the case of *Plessy* v. *Ferguson, supra,* involving not education but transportation. American courts have since labored with the doctrine for over half a century. In this Court, there have been six cases involving the "separate but equal" doctrine in the field of public education. In *Cumming* v. *County Board of Education,* 175 U.S. 528, and *Gong Lum* v. *Rice,* 275 U.S. 78, the validity of the doctrine itself was not challenged. In more recent cases, all on the graduate school level, inequality was found in that specific benefits enjoyed by white students were denied to Negro students of the same educational qualifications. *Missouri ex rel. Gaines* v. *Canada,* 305 U.S. 337; *Sipuel* v. *Oklahoma,* 332 U.S. 631; *Sweatt* v. *Painter,* 339 U.S. 629; *McLaurin* v. *Oklahoma State Regents,* 39 U.S. 637. In none of these cases was it necessary to re-examine the doctrine to grant relief to the Negro plaintiff. And in *Sweatt* v. *Painter, supra,* the Court expressly reserved decision on the question whether *Plessy* v. *Ferguson* should be held inapplicable to public education.

In the instant cases, that question is directly presented. Here, unlike *Sweatt* v. *Painter,* there are findings below that the Negro and white schools involved have been equalized, or are being equalized, with respect to buildings, curricula, qualifications and salaries of teachers, and other "tangible" factors. Our decision, therefore, cannot turn on merely a comparison of these tangible factors in the Negro and white schools involved in each of the cases. We must look instead to the effect of segregation itself on public education.

In approaching this problem, we cannot turn the clock back to 1868 when the Amendment was adopted, or even to 1896 when *Plessy* v. *Ferguson* was written. We must consider public education in the light of its full development and its present place in American life throughout the Nation. Only in this way can it be determined if segregation in public schools deprives these plaintiffs of the equal protection of the laws.

Today, education is perhaps the most important function of state and local governments. Compulsory school attendance laws and the great expenditures for education both demonstrate our recognition of the importance of education to our democratic society. It is required in the performance of our most basic public responsibilities, even service in the armed forces. It is the very foundation of good citizenship. Today it is a principal instrument in awakening the child to cultural values, in preparing him for later professional training, and in helping him to adjust normally to his environment. In these days, it is doubtful that any child may reasonably be expected to succeed in life if he is denied the opportunity of an education. Such an opportunity, where the state has undertaken to provide it, is a right which must be made available to all on equal terms.

We come then to the question presented: Does segregation of children in public schools solely on the basis of race, even though the physical facilities and other "tangible" factors may be equal, deprive the children of the minority group of equal educational opportunities? We believe that it does.

In *Sweatt* v. *Painter, supra,* in finding that a segregated law school for Negroes could not provide them equal educational opportunities, this Court relied in large part on "those qualities which are incapable of objective measurement but which make for greatness in a law school." In *McLaurin* v. *Oklahoma State Regents, supra,* the Court, in requiring that a Negro admitted to a white graduate school be treated like all other students, again resorted to intangible considerations: ". . . his ability to study, to engage in discussions and exchange views with other students, and, in general, to learn his profession." Such considerations apply with added force to children in grade and high schools. To separate them from others of similar age and qualifications solely because of their race generates a feeling of inferiority as to their status in the community that may affect their hearts and minds in a way unlikely ever to be undone. The effect of this separation on their educational opportunities was well stated by a finding in the Kansas case by a court which nevertheless felt compelled to rule against the Negro plaintiffs:

> Segregation of white and colored children in public schools has a detrimental effect upon the colored children. The impact is greater when it has the sanction of the law; for the policy of separating the races is usually interpreted as denoting the inferiority of the negro group. A sense

of inferiority affects the motivation of a child to learn. Segregation with the sanction of law, therefore, has a tendency to [retard] the educational and mental development of negro children and to deprive them of some of the benefits they would receive in a racial[ly] integrated school system.

Whatever may have been the extent of psychological knowledge at the time of *Plessy* v. *Ferguson,* this finding is amply supported by modern authority. Any language in *Plessy* v. *Ferguson* contrary to this finding is rejected.

We conclude that in the field of public education the doctrine of "separate but equal" has no place. Separate educational facilities are inherently unequal. Therefore, we hold that the plaintiffs and others similarly situated for whom the actions have been brought are, by reason of the segregation complained of, deprived of the equal protection of the laws guaranteed by the Fourteenth Amendment. This disposition makes unnecessary any discussion whether such segregation also violates the Due Process Clause of the Fourteenth Amendment.

Because these are class actions, because of the wide applicability of this decision, and because of the great variety of local conditions, the formulation of decrees in these cases presents problems of considerable complexity. On reargument, the consideration of appropriate relief was necessarily subordinated to the primary question—the constitutionality of segregation in public education. We have now announced that such segregation is a denial of the equal protection of the laws. In order that we may have the full assistance of the parties in formulating decrees, the cases will be restored to the docket, and the parties are requested to present further argument on Questions 4 and 5 previously propounded by the Court for the reargument this Term. The Attorney General of the United States is again invited to participate. The Attorneys General of the states requiring or permitting segregation in public education will also be permitted to appear as *amici curiae* upon request to do so by September 15, 1954, and submission of briefs by October 1, 1954.

It is so ordered.

2. THE CULTURAL DIVERSITY OUTLOOK

a. John Dewey

I want to mention only two elements in the nationalism which our education should cultivate. The first is that the American nation is itself complex and compound. Strictly speaking, it is inter-racial and international in its make-up. It is composed of a multitude of peoples speaking different tongues, inheriting diverse traditions, cherishing varying ideals of life. This fact is basic to our nationalism as distinct from that of other peoples. Our national motto, "One from Many," cuts deep and extends far. It denotes a fact which doubtless adds to the difficulty of getting a genuine unity. But it also immensely enriches the possibilities of the result to be attained. No matter how loudly any one proclaims his Americanism, if he assumes that any one racial strain, any one component culture, no matter how early settled it was in our territory, or how effective it has proved in its own land, is to furnish a pattern to which all other strains and cultures are to conform, he is a traitor to an American nationalism. Our unity cannot be a homogeneous thing like that of the separate states of Europe from which our population is drawn; it must be a unity created by drawing out and composing into a harmonious whole the best, the most characteristic, which each contributing race and people has to offer.

I find that many who talk the loudest about the need of a supreme and unified Americanism of spirit really mean some special code or tradition to which they happen to be attacht. They have some pet tradition which they would impose upon all. In thus measuring the scope of Americanism by some single element which enters into it they are themselves false to the spirit of America. Neither Englandism nor New-Englandism, neither Puritan nor Cavalier, any more than Teuton or Slav, can do anything but furnish one note in a vast symphony.

The way to deal with hyphenism, in other words, is to welcome it, but to welcome it in the sense of extracting from each people its special good, so that it shall surrender into a common fund of wisdom and ex-

From John Dewey, "Nationalizing Education," *Journal of Proceedings of the 54th Annual Meeting of the National Education Association of the United States,* New York, New York, July 1–8, 1916, pp. 184–89.

perience what it especially has to contribute. All of these surrenders and contributions taken together create the national spirit of America. The dangerous thing is for each factor to isolate itself, to try to live off its past, and then to attempt to impose itself upon other elements, or, at least, to keep itself intact and thus refuse to accept what other cultures have to offer, so as thereby to be transmuted into authentic Americanism.

In what is rightly objected to as hyphenism, the hyphen has become something which separates one people from other peoples, and thereby prevents American nationalism. Such terms as Irish-American or Hebrew-American or German-American are false terms because they seem to assume something which is already in existence called America, to which the other factor may be externally hitcht on. The fact is, the genuine American, the typical American, is himself a hyphenated character. This does not mean that he is part American and that some foreign ingredient is then added. It means that, as I have said, he is international and interracial in his make-up. He is not American plus Pole or German. But the American is himself Pole-German-English-French-Spanish-Italian-Greek-Irish-Scandinavian-Bohemian-Jew- and so on. The point is to see to it that the hyphen connects instead of separates. And this means at least that our public schools shall teach each factor to respect every other, and shall take pains to enlighten all as to the great past contributions of every strain in our composite make-up. I wish our teaching of American history in the schools would take more account of the great waves of migration by which our land for over three centuries has been continuously built up, and made every pupil conscious of the rich breadth of our national make-up. When every pupil recognizes all the factors which have gone into our being, he will continue to prize and reverence that coming from his own past, but he will think of it as honored in being simply one factor in forming a whole nobler and finer than itself.

In short, unless our education is nationalized in a way which recognizes that the peculiarity of our nationalism is its internationalism, we shall breed enmity and division in our frantic efforts to secure unity. The teachers of the country know this fact much better than do many of its politicians. While too often politicians have been fostering a vicious hyphenatedism and sectionalism as a bid for votes, teachers have been engaged in transmuting beliefs and feelings once divided and opposed, into a new thing under the sun—a national spirit inclusive not exclusive, friendly not jealous. This they have done by the influence of personal contact, co-operative intercourse, and sharing in common tasks and hopes. The teacher who has been an active agent in furthering the common struggle of native-born, African, Jew, Italian, and perhaps a score of other peoples, to attain emancipation and enlightenment will never become a party to a conception of America as a nation which conceives of its history and its hopes as less broad than those of humanity—let politicians clamor for their own ends as they will.

The other point in the constitution of a genuine American nationalism to which I invite attention is that we have been occupied during the greater part of our history in subduing nature, not one another or other peoples. I once heard two foreign visitors coming from different countries discuss what had been imprest upon them as the chief trait of the American people. One said vigor, youthful and buoyant energy. The other said it was kindness, the disposition to live and let live, the absence of envy at the success of others. I like to think that while both of these ascribed traits have the same cause back of them, the latter statement goes deeper. Not that we have more virtue, native or acquired, than others, but that we have had more room, more opportunity. Consequently, the same conditions which have put a premium upon active and hopeful energy have permitted the kindlier instincts of man to express themselves. The spaciousness of a continent not previously monopolized by man has stimulated vigor and has also diverted activity from the struggle against fellow-man into the struggle against nature. When men make their gains by fighting in common a wilderness, they have not the motive for mutual distrust which comes when they get ahead only by fighting one another. I recently heard a story which seems to me to have something typical about it. Some manufacturers were discussing the problem of labor. They were loud in their complaints. They were bitter against the exactions of unions, and full of tales of an inefficiency which seemed to them calculated. Then one of them said: "Oh, well! Poor devils! They haven't much of a chance and have to do what they can to hold their own. If we were in their place, we should be just the same." And the others nodded assent and the conversation lapst. I call this characteristic, for if there was not an ardent sympathy, there was at least a spirit of toleration and passive recognition.

But with respect to this point as well as with respect to our composite make-up, the situation is changing. We no longer have a large unoccupied continent. Pioneer days are past, and natural resources are possest. There is danger that the same causes which have set the hand of man against his neighbor in other countries will have the same effect here. Instead of sharing in a common fight against nature, we are already starting to fight against one another, class against class, haves against have-nots. The change puts a definite responsibility upon the schools to sustain our true national spirit. The virtues of mutual esteem, of human forbearance, and well-wishing, which in our earlier days were the unconscious products of circumstances, must now be the conscious fruit of an education which forms the deepest springs of character.

Teachers above all others have occasion to be distrest when the earlier idealism of welcome to the opprest is treated as a weak sentimentalism, when sympathy for the unfortunate and those who have not had a fair chance is regarded as a weak indulgence fatal to efficiency. Our traditional disposition in these respects must now become a central motive in public education, not at a matter of condescension or patronizing, but as essential to the maintenance of a truly American spirit. All this puts a responsibility upon the schools which can be met only by widening the scope of educational facilities. The schools have now to make up to the disinherited masses by conscious instruction, by the development of personal power, skill, ability, and initiative, for the loss of external opportunities consequent upon the passing of our pioneer days. Otherwise power is likely to pass more and more into the hands of the wealthy, and we shall end with this same alliance between intellectual and artistic culture and economic power due to riches, which has been the curse of every civilization in the past, and which our fathers in their democratic idealism thought this nation was to put an end to.

Since the idea of the nation is equal opportunity for all, to nationalize education means to use the schools as a means for making this idea effective. There was a time when this could be done more or less well simply by providing schoolhouses, desks, blackboards, and perhaps books. But that day has past. Opportunities can be equalized only as the schools make it their active serious business to enable all alike to become masters of their own industrial fate. That growing movement which is called industrial or vocational education now hangs in the scales. If it is so constructed in practice as to produce merely more competent hands for subordinate clerical and shop positions, if its purpose is shaped to drill boys and girls into certain forms of automatic skill which will make them useful in carrying out the plans of others, it means that, instead of nationalizing education in the spirit of our nation, we have given up the battle, and decided to refeudalize education.

b. Stokely Carmichael and Charles V. Hamilton

The adoption of the concept of Black Power is one of the most legitimate and healthy developments in American politics and race relations in our time. The concept of Black Power speaks to all the needs mentioned in this chapter. It is call for black people in this country to unite, to recognize their heritage, to build a sense of community. It is a call for black people to begin to define their own goals, to lead their own organizations and to support those organizations. It is a call to reject the racist institutions and values of this society.

The concept of Black Power rests on a fundamental premise: *Before a group can enter the open society, it must first close ranks.* By this we mean that group solidarity is necessary before a group can operate effectively from a bargaining position of strength in a pluralistic society. Traditionally, each new ethnic group in this society has found the route to social and political viability through the organization of its own institutions with which to represent its needs within the larger society. Studies in voting behavior specifically, and political behavior generally, have made it clear that politically the American pot has not melted. Italians vote for Rubino over O'Brien; Irish for Murphy over Goldberg, etc. This phenomenon may seem distasteful to some, but it has been and remains today a central fact of the American political system. There are other examples of ways in which groups in the society have remembered their roots and used this effectively in the political arena. Theodore Sorensen describes the politics of foreign aid during the Kennedy Administration in his book *Kennedy:*

> No powerful constituencies or interest groups backed foreign aid. The Marshall Plan at least had appealed to Americans who traced their roots to the Western European nations aided. But there were few voters who identified with India, Colombia or Tanganyika [p. 351].

The extent to which black Americans can and do "trace their roots" to Africa, to that extent will they be able to be more effective on the political scene.

A white reporter set forth this point in other terms when he made the following observation about white Mississippi's manipulation of the anti-poverty program:

> The war on poverty has been predicated on the notion that there is such a thing as a community which can be defined geographically and mobilized for a collective effort to help the poor. This theory has no relationship to reality in the deep South. In every Mississippi county there are two communities. Despite all the pious platitudes of the moderates on both sides, these two communities habitually see their interests in terms of conflict rather than cooperation. Only when the Negro community can muster enough political, economic and professional strength to compete on somewhat equal terms, will Negroes believe in the possibility of true cooperation and whites accept its necessity. En route to integration, the Negro community needs to develop a greater independence—a chance to run its own affairs and not cave in whenever "the man" barks—or so it seems to me, and to most of the knowledgeable people with whom I talked in Mississippi. To OEO, this judgment may sound like black nationalism. . . .[1]

The point is obvious: black people must lead and run their own organizations. Only black people can convey the revolutionary idea— and it is a revolutionary idea—that black people are able to do things themselves. Only they can help create in the community an aroused and continuing black consciousness that will provide the basis for political strength. In the past, white allies have often furthered white supremacy without the whites involved realizing it, or even wanting to do so. Black people must come together and do things for themselves. They must achieve self-identity and self-determination in order to have their daily needs met.

Black Power means, for example, that in Lowndes County, Alabama, a black sheriff can end police brutality. A black tax assessor and tax collector and county board of revenue can lay, collect, and channel tax monies for the building of better roads and schools serving black people. In such areas as Lowndes, where black people have a majority, they will attempt to use power to exercise control. This is what they seek: control. When black people lack a majority, Black Power means proper representation and sharing of control. It means the creation of power bases, of strength, from which black people can press to change local or nation-wide patterns of oppression—instead of from weakness.

It does not mean *merely* putting black faces into office. Black visibility is not Black Power. Most of the black politicians around the country today are not examples of Black Power. The power must be that of a community, and emanate from there. The black politicians

[1] Christopher Jencks, "Accommodating Whites: A New Look at Mississippi," *The New Republic* (April 16, 1966).

must start from there. The black politicians must stop being representatives of "downtown" machines, whatever the cost might be in terms of lost patronage and holiday handouts.

Black Power recognizes—it must recognize—the ethnic basis of American politics as well as the power-oriented nature of American politics. Black Power therefore calls for black people to consolidate behind their own, so that they can bargain from a position of strength. But while we endorse the *procedure* of group solidarity and identity for the purpose of attaining certain goals in the body politic, this does not mean that black people should strive for the same kind of rewards (i.e., end results) obtained by the white society. The ultimate values and goals are not domination or exploitation of other groups, but rather an effective share in the total power of the society.

Nevertheless, some observers have labeled those who advocate Black Power as racists; they have said that the call for self-identification and self-determination is "racism in reverse" or "black supremacy." This is a deliberate and absurd lie. There is no analogy—by any stretch of definition or imagination—between the advocates of Black Power and white racists. Racism is not merely exclusion on the basis of race but exclusion for the purpose of subjugating or maintaining subjugation. The goal of the racists is to keep black people on the bottom, arbitrarily and dictatorially, as they have done in this country for over three hundred years. The goal of black self-determination and black self-identity—Black Power—is full participation in the decision-making processes affecting the lives of black people, and recognition of the virtues in themselves as black people. The black people of this country have not lynched whites, bombed their churches, murdered their children and manipulated laws and institutions to maintain oppression. White racists have. Congressional laws, one after the other, have not been necessary to stop black people from oppressing others and denying others the full enjoyment of their rights. White racists have made such laws necessary. The goal of Black Power is positive and functional to a free and viable society. No white racist can make this claim.

A great deal of public attention and press space was devoted to the hysterical accusation of "black racism" when the call for Black Power was first sounded. A national committee of influential black churchmen affiliated with the National Council of Churches, despite their obvious respectability and responsibility, had to resort to a paid advertisement to articulate their position, while anyone yapping "black racism" made front-page news. In their statement, published in the *New York Times* of July 31, 1966, the churchmen said:

> We, an informal group of Negro churchmen in America, are deeply disturbed about the crisis brought upon our country by historic distortions

of important human realities in the controversy about "black power." What we see shining through the variety of rhetoric is not anything new but the same old problem of power and race which has faced our beloved country since 1619.

. . . The conscience of black men is corrupted because having no power to implement the demands of conscience, the concern for justice in the absence of justice becomes a chaotic self-surrender. Powerlessness breeds a race of beggars. We are faced with a situation where powerless conscience meets conscienceless power, threatening the very foundations of our Nation.

We deplore the overt violence of riots, but we feel it is more important to focus on the real sources of these eruptions. These sources may be abetted inside the Ghetto, but their basic cause lies in the silent and covert violence which white middle class America inflicts upon the victims of the inner city.

. . . In short, the failure of American leaders to use American power to create equal opportunity *in life* as well as *law*, this is the real problem and not the anguished cry for black power.

. . . Without the capacity to participate with power, i.e., to have some organized political and economic strength to really influence people with whom one interacts, integration is not meaningful.

. . . America has asked its Negro citizens to fight for opportunity as *individuals*, whereas at certain points in our history what we have needed most has been opportunity for the *whole group*, not just for selected and approved Negroes.

. . . We must not apologize for the existence of this form of group power, for we have been oppressed as a group and not as individuals. We will not find our way out of that oppression until both we and America accept the need for Negro Americans, as well as for Jews, Italians, Poles, and white Anglo-Saxon Protestants, among others, to have and to wield group power.

It is a commentary on the fundamentally racist nature of this society that the concept of group strength for black people must be articulated—not to mention defended. No other group would submit to being led by others. Italians do not run the Anti-Defamation League of B'nai B'rith. Irish do not chair Christopher Columbus Societies. Yet when black people call for black-run and all-black organizations, they are immediately classed in a category with the Ku Klux Klan. This is interesting and ironic, but by no means surprising: the society does not expect black people to be able to take care of their business, and there are many who prefer it precisely that way.

In the end, we cannot and shall not offer any guarantees that Black Power, if achieved, would be non-racist. No one can predict human behavior. Social change always has unanticipated consequences. If black racism is what the larger society fears, we cannot help them. We can only state what we hope will be the result, given the fact that the present situation is unacceptable and that we have no real alternative but to work for Black Power. The final truth is that the white society is not entitled to reassurances, even if it were possible to offer them.

. . .

Next, we must deal with the term "integration." According to its advocates, social justice will be accomplished by "integrating the Negro into the mainstream institutions of the society from which he has been traditionally excluded." This concept is based on the assumption that there is nothing of value in the black community and that little of value could be created among black people. The thing to do is siphon off the "acceptable" black people into the surrounding middle-class white community.

The goals of integrationists are middle-class goals, articulated primarily by a small group of Negroes with middle-class aspirations or status. Their kind of integration has meant that a few blacks "make it," leaving the black community, sapping it of leadership potential and know-how. . . . [T]hose token Negroes—absorbed into a white mass— are of no value to the remaining black masses. They become meaningless show-pieces for a conscience-soothed white society. Such people will state that they would prefer to be treated "only as individuals, not as Negroes"; that they "are not and should not be preoccupied with race." This is a totally unrealistic position. In the first place, black people have not suffered as individuals but as members of a group; therefore, their liberation lies in group action. This is why SNCC—and the concept of Black Power—affirms that helping *individual* black people to solve their problems on an *individual* basis does little to alleviate the mass of black people. Secondly, while color blindness *may* be a sound goal ultimately, we must realize that race is an overwhelming fact of life in this historical period. There is no black man in this country who can live "simply as a man." His blackness is an ever-present fact of this racist society, whether he recognizes it or not. It is unlikely that this or the next generation will witness the time when race will no longer be relevant in the conduct of public affairs and in public policy decision-making. To realize this and to attempt to deal with it does not make one a racist or overly preoccupied with race; it puts one in the forefront of a significant *struggle*. If there is no intense struggle today, there will be no meaningful results tomorrow.

"Integration" as a goal today speaks to the problem of blackness not only in an unrealistic way but also in a despicable way. It is based on complete acceptance of the fact that in order to have a decent house or education, black people must move into a white neighborhood or send their children to a white school. This reinforces, among both black and white, the idea that "white" is automatically superior and "black" is by definition inferior. For this reason, "integration" is a subterfuge for the maintenance of white supremacy. It allows the nation to focus on a handful of Southern black children who get into white schools at a great price, and to ignore the ninety-four percent who are left in un-improved all-black schools. Such situations will not change until black people become equal in a way that means something, and integration ceases to be a one-way street. Then integration does not mean draining skills and energies from the black ghetto into white neighborhoods. To sprinkle black children among white pupils in outlying schools is at best a stop-gap measure. The goal is not to take black children out of the black community and expose them to white middle-class values; the goal is to build and strengthen the black community.

"Integration" also means that black people must give up their identity, deny their heritage. We recall the conclusion of Killian and Grigg: "At the present time, integration as a solution to the race problem demands that the Negro foreswear his identity as a Negro." The fact is that integration, as traditionally articulated, would abolish the black community. The fact is that what must be abolished is not the black community, but the dependent colonial status that has been inflicted upon it.

The racial and cultural personality of the black community must be preserved and that community must win its freedom while preserving its cultural integrity. Integrity includes a pride—in the sense of self-acceptance, not chauvinism—in being black, in the historical attainments and contributions of black people. No person can be healthy, complete and mature if he must deny a part of himself; this is what "integration" has required thus far. This is the essential difference between integration as it is currently practiced and the concept of Black Power.

PEDAGOGICAL MODEL:
The People as Teacher

TECHNICAL AND SOCIAL QUALIFICATIONS
OF THE RULER-TEACHER
George A. Coe

"We, The People," as Educator

If the sovereign were an absolute monarch or a dictator, he could fulfil his function as educator with relative ease. For teaching would take the form of propaganda, pure and simple. The objectives would be fixed by a dictum from the head of the state; the specific content and methods would be found by psychological research and testing.[1] Teachers would follow a straight line, looking neither to the right hand nor to the left for problems or issues. The handling of human nature in pupils would, of course present secondary problems, but never the primary puzzle of tangled values in the state or in society. If the sovereign should discover such problems, and change his mind, an order would go down the line to modify the system accordingly.

But when sovereignty inheres in the people—in the very procession that is moving into and out of the schools—then the teacher and the taught, the ruler and the ruled, are not two but one, and education becomes a part of the process whereby the ruler-teacher makes up his mind and changes it. Propaganda, which presumes that some one rules without obeying while others obey without ruling, is now out of place.

We have arrived at the difficult notion that the whole people is teacher of the whole people through some of the same people to whom are committed special educational functions. These special functions are distributed among officials in a sort of hierarchical order. The people

---

From George A. Coe, *Education for Citizenship: The Sovereign State as Ruler and a Teacher* (N.Y.: Charles Scribner's Sons, 1932), pp. 100–103, 111–15. Copyright 1932. Reprinted with permission of the Charles Scribner's Sons.

---

[1] By the way, how and to what extent does our American movement for tests and measurements reflect an educational standpoint different from that of an absolute monarchy?

adopt a constitution and elect the legislature; the legislature provides the legal framework and the necessary compulsion (of pupils at one extreme, and of taxable property at the other); school departments and boards administer the laws by establishing particular schools and by managing the funds for administering them; teachers by profession, at last, deal with pupils face to face. All these are organs through which "we, the people," carry on the education of "us, the people." Organs, not tools, for the "we" is there in every one of them, and every one, even the pupil, wields original discretion. The old conception of the master-and-servant relation does not apply. Indeed, we are approaching a stage —the adult education movement—at which the adults who through their votes have legal control of the school teacher will in large numbers come to him for instruction concerning their own functions as rulers!

In general, we may expect the educational consciousness to become more and more specific as we move from public opinion and majority votes of the populace to legislatures, then to boards, and finally to teachers. Increasing focalization of function is obvious in matters that concern the technic of teaching. Here, clearly, legislatures are not within the sphere of their competence as educators, and boards of education, if they are wise, will in this respect learn from the teachers whom they employ. But the relation is not merely that of client to technician. At every level of authority direct knowing, feeling, and judging with respect to public interests must be assumed to be a part of the educator's job. In this respect, too, we may look for increasing focalization of function as we proceed from the general public, through legislatures and boards, to the teacher who is in daily contact with pupils.

The legislature, then, needs to be thought of as educator, not merely as law-maker, and the board of education also as educator, not merely as administrator of school laws and funds. Both have discretionary authority in education, which means that they can legally do what is either foolish or wise. The question is, What is the special competence of each? What range of initiative and of discretion will wise legislatures and boards assume for themselves, and what will they pass on to teachers?

The base line for an answer to this question lies in the fact that teachers cannot effectively produce good citizenship through teaching unless they themselves not only know, feel, and judge public interests, but also draw pupils into a fellowship of such knowledge, appreciation, and judgment. This is the job of the citizen-schoolmaster. He is, indeed, a proxy of the public, but a proxy with discretionary powers that permeate not only methods, but also the content of instruction, and even the objectives of the school. The scope of his discretion, like that of the legislature and of the board of education, cannot be strictly defined. The schoolmaster must be trusted, not merely as a techician in the narrow

sense, but also as a citizen, and in fact a more-than-ordinary citizen. He
is to hold himself responsible for expertness in citizenship. He is not
to be an echo of the populace, but rather an incarnation of the better
self of the populace, or—if you prefer—a leader in the expedition of
civilization.

But does the sovereign people desire this leadership? Does it recognize any such better self, and will it tolerate and even pay for the judgments upon itself that this view of the public schools implies? A notion
is floating around that leadership of the masses towards any excellence
must be bestowed from outside, that it cannot arise from within. To this
a retort might be made that every individual of "light and leading" has
sprung, as a matter of fact, from the mass—he has not come to us from
some other planet—and that qualities like his own continually sprout
from the main stock of humanity. What is equally important, within the
mass there is some spontaneous and general recognition of excellence,
together with capacity for growth in appreciation. A school teacher who
is known to be inferior in intelligence or character to the average of
his community would not be tolerated; he must be above the average
in order to be acceptable. Any one who understands parents knows that
they are willing—the generality of them—to have the schools uphold
standards that condemn their own habitual conduct. Indeed, the schools
are expected (whether wisely so or not) to be silent about many current
faults of individuals, of society, and of the state, lest the young should
take these faults as normal! The public schools are society implicitly
accusing itself, and explicitly seeking to transcend itself.

. . .

Civic Intelligence in the Training of Teachers

The following question was put to the head of a large training
school in one of our great cities: "What preparation are your students
here receiving for handling the technical aspects of character education?"
The reply was substantially as follows: "I regret to say, scarcely any at
all. We endeavor to maintain among our students a high standard of
conduct and character, and in this I believe that we succeed. But, as far
as instruction is concerned, we are obliged to keep our noses to the
grindstone of an official syllabus of studies." This was an institution for
undergraduate instruction, no doubt a typical one.

In institutions for graduate students of education a somewhat less
rudimentary state of affairs is likely to be found. For study of the philosophy of education, or of method in teaching, or of the life of children
and youth, commonly opens at least some questions as to how character

is formed and how personality becomes socialized. But as yet, even in graduate schools, two essentials remain unassured. A citizen's outlook and inlook with respect to the present conditions of our society—such intelligence as defines the problems into which young citizens are about to move—has no such prominence as the more mechanical aspects of teaching-technic and administration-technic. In the second place, there is slight assurance that present experience within the society that constitutes a teachers' college will be of the American-citizenship type. This point is so important that a sharp word concerning it will not be out of place.

Even in graduate schools or colleges of education, authority is usually of the overhead variety, an obvious hang-over from monarchical, aristocratic, and paternalistic traditions. The students, though they are full-fledged citizens, are not represented in the faculty nor in the board of control by delegates of their own choosing; no, they have no representation whatever. Everything is matured—rather, supposed to be! before it is handed out to the students; they are still school children in the old sense of the term, that is, the sense that it had before even elementary schools adopted the principle of self-government.

Does this appear to be an exaggeration? If so, consider this fact: Institutions of this class can be found in which the board of control hands down rules for the conduct of students in the halls and on the grounds of the college! It would be interesting to know in just how many teachers' colleges the students exercise the prerogatives of citizens to anything like the extent that pupils in well-managed high schools exercise them.

What should be expected, of course, is no mere repetition of practice in even the best of the lower schools, but advanced practice upon the same principles. Students in teachers' colleges should have a hand in determining the curriculum of their college, the budget, appointments to the faculty, and relations to the legislature, to donors, and to the school system. That is, these young men and women, who are destined to be leaders in the making of citizens, should have experience, within their own sphere, as makers of the American state.

What has been said concerning training schools and teachers' colleges applies in principle to departments of education in colleges and universities. Never yet have the presumptions of democracy been accepted or even understood in these institutions. Even state universities, which supposably have a direct and conscious political function, are not, as they should be, junior states within the state. Consequently, departments of education naturally become vocational in a narrow sense, the sense, namely, of preparing young people to make their living by teaching, and the sign and seal of competency is a license to teach.

The Nation, as Both Ruler and Ruled, Both Teacher and Taught

To many persons, no doubt, deliberate self-education by a democratic society is chimerical. Can one rise by pulling upon one's boot-straps? The tradition of the schools presents the picture of a ruling class, the teachers, imposing their wisdom upon a ruled class, the pupils. Similarly, wisdom in a statesman traditionally consists, in part, in making the masses accept what they do not choose nor understand. Indeed, what is called statesmanship involves having two sets of principles, one set avowed only in inner state circles (such principles as appear now and then when diplomatic correspondence or hitherto secret state documents are published), the other set made up of reasons or incentives offered to the people to induce them to accept the consequences of designs that are only partly disclosed. Secret diplomacy, and secrecy in the management of domestic concerns are still in the order of the day, even in governments called popular. Who does not know that partly platforms aim at popularity rather than at true self-disclosure? Who does not know that much legislation and much administration have an esoteric side? The President of the United States himself, besides keeping some affairs of state secret not only from the people but also from the Congress, speaks in two voices to the public through the press. In one voice he states what he is willing to have printed as his words, therefore what he is willing to stand by; in the other voice he says what he is willing or desirous to have printed, but not as his words, for he may have occasion to repudiate them! So full of the duplicity of monarchs is our own political management.

This duplicity affects our education for citizenship. Not yet do we really intend that the young shall come to full political maturity; not yet do we effectively believe that the people can manage themselves through their own intelligence. That is, not yet have we grasped the political and the educational significance of the fact that here is a nation that is at the same time both ruler and ruled, both teacher and taught.

A man cannot reach the sky by pulling upon his boot-straps, it is true, but a bird can fly by pulling upon certain of its own tendons. Capacity to aspire and to make aspiration effective is not a class-prerogative, but a prerogative of the whole people. We can rise by virtue of our own inherent qualities; we do not have to be lifted, and we have no historical reason for trusting any class as authoritative lifters. Education for citizenship, accordingly, can become a process whereby, through cooperation of pupils, teachers, governmental agencies, and the public, the state continually rises into new life.

Part V

PROGRESSIVISM

Introduction

The ideology of Progressivism emerged as a social force during the later decades of the nineteenth century. America had witnessed the growth of the industrial system, accompanied by an influx of immigrants and increasing urbanization. Confronted by vast social, political, and economic problems, the progressivists sought to ameliorate conditions by reforming various societal institutions. Structural changes, they believed, would adapt the system to the ever-changing social milieu and make it responsive to the needs of the citizens. Institutions thus could be "humanized."

The progressive movement did not intend to destroy either capitalism or technology. Even the movement's most vociferous members, the "muckrakers," would have agreed with President Theodore Roosevelt's oft-quoted assertion that the progressivists were not against wealth, but misconduct. By enhancing the power of the government, the progressivists sought to control the nearly anarchical laissez-faire capitalism of the industrial Barons and thus to create a more rational and humane social order. Enamored of the increasing achievements of science and technology, they wished to apply similar techniques to solving society's pressing social problems.

Within traditional political categories, the progressivists would be classified as liberals. Rejecting both the "rugged individualism" of Social Darwinism and the revolutionary class conflict of Marxism, they advocated social change in a planned, organized, and orderly way. Social progress must be evolutionary and must be achieved by working democratically within the system to change it. In short, the progressivists were practical idealists when it came to social issues.

Adhering to the old adage that moderation is the mother of virtue, progressivists dismiss both the rigid formalism of Puritanism and the rebellious individualism of Romanticism. They believe that Puritanism boarders on tyranny, Romanticism on anarchy. Questions of value and ethical decisions may be open to individual response, but choices must be made within the social context with careful consideration given to the consequences of one's decision. Because man is by nature a social animal, the progressivists assert, the consequences of an individual's actions often effect other individuals. For this reason many decisions should be group decisions.

Coming largely from the middle and upper-middle classes, the Progressivists could afford the luxury of social liberalism and activism. Their activism, however, was generally of the "armchair" variety, for they used their middle-class skills of writing and organizing and their middle-class positions in journalism, law, and education to further the cause of civil liberties and social change.

In the field of education, progressivists provided the major impetus for a revolt against formalism and tradition. They rejected both faculty psychology and stimulus-response behaviorism. Consequently, they dismissed rote memorization, repetitive skill practices, and rigidly controlled structural learning. By placing an emphasis upon learning rather than teaching, on the child rather than the subject, they sought to create a meaningful education system directed to satisfying individualized needs and geared to industrialized interests. To facilitate the achievement of these aims the progressivists attempted to integrate the school and the community and to provide a more permissive atmosphere for learning based upon cooperative group endeavors. Education, they believed, should not be a preparation for life, but life itself.

The progressive movement that emerged at the turn of the century was shattered by America's entry into World War I, a subject about which members of the movement vehemently disagreed. The quasi missionary zeal of some of the progressivists and much of their rhetoric about social reform were mobilized for the war effort, and when the war and President Wilson were repudiated, so was the reform movement. Seeking a "return to normalcy," the American citizenry elected Warren G. Harding and plunged into the "Roaring Twenties," a decade characterized by an apolitical atmosphere in which many individuals pursued the affluent life of personal pleasures.

In this context American intellectuals generally showed little interest in political and economic issues; the major thrust of their criticism was directed toward the culture of puritan Babbittry. Many reformers, disillusioned with social activism, became interested in inner freedom, creative self-expression, and the psychological theories of Sigmund Freud. It was widely felt that social reform, if it were to be accomplished, would result from personal liberation.

The spirit of the times obviously influenced the progressive education movement. Progressivists ignored the political dimension of Dewey's thought and focused upon his concern for child development. Harold Rugg and Anne Shumaker captured the new direction of Progressivism with their book *The Child-Centered School*. According to this theory, the child should be permitted to engage in a variety of artistic endeavors that would promote creative self-expression.

The twenties ended with the Great Depression. In an attempt to deal with the resulting socioeconomic chaos, George Counts, in a pamphlet entitled *Dare the Schools Build a New Social Order?* expressed the sentiments of a growing number of Progressive educators. He, along with other social reconstructionists, criticized the progressive movement in education for its lack of interest in economic and political issues, and demanded that progressive educators return to the social and political emphasis of Dewey.

The third branch of Progressivism in education emerged during the mid 1940s. As America shifted rapidly from a production economy to a consumption economy with an increasing demand for individuals involved in sales and services, the blue-collar urban dweller was replaced by the white-collar suburbanite. Progressive educators met this social change by developing what they called the "life adjustment program" which was designed to prepare individuals for this new life style. It emphasized group dynamics, personality development, and vocational guidance.

In the 1950s Progressivism was severely castigated by the adherents of both classicism (Arthur Bestor) and Scientism (Admiral Rickover). In the next decade, however, Progressivism reappeared as a significant force in American education. As middle-class criticism against traditional education increases, the ideology of Progressivism continues to gain adherents. Recently, for example, progressivists have been instrumental in popularizing the concepts of open classrooms, student participation, team teaching, encounter groups, and many versions of "free" (or "new") schools.

The good life envisioned by the progressivists was a life governed by reason and social responsibility. Their perception of this life, as George E. Mowry points out in the first article of this section, was greatly influenced by their middle-class WASP (white Anglo-Saxon Protestant) origins. Although restricted to the progressivists of California, Mowry's research aptly depicts many of the elements shared by all adherents to the ideology of Progressivism; they are individuals of moderate persuasion, interested in social reform based upon a flexible, secular morality.

The Creed, represented by the essay of John Dewey, expresses the progressivist's faith in reason and education. By fostering an environment conducive to individual growth through cooperative endeavors and meaningful experiences, the schools, Dewey argues, will serve to promote social progress. Furthermore, Dewey's article illustrates the compatibility of Progressivism with the ideologies of Scientism and Educationism.

The first three selections in the section entitled "An Historical Perspective" reflect the three major foci of Progressivism in the field of education. Excerpts from *The Child-Centered School* by Harold Rugg and Anne Shumaker express the beliefs of those interested in fostering the child's creative self-expression. The criticism of this approach is illustrated in the selection from George Counts' *Dare the Schools Build a New Social Order?* Here we see the social reconstructionist's emphasis on the school's role in social and political reform. The third selection, taken from the *Report of the National Conference on Life Adjustment Education*, exemplifies the concerns of those Progressivists interested in the education of the "forgotten majority." Life adjustment education was designed to prepare the "average" student for life in the ever-growing world of the white-collar worker.

In the final selection in this segment, Mario D. Fantini, an outspoken advocate of Progressivism, contrasts the traditional concept of education (closed classroom) with the Progressivist's concept of the "open classroom." The essay illustrates many of the fundamental elements in the ideology of Progressivism: the teacher as a facilitator; a curriculum comprised of cooperative, group projects; a program based upon process, creativity, and growth; and the school as a miniature society

The last two essays in Part V describe the role of the teacher as perceived by adherents to the ideology of Progressivism. From this perspective the teacher functions as a facilitator—an individual who plans, organizes, and manages the learning process. Rather than being an individual who transfers knowledge to the students, the teacher facilitates the cooperative group enterprise commonly referred to as education.

AN ANALYTICAL VIEW: A Brief Survey

THE CALIFORNIA PROGRESSIVE AND HIS RATIONALE: A STUDY IN MIDDLE CLASS POLITICS
George E. Mowry

Considering the fact that the origins of early twentieth-century progressivism lay in the agrarian Middle West, California in 1905 did not seem to be the logical place for the projection of the doctrines first associated with the names of William J. Bryan, Robert M. La Follette, George W. Norris, and Albert B. Cummins. For in almost every important particular, the state offered more contrasts to the land of William Allen White than it did similarities. As opposed to the relatively homogenous population of the corn and wheat belt states, there existed in California a veritable welter of first and second generation immigrants. Contrasted with the middle western one-farm, one-family type of staple agriculture, the California countryside was characterized by the tremendous holdings of corporations and cattle and lumber men on the one hand, and by the smaller but intensively cultivated fruit and vegetable plats on the other. Irrigation on the latter was but one factor in producing extremely high cost land as well as a high rate of absentee ownership and an itinerant labor force. By 1905 factories in the fields had already made their appearance south of the Tehachapi and in the San Joaquin and lesser valleys of the state.

By 1910, 60 per cent of California's population was urban, and to make the comparison with the progressive Middle West a little sharper, almost one half of the state's population in the same year lived in the three metropolitan counties of San Francisco, Los Angeles, and Alameda. Moreover, throughout these urban districts organized labor was on the move as it was in few other places in the nation. After the general strike of 1901, San Francisco was often called "the most closed shop city in the

From George E. Mowry, "The California Progressive and His Rationale: A Study in Middle Class Politics," *Mississippi Valley Historical Review*, XXXVI (September, 1949), 239–50. Reprinted by permission of the author and the Organization of American Historians.

country." And while Harrison Gary Otis and the Los Angeles Merchants and Manufacturers Association had managed to preserve an open shop town, organized labor never gave up its fight to break through this antiunion domination. In fact, one of the two basic state-wide conflicts in California from 1905 to 1916 was the continuous and often bloody struggle between organized capital and organized labor.

The second great state-wide clash of interests in California during these years was the one between the Southern Pacific Railroad and the state's farmers, shippers, merchants, and the ratepaying public. Until Hiram Johnson's victory in 1910, the one constant and almost omnipotent factor in California politics was the railroad. So deep were the tentacles of the "Octopus" sunk into the commonwealth that its agents even selected the receiving surgeons of city hospitals to insure favorable medical evidence whenever accidents occurred on the company's property. During the years before 1910, numerous economic and political groups had fought the railroad. But through its own powerful political machine, through extensive nonpartisan corruption, and through careful nurture of the state's widespread gambling, liquor, and vice interests, the Southern Pacific weathered every popular storm. Until 1910 its rule was disputed only in a few local communities and in San Francisco.

In the Paris of the West, as San Francisco proudly styled itself, the Union Labor party ruled from 1901 to 1911. But far from contributing to honest, efficient, and responsible government, the Union Labor machine, under the able but cancerously corrupt Abraham Reuf, turned out to be a partner in pelf with the railroad. Often for a cash consideration Reuf's "pack of hounds" supplied the votes for the continuing control of the Southern Pacific. The only other force in the state, with the exception of the rising progressives, capable of voicing much protest was the Socialist party. At the crest of their power in 1911, the California Socialists elected a mayor of Berkeley and came within an eyelash of winning control of the city of Los Angeles. But for one reason or another the Socialists were never able to summon up the strength to win a major victory, and it remained for the progressives alone to challenge the Southern Pacific machine.

Just what was a California progressive before he took office in 1910 and before power and the exigencies of politics altered his beliefs? What were his springs of action, his personal aspirations, and his concepts of what constituted the good society? The rest of this paper is devoted to an attempt to answer these questions in the hope that it may shed some light on the origins of progressivism, not only in California but in the rest of the nation as well, and perhaps even direct a few faint rays on the class structuring of American politics before 1917.

Fortunately, the men who first organized the California progressive movement were both literate and historically minded. The nine solid collections of personal manuscripts they so considerately left behind them, the diaries, documents, and innumerable published articles afford the historian perhaps an unrivaled opportunity in recent American history to inquire into the origins of a grass roots movement. Moreover, this group was small. Fewer than a hundred men attended the two state-wide progressive conferences in 1907 and 1909 before victory swelled the number of the organization's would-be leaders. Of this number, the author has been able to discover biographical data on forty-seven men, which produces in total a striking picture of similarity in background, economic base, and social attitudes. Compositely, the California progressive was a young man often less than forty years old. A majority of them was born in the Middle West, principally in Indiana, Illinois, Wisconsin, and Iowa. A good minority was native to the state. Almost all carried north European names and many of them, with two notable exceptions, were of old American stock.

The long religious hand of New England rested heavily upon California progressivism as it has on so many American movements. Of the twenty-two progressives indicating a religious affiliation in their biographies, seven were Congregationalists, two were Unitarians, and four were Christian Scientists. Three of every four had a college education, and three of the group had studied in European universities. Occupationally, the California progressive held a significant niche in the American economic structure. In the sample obtained, there were seventeen attorneys, fourteen journalists, eleven independent businessmen and real estate operators, three doctors, and three bankers. At least one half of the journalists owned their own papers or worked for a family enterprise, and the lawyers, with two exceptions, were not practicing politicians. In the entire group apparently only two had any connection with a large industrial or financial corporation save for the ownership of shares. Obviously this was a group of traditional small independent free enterprisers and professional men.

While not wealthy, the average California progressive was, in the jargon of his day, "well fixed." He was more often than not a Mason, and almost invariably a member of his town's chamber of commerce. Finally, by all available evidence he usually had been, at least until 1900, a conservative Republican, satisfied with William McKinley and his Republican predecessors.

Naturally, some fundamental questions arise about these fortunate sons of the upper middle class. Inheriting a secure place in society, earning a reasonably good living and certainly not radical by temperament, what prompted their political revolt and what did they want? The answer to the first of these questions, of course, is clear. The California progressive reacted politically when he felt himself and his group being hemmed in and his place in society threatened by the monopolistic corporation on one side and organized labor and socialism on the other. Proof for this general conclusion is not hard to find. The earliest manifestation of what later became progressivism in California is apparent in two local movements starting in 1906, one aimed against the Southern Pacific political machine in Los Angeles and the other against the control of the Union Labor party in San Francisco. From that time until victory in 1910, the progressive literature was full of criticism for both politically organized capital and politically organized labor.

The adverb "politically" in the last paragraph is important, for the progressive revolt was not alone a matter of economics. It might be pointed out that progressivism arose in an extremely prosperous period in California, and that the men who really organized the movement were not employers of any significance. In addition, far from beggaring these lawyers, journalists, and real estate operators, a good case can be made out that the Southern Pacific Railroad actually befriended many of them economically. Moreover, the California progressives never attacked the corporate form of business organization or the labor union as such. And although they believed that the closed shop was "anti-social, dangerous and intrinsically wrong," many of them repeatedly went to the union's defense when industry organized to break the unions and create open shops.

"Modern politics," Henry Adams wrote in his *Education,* "is a struggle not of men but of forces. The men become every year more and more creatures of force massed about central power houses." With the struggle for power between capital and labor penetrating to almost every level of California life in the period, and with the individual more and more ignored, the California progressive was increasingly sensitive to that drift and increasingly determined to stop it if possible. This was obvious in the progressive obsession with the nightmare of class consciousness and class rule. "Class government is always bad government," the progressive Los Angeles *Express* vehemently declared as it exclaimed that "unions had no more right to usurp the management of public affairs than had the public service corporations." Chester Rowell, probably the most intelligent of the California progressives, went on to gloss that statement. "Class prejudice among the business men," he wrote, "excuses bribery and sanctifies lawlessness and disorder among labor. When the spectre of class rule is raised, then all questions of truth, right, and policy disappear, and the contest is no longer over what shall be the government but wholly who shall be it." This class spirit on both sides, the editor of the Fresno *Republican* lamented, "is destroying American liberty." When it became predominant he predicted American institutions would have to be changed. "For upon that evil day reform ends and nothing but revolution is possible."

Clearly what troubled these independent progressives about both organized capital and labor was not alone a matter of economics but included questions of high politics, as well as group prestige, group morality, and group power. Involved also was the rising threat to an old American way of life which they represented and which they enthusiastically considered good.

The progressives were members of an old group in America. Whether businessmen, successful farmers, professional people, or politicians, they had engaged in extremely individualistic pursuits and had since the decline of the colonial aristocracy supplied most of the nation's intellectual, moral, and political leadership. Still confident that they possessed most of society's virtues, the California progressives were acutely aware in 1905 that many of society's rewards and badges of merit were going elsewehere. Although finely educated, they were all but excluded from politics unless they accepted either corporate or labor domination, a thing they were exceedingly loath to do. Their church, their personal morality, and their concept of law, they felt, were demeaned by the crude power struggle between capital and labor. Before the days of the Rotarians and kindred organizations they were excluded from, or did not care to participate in, either the Union League Club or the union labor hall.

On the defensive for the first time since the disappearance of the old aristocracy, this class of supreme individualists rationally enough developed a group consciousness themselves. Although generally overlooked by the historian, this consciousness had already evolved among some farming elements in the Populist period. Nothing else can be concluded from the words of the official organ of the Michigan State Farmers' Alliance. "It has been truly said," remarked that paper, "that the People's Party is the logical and only nucleus for every element of the American population that stands for social stability and constitutional rights. It is the bulwark against anarchy of the upper and lower scum of society." Now in the twentieth century, flanked by organized labor on the one side and organized capital on the other, the urban California progressives took up that song. Their letters, journals, and speeches are full of the phrases, "Our crowd," "the better element," and "the good people of the state." Even their political enemies recognized their separateness as indicated by the names they conferred upon them. The phrases "Goo-goo" and "Our Set" dripped with ridicule. But they also indicated an awareness of the progressives' claim to ethical and political superiority. Finally, no clearer expression of the progressives' self-confidence in their own moral elevation and their contempt for the classes above and below them can be found than that in an editorial of their state-wide organ, the *California Weekly.* "Nearly all the problems which vex society," this illuminating item ran, "have their sources above or below the middle class man. From above come the problems of predatory wealth. . . . From below come the problems of poverty and of pigheaded and of brutish criminality." Despite the fact that it was made up of extremely individualistic elements, this was unmistakably an expression of a social group on the march.

The California progressive, then, was militantly opposed to class control and class consciousness when it emanated from either below or above him. This was his point of opposition. What was his positive creed? In the first place this "rank individualist," as he gladly styled himself, was in most cases an extremely religious man. His mind was freighted with problems of morality, his talk shot full of biblical allusions. He often thought of the political movement he had started as a part of the "Religion Forward Movement." As early as 1903 Arthur J. Pillsbury, who was later to become a leading progressive, praised Theodore Roosevelt for coming nearer "to exemplifying the New England conscience in government than any other president in recent times."

But if the religion of the California progressive was old American in its form, much of its content was a product of his recent past. Gone was the stern God of the Puritan, the abiding sense of tragedy, and the inherent evilness of man. As William Allen White later wrote, the cult of the hour was "to believe in the essential nobility of man and the wisdom of God." With an Emersonian optimism, the California progressive believed that evil perished and good would triumph. Under the influence of Darwinism, the rising social sciences, and a seemingly benign world, the progressive had traded some of his old mystical religion for a new social faith. He was aware that evil still existed, but it was a man-made thing and upon earth. And what man created he could also destroy. For the then present sinful condition of man was the result of his conditioning. As Fremont Older's San Francisco *Bulletin* editorialized, "the basic idea behind this age of liberalism is the simple one that all men, prisoners and free, rich and poor are basically alike in spirit. The difference usually lies in what happens to them." And from that, one could conclude that when all men were given justice most of them would return justice to society. The progressive, then, not only wanted to abolish a supernatural hell; he was intent upon secularizing heaven.

There were, of course, individual variations from these generalizations. Chester Rowell, for one, while agreeing that men should not be treated as free moral agents, protested against considering them as "mere creatures of environment." "If we try to cure the trouble by curing the environment," Rowell argued, "we shall never go far enough, for however much we protect men from temptation there will be some left and men will fall to that. . . . Dealing with society the task is to amend the system. But dealing with the individual man the task is to reiterate forever, 'thou shall not steal' and tolerate no exceptions." But Rowell was more of a child of his age than even he himself realized. Despite his strictures on the sinfulness of man, one found him writing later that William H. Taft's peace treaties made international war impossible because "the moral influence on nations (for peace) would be tantamount to compulsion."

"The way to have a golden age," one progressive novelist wrote, "is to elect it by an Australian ballot." This was an extreme affirmation of democracy, but it followed logically from the progressive belief in the fundamental goodness of the individual. For according to progressive thought, behind every political question was a moral question whose answer "could safely be sought in the moral law." Since all men were moral agents, then public opinion was the final distillate of moral law. "It was a jury that can not be fixed," according to Lincoln Steffens, and indeed to some progressives, "God moving among men." Thus Charles D. Willard objected to Theodore Roosevelt's characterization of democracy as just a means to an end. To Willard democracy was a positive moral force in operation, a good in itself. "It is," he wrote, "a soul satisfying thing."

Back in the 1890's Senator John J. Ingalls of Kansas had remarked that "the purification of politics is an iridescent dream." Dream or not, that was one of the major goals of the California progressive a decade later. There was but one law for him—that of the churchgoing middle class—and he was convinced that it should be applied equally to the home, to government, and occasionally even to business. It was in this spirit that Hiram Johnson admonished his followers to forget how to make men richer and concentrate on how to make them better. This attitude helps to explain much of the progressive interest in sumptuary legislation. Individualism was a sacred thing as long as it was moral individualism; otherwise it needed to be corrected. Thus the progressive proposals for the abolition of prize fighting, "a form of social debauchery," gambling, slang, "since it is a coverup for profanity," prostitution, and the liquor traffic. And thus their demands for the censorship of literature, the drama, and social dancing.

In protest against these "holier than thou people" among his fellow progressives, Charles J. McClatchey, owner of the Sacramento *Bee,* wrote that he was his "brother's keeper only in so far as I should set him a good example." And though most progressives vehemently denied the full import of this statement when applied to morality, the majority of them was not in complete disagreement with McClatchey's views when they were applied to economics. Good Christian as he was, and on the whole benevolent, the California progressive did not quarrel with the doctrine of wardship provided it was not pushed too far. Thus he stood ready in 1910 to protect obviously handicapped individuals. And he was ready and even eager to eradicate what he called "special privilege," which to his mind was the fundamental factor in limiting opportunity for the man on the bottom to make his way economically upward. A few individuals on the left of the movement, like Congressman William Kent, felt that soon "property rights were going to tumble about the heads of the men who had built themselves pyramids of money in a desert of want and suffering." And Older raised the disturbing question of why men should be paid fortunes who had been lucky enough to be born with brains or in fortunate environments. One might as well go back to the feudal system, Older answered himself, because there was no more personal merit "in having talent than in having a noble lineage." But for the most part, the progressive majority was content with the basic concepts of the economic system under which 1910 American capitalism awarded its profits and pains.

What the progressive did object to in the year of his triumph was not 1910 capitalism as such but rather the ideological, moral, and political manifestations arising from that system. He was confident, at least in 1910, that there was not an inevitable causal relation between them. And he felt confident that he could cure these ills of society through the political method and through preaching and legislating morality.

The California progressive, then, wanted to preserve the fundamental pattern of twentieth-century industrial society at the same time he sought to blot out the rising clash of economic groups, and for that matter, the groups themselves as conscious economic and political entities. But he sought to do all this, at least before he had actually taken power, without profound economic reform. "The people," Rowell wrote sometime after the sweeping progressive victory in 1910, "elected Governor Johnson to get moral and political reform." The word "economic" was significantly absent from the statement.

From today's dark vantage point, the progressive aim of a capitalist commonwealth,

> Where none were for a class and all were for the state,
> Where the rich man helped the poor and the poor man loved the great,

may seem incredibly naïve. His stress on individualism in a maturing industrial economy was perhaps basically archaic. His refusal or inability to see the connection between the economic institutions and the rising class consciousness indicated a severe case of social myopia. His hopes to avert class strife by political and moral reform alone were scarcely realistic. And paradoxical in extreme was his antipathy to the class consciousness of organized capital and labor without his being aware of his own intense group loyalties.

When the California progressives confidently took control of the state in 1910, the road ahead was uncertain indeed. What, for example, would happen to the fundamental beliefs of this group if they found their ends could not be achieved without substantial economic reform, or, if in spite of their efforts, labor through one program or another threatened their economic and political estate, or if many of them became economically and psychologically absorbed by the advancing corporate system, or again in a less prosperous age than 1910, if the clash between economic groups for a livelihood created an intense social friction? Would their moral calculus, their spirit of benevolence, their faith in men, and their reverence for democracy still persist? The answers to these questions, of course, lay beyond 1910 and belong to another story, another chapter.

But the composite California progressive in 1910 was perhaps the best his economic and social group produced. He was educated, intelligent, able. A man of unquestioned sincerity and public integrity, he was also benevolently aware of the underprivileged groups around him. Devoted to the extension of political democracy and civil rights, he stood as a worthy representative of that long historical lineage of Americans who had dreamed and worked for a better commonwealth. If such a small group is ever able to amend or to alter a little the drift of society, the California progressive's chances seemed better than an even bet.

THE CREED: Progressivist Admonitions

MY PEDAGOGIC CREED
John Dewey

Article I—What Education Is

I believe that all education proceeds by the participation of the individual in the social consciousness of the race. This process begins unconsciously almost at birth, and is continually shaping the individual's powers, saturating hs consciousness, forming his habits, training his ideas, and arousing his feelings and emotions. Through this unconscious education the individual gradually comes to share in the intellectual and moral resources which humanity has succeeded in getting together. He becomes an inheritor of the funded capital of civilization. The most formal and technical education in the world cannot safely depart from this general process. It can only organize it or differentiate it in some particular direction.

I believe that the only true education comes through the stimulation of the child's powers by the demands of the social situations in which he finds himself. Through these demands he is stimulated to act as a member of a unity, to emerge from his original narrowness of action and feeling, and to conceive of himself from the standpoint of the welfare of the group to which he belongs. Through the responses which others make to his own activities he comes to know what these mean in social terms. The value which they have is reflected back into them. For instance, through the response which is made to the child's instinctive babblings the child comes to know what those babblings mean; they are transformed into articulate language and thus the child is introduced into the consolidated wealth of ideas and emotions which are now summed up in language.

I believe that this educational process has two sides—one psychological and one sociological; and that neither can be subordinated to the other

From John Dewey, "My Pedagogic Creed," *The School Journal*, LIV, No. 3 (January 16, 1897), 77–80.

or neglected without evil results following. Of these two sides, the psy-chological is the basis. The child's own instincts and powers furnish the material and give the starting point for all education. Save as the efforts of the educator connect with some activity which the child is carrying on of his own initiative independent of the educator, education becomes reduced to a pressure from without. It may, indeed, give certain external results, but cannot truly be called educative. Without insight into the psychological structure and activities of the individual, the educative process will, therefore, be haphazard and arbitrary. If it chances to coincide with the child's activity it will get a leverage; if it does not, it will result in friction, or disintegration, or arrest of the child nature.

I believe that knowledge of social conditions, of the present state of civilization, is necessary in order properly to interpret the child's powers. The child has his own instincts and tendencies, but we do not know what these mean until we can translate them into their social equivalents. We must be able to carry them back into a social past and see them as the inheritance of previous race activities. We must also be able to project them into the future to see what their outcome and end will be. In the illustration just used, it is the ability to see in the child's babblings the promise and potency of a future social intercourse and conversation which enables one to deal in the proper way with that instinct.

I believe that the psychological and social sides are organically related and that education cannot be regarded as a compromise between the two, or a superimposition of one upon the other. . . .

In sum, I believe that the individual who is to be educated is a social individual and that society is an organic union of individuals. If we eliminate the social factor from the child we are left only with an abstraction; if we eliminate the individual factor from society, we are left only with an inert and lifeless mass. Education, therefore, must begin with a psychological insight into the child's capacities, interests, and habits. It must be controlled at every point by reference to these same considerations. These powers, interests, and habits must be con-tinually interpreted—we must know what they mean. They must be trans-lated into terms of their social equivalents—into terms of what they are capable of in the way of social service.

Article II—What the School Is

I believe that the school is primarily a social institution. Education being a social process, the school is simply that form of community life in which all those agencies are concentrated that will be most effective in bringing the child to share in the inherited resources of the race, and to use his own powers for social ends.

I believe that education, therefore, is a process of living and not a preparation for future living.

I believe that the school must represent present life—life as real and vital to the child as that which he carries on in the home, in the neighborhood, or on the playground.

. . .

I believe that much of present education fails because it neglects this fundamental principle of the school as a form of community life. It conceives the school as a place where certain information is to be given, where certain lessons are to be learned, or where certain habits are to be formed. The value of these is conceived as lying largely in the remote future; the child must do these things for the sake of something else he is to do; they are mere preparation. As a result they do not become a part of the life experience of the child and so are not truly educative.

I believe that the moral education centers upon this conception of the school as a mode of social life, that the best and deepest moral training is precisely that which one gets through having to enter into proper relations with others in a unity of work and thought. The present educational systems, so far as they destroy or neglect this unity, render it difficult or impossible to get any genuine, regular moral training.

. . .

Article III—The Subject-Matter of Education

I believe that the social life of the child is the basis of concentration, or correlation, in all his training or growth. The social life gives the unconscious unity and the background of all his efforts and of all his attainments.

I believe that the subject-matter of the school curriculum should mark a gradual differentiation out of the primitive unconscious unity of social life.

I believe that we violate the child's nature and render difficult the best ethical results, by introducing the child too abruptly to a number of special studies, of reading, writing, geography, etc., out of relation to this social life.

I believe, therefore, that the true center of correlation on the school subjects is not science, not literature, nor history, nor geography, but the child's own social actviities.

. . .

I believe finally, that education must be conceived as a continuing reconstruction of experience, that the process and the goal of education are one and the same thing.

I believe that to set up any end outside of education, as furnishing its goal and standard, is to deprive the educational process of much of its meaning and tends to make us rely upon false and external stimuli in dealing with the child.

Article IV—The Nature of Method

I believe that the question of method is ultimately reducible to the question of the order of development of the child's powers and interests. The law for presenting and treating material is the law implicit within the child's own nature. Because this is so I believe the following statements are of supreme importance as determining the spirit in which education is carried on:

I believe that the active side precedes the passive in the development of the child nature; that expression comes before conscious impression; that the muscular development precedes the sensory; that movments come before conscious sensations; I believe that consciousness is essentially motor or impulsive; that conscious states tend to project themselves in action.

I believe that the neglect of this principle is the cause of a large part of the waste of time and strength in school work. The child is thrown into a passive, receptive, or absorbing attitude. The conditions are such that he is not permitted to follow the law of his nature; the result is friction and waste.

.   .   .

I believe that only through the continual and sympathetic observation of childhood's interests can the adult enter into the child's life and see what it is ready for, and upon what material it could work most readily and fruitfully.

I believe that these interests are neither to be humored nor repressed. To repress interest is to substitute the adult for the child, and so to weaken intellectual curiosity and alertness, to suppress initiative, and to deaden interest. To humor the interests is to substitute the transient for the permanent. The interest is always the sign of some power below; the important thing is to discover this power. To humor the interest is to fail to penetrate below the surface and its sure result is to substitute caprice and whim for genuine interest.

I believe that the emotions are the reflex of actions.

I believe that to endeavor to stimulate or arouse the emotions apart from their corresponding activities, is to introduce an unhealthy and morbid state of mind.

I believe that if we can only secure right habits of action and thought, with reference to the good, the true, and the beautiful, the emotions will for the most part take care of themselves.

I believe that next to deadness and dullness, formalism and routine, our education is threatened with no greater evil than sentimentalism.

I believe that this sentimentalism is the necessary result of the attempt to divorce feeling from action.

Article V—The School and Social Progress

I believe that education is the fundamental method of social progress and reform.

I believe that all reforms which rest simply upon the enactment of law, or the threatening of certain penalties, or upon changes in mechanical or outward arrangements, are transitory and futile.

I believe that education is a regulation of the process of coming to share in the social consciousness; and that the adjustment of individual activity on the basis of this social consciousness is the only sure method of social reconstruction.

I believe that this conception has due regard for both the individualistic and socialistic ideals. It is duly individual because it recognizes the formation of a certain character as the only genuine basis of right living. It is socialistic because it recognizes that this right character is not to be formed by merely individual precept, example, or exhortation, but rather by the influence of a certain form of institutional or community life upon the individual, and that the social organism through the school, as its organ, may determine ethical results.

I believe that in the ideal school we have the reconciliation of the individualistic and the institutional ideals.

I believe that the community's duty to education is, therefore, its paramount moral duty. By law and punishment, by social agitation and discussion, society can regulate and form itself in a more or less haphazard and chance way. But through education society can formulate its own purposes, can organize its own means and resources, and thus shape itself with definiteness and economy in the direction in which it wishes to move.

· · ·

I believe, finally, that the teacher is engaged, not simply in the training of individuals, but in the formation of the proper social life.

I believe that every teacher should realize the dignity of his calling; that he is a social servant set apart for the maintenance of proper social order and the securing of the right social growth.

I believe that in this way the teacher always is the prophet of the true God and the usherer in of the true kingdom of God.

REPRESENTATIVE EXPRESSIONS:
An Historical Perspective

1. "NEW ARTICLES OF FAITH"
Harold Rugg and Ann Shumaker

Freedom vs. Control

And the first of these articles of faith is freedom. "Free the legs, the arms, the larynx of a child," say these advocates of the new education, "and you have taken the first step towards freeing his mind and spirit."

Hence the revolution in school furniture, schedules of work, all the paraphernalia of administration. Fixed seats nailed to the floor, lock-step precision, rigidity, conformity, are disappearing. In their places are coming the informal, intimate atmosphere—the air of happy, cheerful living. Light, movable tables and chairs that may be shoved aside at any time to make room for work or play; children moving freely about, talking with one another, leaving the room to go to other parts of the building relatively at their discretion. The fixed, elaborate machinery of mass education is being abandoned: large classes; emphasis upon grades; housing in stereotyped, barrack-like buildings; adherence to strict time schedules; the oppressive silence of restraint; the labored compulsion—all the stringent coercion of the old order is passing.

The new freedom reveals itself, therefore, in an easier, more natural group life. At great expense to itself it maintains mere corporal's guards of classes—ten, twelve, fifteen, rarely over twenty pupils—in sharp contrast to the huge regiments of the formal, graded school. Thus the formal question-and-answer recitation is giving way to the free interchange of thought in group conferences and progress through individual work.

Freedom to develop naturally, to be spontaneous, unaffected, and unselfconscious, is, therefore, the first article of faith.

From Harold Rugg and Ann Shumaker, *The Child-Centered School* (New York: World Book Company, 1928), pp. 55–69. Reprinted with permission.

Child Initiative *vs.* Teacher Initiative

What is this new freedom based upon? Nothing less than the reorientation of the entire school around the child. These schools are child-centered institutions in contrast to the teacher-centered and principal-centered schools of the conventional order. They believe that the ability to govern one's self grows only through the practice of self-government. They have learned wisely the lesson of democracy in the western world; namely, that no people, however potentially able, will learn how to carry on its collective affairs except under freedom to practice self-government. Wherever adult societies have imposed democratic forms of government on a people uneducated in democracy, chaos has resulted. Throughout a century of national history in America our schools have adopted the form and the catch slogans of democracy, but never its true technique.

In this respect, however, another day has come in the new schools. These schools believe that boys and girls should share in their own government, in the planning of the program, in the administering of the curriculum, in conducting the life of the school. In the elementary division of some of these schools, during an informal morning discussion period, children, with the teacher as a wise but inconspicuous adult member of the group, consider together what they are to undertake during the day. The routine needs of the school, as well as the lesson assignments, the planning of excursions and exhibits, and the criticism of reports are taken over by the pupils. This is, indeed, a revolution in educational procedure and stands in sharp contrast to the conventional mode of conducting a school.

The difference in amount of work done by teachers and pupils respectively under these two plans of work—the pupil-initiating plan *vs.* the teacher-initiating plan—is conspicuous. In the formal school of today the teacher still does the thinking, planning, and initiating. Pupils are passive, quiescent, generally uninterested if not actively antagonistic. Learning is at a low ebb, if not at a standstill. In the child-centered school, however, pupils are alive, active, working hard, inventing, organizing, contributing original ideas, assembling materials, carrying out enterprises. As individuals and as social groups pupils grow, and they grow in the capacity to govern themselves, to organize machinery for handling their collective affairs, as well as in individual capacity for creative self-expression. So it is that the true theory of democracy is being put into practice in these new schools.

This centering of responsibility and initiative in the pupil brings into the forefront the child's own needs. His immediate interests are to furnish the starting point of education, according to the new schools. But, even of the most rebellious reformers, few advocate that the entire work of the school be based solely upon these naïve and spontaneous interests of children. However, the last twenty-five years of experimentation have undoubtedly contributed no more revolutionary articles of faith than that involved in this reorientation of the school about the child.

The Active School

Freedom, pupil initiative—therefore, the active school.

Naturally, from the free atmosphere in which pupil initiative plays the chief rôle it is but a next step to pupil activity. In these free, child-centered schools, therefore, pupils are active—physically active, mentally active, artistically active. There is a large amount of actual physical exertion, of overt bodily movement, of a wide variety of sensory contacts, of the type of energy-release which is ordinarily designated as play. Hence the terms, "activity schools," "play schools," and so on.

Education is to be based on child experience—experience not only in the physical sense but in the intellectual and emotional sense too. Thus do these child-centered schools want experience to be real. They depend as little as possible upon described experience. The wiser among their leaders know, of course, that in the adult world much real experience is abstract, described, vicarious, verbal. Therefore the child who is growing toward adulthood will appropriate to his uses an increasingly larger amount of described experience. In the higher reaches of the school, indeed, many described experiences must be made the very center of educational development. However, as far as possible, and predominantly in the lower years of the child-centered schools, real life is reproduced in physical miniature. Excursions are made into the neighborhood, the community. The scholastic environment is extended outward to include *realia* of a variegated sort, and within the school itself plants, animals, tools, materials, machines, are provided to stimulate activity and to give rise to interests which will require activity in their development. Much free play is permitted for the experiences in self-direction it affords.

Now the most deep-seated tendency in human life is movement, impulse, activity. The new schools, therefore, are experimenting vigorously with this fundamental psychological law—that the basis of all learning is reaction. That they are making a contribution is unquestioned.

In the formal schools the conditions of true growth were exactly reversed. One found outward quiet, orderliness, apparent concentration, little physical movement. Actually, however, this condition was one of restlessness, of much inner activity—a continual mutiny against the aims of the school. The iron rule of the school succeeded only in inhibiting the outward symptoms of inattention. There was fidgeting, uneducative scattering of interest and attention, and little conscious reflection on the matters in hand.

The new schools, with freedom of activity and movement, with apparent lack of concentration, produce nevertheless a much more truly educative absorption. The newer education regards the active child as the truly growing child. Not activity for activity's sake—energy exploding in random movements—but activity which is a growing toward something more mature, a changing for the better. The true criterion of educative activity is prolonged attention and concentrated effort. Such then is the activity which the new education writes into its articles of faith.

Child Interest as the Basis of the New Educational Program

Freedom, not restraint.
Pupil initiative, not teacher initiative.
The active, not the passive, school.
There is a fourth new article of faith—child interest as the orienting center of the school program.

In the formal schools, even in those of today, the program of the child's education is organized about school subjects. Not so in the new schools. We find a new educational vocabulary exponential of a unique educative program. Compare the schedules of the new and the old schools. What a difference! The logically arranged subjects of the past —reading, writing, arithemtic, spelling, geography, history—are replaced by projects, units of work, creative work periods, industrial arts, creative music, story hour, informal group conferences, and other vastly intriguing enterprises.

This curriculum does not look well on paper. It is a chaos of irregular time allotments. School principals might have a difficult time trying to fit the orderly movement of a large school into it. But it does give promise of active learning.

The new school is setting up a program of work which has a personal connection with the immediate life of the child. It starts from his needs and interests. The units of the new program approximate as nearly as possible what to the children are real-life situations. Hence the new school organizes its program around the centers of interest rather than around academic subjects. Wherever school subjects, however, coincide with life needs, then the new centers of interest coincide with the old school subjects; for example, the subjects of reading and creative music, the story hour. But because the formal school subjects were the product of academic research interests, most of them do not coincide with life interests, either of children or of adults. Hence in the new educational order they must go. This new plan of organizing the curriculum around units of pupil activity gives greater promise of widespreading, educational achievement for the pupil than does the dry, intellectualized, logical arrangement of subjects-to-be-learned of the old school. It is vitalized by interesting and purposeful activity that has an intimate connection with the child's personal life.

That the new schools are evolving an educational program in which school subjects are rejected in favor of broader and more integrative centers of work is illustrated also in the tendency to organize materials in a few broad departments of knowledge. The old school organized knowledge into many minute, disparate, academic departments. In the upper grades of some of the new schools the initiating center of organization is the interest of the child in some contemporary institution or problem. In the lower grades the focus is the immediate school scene. In the higher grades the emphasis shifts to adult society; in the foreground always stand the fundamental movements or trends, the crucial institutions or problems of contemporary life.

All this does not mean that the new school entirely avoids school subjects, but the subjects in these schools differ materially from those of the formal school. The new-school subjects represent new departmentalizations of knowledge which include a broad view of race experience rather than mere devitalized definitions and long lists of factual enumerations. They are concerned at bottom with big concepts, themes, movements, that explain broad, fundamental phases of human life.

The old school spent its time and energy in drilling pupils into a state of passable efficiency in minimal essentials. The new school treats these minimal essentials, which are largely skills, as by-products of the educative situation. Usually it has succeeded in teaching them much more adequately than the old school, and in less time.

Creative Self-Expression

"I would have a child say not, 'I know,' but 'I have experienced.'"

Education as conformity *vs.* education as creative self-expression, adaptation and adjustment *vs.* creative experience—these are some of the phrases which are recurring with accumulating momentum in the discussions of the new education.

We find as sharp a contrast in theory between the old and the new at this point in our analysis as in our consideration of other aspects. The spirit of the old school was centered about social adjustment, adaptation to the existing order. The aim of conventional education was social efficiency. Growth was seen as increasing power to conform, to acquiesce to a schooled discipline; maturity was viewed from the standpoint of successful compliance with social demands.

In the new school, however, it is the creative spirit from within that is encouraged, rather than conformity to a pattern imposed from without. The success of the new school has been startling in eliciting self-expression in all of the arts, in discovering a marvelously creative youth. The child as artist, poet, composer, is coming into his own.

This success is due not so much to the changed viewpoint concerning the place of art in education as to the whole new theory of self-expression, the emphasis on the place of creative originality in life. Art in the new school is permitted; in the old it was imposed. The new school assumes that every child is endowed with the capacity to express himself, and that this innate capacity is immensely worth cultivating. The pupil is placed in an atmosphere conducive to self-expression in every aspect. Some will create with words, others with light. Some will express themselves through the body in the dance; others will model, carve, shape their ideas in plastic materials. Still others will find expression through oral language, and some through an integrated physical, emotional, and dramatic gesture. But whatever the route, the medium, the materials—each one has some capacity for expression.

The artist in Everyman's child is being discovered, not only in the unusual, the gifted, the genius; the lid of restraint is being lifted from the child of the common man in order that he may come to his own best self-fulfillment. The new schools are providing "drawing-out" environments in sharp contrast to the "pouring-in" environments of the old.

Art in the new schools is naïve, neo-primitive. The child is permitted to set his own standards as he works. The "masters" are not set out to be worshiped respectfully—they are admired in the frank and critical spirit of intimate companionship. Appreciation of the finished works of genius is best built up, say the new schools, by first encouraging the creative products of the child's own pen, voice, brush. The emphasis is not upon finished work, skill, and technical perfection, but upon the release of the child's creative capacities, upon growth in his power to express his own unique ideas naturally and freely, whatever the medium.

Personality and Social Adjustment

The leaders of our schools are confronted by no more important and overwhelming problem than that of providing an environment by which each child can learn to live with others and yet retain his personal identity. To live with others, learn how to adjust himself to them, and yet grow in the confident knowledge that he, like each of them, is a unique individuality, a rare personality; to live with others and yet grow in the assurance that he too is superior, that he, and he alone, is distinctive in some trait or traits and that he has something unique to contribute to the groups in which he lives. How are the new and the old schools trying to solve this problem?

The old school, with its mass-education machinery, seemed to treat children in social groups, to develop social attitudes, but in reality it sacrificed the individual to mythical group needs. Social contacts during school hours were dominated by an arbitrary authority—the teacher—and had to conform to a rigid formality in order that discipline might be maintained. The old school, therefore, left the child entirely unaided in coping with social situations. Under mass education—hyper-intellectual, hyper-individualistic—with pupils isolated in seats, no opportunity was offered to practice cooperative living except in the undirected out-of-school contacts. The child was not assisted in learning to work effectively with a group at a common interest. A false notion of individuality was erected; namely, that superiority could be asserted only through personal competition. The old school over-emphasized competition because it was a convenient, effective, and inexpensive device for attaining greater effort from pupils. However, it was often used at the cost of successful social living.

The new school, on the other hand, encourages the child to be a distinct personality, an individualist, to believe in his ability—but of course not to an unjustifiable degree. It sets up situations which provide constant practice in cooperative living. It encourages activities in which he can make a personal contribution to group enterprises; in which he has social experiences, graded to fit his level of social development; in which he feels himself an accepted and respected member of a society of which he himself approves.

The new school bridges the gap, therefore, between the development of individuality on the one hand and successful social participation on the other by insisting that the true development of the individual and the fulfillment of personality are best attained as one expresses himself most successfully and adequately *with* others and *toward* others.

How does the new school propose to secure this cooperative endeavor?

It does so by means of a wide variety of group activities. Dramatics which require concerted effort toward a common goal; assemblies through which frequent interchange of mutually interesting ideas takes place; student committees and clubs managing student affairs; miniature social organizations and group games—these are some of the social situations which the new school deliberately encourages. The group dance also is coming into its own as a vehicle for more than rhythmic physical development. Indeed, rhythmics gives promise of usurping the place in the lower school that has formerly been given to competitive athletics. Active experience in grace and physical poise, as an agency for the education of personality of each and every individual, is the aim, rather than development of a few stellar performers with the mass remaining mere passive, untransformed observers.

The new school has no extracurricular activities. These group activities are a regular and important part of school life—they are not a side issue indulged in at the end of the day or week as unrelated recreation or relief from the real business of the school.

Again, where the old school maintained a noisy silence as the ideal schoolroom atmosphere, the new removes the ban from speech, encourages communication as a vehicle for social understanding and personal development. Indeed the new school has gone so far in this respect as to be accused at times of being garrulous. However, it is well known that practice in the free use of language, with guidance, helps to develop qualities desirable for successful social living. Fluent, natural speech is the basis for effective self-expression and mutual understanding.

In ways like these the new school is evolving its informal real-life organization, encouraging common aims and purposes, the interpenetration of minds, producing in the school a life of happy intimacy—creating a "wholesome medium for the most complete living." [1]

[1] Tippett, James S., and Others, *Curriculum Making in an Elementary School* (Ginn & Co., Boston, 1927), page 8.

2. DARE THE SCHOOL BUILD A NEW SOCIAL ORDER?
George S. Counts

Like all simple and unsophisticated peoples we Americans have a sublime faith in education. Faced with any difficult problem of life we set our minds at rest sooner or later by the appeal to the school. We are convinced that education is the one unfailing remedy for every ill to which man is subject, whether it be vice, crime, war, poverty, riches, injustice, racketeering, political corruption, race hatred, class conflict or just plain original sin. We even speak glibly and often about the general reconstruc-

From George S. Counts, *Dare the School Build a New Social Order?* John Day Pamphlets, No. 11 (New York: John Day, 1932), pp. 3–10.

tion of society through the school. We cling to this faith in spite of the fact that the very period in which our troubles have multiplied so rapidly has witnessed an unprecedented expansion of organized education. This would seem to suggest that our schools, instead of directing the course of change, are themselves driven by the very forces that are transforming the rest of the social order.

The bare fact, however, that simple and unsophisticated peoples have unbounded faith in education does not mean that the faith is untenable. History shows that the intuitions of such folk may be nearer the truth than the weighty and carefully reasoned judgments of the learned and the wise. Under certain conditions education may be as beneficent and as powerful as we are wont to think. But if it is to be so, teachers must abandon much of their easy optimism, subject the concept of education to the most rigorous scrutiny, and be prepared to deal much more fundamentally, realistically, and positively with the American social situation than has been their habit in the past. Any individual or group that would aspire to lead society must be ready to pay the costs of leadership: to accept responsibility, to suffer calumny, to surrender security, to risk both reputation and fortune. If this price, or some important part of it, is not being paid, then the chances are that the claim to leadership is fraudulent. Society is never redeemed without effort, struggle, and sacrifice. Authentic leaders are never found breathing that rarefied atmosphere lying above the dust and smoke of battle. With regard to the past we always recognize the truth of this principle, but when we think of our own times we profess the belief that the ancient roles have been reversed and that now prophets of a new age receive their rewards among the living.

That the existing school is leading the way to a better social order is a thesis which few informed persons would care to defend. Except as it is forced to fight for its own life during times of depression, its course is too serene and untroubled. Only in the rarest of instances does it wage war on behalf of principle or ideal. Almost everywhere it is in the grip of conservative forces and is serving the cause of perpetuating ideas and institutions suited to an age that is gone. But there is one movement above the educational horizon which would seem to show promise of genuine and creative leadership. I refer to the Progressive Education movement. Surely in this union of two of the great faiths of the American people, the faith in progress and the faith in education, we have reason to hope for light and guidance. Here is a movement which would seem to be completely devoted to the promotion of social welfare through education.

Even a casual examination of the program and philosophy of the Progressive schools, however, raises many doubts in the mind. To be sure, these schools have a number of large achievements to their credit. They have focused attention squarely upon the child; they have recognized the fundamental importance of the interest of the learner; they have defended the thesis that activity lies at the root of all true education; they have conceived learning in terms of life situations and growth of character; they have championed the rights of the child as a free personality. Most of this is excellent, but in my judgment it is not enough. It constitutes too narrow a conception of the meaning of education; it brings into the picture but one-half of the landscape.

If an educational movement, or any other movement, calls itself progressive, it must have orientation, it must possess direction. The word itself implies moving forward, and moving forward can have little meaning in the absence of clearly defined purposes. We cannot, like Stephen Leacock's horseman, dash off in all directions at once. Nor should we, like our presidential candidates, evade every disturbing issue and be all things to all men. Also we must beware lest we become so devoted to motion that we neglect the question of direction and be entirely satisfied with movement in circles. Here, I think, we find the fundamental weakness, not only of Progressive Education, but also of American education generally. Like a baby shaking a rattle, we seem to be utterly content with action, provided it is sufficiently vigorous and noisy. In the last analysis a very large part of American educational thought, inquiry, and experimentation is much ado about nothing. And, if we are permitted to push the analogy of the rattle a bit further, our consecration to motion is encouraged and supported in order to keep us out of mischief. At least we know that so long as we thus busy ourselves we shall not incur the serious displeasure of our social elders.

The weakness of Progressive Education thus lies in the fact that it has elaborated no theory of social welfare, unless it be that of anarchy or extreme individualism. In this, of course, it is but reflecting the viewpoint of the members of the liberal-minded upper middle class who send their children to the Progressive schools—persons who are fairly well-off, who have abandoned the faiths of their fathers, who assume an agnostic attitude towards all important questions, who pride themselves on their open-mindedness and tolerance, who favor in a mild sort of way fairly liberal programs of social reconstruction, who are full of good will and humane sentiment, who have vague aspirations for world peace and human brotherhood, who can be counted upon to respond moderately to any appeal made in the name of charity, who are genuinely distressed at the sight of unwonted forms of cruelty, misery, and suffering, and who perhaps serve to soften somewhat the bitter clashes of those real forces that govern the world; but who, in spite of all their good qualities, have no deep and abiding loyalties, possess no convictions for which they would sacrifice over-much, would find it hard to live without their customary material comforts, are rather insensitive to the accepted forms of social injustice, are content to play the role of interested spectator in the drama of human history, refuse to see reality in its harsher and more disagreeable forms, rarely move outside the pleasant circles of the class to which they belong, and in the day of severe trial will follow the lead of the most powerful and respectable forces in society and at the same time find good reasons for so doing. These people have shown themselves entirely incapable of dealing with any of the great crises of our time—war, prosperity, or depression. At bottom they are romantic sentimentalists, but with a sharp eye on the main chance. That they can be trusted to write our educational theories and shape our educational programs is highly improbable.

Among the members of this class the number of children is small, the income relatively high, and the economic functions of the home greatly reduced. For these reasons an inordinate emphasis on the child and child interests is entirely welcome to them. They wish to guard their offspring from too strenuous endeavor and from coming into too intimate contact with the grimmer aspects of industrial society. They wish their sons and daughters to succeed according to the standards of their class and to be a credit to their parents. At heart feeling themselves members of a superior human strain, they do not want their children to mix too freely with the children of the poor or of the less fortunate races. Nor do they want them to accept radical social doctrines, espouse unpopular causes, or lose themselves in quest of any Holy Grail. According to their views education should deal with life, but with life at a distance or in a highly diluted form. They would generally maintain that life should be kept at arm's length, if it should not be handled with a poker.

If Progressive Education is to be genuinely progressive, it must emancipate itself from the influence of this class, face squarely and courageously every social issue, come to grips with life in all of its stark reality, establish an organic relation with the community, develop a realistic and comprehensive theory of welfare, fashion a compelling and challenging vision of human destiny, and become less frightened than it is today at the bogies of imposition and indoctrination. In a word, Progressive Education cannot place its trust in a child-centered school.

This brings us to the most crucial issue in education—the question of the nature and extent of the influence which the school should exercise over the development of the child. The advocates of extreme freedom have been so successful in championing what they call the rights of the child that even the most skillful practitioners of the art of converting others to their opinions disclaim all intention of molding the learner. And when the word indoctrination is coupled with education there is scarcely one among us possessing the hardihood to refuse to be horrified. This feeling is so widespread that even Mr. Lunacharsky, Commissar of Education in the Russian Republic until 1929, assured me on one occasion that the Soviet educational leaders do not believe in the indoctrination of children in the ideas and principles of communism. When I asked him whether their children become good communists while attending the schools, he replied that the great majority do. On seeking from him an explanation of this remarkable phenomenon he said that Soviet teachers merely tell their children the truth about human history. As a consequence, so he asserted, practically all of the more intelligent boys and girls adopt the philosophy of communism. I recall also that the Methodist sect in which I was reared always confined its teachings to the truth!

The issue is no doubt badly confused by historical causes. The champions of freedom are obviously the product of an age that has broken very fundamentally with the past and is equally uncertain about the future. In many cases they feel themselves victims of narrow orthodoxies which were imposed upon them during childhood and which have severely cramped their lives. At any suggestion that the child should be influenced by his elders they therefore envisage the establishment of a state church, the formulation of a body of sacred doctrine, and the teaching of this doctrine as fixed and final. If we are forced to choose between such an unenlightened form of pedagogical influence and a condition of complete freedom for the child, most of us would in all probability choose the latter as the lesser of two evils. But this is to create a wholly artificial situation: the choice should not be limited to these two extremes. Indeed today neither extreme is possible.

I believe firmly that a critical factor must play an important role in any adequate educational program, at least in any such program fashioned for the modern world. An education that does not strive to promote the fullest and most thorough understanding of the world is not worthy of the name. Also there must be no deliberate distortion or suppression of facts to support any theory or point of view. On the other hand, I am prepared to defend the thesis that all education contains a large element of imposition, that in the very nature of the case this is inevitable, that the existence and evolution of society depend upon it, that it is consequently [1] eminently desirable, and that the frank acceptance of this fact by the educator is a major professional obligation. I even contend that failure to do this involves the clothing of one's own deepest prejudices in the garb of universal truth and the introduction into the theory and practice of education of an element of obscurantism.

---

[1] Some persons would no doubt regard this as a *non sequitur,* but the great majority of the members of the human race would, I think, accept the argument.

3. REPORT OF THE NATIONAL CONFERENCE ON
LIFE ADJUSTMENT EDUCATION (PROSSER RESOLUTION)

Original Form of Prosser Resolution:

"It is the belief of this conference that, with the aid of this report in final form, the vocational school of a community will be able better to prepare 20 percent of the youth of secondary school age for entrance upon desirable skilled occupations; and that the high school will continue to prepare another 20 percent for entrance to college. We do not believe that the remaining 60 percent of our youth of secondary school age will receive the life adjustment training they need and to which they are entitled as American citizens—unless and until the administrators of public education with the assistance of the vocational education leaders formulate a similar program for this group.

"We therefore request the U.S. Commissioner of Education and the Assistant Commissioner for Vocational Education to call at some early date a conference or a series of regional conferences between an equal number of representatives of general and of vocational education—to consider this problem and to take such initial steps as may be found advisable for its solution."

. . .

It was the consensus of those participating in the regional conferences:

1. That secondary education today is failing to provide adequately and properly for the life adjustment of perhaps a major fraction of the persons of secondary school age.
2. That public opinion can be created to support the movement to provide appropriate life adjustment education for these youth.
3. That the solution is to be found in the provision of educational experiences based on the diverse individual needs of youth of secondary-school age.
4. That a broadened viewpoint and a genuine desire to serve all youth is needed on the part of teachers and of those who plan the curriculums of teacher-training institutions.

From *Report of the National Conference on Life Adjustment Education (Prosser Resolution),* Office of Education, Chicago, May 8–10, 1947, pp. 17, 18–19, 48–49, 97–99.

5. That local resources must be utilized in every community to a degree as yet achieved only in a few places.
6. That functional experiences in the areas of practical arts, home and family life, health and physical fitness, and civic competence are basic in any program designed to meet the needs of youth today.
7. That a supervised program of work experience is a "must" for the youth with whom the Resolution is concerned.
8. That one of the principal barriers to the achievement of the ideals of the Resolution is the multiplicity of small, understaffed and under-financed school districts in this Nation.
9. That an intimate, comprehensive, and continuous program of guidance and pupil personnel services must constitute the basis on which any efforts to provide life adjustment education must rest.

Characteristics of the Youth with Whom the Resolution Is Concerned

The characteristics of those youth of high school age whose needs are not being met by existing school programs cannot, of course, be specifically described, because they cannot be identified with great accuracy except possibly in retrospect. For an individual 18 or 19 years of age a fair evaluation of the adequacy of his schooling during the previous 6 years can often be made. Analyses have been made of the schooling of 18- or 19-year-olds concerning the number of years spent in school, achievement in various areas, and judgment as to the value of the schooling. The Regents Inquiry into the Character and Cost of Public Education in the State of New York, which included an analysis of the knowledge, attitudes, and accomplishments of high school graduates, is a good example of such an evaluation. Many of the inadequacies of secondary education were brought out by this survey.

While the naming of inadequacies aids in establishing the type of guidance program and curriculum needed, in general, evaluative studies do not fully answer the question of the type of school that is needed. It is necessary to know the characteristics of individuals at the time they are in school in order to adapt the suggested educational program to them.

The youth with whom we are concerned cannot be identified with great accuracy by any one characteristic. Every single characteristic associated with the youth referred to in the Resolution is also associated with certain of those who are in the college preparatory or vocational programs. However, when a great many of these characteristics are associated with one individual, the chance of that individual's being one who will be inadequately served in our schools, as presently constituted, is high. The identification of these characteristics, then, is extremely important and may serve at least three purposes:

1. Such identification calls attention to factors in the life of youth which are of importance to counselors and others having to do with the pupil personnel program in schools. In fact, the identification of many of the potentially neglected youth can come only through individual diagnoses using measures of the qualities alluded to in the following list of characteristics. . . .

2. Society has the power to change many of the characteristics of youth so that many of our youth will not remain on the potentially neglected list any longer. For example, the handicap of coming from a family of low income can be overcome by society through providing scholarships or through raising the level of the income of families with youth of high-school age.

3. Schools knowing that many pupils have these characteristics can consciously modify their programs so that some of the characteristics may be modified or eliminated. For example, low general intelligence, retardation in school, low achievement test scores, may be improved by better schooling.

To be most helpful in setting up the educational program, including both guidance services and the curriculum, some of the characteristics of this neglected group at 12 years of age and again at 16 years of age are included here. These characteristics are not intended to brand the group as in any sense inferior but rather as different in types of educational services needed; they are significant because their presence in pupils has been found to be associated with maladjustment in school. With this caution the following 11 factors may be used to distinguish the 12-year-olds who are likely to be neglected by the schools.[1] They often, if not usually,

1. Come from families the members of which are engaged in unskilled and semiskilled occupations.
2. Come from families with low incomes.
3. Come from families with low cultural environments.
4. Are retarded in school.

[1] Among the many sources used in developing this list of factors these were particularly helpful:

Dodds, B. L. That All May Learn. *Bulletin of the National Association of Secondary-School Principals,* 23: 1–235, November 1939.

Havighurst, R. J., Prescott, D. A., and Redl, Fritz. Scientific Study of Developing Boys and Girls Has Set Up Guideposts. In General Education in the American High School. Ch. 4. Chicago: Scott, Foresman and Co., 1942, pp. 105–35.

Seymour, H. C. The Characteristics of Pupils Who Leave School Early. Cambridge, Mass., Harvard University, 1940. (Unpublished Doctoral Dissertation).

Warner, W. L., Havighurst, R. J., and Loeb, M. B. Who Shall Be Educated? New York: Harper and Bros., 1944, 190 pp.

5. Begin school later than other children.
6. Make considerably poorer scores on intelligence tests (not only verbal traits but all mental traits).
7. Make considerably lower achievement test scores for age than the average.
8. Make somewhat lower achievement test scores for grade than the average. (Since they are usually retarded their achievement is nearer their grade group than their age group.)
9. Make lower marks than other students.
10. Are less emotionally mature—nervous, feel less secure.
11. Lack interest in school work.

This list of identifying characteristics is not necessarily all-inclusive, but it will be found that most other characteristics noted about this group will fit under these 11.

Work Experience, Occupational Adjustment, and Competencies

The Prosser Resolution is concerned with life adjustment training by the high schools for those American youth not served in the vocational or college preparatory programs. The topic, "work experience, occupational adjustment, and competencies," is a vital aspect of the entire problem involved in the Resolution. Life adjustment is impossible unless occupational adjustment occurs.

Since they may change jobs many times during their lives, the boys and girls with whom the Resolution is concerned are likely to need resourcefulness and flexibility in order to achieve occupational adjustment. They will hold jobs for which they can make little specific preparation while they are still in school. If by actual work experience a boy can learn the types of jobs he dislikes, he will have made some progress. If, in addition, he can learn to work 8 hours a day and can attain competence in some one job which he does like, he is well on his way toward occupational adjustment.

. . .

This involves adjustment to many phases of life activity. It certainly has great significance insofar as occupational adjustment is concerned as any type of occupation requires work that meets "productive standards." Work experience, however, does more than prepare one to meet "standards" of efficiency. The youth can learn and the high school must provide more than in the past about safety practices, labor problems, relations with employers, working under directions, holding a job, getting promotions, working with others, a new sense of money values, and the like.

. . .

Significance of Work Experience

The language used in the Prosser Resolution provides a setting that leads the reader to the conclusion that one of the basic factors in education for "life adjustment" is "occupational adjustment." In view of that impression a search was made to discover what educators regarded as an important outcome of "work experience." The following quotations [2] are therefore submitted:

> Young people need to learn to work. Labor is the lot of man, and it has not been recognized as it should have been in arranging institutional education.
> The ability to work steadily for 8 hours is not a natural possession; it has to be acquired.
> By the time a young person reaches adolescence he needs to have opportunities for work if he is to make the transition into adulthood rapidly and efficiently.
> The payment of wages to young people for the labor which they perform contributes to economic adjustment.
> Wages are a means additional to schooling of inducting young people into adulthood.
> With proper social motives a vocation may be made the most compelling purpose of education which we can set before a pupil.
> A democracy will not separate its work and culture.
> All children should be given several types of work experience for its exploratory value so that all may have some understanding of the work of the world.

[2] American Council on Education, The American Youth Commission. What the High Schools Ought to Teach. Washington, D.C., The Council, 1940, pp. 15, 16, 17.
Educational Policies Commission. The Purposes of Education in American Democracy. Washington, D.C., The Commission, 1938, p. 100.
Jacobson, Paul B. Adolescents Need Experience in the Work of Their World. *In* General Education in the American High School, Ch. 11, *op. cit.*, p. 283.

4. OPEN v. CLOSED CLASSROOM
Mario D. Fantini

We hear a great deal these days about the open v. the closed society. In the one camp we have the totalitarian social order, referred to as a "closed" society, wherein individuals are actually subservient to the state.

From Mario D. Fantini, "Open v. Closed Classrooms," *The Clearing House*, 37, No. 2 (October 1962), pp. 67–71. Used by permission of the publisher.

In the other camp we have those societies which value the individual over the state and are referred to as "open" societies. It is said further that in one society the individual is "free"; in the other, that he is not.

The seriousness of the conflict between open and closed societies cannot be slighted because both societies are willing to preserve their prized values even at the expense of an all-out war. Consequently, we are talking about very important concepts. Moreover, there is a parallel between societies and the classrooms in which teachers find themselves. There are also open and closed classrooms, which, in a sense, are miniatures of open and closed societies.

If you were to view the schools in this light, you might examine a classroom and see the teacher in the front of the room talking to the class. The class might be listening and taking notes; if an assignment were being made, the students might be writing down the assignment, after which perhaps certain students might ask questions. Soon the class is over and a new class comes in. The teacher again asks for the homework assignments from the previous day, goes on to some new work, dictates some important facts, asks a few questions on the work which should have been prepared for the day, makes an assignment for the following day, and answers some last minute questions. Then a new group comes in and this pattern is repeated.

You might then examine another room where the teacher is, at first, hard to find. She is in the background, but the students are moving around freely. Various projects are being undertaken by small groups of students, while other students are working alone. In this classroom, there does not seem to be a routinized approach.

In a sense, you could say that these were observations of open and closed classrooms. In the foregoing descriptions, the first exemplified a closed classroom, while the second one approached the open classroom.

It is my assumption that both classrooms are miniature social systems, in which certain values are being developed (whether the teacher realizes it or not) because of the kind of conditions which the teacher has set up. It is my further assumption that the values sponsored by these miniature social systems parallel many of the values which underlie the open and closed societies. It is my belief, also, that there are in operation more of the closed classroom systems than the open classroom systems. If these assumptions are valid, then a possible conclusion is that our schools are actually developing more closed society values than open. This means that American schools are preparing individuals for a closed society, when it is obvious that the schools should be doing just the opposite.

Why do we seem to have more closed than open classrooms? For one reason, the closed system seems to be much more systematic. It appears to be more logical. Since we seem to have inherited this pattern, this seems to be the "way to do it"; so this structure is perpetuated. Since in the closed classroom system the teacher is the center of attraction, this becomes a teachercentric type of arrangement. The individuals, the learners, take their signals largely from the teacher. You can compare this with the closed society, in which the individual takes his signals from the state. Thus, the model projected here is based on the assign-recite-test sequence. This is the normal methodology. Conformity is being fostered because of the teacher-ascribed standards, which are supposedly sanctioned as being objective. The individual here is in competition with others. The climate fostered here is one in which the prize is on convergent values. The individual must conform or he does not succeed. These convergent values breed conformity, so that ultimately you have a miniature conforming classroom society.

In a closed classroom, such student questions as these are typical: "How long do you want this assignment?" "May we use other textbooks?" "Do you want a bibliography?" The emphasis on these questions is to get permission from the teacher in order to proceed. The teacher is the source of "truth." As long as one goes along with the values and standards that the teacher has imposed, he will gain status and recognition and thereby succeed. The ironic aspect here is that we are making conformists of bright students, those very students who may be called upon to give us the creative leadership we need on a national level. Some students do rebel against the system. These become "outsiders" and usually fail. Most learners conform to the system and, in the process of conforming, internalize these convergent values which, in turn, become an excellent orientation for participation in a closed society.

Moreover, in the closed system the important thing is to *acquire knowledge*—that is, you must know *about* subject matter. The knowing about subject matter is what will be tested, and if the recall is good, the learner will be rewarded. The entire approach in the closed classroom is deductive; the *answers* are more important than the *process* for achieving answers. In all probability, facts will be emphasized at the expense of the conceptual structure. The school administration seems to be satisfied with this operation because it creates little organizational conflict. Parents do not object since this is the same pattern to which they themselves were exposed.

The open classroom, on the other hand, is a replica of an open society and, hopefully, can develop those values needed to support and advance an open society—that is, freedom with self-direction. In the open classroom the teacher is largely in the background and the situation is one in which the pupils are the center of attraction. This is the pupil-centric structure. The important value which is developed here is creative self-expression. Just as the center of the open society is the individual and not the state, the center of the open classroom is the student and not the teacher. The climate being fostered is one which permits the development of the creative person and the inner-directed person (to use Riesman's term), since the individual takes his signals from within himself. He is competing with himself, and not with others, so that standards are actually relative to the individual. Critical thinking is being fostered because the process here is *inductive*. It is a search. It is the process of exploration. The answer is not given first; rather, the learner must attempt to discover new ideas and new concepts which will give meaning to further performance.

In the open classroom, the process is valued as much as the product. Further, the open classroom is more prone to be action oriented than is the closed system, where the learner is passive and the teacher is the dominant force. The open classroom swings the emphasis from teaching to learning, to those conditions which surround learning for each student.

If you were able to move through the school systems in our country, you would not find it difficult to determine whether the emphasis is more on the open or closed classroom systems. Certainly there are values to both, but this is not the major point that is being discussed here. What is being suggested is that an important relationship exists between the classroom and society. Ultimately, what is being learned in the classroom should prepare individuals for competent societal roles. The values of freedom, creativity, and self-direction, so basic to our society, do not just happen. They are developed, and the classroom is one of the important laboratories in the process. Not being cognizant of the values being developed in the classroom is to damage the foundations of a free society. The emphasis today in a free society is on the development of creative individuals. Everyone has the potential for creativity and everyone has a potential for excellence in some area of human endeavor. Each person is born with a particular set of abilities which can be developed to the fullest if the school would provide favorable conditions which foster this development. The emphasis on the creative individual, it seems to me, is founded on an important philosophical position which states that in our type of civilization, the dignity and worth of the individual are supreme. Under this concept, the individual, because of his uniqueness, has the ability to express himself in a unique way. The fruits of his uniqueness can lead to creative expression, whether it be in music, in dance, or in play-acting. This development, it seems to me, is more likely to find expression in the open classroom environment.

If you stand apart to view the educational process as it takes place in the schools, you can see a kind of continuum from the open to the closed system. It is surprising how we begin our education with an open system and gradually proceed to a more closed type of classroom system. For example, the kindergarten is an excellent model of the open classroom, but as we move through the grades the situation changes. What we are doing actually, instead of nurturing creativity, is creating conditions that stymie creative growth.

However, the open system is not a panacea and there are certain important arguments against the open classroom systems. The first is that it is difficult for a teacher to control an open system—that it lacks discipline—that there is a lack of teacher control. The argument continues that in the absence of someone in charge in the room, utter chaos would follow. For example, it is often cited that the teacher who is weak and does not have authority is subjected to behavior abuses because of lack of control.

My answer to this argument would be that in an open society, the highest form of discipline is not imposed discipline but self-discipline; i.e., the internalization of a certain set of values which give meaning and purpose to behavior. This is the sought for kind of ideal. If this is not true, then the argument is really in favor of a nation of followers. One of the most severe criticisms of our times is that we have become a nation of conformists. If you were to look back in time, a counter argument could be raised, based on the school years; i.e., retracing the causes of conformity could lead logically to the classroom and to the lack of sufficient opportunities to exercise and to internalize types of behavior patterns which would develop self-direction. Consequently, since the development of self-discipline is inherent in the open system, its practice should be encouraged. Conversely, the closed system is more likely to sponsor the other-directed orientation.

Another argument that is often cited is that the open system is one that is more apt not to cover the subject matter that needs to be covered. The knowledge which we should be giving to the students would not be taught under an open system. The argument continues that it is important to outline the course work in a logical fashion and to cover a certain amount of work each day so that, over a period of time, the essentials are covered.

However, if you examine knowledge today, you realize that it is expanding at a geometric rate. It is impossible to expect one person to know all. Moreover, the nature of knowledge is changing. The orientation of many teachers took place at a time when knowledge was not expanding at a geometric rate, and there is no guarantee that the teacher has kept up with changing perspectives in his own discipline. Consequently, it is not knowledge that is important, but the ideas and concepts which underlie the change in the framework of knowledge. This is the very thing that an open classroom seeks—to give the person, through the process of inquiry, the method for discovering the big ideas which have given meaning to change. In addition, those who would argue that knowledge would be neglected under an open system, at the same time underestimate value development. The open classroom system stimulates the process for development of such values as freedom, critical thinking, self-direction, creativity, and cooperation—those very values which give meaning and direction to democratic functioning. Students in this open system are experiencing patterns of behavior which are more like the ideals of the open and free society in which they will eventually become members.

An argument often cited against closed systems is that the closed system is more prone to developing a passive individual. Since the teacher is the center of dominance in the closed system, the student's role is primarily passive. The student is the recipient of a flow of communication from the teacher. By contrast, the learner in the open system is quite active because he must go through the process of exploring and discovering. Moreover, this active process, encouraged by the open system, serves also to fortify the learner with a particular method for discovering answers to problems, which is based on a major tool of science—the scientific method. The breakthroughs which we have in the field of science are largely attributable to increased sophistication in the implementation of this method. Actually, an open classroom is fortifying the learner with tools for problem solving in an age when it is necessary for a person to be able to think through the complexities of modern life to the degree, at least, of gaining insights which would enable him to recognize the significant from the insignificant. These are all attributes which are possible of development in a classroom which takes on the characteristics more of an open than of a closed system.

The question arises, "Why are there not more open than closed classroom systems?" This is, again, a complex problem. One answer is that this would necessitate a new orientation for most teachers. It is actually a much more difficult challenge to create the learning environment of an open classroom. For example, as a new teacher moves into the school situation, he becomes a member of a social system. He usually is not in a position to initiate change, and must go along with the norms of the system. The process of shifting a classroom situation from a closed to an open one is often fraught with hazards for the beginner. It may be that over a period of time the beginner succumbs to the pressures of the system. More likely, however, the closed system is found to be the easier way out. The closed system seems to be more definite. The teacher sees the logic of the approach more readily. He feels more satisfaction in having covered a given body of subject matter and in testing the student to see what he has learned. He seems to get more reward out of knowing his place in teaching.

The open system, on the other hand, is difficult to assess in terms of the teacher's role. The teacher in the open system is more of a climate setter, one who, while remaining in the background, is actually the agent who brings into the classroom environment all of the resources which implement learning.

Whether we realize it or not, education is playing a vital role in terms of national purpose. We are getting an awakening of the importance of education in the total process of developing an ideal type of society. Sooner or later we must come to the conclusion that schools have specific and major functions in society, and that this function concerns itself mainly with socializing all the citizens to perform effectively and maturely in the society in which they will function. That is, the school should attempt to develop the individual to the fullest, because, as a self-realizing individual, he will best make a contribution to the development of a free and open civilization.

Certainly, we are hopeful that the schools will develop the kind of individual who has social responsibility, one who feels deeply for humanity. In order to develop the kind of individual called for in this type of free order, the schools have a vital role to perform.

As we examine the educational process closely, it becomes apparent that serious consideration should be given to the nature of the teaching front, to that environmental situation in which teaching and learning take place. Hopefully, that direction will be more toward the model of the open classroom system.

PEDAGOGICAL MODEL:
The Teacher as Facilitator

1. CHECK YOUR INQUIRY-TEACHING TECHNIQUE
Mary Sugrue and Jo A. Sweeney

As a teacher, are you concerned with helping your pupils become better thinkers? Do you want students to gain in their ability to utilize knowledge independently and effectively? If so, you may find this check list of classroom behaviors helpful to you.

Read each described classroom behavior carefully; then ask yourself: When my classroom is in normal operation, does the behavior described occur regularly, frequently, sometimes, or seldom? Check the space which you think best describes the normal operation of your classroom. When you have finished, give yourself four points for each item marked "regularly"; three points for "frequently"; two for "sometimes"; and one for "seldom." Fifty points or less means lots of room for improvement; 51–85, you're coming along; 86–110, you're better than most; 111–136, you've mastered inquiry techniques.

Don't be discouraged if you didn't score as well as you wished. Fill out the check list again a month from now and see how much you've improved.

Am I an Inquiry Teacher?

	Regularly	Frequently	Some-times	Seldom
As Planner — I focus on lessons involving exploration of significant ideas, concepts, or problem areas that can be investigated at many levels of sophistication.	——	——	——	——

From Mary Sugrue and Jo A. Sweeney, "Check Your Inquity-Teaching Technique," *Today's Education* 62 (May 1969), pp. 43–44. Reprinted with permission.

	Regularly	Frequently	Some-times	Seldom

As Planner

I prepare for a broad range of alternative ideas and values which the students may raise related to a central topic.

| | ___ | ___ | ___ | ___ |

I select materials and learning experiences to stimulate student curiosity and support student investigation.

| | ___ | ___ | ___ | ___ |

I make available a wide variety of resources and material for student use.

| | ___ | ___ | ___ | ___ |

Skill-building exercises are tied directly to ongoing learnings where they can be utilized and applied.

| | ___ | ___ | ___ | ___ |

As Introducer

My introductory lessons present some problem, question, contradiction, or unknown element that will maximize student thinking.

| | ___ | ___ | ___ | ___ |

My aim is for students to react freely to the introductory stimulus with little direction from me.

| | ___ | ___ | ___ | ___ |

I encourage many different responses to a given introductory stimulus and am prepared to deal with alternative patterns of exploration.

| | ___ | ___ | ___ | ___ |

As Questioner and Inquiry Sustainer

The students talk more than I do.

| | ___ | ___ | ___ | ___ |

Students are free to discuss and interchange their ideas.

| | ___ | ___ | ___ | ___ |

When I talk, I "question," not "tell."

| | ___ | ___ | ___ | ___ |

I consciously use the ideas students have raised and base my statements and questions on their ideas.

| | ___ | ___ | ___ | ___ |

I redirect student questions in such a way that students are encouraged to arrive at their own answers.

| | ___ | ___ | ___ | ___ |

My questions are intended to lead the pupils to explore, explain, support, and evaluate their ideas.

| | ___ | ___ | ___ | ___ |

I encourage students to move evaluate the adequacy of grounds provided for statements made by them or by others.

| | ___ | ___ | ___ | ___ |

		Regularly	Frequently	Some-times	Seldom

As Manager

Students gain understanding and practice in logical and scientific processes of acquiring, validating, and using knowledge. ____ ____ ____ ____

My questions lead the students to test the validity of their ideas in a broad context of experience. ____ ____ ____ ____

I encourage students to move from examination of particular cases to more generalized concepts and understandings. ____ ____ ____ ____

I emphasize learning and the use of ideas, rather than managerial functions, such as discipline and record keeping. ____ ____ ____ ____

I allow for flexible seating, student movement, and maximum student use of materials and resources. ____ ____ ____ ____

Class dialogue is conducted in an orderly fashion that emphasizes courtesy and willingness to listen to each person's ideas. ____ ____ ____ ____

Students are actively involved in the planning and maintenance of the total classroom environment. ____ ____ ____ ____

I foster balanced participation by encouraging the more reticent students to take an active role in classroom activities. ____ ____ ____ ____

As Rewarder

I encourage and reward the free exchange and testing of ideas. ____ ____ ____ ____

I emphasize the internal rewards that spring from the successful pursuit of one's own ideas. ____ ____ ____ ____

I avoid criticizing or judging ideas offered by students. ____ ____ ____ ____

Each student's contribution is considered legitimate and important. ____ ____ ____ ____

I evaluate students on growth in many aspects of the learning experience, rather than simply on the basis of facts acquired. ____ ____ ____ ____

I emphasize that concepts, social issues, policy decisions, attitudes, and values are legitimate areas for discussion. ____ ____ ____ ____

	Regularly	Frequently	Some-times	Seldom
As Value Investigator — All topics are critically examined, not "taught" as closed issues with a single "right" solution.	___	___	___	___
Use of unfounded, emotionally charged language is minimized in discussing attitudes and values.	___	___	___	___
I encourage the students to explore the implications of holding alternative value and policy positions.	___	___	___	___
I make the students aware of personal and social bases for diversity in attitudes, values, policies.	___	___	___	___
I encourage the students to arrive at value and policy positions of their own that they understand and can defend.	___	___	___	___

2. WHAT IS TEAM TEACHING?
J. Lloyd Trump

What is in a name? Usually there is more than that which meets the eye or ear. Certainly that is the case with "team teaching." This rubric means different things to various persons. Some regard it as a recent educational fad, something to brag about to colleagues in the next professional meeting. To others team teaching is a dragon that threatens the sanctity of the self-contained classroom and therefore is an enemy to be attacked with every weapon at hand. Still others regard it as a basic step in a long overdue educational revolution.

What *is* team teaching? What is it *not?* What should it *be?* This article aims to give workable answers to those questions.

"What Is Team Teaching?"

I prefer a relatively broad definition of team teaching. The term might apply to an arrangement whereby two or more teachers and their

From J. Lloyd Trump, "What is Team Teaching?" *Education* (February 1965). Reprinted with permission of the Bobbs-Merrill Company, Inc.

aides, in order to take advantage of their respective competencies, plan, instruct, and evaluate, in one or more subject areas, a group of elementary or secondary students equivalent in size to two or more conventional classes, making use of a variety of technical aids to teaching and learning in large-group instruction, small-group discussion, and independent study. Let us now analyze the various components.

Cooperative Activity

Team teaching is a cooperative activity. Teaching teams may involve all the teachers in a school or only a part of them. Each teacher does what he is most interested in and most able to do in the instructional system which the team develops and uses.

The members of a given team may come from within a subject department in the school, or the team may cut across subject lines. Teams that cut across subject lines tend to plan instruction that recognizes the inter-relatedness of subject content. In this regard, they have some of the same objectives as the core or common learnings curricular approaches.

Which type of team is better? Present research provides no answer. School philosophy and staff preferences control the local decision. Personally, I prefer teams that cut across subject lines. Teachers still work in their specialities, while they benefit from group planning. I have seen excellent as well as ineffective teams of both types.

A given team preferably includes older, more experienced teachers as well as beginners and less experienced ones. A diverse group thus benefits from contacts with each other.

The team needs to select a leader to preside at their planning and evaluating sessions. I do not favor too much formalization of this position or paying extra salary for it. The position of team leader is not analogous to that of a department chairman.

Involves Assistance

Team teaching involves providing assistance. A basic purpose of team teaching is to emphasize the truly professional role of the teacher. Therefore, a team needs the help of general aides, clerks, and instruction assistants.

Actually, general aides may not be assigned to specific teams because their functions may be school wide. General aides, unlike clerks or instruction assistants, do not possess specific educational qualifications. They are employed to assist in supervising playgrounds, taking tickets, storing materials, supervising non-specialized activities such as games and assemblies, and the like.

Instruction assistants are persons qualified in a given subject area but who do not possess the certification requirements of professional teachers. Typically the instruction assistant has at least a college minor in the subject area of the team to which he is attached. These assistants' tasks include helping to assemble materials, supervising independent study workrooms, and assisting with evaluation.

There are three major sources of instruction assistants: housewives, advanced college students, and retired teachers. They are employed on an hourly basis—typically 10–20 hours per week. Some of the work is done at home or in libraries or museums. The average pay is around two dollars per hour.

Clerical assistants type and duplicate materials, keep records, assist in supervising large groups, take attendance, pass out materials, check objective tests, and perform other duties.

Special consultants provide another type of assistance. If someone in the community is better qualified than any member of the team to make a presentation on a particular subject, he is invited to assume that responsibility. Both a visual and sound record is made of the presentation so that the material is available for further study or use without asking the consultant to return repeatedly. The team needs to assemble a file of available consultants with appropriate notations regarding specialized competencies. Taking a census of the community to assemble the consultant file is an appropriate activity of the PTA, student council, or service club.

These assistants are selected as carefully as teachers. They have essential tasks to do and must be competent to do them. Some assistants will become professional teachers. They are paid employees rather than voluntary workers so the school has legal control over them and legal protection for employing them.

Changes in laws or regulations in some states or cities are needed to facilitate the employment of assistants. Bus drivers and custodians are already provided for to supervise and/or deal with students. This precedent can be extended.

Technical Aids

Team teaching requires the use of aids. The instructional set-up is not complete without appropriate tools. Without technical aids, a large group presentation may be no better than the conventional lectures which teachers give in ordinary classes. The large group presentation space must include an overhead projector, other projectors, television, recorders, and possibly a flannel board.

All students must be able to hear and see very well. That requirement rules out the use of conventional maps, chalkboards, and small pictures in the large group setting. The screen must be reasonably large and tilted properly to minimize the keystone effect and facilitate better viewing. Chest microphones and adequate public address systems are other essentials.

The independent study workrooms need projection and recording devices that students can operate themselves, books and printed materials, programed instruction devices, and the specialized tools of the subject. For example, a social studies workroom needs typewriters, calculating machines, duplicating equipment, materials for making charts and maps, maps and globes, and preferably a teletype machine. The science workroom needs, in addition to the usual laboratory equipment, places where students can listen to recordings, look at projected materials, read, and write. Rooms utilized for remedial work in reading employ a variety of technical devices such as tachistoscopes, reading accelerators, program materials, and the like.

Small discussion rooms need tables, chairs and a chalkboard.

Instructional Reorganization

Team teaching involves reorganization of instruction. It attempts to use teachers' professional talents better. Teachers now lecture, present, demonstrate, and test in conventional classes an average of about one-half the time they spend with their students. Most of the remaining time the teachers use to conduct oral quizzes (erroneously called, classroom discussion) and to supervise study. One teacher and the usual 30 students in a "self-sufficient" classroom is not the best setting for discussion and study. Moreover, it is needlessly wasteful of teacher time and energy for the other activities wherein research shows class size is irrelevant to achieving the instructional purposes involved.

Teams of teachers plan which purposes are served best by large-group instruction, small-group discussion, and independent study. Also, the teams plan *who* will do *what* in the altered organizational program.

The best teaching the team can muster is used in large group instruction. This instruction may combine the use of personal presentation by a team member, a film, filmstrip, tape, or TV program, or the use of a consultant from outside the school. In any event, the instruction aims to motivate students, to bring them knowledge not readily available elsewhere, and to indicate what students are to do during independent study.

Giving written tests and using some types of programed materials are other large group activities.

The size of the group depends on the number of students available, the size of the room, and teacher preferences. The crucial elements are that all students can hear and see well and that the quality of the presentation is the best possible.

Independent study is either on an individual or group basis. Here is where students cover the essential knowledge and skills of the course and then hopefully go on to further creative and depth studies, each according to his own motivations and talents. Groups for remedial work or advanced study are organized as needed. Team teachers plan, sometimes personally prepare, and help to assemble a variety of materials for students to use in various resource centers. The students listen to tapes and records, view films, filmstrips, and visual materials, read, write, think, and work with the "tools of the trade" in the subject fields. Mostly, instruction assistants conduct the routine supervision of students and arrange appointments with professional teachers as needed.

Small group discussion develops communication skills, teaches problem solving and critical thinking, and encourages better interpersonal relations. Team teachers spend much of their teaching time meeting with students in groups of 15 or under to accomplish the listed goals in all subjects.

Flexible Schedule

Team teaching requires a flexible schedule. Members must decide *who* does *what* with *which* groups of students, and also *when* and for *how long*. The conventional rigid schedule which students follow day after day, changing their places automatically as the programed clock rings bells, is replaced. Control over time is given to the teaching teams for daily or weekly changes. Students also need the privilege of changing the amounts of time and locale of their independent study, subject to the approval of teachers and counselors. Time varies with the purposes of teaching and learning in the team teaching situation.

Different Approach

Team teaching is a different approach to teaching roles and to evaluation. Team members constantly meet to define and evaluate their changed teaching roles with respect to large groups, small groups, and independent study. Team teaching will not be more effective if teaching methods are the same as in conventional classrooms.

Team evaluation of individual pupil progress is another ingredient of team teaching. Tests reveal the gains pupils make in achieving the essential facts, understandings, and skills of the different courses. Team members report on changes in pupil behavior as observed in small groups. Scaling techniques reveal accomplishments in independent study. Anecdotal reports are received and interpreted by each team member who bears responsibility for the portion of the team's students assigned to him. Comprehensive reports provide discrete, significant information on the accomplishment of goals to pupils, parents, employers, and colleges.

Different Spending Habits

Team teaching involves spending money differently. It requires analysis of the financial feasibility of making changes. The team saves money with large-group instruction, by using less costly clerks and instruction assistants, by permitting students to learn more by themselves under the supervision of assistants, and by using educational facilities (buildings and teaching tools) more efficiently. The team spends more money on small groups, on reducing the hours teachers are scheduled with groups, and on the use of technical aids to teaching and learning. The savings can approximately offset the added costs if the team plans its work carefully.

What Team Teaching Is Not

Team teaching does not mean, for example, 3 teachers and 90 students who occasionally come together for a presentation to the total group and then return to their respective classes of 30. This simple variation of class size is not likely to produce any more gains for teachers or pupils than the hundreds of class size studies conducted in this country and in others for many years.

Moreover, team teaching does not mean merely changing standard size classes of 30 each to classes of 120, 15, and individual study without changing what teachers and students do. What teachers today call "class discussion" is inappropriate for large groups. Similarly, their typical lectures given to small classes are inadequate. A small-group session is largely wasted if teachers continue to conduct oral quizzes or lectures. Independent study involves more for students than conventional homework or merely reading books and filling in blanks.

Team teaching is not limited either to secondary or elementary age students. Nor is it limited to the academically able or the highly motivated pupils. It is not appropriate only for some subjects, but rather works well in all of them since the principles of teaching and learning are similar.

Certainly team teaching is not an effort to increase the routine duties of teachers. However, it is not only an effort to reduce the total hours per week that teachers spend in their professional tasks.

Team teaching is not per se an effort to solve the teacher shortage problem except as it identifies more stimulating and professional roles. It is not merely changing teacher-pupil ratio for the sake of juggling numbers.

Above all, team teaching is not a fad to be engaged in simply because others are doing it or as a temporary expedient to solve a building shortage or financial problems because a referendum did not pass. Team teaching is not a superficial arrangement for educators and communities that have not thought deeply or carefully considered their convictions about how to improve educational quality.

What Team Teaching Should Be

United States education knows no shortages of innovation and experimentation. Long before Sputnik, this constant search for better educational quality accounted for the superiority of our schools. Nowhere in the world have so many been educated so well.

Team teaching, like other innovations past and present, succeeds only to the extent that conditions such as the following are met:

1. The broad implications of the change are realized and met.
2. Teachers are reeducated on the job prior to and during the change.
3. Evaluation changes proceed along with the innovations.
4. Shortcomings are remedied as soon as they are discovered.
5. Appropriate facilities are obtained.
6. The financial implications are considered so that the new procedures are reasonable in their demands for added expenditures.
7. Adequate, honest, easily understood information about the changes is provided to lay and professional groups.

Team teaching constitutes a basic, broad-scoped educational reorganization designed to improve the conditions for teaching and learning and to improve markedly the achievement of educational goals long held by perceptive educators. That is what team teaching can and should be. If it is less than that, those who plan and direct programs should take another look and try again.

Part VI

EDUCATIONISM

Introduction

The ideology of Educationism has been instrumental in the development of America's vast system of formal public schooling. Aided by the demands of a country concerned about social cohesion and goaded by the manpower needs of our industrial system, educationists have provided a rationale for a continuing extension of formal schooling.

The basic elements of Educationism include formalism, institutionalism, and professionalism. Adherents to this ideology believe that learning must be formalized, that education must occur within an institution and that the process must be controlled by professionally trained personnel. These elements, educationists assert, are necessary prerequisites for social progress.

Since its inception in seventeenth-century Puritan New England, formal education has been viewed as a major instrument in the process of acculturation and as one of the primary means of creating social cohesion. This function of the schools was emphasized again after the American Revolution and during the period of increased immigration in the nineteenth century.

Formal schooling is sometimes viewed as a panacea for social ills. Educationists generally believe that such problems as drug use, unemployment, racism, poverty, and venereal disease could be solved if formal schooling were to receive adequate support. In addition, they certainly would agree with Jefferson's equation of education with political freedom. Without schooling the American citizenry would be victimized by demagogues, but schooling will guarantee an enlightened citizenry whose wisdom will be reflected in their choice of political office-holders and their awareness of political issues.

Literacy continues to be a major concern of educationists. Indeed, they believe that civilization is founded upon literacy; without it, a "civilized" populace would quickly regress to barbarism and savagery. The emphasis on literacy, however, is not directly related to intellectualism. In fact, many educationists have been more or less accurately described as anti-intellectual. Although the controversy between the "intellectuals" and the "anti-intellectuals" is to be found within the ranks of the educationists, it is carried on most intensely in conflicts between educationists and academicians. While academicians castigate educationists for their lack of intellectual rigor, educationists condemn academicians for their failure to be concerned with learning. Educationists maintain that subject matter knowledge is only one of many factors to be considered when judging teachers; academicians answer that the application of the principles of Educationism produces teachers whose technical proficiency at teaching does not make up for their inadequate grasp of the subject matter to be taught. This debate goes on endlessly and there is much to be said on both sides.

The ideology of Educationism has been enhanced enormously by industrialization. Historically, the importance of formal schooling has depended inversely upon the strength of familial influence. As the importance of the family diminishes, a consequence of industrialization, the significance of schooling increases. With the development of day care centers and Head Start programs, the importance of schooling continues to increase as it did when the extended family was replaced by the nuclear family.

Automation and cybernetics have created a labor market that demands a smaller work force having higher levels of skills. Formal schooling provides an alternative to the declining demands of the labor market by occupying young people who otherwise would be thrown into the job market. In addition, it is used to train and certify those who enter the work force. These factors have been responsible for creating a credential-oriented society. Inasmuch as credentialization is largely determined by formal schooling, the ideology of Educationism has been significantly enhanced by this trend.

Because formal schooling has become the major factor in determining social mobility, the schools have become centers of controversy. Racial and/or ethnic minority groups, realizing the increased importance of schooling, have become quite concerned about school policy and the concept of "good schools" has become a national issue.

Many educationists, feeling threatened by "outside" demands and a "taxpayers' revolt," yet aware of their recently acquired prestige, have found it necessary to unite in order to protect and consolidate their recent gains. Considering themselves to be professionals, they generally have supported the National Education Association (NEA). Recently, however, victories of the American Federation of Teachers (AFT) have influenced the direction of the NEA. Both organizations continue to emphasize the concept of professionalism and the differences between their means of attaining professional status has diminished.

Because educationists have access to a vast formal system that can be used to promote specific causes, they are constantly beleaguered by individuals and/or groups representing various ideological persuasions. Controversy becomes exceptionally intense when these individuals and/or groups believe their ideological stance is being threatened. On a national level, superpatriots and adherents to Scientism, for example, successfully influenced school policy following the Soviet Union's launching of Sputnik. On a local level, puritans and progressivists have engaged in ideological conflicts concerning such controversial issues as sex education.

In addition to the controversy created in the schools by "outside" ideological influences, educationists themselves disagree about many issues directly related to their own ideology. The eclectic nature of Educationism is reflected in the many attempts to define the specific aims of education. Educationists all agree, for example, that formal schooling will enrich the lives of the students. But, should formal schooling minimize or maximize cultural differences? Should it be an equalizer or should it promote an aristocracy of talent? Failing to achieve any modicum of consensus on these specific questions, educationists have developed a list of general aims, such as "citizenship" and "democracy," that remain rather abstract and vague. Attempts to clarify these aims create additional controversy when "outside" ideological commitments are involved, so that educationists continue to frustrate the true believers of all ideological persuasions.

In the first selection of Part VI, Educationism, Professors V. T. Thayer and Martin Levit examine the interrelationship of the school and the society in order to arrive at a scholarly overview of the American faith in education. As the reader will note, the ideology of Educationism has been instrumental in forging and propagating this questionable but enduring belief.

The ideological creed is exemplified in the Code of Ethics developed by the Committee on Professional Ethics of the National Education Association. The Code illustrates the educationists' concern for formalism, institutionalism, and professionalism.

Few individuals have so fervently espoused the tenets of Educationism as Horace Mann. His "common school" crusade, as it was so aptly termed, focused upon the absolute necessity of universal, compulsory, tax-supported formal schooling. "Education," Mann asserted in his twelfth Annual Report on Education (1848), "is the great equalizer of men, the balance wheel of the social machinery." In addition, he believed, as other educationists do, that formal schooling would eliminate poverty, create a respect for private property, develop a sense of moral responsibility and tolerance, and produce a politically enlightened citizenry.

By the mid-ninetenth century numerous normal schools were established to meet the ever-increasing demand for public school teachers. Individuals, predominantly women from rather humble socioeconomic origins, enrolled in the two-year certification programs offered by these institutions. The normal schools, later to be known as state teachers colleges, emphasized the middle-class puritan virtues and the concept of the teacher as a moral exemplar. This emphasis is illustrated in the excerpts from an article by David Page, a principal of a normal school in Albany, New York. His admonishments to teachers in 1849 continue to be relevant to educationists today.

The next selection, the Cardinal Principles of Secondary Education, illustrates the educationists' continuing attempt to define and clarify the aims of the immense bureaucratic system of formal schooling. The reader will note that the aims are characterized by their generality and their inclusiveness. This may not result in clarity, but it does obviate potential ideological conflicts.

Although both Booker T. Washington and W. E. B. DuBois may have agreed that education could be an equalizer, they vociferously disagreed about the type of education best suited for black people. Washington called for practical vocational education for the masses of black people, whereas DuBois demanded a vigorous intellectual education, especially for the "talented tenth." The essence of their debate retains significance for modern educationists, who continue to disagree about the nature of education. To what extent should formal schooling be directed toward job training? Should students be tracked according to ability? Should formal schooling serve to "sort and select" individuals according to their "probable destinies"?

The consequences of court decisions oft-times profoundly influence the thoughts and actions of educationists. In the next selection, *Plessy v. Ferguson* (1895), the majority opinion of the United States Supreme Court affirmed a lower court decision that "separate but equal" facilities were, in fact, constitutional. Although the decision concerned passenger train coaches, it legitimized the concept of "separate but equal" in other areas of society, including public schooling. Justice Harlan's dissenting opinion foreshadowed the 1954 *Brown et al. v. Board of Education of Topeka et al.* case (see selection in Part IV, Nationalism) in which the court ruled that separate facilities are inherently unequal. Recently, these decisions have been further complicated by the issue of busing "to achieve racial balance." Educationists continue to be surrounded by controversy.

The issue of unionism has become increasingly important to Educationists. Faced with controversy surrounding the school system and a taxpayers' revolt, educationists have turned to organized action as a means of exerting influence. Perceiving themselves as professionals, educationists in the past generally refused to join the teachers' union, the American Federation of Teachers, but today an increasing number has accepted the concept of unionism. This concept, described in the article by Donald L. Conrad, a member of National Education Association, has been elaborated in such a way as to incorporate the views of both the AFT and the NEA. The emphasis is placed upon professionalism yet allows collective bargaining and strikes or "work stoppages."

From the ideological perspective of Educationism, the teacher is viewed as a professional. In an excerpt from his book *The Future of Public Education,* Myron Lieberman examines the ideal role of the teacher as professional and advocates the continuing professionalization of education. Most educationists would avidly agree with Professor Lieberman.

AN ANALYTICAL VIEW: A Brief Survey

FAITH IN EDUCATION
V. T. Thayer & Martin Levit

A Common Faith

From their earliest establishment, settlements upon the American continent have been characterized by diversity. Varying in national origin and ethnic background, in religion, language, and customs, Americans have always faced problems of forging unity from difference and stability from change.

The schools of America have played a major role in the process of evolving a common culture. Even in the relatively homogeneous communities of seventeenth-century New England, schools were established to realize objectives more comprehensive than those of similar institutions in England and on the Continent. High on the list was the resolve to offset the disintegrating effects of new living conditions upon family life and long-established values. While less ambitious, legislation for education in the Middle and Southern colonies during the colonial period had much the same purpose.

The school's share in the development of American civilization has been continually growing. The transition from a predominantly rural and agricultural society to one industrial and urban has called for ever higher levels of education for ever more people; this extension of educational opportunities, in turn, has resulted in a level of productivity that has permitted—indeed, required—larger numbers to prolong their education. The developing American economy has given rise to a new class structure, to new professional and managerial positions, and to a socioeconomic mobility closely identified with democracy and access to

From V. T. Thayer and Martin Levit, *The Role of the School in American Society* (N.Y.: Dodd, Mead & Company, Inc., 1960), pp. 3–15. Copyright © 1960 Dodd, Mead & Company, Inc. Reprinted by permission of Dodd, Mead & Company.

the "good life" by an ever-increasing proportion of the population.

In international relations the American dream of individual liberty and progress has been translated into revolution, expansionism, and a general belief in the Manifest Destiny of the United States to carry its way of life to other lands. In the course of these changes, the schools have been called upon to help develop a spirit of national unity, to instruct students in the changing definitions of allies and enemies, and, in recent decades, to provide the trained manpower essential for the specialized needs of a modern great power.

At different periods and under differing conditions the individual equipment required for effective participation in American life has varied from the barest literacy to the acquisition of complex technical and professional skills; from a high level of personal ambition and a disciplined zest for work (that is, from the ability to play a lone hand successfully) to ability to get along well with people; from a modicum of knowledge and a maximal acceptance of the status quo to competent inquiry into the problems of impending change. Again, the schools have been asked to contribute by providing the means for the individual's acquisition of skills for today's needs.

Often the shifting and contradictory demands upon the schools, as well as their admitted failures and defects, have resulted in waves of criticism against the schools. Generally speaking, however, criticism has reflected less a lack of faith in public education itself than conflict and division with respect to the *ends* the schools should serve and the *methods* they should employ to realize these ends. These social conflicts and divisions find their correlates today in the confused and contradictory beliefs of many individuals as to the function of education in American society.

Historians tell us that in appending their names to the Declaration of Independence, with its revolutionary assertion that "all men are created equal" and are "endowed . . . with certain unalienable Rights," the members of the Continental Congress had in mind no more than the principle that all men are equal in the sight of the law and should be so treated by government. Very quickly, however, under the unique conditions of American life, there developed a mutually sustaining relationship between popular psychology and the material conditions of living. Life in the United States seemed to confirm the theory that all men are born essentially equal in their potentialities. As a result, within seventy years of the signing of the Declaration of Independence, that vigorous advocate of public schools, Horace Mann, could assert, with little fear of contradiction that "there is by nature little or perhaps no distinction among men with respect to their original power of intellect. The seeds of knowledge, of refinement, and of literary excellence are implanted with a liberality, nearly or completely equal, in the mind of the ignorant peasant, and in the mind of the most profound philosopher."

The School as an Open Frontier

Life on the ever-expanding frontier, with its democratic faith in the potentialities of each individual, seemingly reinforced this assumption of original equality among men. The frontier invited the oppressed and the underprivileged of the earth to seek their fortunes in America. So alluring, indeed, was this invitation that in the colonial period many an ambitious soul became a bonded servant, subject to purchase and sale, in order to pay for his passage from Europe to America. Others cheerfully accepted the hardships involved in clearing the forests and breaking virgin soil in order to insure for themselves and their children a fresh start in life. For a period these opportunities derived principally and directly from the open country, but in the course of time the opportunities of an industrial economy proved equally attractive. With the exploitation of these later opportunities, however, both general and technical education assumed ever more importance.

The agricultural and industrial attractions of the frontier thus led Americans to ascribe to education, and, in particular, to a system of tax-supported education on all levels—elementary, secondary, and higher—a status unique in history.

This is not to say that determination of an "adequate" education has been the same at all times or in all places. The level for functional literacy, for example, and for other skills essential for individual competence in practical affairs has risen with developments in the American economy. It once involved little more than the ability to write one's name and to read the simplest sentences. Later, the mastery of the three R's to a degree somewhat less than that now provided in the curriculum of the elementary school became a minimum requirement, with the result that throughout the nineteenth century the term "common school" was used to designate the elementary school. In the early 1900s the junior high school came into existence with a view to providing a "terminal education" for a rapidly expanding school population. But after a relatively short period, the need for further schooling was recognized. Soon the upper years of the secondary school were confronted with a similar obligation, and it is today widely recognized that graduation from the secondary school constitutes an inadequate preparation for successful and responsible participation in contemporary life. Indeed, with the emergence of the junior college, terminal education has invaded the college years.

Paralleling, or should we say supporting, these increasing demands for additional formal schooling has been confidence in the magical powers of an education. Often this has been of a materialistic and narrowly practical character. The school was conceived of as a great democratic opportunity, an agency designed to enable those who wanted to better their lot in life to do so. Poor and rich alike might attend it and thus acquire the information and training indispensable for individual advancement.

Some see in this faith in education little more than an expression of the materialism that dominates American life. That there has been and still is a materialistic core to it is no doubt true. Horace Mann, for example, despite his idealism, was shrewd enough to know that his fellow citizens required hard-headed arguments if they were to agree to tax themselves on behalf of public schools. Consequently, he sought to demonstrate that ". . . education has a market value; that it is so far an article of merchandise, that it may be turned to pecuniary account; it may be minted, and will yield a larger amount of statuable coin than common bullion. . . . The aim of industry is served, and the wealth of the country is augmented, in proportion to the diffusion of knowledge."

Witness, too, the numerous publications throughout the years that, presenting evidence of the financial rewards that come with schooling, are designed to persuade youth to resist the inducements of immediate earnings out of school. One typical set of figures compares the annual mean incomes for males twenty-five years of age and over by years of school completed. These statistics indicate that college graduates earn well over three times more than those who have had less than eight years of schooling, well over twice as much as those with just eight years of schooling, and about 40 per cent more than high school graduates. Moreover, since 1939 the differences between these incomes have been increasing.[1]

Or, take the results of a national poll conducted in 1963 by the Survey Research Center of the University of Michigan. The survey found that 96 per cent of the public believes a college education is more important now than it was about thirty years ago. Of those polled, 72 per cent believe that the most important benefit from a college education is "training for a good job." The reasons given next most frequently for going to college were "social acceptance" and "getting to know the right people."

We agree that these expressions of faith in education are materialistic. It is easy, however, to oversimplify one's judgments. Frequently, an educated man is able to enjoy the refinements of living commonly denied to those who "work with their hands." Moreover, this way of life might well include nonmaterialistic as well as materialistic values. And often

---

[1] U.S. Office of Education, *Digest of Educational Statistics* (Washington, D.C.: Government Printing Office, 1964), p. 126.

his work is more stimulating and, therefore, enjoyable in itself. It is not uncommon for the "cultured," or the fortunate possessor of conditions that make for ease and comfort, to condemn as evidence of the "materialistic spirit of the times" the strivings of a submerged group for similar refinements of living!

Broad relations among certain educational, economic, political, and intellectual factors suggest that a rigid division between so-called "materialistic" and "higher" values may be misleading. It is clearly false, for example, that among nations a high degree of social mobility and the widespread availability of education are invariably associated with a high level of political democracy.[2] On the other hand, it is quite generally true that a low level of political democracy is associated with a low level of social mobility and with limited educational opportunities.[3] An extensive and careful comparison of preindustrial and industrial societies reveals the key role played by industrialization in increasing social mobility and the proportions of middle- and upper-class occupations.[4] In the United States there has been a close association between movements directed at expanding educational opportunities and movements toward political, social, and economic reforms.[5]

Although the economic motive for education is a dominant drive, education often has expanded more than economic horizons. Many studies have revealed that people of lower-class status who have had a limited education strongly tend to favor intolerant, authoritarian forms of political and religious behavior.[6] Even when individuals are grouped according to social class status, persons within each class who have higher levels of education tend to be characterized by more liberal and humanitarian attitudes, greater cultural awareness, and a higher level of interest in civic and international affairs.[7] Level of education seems to be asso-

[2] See, for example, Seymour M. Lipset, "The Value Patterns of Democracy: A Case Study in Comparative Analysis," *American Sociological Review*, August 1963, pp. 515–31.

[3] See John Vaizey, "Comparative Notes on Economic Growth and Social Change in Education," *Comparative Education Review*, June 1961, pp. 7–12. See also Theodore L. Reller and Edgar L. Morphet, eds., *Comparative Educational Administration* (Englewood Cliffs, N.J.: Prentice-Hall, Inc., 1962), pp. 375, 377.

[4] Robert M. Marsh, "Values, Demand and Social Mobility," *American Sociological Review*, August 1963, pp. 565–75.

[5] For an excellent analysis of these movements, see Rush Welter, *Popular Education and Democratic Thought in America* (New York: Columbia University Press, 1962).

[6] For a review of some relevant studies, see Melvin L. Kohn, "Social Class and Parent-Child Relationships: An Interpretation," *American Journal of Sociology*, January 1963, pp. 475–79.

[7] Burton R. Clark discusses some of these studies in his book *Educating the Expert Society* (San Francisco: Chandler Publishing Company, 1962), pp. 30–37. See also Robert M. Frumkin, "Dogmatism, Social Class, Values, and Academic Achievement in Sociology," *Journal of Educational Sociology*, May 1961, pp. 398–403.

ciated with these characteristics and values even when such variables as age, occupation, and income are controlled or taken into account.

These findings do not justify the claim that more formal education produces unadulterated virtues. Nor can one assume that the person who defends, say, the political rights of other persons necessarily has a profound understanding of why he does or should defend those rights. Moreover, like other American institutions, education is heavily endowed with various brands of anti-intellectualism.[8] Indeed . . . we will argue that the schools have often repressed rather than released critical intelligence and creative, contemplative tendencies.

At all events, it is well to recognize that the schooling an individual prizes initially for its promise to better his status economically may also open his eyes to values to which he had previously been blind. We can thus draw the moral that one possible way to transform the material aspirations of an individual or a people into values of a higher order is to provide more education. In the case of an individual as well as a group, economic well-being constitutes a soil more favorable than poverty and undernourishment for the cultivation of the values of a liberal education.

Free Schools and the Conservation of Values

Thus far we have emphasized the individualistic expression of the American's faith in education. This is but half the story. Equally significant has been a vision of the social mission of the school.

The social conception of the functions of education in America dates from the origin of the first schools. In New England and the Middle Colonies a primary purpose in establishing schools was to insure the perpetuation of the religious faith of the community. To be sure, what constituted religious truth varied as one moved from one colony to another. In New England, to which the Puritan had journeyed, impelled by the conviction that "the God of Heaven had carried a nation into the wilderness upon the designs of a glorious transformation," schools were a major means for insuring allegiance to what Cotton Mather also described as "the pure and full dispensations of the Gospel." [9]

---

[8] See Richard Hofstadter, *Anti-intellectualism in American Life* (New York: Alfred A. Knopf, 1963), chaps. XII–XIV.

[9] . . . we shall return to the influence of early religious motives upon education. However, it may be well to state here that religious ardor waned after the middle of the seventeenth century, and that in both early and later expressions, religious motives were often used to justify concerns other than religious. Nevertheless, the early colonial mind generally identified social health with religious orthodoxy and, as Oscar Handlin states, "seventeenth century schools [were] mainly religious in orientation . . . the Bible was the primary text." (See his *The Americans: A New History of the People of the United States* [Boston: Little, Brown and Company, 1963],

Similar motives prompted the good people of the Middle Colonies to establish schools, but heterogeneity of religious faith rather than homogeneity prevailed. Each community in this checkered pattern was convinced of the validity of its own faith, and schools were recognized as essential in order to perpetuate "truth" in competition with "error." Thus schooling, both in subject matter and method, served the commonly accepted purpose of education for conformity. So axiomatic was this conception of education, even with respect to higher education, that the authors of Statutes of the College of William and Mary were constrained to enjoin instructors to "take special care that if the author is never so well approved on other accounts, he [the Master] teach no such part of him to his scholars as insinuates against religion and morals." [10]

With the advent of manhood suffrage and the increasing participation of the common man in government, the attempt to use education as a means of forming the mind of the young assumed political importance. Members of the upper classes now envisaged the possibility of government by "the mob." As Catherine Beecher put it, the common people had become masters, and consequently "the education of the common people . . . is the point around which the wisest heads, the warmest hearts, the most powerful energies should gather for conservation, for planning, for unity of action, and for persevering enterprise."

As Richard D. Mosier amply illustrates in his careful study of the influence of the McGuffey readers, the compilers of these books turned to the Beechers, along with many others, for material with which to influence the minds of the young, and thus "safeguard[ed] established institutions from the inroads of Jacksonian hordes" by instilling the proper political as well as social and moral concepts.[11]

There is a temptation to see (as some critics have done) in this deliberate and earnest effort to form the minds of the young the selfish attempts of once dominant groups to perpetuate their ideals and ways of living in a shifting and changing situation. Although partially true, this explanation fails to do justice to the generous aspirations of many a pioneer in early American education. Some of these people were ardently committed to change, and saw in public education an instrument

---

p. 121.) It is possible that some current skepticism concerning the potency of the religious motive in the colonial period is, in part, a reflection of certain contemporary attitudes that find their expression in historical interpretation.

[10] See Elmer Ellsworth Brown, *The Making of Our Middle Schools* (New York: Longmans, Green & Company, 1914), chap. VII, for an excellent account of education in colonial schools. See also Adolphe Meyer, *An Educational History of the American People* (New York: McGraw-Hill, Inc., 1957), chap. VI.

[11] *Making the American Mind* (New York: Kings Crown Press, 1947), chaps. I, IV.

with which to insure for all the blessings commonly enjoyed only by the few. Certainly we should hesitate to describe the motivations of Horace Mann and Henry Barnard exclusively in terms of class consciousness, even though their concepts of the good life may have been identical with the virtues and values of one class of society rather than another.[12] It is more accurate to credit them with insight, rare in their day, into the relationship between free schools and a free society.

At the same time, profiting from the record, we can identify an excess of optimism in some of the arguments put forth in support of a system of tax-supported schools. Thus, we find Horace Mann looking to popular education as an automatic cure for the dangers that follow from an excess of wealth in one class and poverty in another. "Education," he asserted in his famous report of 1848 to the Massachusetts State Board of Education, "is the great equalizer of men, the balance wheel of the social machinery."

Not all individuals, however, are equally moved by broad, general social objectives. They require more direct and immediate evidence of ways in which new proposals will better their lot. The advocates of free schools early in the nineteenth century were keenly aware of this fact. Accordingly, not only educators, such as Horace Mann and Henry Barnard in the North, Caleb Cushing in the South, and Calvin Stowe in the West, but liberal-minded laymen, labor leaders, and statesmen emphasized the practical importance of a free education in a free society. To stubborn objectors, such as the irate Rhode Island farmer who threatened to do bodily harm to Henry Barnard for "preaching such a horrible heresy as the partial confiscation of one man's property to educate another man's children," [13] the advocates of tax-supported schools put this question: "Which do you prefer: to tax yourselves for jails or for schools?"

Thaddeus Stevens employed this argument most effectively in the Pennsylvania legislature in 1834, when engaged in one of the most dramatic and influential battles over the issues of free education. In an address later printed and distributed widely throughout the country, Stevens answered virtually all the common objections to publicly supported education and also demonstrated the benefits that would flow from it.

To the argument that it is unjust, if not immoral, to tax people to provide educational facilities from which they can observe no direct or

---

[12] For an excellent presentation of these views, see Merle Curti, *The Social Ideas of American Educators* (New York: Charles Scribner's Sons, 1935), chaps. III, IV.

[13] Edgar W. Knight, *Education in the United States* (Boston: Ginn & Company, 1934), p. 250.

indirect return, Stevens replied that it is nevertheless for their own benefit since it sustains government and the laws that protect their lives and property. Furthermore, inquired Stevens, why not urge the same objections to other taxes? "The industrious, thrifty, rich farmer" pays taxes to support courts, jails, sheriffs, and other officials whom he will probably never use, "but loudly complains of that which goes to prevent his fellow-being from becoming a criminal and to obviate the necessity of these humiliating institutions." [14]

The virtues of an education for citizenship, as Thaddeus Stevens and his associates envisaged it, were essentially political. It is understandable, therefore, that a predominantly rural population, accustomed to relatively simple institutions and face-to-face relations with their public servants, should have remained skeptical of the indispensable character of formal education. For many decades, in fact, the friends of tax-supported schools were confronted with arguments similar to those of a rural correspondent for a Raleigh (N.C.) newspaper who inquired whether it might not be of as much advantage to young people, as well as to the state, "if they should pass their days in the cotton patch, or at the plow, or in the cornfield, instead of being mewed up in a schoolhouse where they are earning nothing." [15]

In the rapidly growing cities of America the importance of schooling was more obvious. Here the children of immigrants, together with the children of families accustomed only to rural living, were growing up under slum conditions. This fact profoundly disturbed many who were accustomed to thinking of America as a land of open opportunities and who were resolved to keep it so. To these individuals—representatives of labor, humanitarians, statesmen, educators—we are indebted for the concept of the school as an agency designed to serve the children of all classes in much the same way as the open country with its free land had long served adults by providing an opportunity to better their status in life. Out of their efforts came, eventually, the decision of all states in the Union to provide schooling free to all able and willing to profit therefrom.

Nor did schools fail in this objective. They were so conspicuously successful that with steady progress in industrialization and the gradual transformation of a predominantly rural and agricultural economy into an urban and industrial economy a schooling that was once optional for the young became compulsory. Massachusetts was the first state to set this example with the passage of a compulsory school attendance law in 1852. Other states followed with varying degrees of rapidity. In 1918

[14] Thomas Frederick Woodley, *Thaddeus Stevens* (Harrisburg, Pa.: Telegraph Press, 1934), pp. 153–67.
[15] Knight, *op. cit.*, p. 244.

the circle was complete when Mississippi, the last of the states to do so, finally adopted its compulsory school attendance law.[16]

Many of the conditions that seemed to dictate free education and, later, compulsory school attendance likewise suggested an ever enlarging area of responsibility for the school. For children of the foreign-born and children of underprivileged rural families the school has functioned as a melting pot in the sense that it has striven to instill in the young ideas and ideals, specific habits and dispositions of ways of life unlike their original backgrounds. Indeed, the process of assimilation has not infrequently been carried so far that the school has been charged with creating unfortunate gaps between the generations, with the further result that potential contributions of peoples from widely different cultures have been lost to American life.

Be this as it may, economic, social, and political life since the day of Thaddeus Stevens has complicated and extended the services of the school far beyond what Stevens and his fellow pioneers envisaged. Today even many traditionalists who would restrict the schools largely to the teaching of "basic subjects" and "fundamental disciplines" think of these subjects in ways that go far beyond most nineteenth-century and early twentieth-century conceptions of subject matter. Arithmetic, for example, may be seen not as merely a collection of numbers, tables, and simple mathematical operations, but as an example of inductive and deductive modes of thought and of other logical concepts and operations.[17] Or American history may be seen as loaded and spiced with problems of causation, interpretation, and verification.[18]

Moreover, many traditionalists assume or assert that the schools should perform functions that would have seemed preposterous in, say, 1875 to many reformers urging an expansion of educational functions. . . .

The world today is one of science and technology, of accelerating change, of complex and closely knit parts. These descriptions help explain the rapid decline of "common sense" and traditional practices as sufficient responses and the increasingly central role of education in our times. Whether we desire wealth and security or an understanding of ourselves and society, we turn to education to find ways and means.

[16] It is one thing to pass a law and altogether another to provide adequately for its enforcement. In a number of instances states made no provision for the enforcement of these acts. Even today considerable variation exists as to the years covered by compulsory acts and the means of enforcement.

[17] Stewart S. Cairns, "Mathematics," in James D. Koerner, ed., *The Case for Basic Education: A Program of Aims for Public Schools* (Boston: Little, Brown and Company, 1959), pp. 155–69.

[18] Ray A. Billington, "American History," in Koerner, *op. cit.*, pp. 27–48.

The American's faith in education, then, has both persisted and expanded throughout the years. However, as a result of the uses to which this faith has been put, problems have arisen. Principles and procedures that in a simple and relatively homogeneous community seemed self-evident have become less so—have even become questionable—in today's complex and heterogeneous society. Take for illustration the colonial concept of teaching as synonymous with the instilling of approved ideas in the minds of the young. This was once widely accepted as the legitimate function of the school. This concept of education, however, is difficult to apply once communities become genuinely heterogeneous in politics, in religion, and in social and cultural background.

Out of the practical necessity of maintaining peace and furthering understanding within diversity in American life has emerged the concept of freedom of thought and expression and the discipline of free inquiry as an essential value in American society. This second tradition is the younger, although older by far than the public school, and is grounded in principles sanctioned by the federal Constitution.

Thus it is that two traditions in education are in conflict, each contending for a central position in the school: one a tradition of conformity and orthodoxy, the other a tradition of free inquiry, each with its appropriate discipline of thought. One of the problems in present-day education is to determine the relations that should obtain between these two traditions and the educational procedures that derive from each.

Consistent with the first tradition is the tendency of earnest individuals and groups to use education as an instrument for implanting in the minds of the young the information and conviction that these elders believe to be all-important.

The second tradition has the problem of rendering more explicit than it has done thus far the relation of the discipline of free inquiry to the entire program of the school and to areas of knowledge not visibly subject to change as well as to areas still uncertain and controversial.

The adherents of both traditions are, however, as one in their faith in education. To this faith, in large measure, we may ascribe the phenomenal growth and development of the public school system of the United States.

THE CREED: Educationist Admonitions

NATIONAL EDUCATION ASSOCIATION
Code of Ethics

Preamble

We, professional educators of the United States of America, affirm our belief in the worth and dignity of man. We recognize the supreme importance of the pursuit of truth, the encouragement of scholarship, and the promotion of democratic citizenship. We regard as essential to these goals the protection of freedom to learn and to teach and the guarantee of equal educational opportunity for all. We affirm and accept our responsibility to practice our profession according to the highest ethical standards.

We acknowledge the magnitude of the profession we have chosen, and engage ourselves, individually and collectively, to judge our colleagues and to be judged by them in accordance with the applicable provisions of this code.

Principle I

COMMITMENT TO THE STUDENT

We measure success by the progress of each student toward achievement of his maximum potential. We therefore work to stimulate the spirit of inquiry, the acquisition of knowledge and understanding, and the thoughtful formulation of worthy goals. We recognize the importance of cooperative relationships with other community institutions, especially the home.

In fulfilling our obligations to the student, we—

1. Deal justly and considerately with each student.

Committee on Professional Ethics, National Education Association. Reprinted by permission.

2. Encourage the student to study varying points of view and respect his right to form his own judgment.

3. Withhold confidential information about a student or his home unless we deem that its release serves professional purposes, benefits the student, is required by law.

4. Make discreet use of available information about the student.

5. Conduct conferences with or concerning students in an appropriate place and manner.

6. Refrain from commenting unprofessionally about a student or his home.

7. Avoid exploiting our professional relationship with any student.

8. Tutor only in accordance with officially approved policies.

9. Inform appropriate individuals and agencies of the student's educational needs and assist in providing an understanding of his educational experiences.

10. Seek constantly to improve learning facilities and opportunities.

Principle II

COMMITMENT TO THE COMMUNITY

We believe that patriotism in its highest form requires dedication to the principles of our democratic heritage. We share with all other citizens the responsibility for the development of sound public policy. As educators, we are particularly accountable for participating in the development of educational programs and policies and for interpreting them to the public.

In fulfilling our obligations to the community, we—

1. Share the responsibility for improving the educational opportunities for all.

2. Recognize that each educational institution may have a person authorized to interpret its official policies.

3. Acknowledge the right and responsibility of the public to participate in the formulation of educational policy.

4. Evaluate through appropriate professional procedures conditions within a district or institution of learning, make known serious deficiencies, and take any action deemed necessary and proper.

5. Use educational facilities for intended purposes consistent with applicable policy, law, and regulation.

6. Assume full political and citizenship responsibilities, but refrain from exploiting the institutional privileges of our professional positions to promote political candidates or partisan activities.

7. Protect the educational program against undesirble infringement.

Principle III

COMMITMENT TO THE PROFESSION

We believe that the quality of the services of the education profession directly influences the future of the nation and its citizens. We therefore exert every effort to raise educational standards, to improve our service, to promote a climate in which the exercise of professional judgment is encouraged, and to achieve conditions which attract persons worthy of the trust to careers in education. Aware of the value of united effort, we contribute actively to the support, planning, and programs of our professional organizations.

In fulfilling our obligations to the profession we—

1. Recognize that a profession must accept responsibility for the conduct of its members and understand that our own conduct may be regarded as representative.
2. Participate and conduct ourselves in a responsible manner in the development and implementation of policies affecting education.
3. Cooperate in the selective recruitment of prospective teachers and in the orientation of student teachers, interns, and those colleagues new to their positions.
4. Accord just and equitable treatment to all members of the profession in the exercise of their professional rights and responsibilities, and support them when unjustly accused or mistreated.
5. Refrain from assigning professional duties to non-professional personnel when such assignment is not in the best interest of the student.
6. Provide, upon request, a statement of specific reason for administrative recommendations that lead to the denial of increments, significant changes in employment, or termination of employment.
7. Refrain from exerting undue influence based on the authority of our positions in the determination of professional decisions by colleagues.
8. Keep the trust under which confidential information is exchanged.
9. Make appropriate use of time granted for professional purposes.
10. Interpret and use the writings of others and the findings of educational research with intellectual honesty.
11. Maintain our integrity when dissenting by basing our public criticism of education on valid assumptions as established by careful evaluation of facts or hypotheses.
12. Represent honestly our professional qualifications and identify ourselves only with reputable educational institutions.
13. Respond accurately to requests for evaluation of colleagues seeking professional positions.

14. Provide applicants seeking information about a position with an honest description of the assignment, the conditions of work, and related matters.

Principle IV

COMMITMENT TO PROFESSIONAL EMPLOYMENT PRACTICES

We regard the employment agreement as a solemn pledge to be executed both in spirit and in fact in a manner consistent with the highest ideals of professional service. Sound professional personnel relationships with governing boards are built upon personal integrity, dignity, and mutual respect.

In fulfilling our obligations to professional employment practices, we—

1. Apply for or offer a position on the basis of professional and legal qualifications.
2. Apply for a specific position only when it is known to be vacant and refrain from such practices as underbidding or commenting adversely about other candidates.
3. Fill no vacancy except where the terms, conditions, policies, and practices permit the exercise of our professional judgment and skill, and where a climate conducive to professional service exists.
4. Adhere to the conditions of a contract or to the terms of an appointment until either has been terminated legally or by mutual consent.
5. Give prompt notice of any change in availability of service, in status of applications, or in change in position.
6. Conduct professional business through the recognized educational and professional channels.
7. Accept no gratuities or gifts of significance that might influence our judgment in the exercise of our professional duties.
8. Engage in no outside employment that will impair the effectiveness of our professional service and permit no commercial exploitation of our professional position.

REPRESENTATIVE EXPRESSIONS:
An Historical Perspective

1. TWELFTH ANNUAL REPORT ON EDUCATION (1848)

Under the providence of God, our means of education are the grand machinery by which the "raw material" of human nature can be worked up into inventors and discoverers, into skilled artisans and scientific farmers, into scholars and jurists, into the founders of benevolent institutions, and the great expounders of ethical and theological science. By means of early education, those embryos of talent may be quickened which will solve the difficult problems of political and economical law; and by them, too, the genius may be kindled which will blaze forth in the poets of humanity. Our schools, far more than they have done, may supply the presidents and professors of colleges, and superintendents of public instruction, all over the land; and send, not only into our sister States, but across the Atlantic, the men of practical science to superintend the construction of the great works of art. Here, too, may those judicial powers be developed and invigorated which will make legal principles so clear and convincing as to prevent appeals to force; and, should the clouds of war ever lower over our country, some hero may be found—the nursling of our schools, and ready to become the leader of our armies, that best of all heroes—who will secure the glories of a peace, unstained by the magnificent murders of the battle-field.

. . .

Without undervaluing any other human agency, it may be safely affirmed that the common school, improved and energized as it can easily be, may become the most effective and benignant of all the forces of civilization. Two reasons sustain this position. In the first place, there is a universality in its operation, which can be affirmed of no other institution whatever. If administered in the spirit of justice and conciliation, all the rising generation may be brought within the circle of its reformatory and elevating influences. And, in the second place, the materials upon

From Horace Mann, *Life and Works of Horace Mann*, Vol. IV (Boston: Lee and Shepard Publishers, 1867), pp. 228, 232–33, 251–52, 283–88, 291, 312–13.

which it operates are so pliant and ductile as to be susceptible of assuming a greater variety of forms than any other earthly work of the Creator. The inflexibility and ruggedness of the oak, when compared with the lithe sapling or the tender germ, are but feeble emblems to typify the docility of childhood when contrasted with the obduracy and intractableness of man. It is these inherent advantages of the common school, which, in our own State, have produced results so striking, from a system so imperfect, and an administration so feeble. In teaching the blind and the deaf and dumb, in kindling the latent spark of intelligence that lurks in an idiot's mind, and in the more holy work of reforming abandoned and outcast children, education has proved what it can do by glorious experiments. These wonders it has done in its infancy, and with the lights of a limited experience; but when its faculties shall be fully developed, when it shall be trained to wield its mighty energies for the protection of society against the giant vices which now invade and torment it,—against intemperance, avarice, war, slavery, bigotry, the woes of want, and the wickedness of waste,—then there will not be a height to which these enemies of the race can escape which it will not scale, nor a Titan among them all whom it will not slay.

I proceed, then, in endeavoring to show how the true business of the schoolroom connects itself, and becomes identical, with the great interests of society. The former is the infant, immature state of those interests; the latter their developed, adult state. As "the child is father to the man," so may the training of the schoolroom expand into the institutions and fortunes of the State.

. . .

Education, then, beyond all other devices of human origin, is the great equalizer of the conditions of men,—the balance-wheel of the social machinery. I do not here mean that it so elevates the moral nature as to make men disdain and abhor the oppression of their fellow-men. This idea pertains to another of its attributes. But I mean that it gives each man the independence and the means by which he can resist the selfishness of other men. It does better than to disarm the poor of their hostility towards the rich: it prevents being poor. Agrarianism is the revenge of poverty against wealth. The wanton destruction of the property of others—the burning of hay-ricks and corn-ricks, the demolition of machinery because it supersedes hand-labor, the sprinkling of vitriol on rich dresses—is only agrarianism run mad. Education prevents both the revenge and the madness. On the other hand, a fellow-feeling for one's class or caste is the common instinct of hearts not wholly sunk in selfish regards for person or for family. The spread of education, by enlarging the cultivated class or caste, will open a wider area over which the social feelings will expand;

and, if this education should be universal and complete, it would do more than all things else to obliterate factitious distinctions in society.

The main idea set forth in the creeds of some political reformers, or revolutionizers, is, that some people are poor *because* others are rich This idea supposes a fixed amount of property in the community, which by fraud or force, or arbitrary law, is unequally divided among men; and the problem presented for solution is, how to transfer a portion of this property from those who are supposed to have too much to those who feel and know that they have too little. At this point, both their theory and their expectation of reform stop. But the beneficent power of education would not be exhausted, even though it should peaceably abolish all the miseries that spring from the co-existence, side by side, of enormous wealth and squalid want. It has a higher function. Beyond the power of diffusing old wealth, it has the prerogative of creating new. It is a thousand times more lucrative than fraud, and adds a thousand-fold more to a nation's resources than the most successful conquests. Knaves and robbers can obtain only what was before possessed by others. But education creates or develops new treasures,—treasures not before possessed or dreamed of by any one.

Moral Education

Moral education is a primal necessity of social existence. The unrestrained passions of men are not only homicidal, but suicidal; and a community without a conscience would soon extinguish itself. Even with a natural conscience, how often has evil triumphed over good! From the beginning of time, wrong has followed right, as the shadow the substance. As the relations of men became more complex, and the business of the world more extended, new opportunities and new temptations for wrong-doing have been created. With the endearing relations of parent and child came also the possibility of infanticide and parricide; and the first domestic altar that brothers ever reared was stained with fratricidal blood. Following close upon the obligations to truth came falsehood and perjury, and closer still upon the duty of obedience to the divine law came disobedience. With the existence of private relations between men came fraud; and with the existence of public relations between nations came aggression, war, and slavery. And so, just in proportion as the relations of life became more numerous, and the interests of society more various and manifold, the range of possible and of actual offences has been continually enlarging. As for every new substance there may be a new shadow, so for every new law there may be a new transgression. No form of the precious metals has ever been used which dishonest men have not counter-feited, and no kind of artificial currency has ever been legalized which rogues have not forged. The government sees the evils that come from the use of intoxicating drinks, and prohibits their sale; but unprincipled men pander to depraved appetites, and gather a harvest of dishonest profits. Instead of licensing lotteries, and deriving a revenue from the sale of tickets, the State forbids the mischievous traffic; but, while law-abiding men disdain to practise an illicit trade, knavish brokers, by means of the prohibition itself, secure a monopoly of the sales, and pocket the infamous gain. The government imposes duties on imported goods: smugglers evade the law, and bring goods into the market clandestinely; or perjurers swear to false invoices, and escape the payment of duty, and thus secure to themselves the double advantage of increased sales, and enhanced profits upon what is sold. Science prepares a new medicine to heal or alleviate the diseases of men; crime adulterates it, or prepares as a substitute some cheap poison that resembles it, and can be sold instead of it. A benefactor of the race discovers an agent which has the marvellous power to suspend consciousness, and take away the susceptibility of pain; a villain uses it to rob men or pollute women. Houses are built; the incendiary burns them, that he may purloin the smallest portion of their goods. The press is invented to spread intelligence; but libellers use it to give wings to slander. And so, throughout the infinitely complex and ramified relations of society, wherever there is a right, there may be a wrong; and wherever a law is made to repress the wrong, it may be evaded by artifice or over-borne by violence. In fine, all means and laws designed to repress in-justice and crime give occasion to new injustice and crime. For every lock that is made, a false key is made to pick it; and, for every Paradise that is created, there is a Satan who would scale its walls. . . .

Against these social vices in all ages of the world, the admonitions of good men have been directed. The moralist has exposed their deformity in his didactic page; the satirist has chastised them in his pungent verse; to the character of a disciple of Jesus. Still they continue to exist; and, to some extent, the Christian minister has exhibited their gross repugnancy to the character of a disciple of Jesus. Still they continue exist; and, to say nothing of heathen nations, the moral condition of all Christendom is, in this respect, like the physical condition of one of the nations that com-pose it,—that extraordinary people, I mean, whose dwellings, whose flocks, whose agriculture, whose merchandise, and who themselves, are below the level of the ocean; and against them, at all times, this ocean rages, and lifts itself up; and whenever or wherever it can find a breach, or make one, it rushes in, and overwhelms men and their possessions in one common inundation. Even so, like a weltering flood, do immoralities and crimes break over all moral barriers, destroying and profaning the securities and the sanctities of life. Now, how best shall this deluge be repelled? What mighty power or combination of powers can prevent its inrushing, or narrow the sweep of its ravages?

The race has existed long enough to try many experiments for the solution of this greatest problem ever submitted to its hands; and the race has experimented, without stint of time or circumscription of space to mar or modify legitimate results. Mankind have tried despotisms, monarchies, and republican forms of government. They have tried the extremes of anarchy and of autocracy. They have tried Draconian codes of law; and, for the lightest offences, have extinguished the life of the offender. They have established theological standards, claiming for them the sanction of divine authority, and the attributes of a perfect and infallible law; and then they have imprisoned, burnt, massacred, not individuals only, but whole communities at a time, for not bowing down to idols which ecclesiastical authority had set up. These and other great systems of measures have been adopted as barriers against error and guilt: they have been extended over empires, prolonged through centuries, and administered with terrible energy; and yet the great ocean of vice and crime overleaps every embankment, pours down upon our heads, saps the foundations under our feet, and sweeps away the securities of social order, of property, liberty, and life.

At length, these experiments have been so numerous, and all of them have terminated so disastrously, that a body of men has risen up in later times, powerful in influence, and not inconsiderable in numbers, who, if I may use a mercantile phrase, would abandon the world as a total loss; who mock at the idea of its having a benevolent or even an intelligent Author or Governor; and who, therefore, would give over the race to the dominion of chance, or to that of their own licentious passions, whose rule would be more fatal than chance.

But to all doubters, disbelievers, or despairers in human progress, it may still be said, there is one experiment which has never yet been tried. It is an experiment, which, even before its inception, offers the highest authority for its ultimate success. Its formula is intelligible to all; and it is as legible as though written in starry letters on an azure sky. It is expressed in these few and simple words: "*Train up a child in the way he should go; and, when he is old, he will not depart from it.*" This declaration is positive. If the conditions are complied with, it makes no provision for a failure. Though pertaining to morals, yet, if the terms of the direction are observed, there is no more reason to doubt the result than there would be in an optical or a chemical experiment.

But this experiment has never yet been tried. Education has never yet been brought to bear with one-hundredth part of its potential force upon the natures of children, and, through them, upon the character of men and of the race. In all the attempts to reform mankind which have hitherto been made, whether by changing the frame of government, by aggravating or softening the severity of the penal code, or by substituting a government-created for a God-created religion,—in all these attempts, the infantile and youthful mind, its amenability to influences, and the enduring and self-operating character of the influences it receives, have been almost wholly unrecognized. Here, then, is a new agency, whose powers are but just beginning to be understood, and whose mighty energies hitherto have been but feebly invoked; and yet, from our experience, limited and imperfect as it is, we do know, that, far beyond any other earthly instrumentality, it is comprehensive and decisive.

. . .

Is any high-minded, exemplary, and conscientious man disposed to believe that this substantial extirpation of social vices and crimes (according to the testimony of the witnesses above referred to) is a Utopian idea, is more than we have any reason to expect while human nature remains as it is, let me use the *ad hominem* argument to refute him. Let me refer him to himself, and ask him why the same influences which have saved him from gaming, intemperance, dissoluteness, falsehood, dishonesty, violence, and their kindred offences, and have made him a man of sobriety, frugality, and probity,—why the same influences which have saved him from ruin, might not, if brought to bear upon others, save them also. So far as human instrumentalities are concerned, we have abundant means for surrounding every child in the State with preservative and moral influences as extensive and as efficient as those under which the present industrious, worthy, and virtuous members of the community were reared. And as to all those things in regard to which we are directly dependent upon the divine favor, have we not the promise, explicit and unconditional, that the men SHALL NOT depart from the way in which they should go, if the children are trained up in it? It has been overlooked that this promise is not restricted to parents, but seems to be addressed indiscriminately to all, whether parents, communities, states, or mankind.

. . .

The very terms "public school" and "common school" bear upon their face that they are schools which the children of the entire community may attend. Every man not on the pauper-list is taxed for their support; but he is not taxed to support them as special religious institutions: if he were, it would satisfy at once the largest definition of a religious establishment. But he is taxed to support them as a *preventive* means against dishonesty, against fraud, and against violence, on the same principle that he is taxed to support criminal courts as a *punitive* means against the same offences. He is taxed to support schools, on the same principle that he is taxed to support paupers,—because a child without education is poorer and more wretched than a man without bread. He is taxed to support schools, on the same principle that he would be taxed to defend the nation against foreign invasion, or against rapine committed by a foreign foe,—because the general prevalence of ignorance, superstition, and vice, will breed Goth and Vandal at home more fatal to the public well-being than any Goth and Vandal from abroad. And, finally, he is taxed to support schools, because they are the most effective means of developing and training those powers and faculties in a child, by which, when he becomes a man, he may understand what his highest interests and his highest duties are, and may be in fact, and not in name only, a free agent. The elements of a political education are not bestowed upon any school child for the purpose of making him vote with this or that political party when he becomes of age, but for the purpose of enabling him to choose for himself with which party he will vote. So the religious education which a child receives at school is not imparted to him for the purpose of making him join this or that denomination when he arrives at years of discretion, but for the purpose of enabling him to judge for himself, according to the dictates of his own reason and conscience, what his religious obligations are, and whither they lead.

2. THEORY AND PRACTICE OF TEACHING: OR, THE MOTIVES AND METHODS OF GOOD SCHOOL-KEEPING
David Page

1. Neatness

This implies cleanliness of the person. If some who assume to teach were not proverbial for their slovenliness, I would not dwell on this point. On this point, however, I must be allowed great plainness of speech, even at the expense of incurring the charge of excessive nicety; for it is by attending to a *few little things* that one becomes a strictly neat person. The morning ablution, then, should never be omitted, and the comb for the hair and brush for the clothes should always be called into requisition before the teacher presents himself to the family, or to his school. Every teacher would very much promote his own health by washing the whole surface of the body every morning in cold water. This is now done by very many of the most enlightened teachers, as well as others. When

From David Page, *Theory and Practice of Teaching: Or, the Motives and Methods of Good School-Keeping* (New York: A. S. Barnes Co., 1849), pp. 40–43.

physiology is better understood, this practice will be far more general. To no class of persons is it more essential than to the teacher; for on account of his confinement, often in an unventilated room, with half a hundred children during the day, very much more is demanded of the exhalents in him than in others. His only safety is in a healthy action of the skin.

The *teeth* should be attended to. A brush and clean water have saved many a set of teeth. It is bad enough to witness the deplorable neglect of these important organs so prevalent in the community; but it is extremely mortifying to see a filthy set of teeth in the mouth of the teacher of our youth. The *nails,* too, I am sorry to say, are often neglected by some of our teachers, till their *ebony tips* are any thing but ornamental. This matter is made worse, when, in the presence of the family or of the school, the penknife is brought into requisition to remove that which should have received attention at the time of washing in the morning. The *teacher* should remember that it is a *vulgar* habit to pare or clean the nails while in the presence of others, and especially during conversation with them.

The teacher should be neat in his *dress.* I do not urge that his dress should be expensive. His income ordinarily will not admit of this. He may wear a very plain dress; nor should it be any way singular in its fashion. All I ask is, that his clothing should be in good taste, and *always clean.* A slovenly dress, covered with dust, or spotted with grease, is never so much out of its proper place, as when it clothes the teacher.

While upon this subject I may be indulged in a word or two upon the use of tobacco by the teacher. It is quite a puzzle to me to tell why any man but a Turk, who may lawfully dream away half his existence over the fumes of this filthy narcotic, should ever use it. Even if there were nothing wrong in the use of unnatural stimulants themselves, the filthiness of tobacco is enough to condemn it among teachers, especially in the form of chewing. It is certainly worth while to ask whether there is not some moral delinquency in teaching this practice to the young, while it is admitted, by nearly all who have fallen into the habit, to be an evil, and one from which they would desire to be delivered. At any rate, I hope the time is coming, when the good taste of teachers, and a regard for personal neatness and the comfort of others, shall present motives sufficiently strong to induce them to break away from a practice at once so unreasonable and so disgusting.

2. Order

In this place I refer to the *system* and regularity so desirable in every teacher. He should practise it in his room at his boarding-house.

Every thing should have its place. His books, his clothing, should all be arranged with regard to this principle. The same habit should go with him to the schoolroom. His desk there should be a pattern of orderly arrangement. Practising this himself, he may with propriety insist upon it in his pupils. It is of great moment to the teacher, that, when he demands order and arrangement among his pupils, they cannot appeal to any breach of it in his own practice.

3. Courtesy

The teacher should ever be courteous, both in his language and in his manners. *Courtesy of language* may imply a freedom from all *coarseness*. There is a kind of communication, used among boatmen and hangers-on at bar-rooms, which should find no place in the teacher's vocabulary. All vulgar jesting, all double-entendres, all low allusions, should be forever excluded from his mouth. And profanity!—can it be necessary that I should speak of this as among the habits of the teacher? Yes, it is even so. Such is the want of moral sense in the community, that men are still employed in some districts, whose ordinary conversation is poisoned with the breath of blasphemy; ay, and even the walls of the schoolroom resound to undisguised oaths! I cannot find words to express my astonishment at the indifference of parents, or at the recklessness of teachers, wherever I know such cases to exist.

Speaking of the *language* of the teacher, I might urge also that it should be both *pure* and *accurate*. Pure as distinguished from all those cant phrases and provincialisms which amuse the vulgar in certain localities; and accurate as to the terms used to express his meaning. As the *teacher teaches* in this, as in every thing, by example as well as by precept, he should be very careful to acquire an unexceptionable use of our language, and never deviate from it in the hearing of his pupils or elsewhere.

3. CARDINAL PRINCIPLES OF SECONDARY EDUCATION

The Goal of Education in a Democracy

Education in the United States should be guided by a clear conception of the meaning of democracy. It is the ideal of democracy that the individual and society may find fulfillment each in the other. Democracy sanctions neither the exploitation of the individual by society, nor the disregard of the interests of society by the individual. More explicitly—

The purpose of democracy is so to organize society that each member may develop his personality primarily through activities designed for the well-being of his fellow members and of society as a whole.

This ideal demands that human activities be placed upon a high level of efficiency; that to this efficiency be added an appreciation of the significance of these activities and loyalty to the best ideals involved; and that the individual choose that vocation and those forms of social service in which his personality may develop and become most effective. For the achievement of these ends democracy must place chief reliance upon education.

Consequently, education in a democracy, both within and without the school, should develop in each individual the knowledge, interests, ideals, habits, and powers whereby he will find his place and use that place to shape both himself and society toward ever nobler ends.

The Main Objectives of Education

In order to determine the main objectives that should guide education in a democracy it is necessary to analyze the activities of the individual. Normally he is a member of a family, of a vocational group, and of various civic groups, and by virtue of these relationships he is called upon to engage in activities that enrich the family life, to render important vocational services to his fellows, and to promote the common welfare. It

From Commission on the Reorganization of Secondary Education, *Cardinal Principles of Secondary Education*, Bulletin 35 (Washington, D.C.: Bureau of Education, 1918), pp. 9–11.

follows, therefore, that worthy home-membership, vocation, and citizenship, demand attention as three of the leading objectives.

Aside from the immediate discharge of these specific duties, every individual should have a margin of time for the cultivation of personal and social interests. This leisure, if worthily used, will recreate his powers and enlarge and enrich life, thereby making him better able to meet his responsibilities. The unworthy use of leisure impairs health, disrupts home life, lessens vocational efficiency, and destroys civic-mindedness. The tendency in industrial life, aided by legislation, is to decrease the working hours of large groups of people. While shortened hours tend to lessen the harmful reactions that arise from prolonged strain, they increase, if possible, the importance of preparation for leisure. In view of these considerations, education for the worthy use of leisure is of increasing importance as an objective.

To discharge the duties of life and to benefit from leisure, one must have good health. The health of the individual is essential also to the vitality of the race and to the defense of the Nation. Health education is, therefore, fundamental.

There are various processes, such as reading, writing, arithmetical computations, and oral and written expression, that are needed as tools in the affairs of life. Consequently, command of these fundamental processes, while not an end in itself, is nevertheless an indipensable objective.

And, finally, the realization of the objectives already named is dependent upon ethical character, that is, conduct founded upon right principles, clearly perceived and loyally adhered to. Good citizenship, vocational excellence, and the worthy use of leisure go hand in hand with ethical character; they are at once the fruits of sterling character and the channels through which such character is developed and made manifest. On the one hand, character is meaningless apart from the will to discharge the duties of life, and, on the other hand, there is no guarantee that these duties will be rightly discharged unless principles are substituted for impulses, however well-intentioned such impulses may be. Consequently ethical character is at once involved in all the other objectives and at the same time requires specific consideration in any program of national education.

This commission, therefore, regards the following as the main objectives of education: 1. Health. 2. Command of fundamental processes. 3. Worthy home-membership. 4. Vocation. 5. Citizenship. 6. Worthy use of leisure. 7. Ethical character.

The naming of the above objectives is not intended to imply that the process of education can be divided into separated fields. This can not be, since the pupil is indivisible. Nor is the analysis all-inclusive. Nevertheless, we believe that distinguishing and naming these objectives will aid in directing efforts; and we hold that they should constitute the principal aims in education.

4. INDUSTRIAL EDUCATION FOR THE NEGRO
Booker T. Washington

One of the most fundamental and far-reaching deeds that has been accomplished during the last quarter of a century has been that by which the Negro has been helped to find himself and to learn the secrets of civilization—to learn that there are a few simple, cardinal principles upon which a race must start its upward course, unless it would fail, and its last estate be worse than its first.

It has been necessary for the Negro to learn the difference between being worked and working—to learn that being worked meant degradation, while working means civilization; that all forms of labor are honorable, and all forms of idleness disgraceful. It has been necessary for him to learn that all races that have got upon their feet have done so largely by laying an economic foundation, and, in general, by beginning in a proper cultivation and ownership of the soil.

Forty years ago my race emerged from slavery into freedom. If, in too many cases, the Negro race began development at the wrong end, it was largely because neither white nor black properly understood the case. Nor is it any wonder that this was so, for never before in the history of the world had just such a problem been presented as that of the two races at the coming of freedom in this country.

For two hundred and fifty years, I believe the way for the redemption of the Negro was being prepared through industrial development.

. . .

Only a short time before his death the late Mr. C. P. Huntington, to whose memory a magnificent library has just been given by his widow to the Hampton Institute for Negroes, in Virginia, said in a public address some words which seem to me so wise that I want to quote them here:

> Our schools teach everybody a little of almost everything, but, in my opinion, they teach very few children just what they ought to know in order to make their way successfully in life. They do not put into their hands the tools they are best fitted to use, and hence so many failures. Many a mother and sister have worked and slaved, living upon

From Booker T. Washington, "Industrial Education for the Negro," in *The Negro Problem,* Booker T. Washington, ed. (New York: James Pott & Company, 1903), pp. 9–10, 14–25, 27–29.

scanty food, in order to give a son and brother a "liberal education," and in doing this have built up a barrier between the boy and the work he was fitted to do. Let me say to you that all honest work is honorable work. If the labor is manual, and seems common, you will have all the more chance to be thinking of other things, or of work that is higher and brings better pay, and to work out in your minds better and higher duties and responsibilities for yourselves, and for thinking of ways by which you can help others as well as yourselves, and bring them up to your own higher level.

Some years ago, when we decided to make tailoring a part of our training at the Tuskegee Institute, I was amazed to find that it was almost impossible to find in the whole country an educated colored man who could teach the making of clothing. We could find numbers of them who could teach astronomy, theology, Latin or grammar, but almost none who could instruct in the making of clothing, something that has to be used by every one of us every day in the year. How often have I been discouraged as I have gone through the South, and into the homes of the people of my race, and have found women who could converse intelligently upon abstruse subjects, and yet could not tell how to improve the condition of the poorly cooked and still more poorly served bread and meat which they and their families were eating three times a day. It is discouraging to find a girl who can tell you the geographical location of any country on the globe and who does not know where to place the dishes upon a common dinner table. It is discouraging to find a woman who knows much about theoretical chemistry, and who cannot properly wash and iron a shirt.

. . .

I would not confine the race to industrial life, not even to agriculture, for example, although I believe that by far the greater part of the Negro race is best off in the country districts and must and should continue to live there, but I would teach the race that in industry the foundation must be laid—that the very best service which any one can render to what is called the higher education is to teach the present generation to provide a material or industrial foundation. On such a foundation as this will grow habits of thrift, a love of work, economy, ownership of property, bank accounts. Out of it in the future will grow practical education, professional education, positions of public responsibility. Out of it will grow moral and religious strength. Out of it will grow wealth from which alone can come leisure and the opportunity for the enjoyment of literature and the fine arts.

. . . I plead for industrial education and development for the Negro not because I want to cramp him, but because I want to free him. I want to see him enter the all-powerful business and commercial world.

. . .

Early in the history of the Tuskegee Institute we began to combine industrial training with mental and moral culture. Our first efforts were in the direction of agriculture, and we began teaching this with no appliances except one hoe and a blind mule. From this small beginning we have grown until now the Institute owns two thousand acres of land, eight hundred of which are cultivated each year by the young men of the school. We began teaching wheelwrighting and blacksmithing in a small way to the men, and laundry work, cooking and sewing and house-keeping to the young women. The fourteen hundred and over young men and women who attended the school during the last school year received instruction—in addition to academic and religious training—in thirty-three trades and industries, including carpentry, blacksmithing, printing, wheelwrighting, harnessmaking, painting, machinery, founding, shoemaking, brickmasonry and brickmaking, plastering, sawmilling, tin-smithing, tailoring, mechanical and architectural drawing, electrical and steam engineering, canning, sewing, dressmaking, millinery, cooking, laundering, housekeeping, mattress making, basketry, nursing, agriculture, dairying and stock raising, horticulture.

Not only do the students receive instruction in these trades, but they do actual work, by means of which more than half of them pay some part or all of their expenses while remaining at the school. Of the sixty buildings belonging to the school all but four were almost wholly erected by the students as a part of their industrial education. Even the bricks which go into the walls are made by students in the school's brick yard, in which, last year, they manufactured two million bricks.

. . .

It seems to me that too often mere book education leaves the Negro young man or woman in a weak position. For example, I have seen a Negro girl taught by her mother to help her in doing laundry work at home. Later, when this same girl was graduated from the public schools or a high school and returned home she finds herself educated out of sympathy with laundry work, and yet not able to find anything to do which seems in keeping with the cost and character of her education. Under these circumstances we cannot be surprised if she does not fulfill the expecations made for her. What should have been done for her, it seems to me, was to give her along with her academic education thorough training in the latest and best methods of laundry work, so that she could have put so much skill and intelligence into it that the work would have been lifted out from the plane of drudgery. The home which she would then have been able to found by the results of her work would have enabled her to help her children to take a still more responsible position in life.

Almost from the first Tuskeegee has kept in mind—and this I think should be the policy of all industrial schools—fitting students for occupations which would be open to them in their home communities.

Many seem to think that industrial education is meant to make the Negro work as he worked in the days of slavery. This is far from my conception of industrial education. If this training is worth anything to the Negro, it consists in teaching him how not to work, but how to make the forces of nature—air, steam, water, horse-power and electricity—work for him. If it has any value it is in lifting labor up out of toil and drudgery into the plane of the dignified and the beautiful. The Negro in the South works and works hard; but too often his ignorance and lack of skill causes him to do his work in the most costly and shiftless manner, and this keeps him near the bottom of the ladder in the economic world.

I close, then, as I began, by saying that as a slave the Negro was worked, and that as a freeman he must learn to work. . . . Our pathway must be up through the soil, up through swamps, up through forests, up through the streams, the rocks, up through commerce, education and religion!

5. THE TALENTED TENTH
W. E. B. DuBois

The Negro race, like all races, is going to be saved by its exceptional men. The problem of education, then, among Negroes must first of all deal with the Talented Tenth; it is the problem of developing the Best of this race that they may guide the Mass away from the contamination and death of the Worst, in their own and other races. Now the training of men is a difficult and intricate task. Its technique is a matter for educational experts, but its objects is for the vision of seers. If we make money the object of man-training, we shall develop money-makers but not necessarily men; if we make technical skill the object of education, we may possess artisans but not, in nature, men. Men we shall have only as we make manhood the object of the work of the schools—intelligence, broad sympathy, knowledge of the world that was and is, and of the relation of men to it—this is the curriculum of that Higher Education which must underlie true life. On this foundation we may build bread winning, skill of hand and quickness of brain, with never a

W. E. B. DuBois, "The Talented Tenth" in *The Negro Problem*, Booker T. Washington, ed. (New York: James Pott & Company, 1903), pp. 33–34, 45, 54–63, 74–75.

fear lest the child and man mistake the means of living for the object of life.

. . .

Can the masses of the Negro people be in any possible way more quickly raised than by the effort and example of this aristocracy of talent and character? Was there ever a nation on God's fair earth civilized from the bottom upward? Never; it is, ever was and ever will be from the top downward that culture filters. The Talented Tenth rises and pulls all that are worth the saving up to their vantage ground. This is the history of human progress; and the two historic mistakes which have hindered that progress were the thinking first that no more could ever rise save the few already risen; or second, that it would better the unrisen to pull the risen down.

How then shall the leaders of a struggling people be trained and the hands of the risen few strengthened? There can be but one answer: The best and most capable of their youth must be schooled in the colleges and universities of the land.

. . . [T]he college-bred Negro . . . is, as he ought to be, the group leader, the man who sets the ideals of the community where he lives, directs its thoughts and heads its social movements. It need hardly be argued that the Negro people need social leadership more than most groups; that they have no traditions to fall back upon, no long established customs, no strong family ties, no well defined social classes. All these things must be slowly and painfully evolved. The preacher was, even before the war, the group leader of the Negroes, and the church their greatest social institution. Naturally this preacher was ignorant and often immoral, and the problem of replacing the older type by better educated men has been a difficult one. Both by direct work and by direct influence on other preachers, and on congregations, the college-bred preacher has an opportunity for reformatory work and moral inspiration, the value of which cannot be overestimated.

It has, however, been in the furnishing of teachers that the Negro college has found its peculiar function. Few persons realize how vast a work, how mighty a revolution has been thus accomplished. To furnish five millions and more of ignorant people with teachers of their own race and blood, in one generation, was not only a very difficult undertaking, but a very important one, in that, it placed before the eyes of almost every Negro child an attainable ideal. It brought the masses of the blacks in contact with modern civilization, made black men the leaders of their communities and trainers of the new generation. In this work college-bred Negroes were first teachers, and then teachers of teachers. And here it is that the broad culture of college work has been of peculiar value. Knowledge of life and its wider meaning, has been the point of the

Negro's deepest ignorance, and the sending out of teachers whose training has not been simply for bread winning, but also for human culture, has been of inestimable value in the training of these men.

In earlier years the two occupations of preacher and teacher were practically the only ones open to the black college graduate. Of later years a larger diversity of life among his people, has opened new avenues of employment.

. . .

The problem of training the Negro is to-day immensely complicated by the fact that the whole question of the efficiency and appropriateness of our present systems of education, for any kind of child, is a matter of active debate, in which final settlement seems still afar off. Consequently it often happens that persons arguing for or against certain systems of education for Negroes, have these controversies in mind and miss the real question at issue. The main question, so far as the Southern Negro is concerned, is: What under the present circumstance, must a system of education do in order to raise the Negro as quickly as possible in the scale of civilization? The answer to this question seems to me clear: It must strengthen the Negro's character, increase his knowledge and teach him to earn a living. Now it goes without saying, that it is hard to do all these things simultaneously or suddenly, and that at the same time it will not do to give all the attention to one and neglect the others; we could give black boys trades, but that alone will not civilize a race of ex-slaves; we might simply increase their knowledge of the world, but this would not necessarily make them wish to use this knowledge honestly; we might seek to strengthen character and purpose, but to what end if this people have nothing to eat or to wear? A system of education is not one thing, nor does it have a single definite object, nor is it a mere matter of schools. Education is that whole system of human training within and without the school house walls, which molds and develops men. If then we start out to train an ignorant and unskilled people with a heritage of bad habits, our system of training must set before itself two great aims—the one dealing with knowledge and character, the other part seeking to give the child the technical knowledge necessary for him to earn a living under the present circumstances. These objects are accomplished in part by the opening of the common schools on the one, and of the industrial schools on the other. But only in part, for there must also be trained those who are to teach these schools—men and women of knowledge and culture and technical skill who understand modern civilization, and have the training and aptitude to impart it to the children under them. There must be teachers, and teachers of teachers, and to attempt to establish any sort of a system of common and industrial school training, without *first* (and I say *first* advisedly) without *first* providing for the higher training of the very best teachers, is simply throwing your money to the winds. School houses do not teach themselves—piles of brick and mortar and machinery do not send out *men*. It is the trained, living human soul, cultivated and strengthened by long study and thought, that breathes the real breath of life into boys and girls and makes them human, whether they be black or white, Greek, Russian or American. . . .

I would not deny, or for a moment seem to deny, the paramount necessity of teaching the Negro to work, and to work steadily and skill-fully; or seem to depreciate in the slightest degree the important part industrial schools must play in the accomplishment of these ends, but I *do* say, and insist upon it, that it is industrialism drunk with its vision of success, to imagine that its own work can be accomplished without providing for the training of broadly cultured men and women to teach its own teachers, and to teach the teachers of the public schools.

But I have already said that human education is not simply a matter of schools; it is much more a matter of family and group life—the training of one's home, of one's daily companions, of one's social class. Now the black boy of the South moves in a black world—a world with its own leaders, its own thoughts, its own ideals. In this world he gets by far the larger part of his life training, and through the eyes of this dark world he peers into the veiled world beyond. . . . You have no choice; either you must help furnish this race from within its own ranks with thoughtful men of trained leadership, or you must suffer the evil con-sequences of a headless misguided rabble.

I am an earnest advocate of manual training and trade teaching for black boys, and for white boys, too. I believe that next to the founding of Negro colleges the most valuable addition to Negro education since the war, has been industrial training for black boys. Nevertheless, I insist that the object of all true education is not to make men carpenters, it is to make carpenters men; there are two means of making the car-penter a man, each equally important: the first is to give the group and community in which he works, liberally trained teachers and leaders to teach him and his family what life means; the second is to give him sufficient intelligence and technical skill to make him an efficient work-man; the first object demands the Negro college and college-bred men—not a quantity of such colleges, but a few of excellent quality; not too many college-bred men, but enough to leaven the lump, to inspire the masses, to raise the Talented Tenth to leadership; the second object de-mands a good system of common schools, well-taught, conveniently lo-cated and properly equipped.

. . .

Men of America, the problem is plain before you. Here is a race transplanted through the criminal foolishness of your fathers. Whether you like it or not the millions are here, and here they will remain. If you do not lift them up, they will pull you down. Education and work are the levers to uplift a people. Work alone will not do it unless inspired by the right ideals and guided by intelligence. Education must not simply teach work—it must teach Life. The Talented Tenth of the Negro race must be made leaders of thought and missionaries of culture among their people. No others can do this work and Negro colleges must train men for it. The Negro race, like all other races, is going to be saved by its exceptional men.

6. PLESSY v. FERGUSON
U. S. Supreme Court

This case turns upon the constitutionality of an act of the General Assembly of the State of Louisiana, passed in 1890, providing for separate railway carriages for the white and colored races. Acts 1890, No. 111, p. 152.

The first section of the statute enacts "that all railway companies carrying passengers in their coaches in this State, shall provide equal but separate accommodations for the white, and colored races, by providing two or more passenger coaches for each passenger train, or by dividing the passenger coaches by a partition so as to secure separate accommodations: *Provided,* That this section shall not be construed to apply to street railroads. No person or persons, shall be admitted to occupy seats in coaches, other than the ones assigned to them, on account of the race they belong to."

By the second section it was enacted "that the officers of such passenger trains shall have power and are hereby required to assign each passenger to the coach or compartment used for the race to which such passenger belongs; any passenger insisting on going into a coach or compartment to which by race he does not belong, shall be liable to a fine of twenty-five dollars, or in lieu thereof to imprisonment for a period of not more than twenty days in the parish prison, and any officer of any railroad insisting on assigning a passenger to a coach or compartment other than the one set aside for the race to which said passenger belongs, shall be liable to a fine of twenty-five dollars, or in lieu thereof to imprisonment for a period of not more than twenty days in the parish prison; and should any passenger refuse to occupy the coach or compartment

Plessy v. Ferguson, 163 U.S. 537 (1895).

to which he or she is assigned by the officer of such railway, said officer shall have power to refuse to carry such passenger on his train, and for such refusal neither he nor the railway company which he represents shall be liable for damages in any of the courts of this State."

The third section provides penalties for the refusal or neglect of the officers, directors, conductors and employés of railway companies to comply with the act, with a proviso that "nothing in this act shall be construed as applying to nurses attending children of the other race." The fourth section is immaterial.

The information filed in the criminal District Court charged in substance that Plessy, being a passenger between two stations within the State of Louisiana, was assigned by officers of the company to the coach used for the race to which he belonged, but he insisted upon going into a coach used by the race to which he did not belong. Neither in the information nor plea was his particular race or color averred.

The petition for the writ of prohibition averred that petitioner was seven eighths Caucasian and one eighth African blood; that the mixture of colored blood was not discernible in him, and that he was entitled to every right, privilege and immunity secured to citizens of the United States of the white race; and that, upon such theory, he took possession of a vacant seat in a coach where passengers of the white race were accommodated, and was ordered by the conductor to vacate said coach and take a seat in another assigned to persons of the colored race, and having refused to comply with such demand he was forcibly ejected with the aid of a police officer, and imprisoned in the parish jail to answer a charge of having violated the above act.

The constitutionality of this act is attacked upon the ground that it conflicts both with the Thirteenth Amendment of the Constitution, abolishing slavery, and the Fourteenth Amendment, which prohibits certain restrictive legislation on the part of the States.

1. That it does not conflict with the Thirteenth Amendment, which abolished slavery and involuntary servitude, except as a punishment for crime, is too clear for argument. Slavery implies involuntary servitude—a state of bondage; the ownership of mankind as a chattel, or at least the control of the labor and services of one man for the benefit of another, and the absence of a legal right to the disposal of his own person, property and services.

. . .

It was intimated, . . . that this amendment was regarded by the statesmen of that day as insufficient to protect the colored race from certain laws which had been enacted in the Southern States, imposing upon the colored race onerous disabilities and burdens, and curtailing their rights in the pursuit of life, liberty and property to such an extent that their freedom was of little value; and that the Fourteenth Amendment was devised to meet this exigency.

So, too, in the *Civil Rights Cases*, 109 U.S. 3, it was said that the act of a mere individual, the owner of an inn, a public conveyance or place of amusement, refusing accommodations to colored people, cannot be justly regarded as imposing any badge of slavery or servitude upon the applicant, but only as involving an ordinary civil injury, properly cognizable by the laws of the State, and presumably subject to redress by those laws until the contrary appears. "It would be running the slavery argument into the ground," said Mr. Justice Bradley, "to make it apply to every act of discrimination which a person may see fit to make as to the guests he will entertain, or as to the people he will take into his coach or cab or car, or admit to his concert or theatre, or deal with in other matters of intercourse or business."

. . .

2. By the Fourteenth Amendment, all persons born or naturalized in the United States, and subject to the jurisdiction thereof, are made citizens of the United States and of the State wherein they reside; and the States are forbidden from making or enforcing any law which shall abridge the privileges or immunities of citizens of the United States, or shall deprive any person of life, liberty or property without due process of law, or deny to any person within their jurisdiction the equal protection of the laws.

. . .

The object of the amendment was undoubtedly to enforce the absolute equality of the two races before the law, but in the nature of things it could not have been intended to abolish distinctions based upon color, or to enforce social, as distinguished from political equality, or a commingling of the two races upon terms unsatisfactory to either. Laws permitting, and even requiring, their separation in places where they are liable to be brought into contact do not necessarily imply the inferiority of either race to the other, and have been generally, if not universally, recognized as within the competency of the state legislatures in the exercise of their police power. The most common instance of this is connected with the establishment of separate schools for white and colored children, which has been held to be a valid exercise of the legislative power even by courts of States where the political rights of the colored race have been longest and most earnestly enforced.

One of the earliest of these cases is that of *Roberts v. City of Boston,* 5 Cush. 198, in which the Supreme Judicial Court of Massachusetts held that the general school committee of Boston had power to make provision for the instruction of colored children in separate schools established exclusively for them, and to prohibit their attendance upon the other schools. "The great principle," said Chief Justice Shaw, p. 206, "advanced by the learned and eloquent advocate for the plaintiff," (Mr. Charles Sumner,) "is, that by the constitution and laws of Massachusetts, all persons without distinction of age or sex, birth or color, origin or condition, are equal before the law. . . . But, when this great principle comes to be applied to the actual and various conditions of persons in society, it will not warrant the assertion, that men and women are legally clothed with the same civil and political powers, and that children and adults are legally to have the same functions and be subject to the same treatment; but only that the rights of all, as they are settled and regulated by law, are equally entitled to the paternal consideration and protection of the law for their maintenance and security." It was held that the powers of the committee extended to the establishment of separate schools for children of different ages, sexes and colors, and that they might also establish special schools for poor and neglected children, who have become too old to attend the primary school, and yet have not acquired the rudiments of learning, to enable them to enter the ordinary schools. Similar laws have been enacted by Congress under its general power of legislation over the District of Columbia, Rev. Stat. D.C. Sections 281, 282, 283, 310, 319, as well as by the legislatures of many of the States, and have been generally, if not uniformly, sustained by the courts.

Laws forbidding the intermarriage of the two races may be said in a technical sense to interfere with the freedom of contract, and yet have been universally recognized as within the police power of the State.

. . .

While we think the enforced separation of the races, as applied to the internal commerce of the State, neither abridges the privileges or immunities of the colored man, deprives him of his property without due process of law, nor denies him the equal protection of the laws, within the meaning of the Fourteenth Amendment, we are not prepared to say that the conductor, in assigning passengers to the coaches according to their race, does not act at his peril, or that the provision of the second section of the act, that denies to the passenger compensation in damages for a refusal to receive him into the coach in which he properly belongs, is a valid exercise of the legislative power. Indeed, we understand it to be conceded by the State's attorney, that such part of the act as exempts from liability the railway company and its officers is unconstitutional. The power to assign to a particular coach obviously implies the power to determine to which race the passenger belongs, as well as the power to determine who, under the laws of the particular State, is to be deemed a white, and who a colored person. This question, though indicated in the brief of the plaintiff in error, does not properly arise upon the unconstitutionality of the act, so far as it requires the railway to provide separate accommodations, and the conductor to assign passengers according to their race.

It is claimed by the plaintiff in error that, in any mixed community, the reputation of belonging to the dominant race, in this instance the white race, is *property*, in the same sense that a right of action, or of inheritance, is property. Conceding this to be so, for the purposes of this case, we are unable to see how this statute deprives him of, or in any way affects his right to, such property. If he be a white man and assigned to a colored coach, he may have his action for damages against the company for being deprived of his so called property. Upon the other hand, if he be a colored man and be so assigned, he has been deprived of no property, since he is not lawfully entitled to the reputation of being a white man.

In this connection, it is also suggested by the learned counsel for the plaintiff in error that the same argument that will justify the state legislature in requiring railways to provide separate accommodations for the two races will also authorize them to require separate cars to be provided for people whose hair is of a certain color, or who are aliens, or who belong to certain nationalities, or to enact laws requiring colored people to walk upon one side of the street, and white people upon the other, or requiring white men's houses to be painted white, and colored men's black, or their vehicles or business signs to be of different colors, upon the theory that one side of the street is as good as the other, or that a house or vehicle of one color is as good as one of another color. The reply to all this is that every exercise of the police power must be reasonable, and extend only to such laws as are enacted in good faith for the promotion of the public good, and not for the annoyance or oppression of a particular class.

.   .   .

So far, then, as a conflict with the Fourteenth Amendment is concerned, the case reduces itself to the question whether the statute of Louisiana is a reasonable regulation, and with respect to this there must necessarily be a large discretion on the part of the legislature. In determining the question of reasonableness it is at liberty to act with reference to the established usages, customs and traditions of the people, and with a view to the promotion of their comfort, and the preservation of the public peace and good order. Gauged by this standard, we cannot say that a law which authorizes or even requires the separation of the two races in public conveyances is unreasonable, or more obnoxious to the Fourteenth Amendment than the acts of Congress requiring separate schools for colored children in the District of Columbia, the constitutionality of which does not seem to have been questioned, or the corresponding acts of state legislatures.

We consider the underlying fallacy of the plaintiff's argument to consist in the assumption that the enforced separation of the two races stamps the colored race with a badge of inferiority. If this be so, it is not by reason of anything found in the act, but solely because the colored race chooses to put that construction upon it. The argument necessarily assumes that if, as has been more than once the case, and is not unlikely to be so again, the colored race should become the dominant power in the state legislature, and should enact a law in precisely similar terms, it would thereby relegate the white race to an inferior position. We imagine that the white race, at least, would not acquiesce in this assumption. The argument also assumes that social prejudices may be overcome by legislation, and that equal rights cannot be secured to the negro except by an enforced commingling of the two races. We cannot accept this proposition. If the two races are to meet upon terms of social equality, it must be the result of natural affinities, a mutual appreciation of each other's merits and a voluntary consent of individuals. As was said by the Court of Appeals of New York in *People v. Gallagher*, 93 N.Y. 438, 448, this end can neither be accomplished nor promoted by laws which conflict with the general sentiment of the community upon whom they are designed to operate. When the government, therefore, has secured to each of its citizens equal rights before the law and equal opportunities for improvement and progress, it has accomplished the end for which it was organized and performed all of the functions respecting social advantages with which it is endowed." Legislation is powerless to eradicate racial instincts or to abolish distinctions based upon physcal differences, and the attempt to do so can only result in accentuating the difficulties of the present situation. If the civil and political rights of both races be equal one cannot be inferior to the other civilly or politically. If one race be inferior to the other socially, the Constitution of the United States cannot put them upon the same plane.

It is true that the question of the proportion of colored blood necessary to constitute a colored person, as distinguished from a white person, is one upon which there is a difference of opinion in the different States, some holding that any visible admixture of black blood stamps the person as belonging to the colored race; others that it depends upon the preponderance of blood; and still others that the predominance of white blood must only be in the proportion of three fourths. But these are questions to be determined under the laws of each State and are not properly put in issue in this case. Under the allegations of his petition, it may undoubtedly become a question of importance whether, under the law of Louisiana, the petitioner belongs to the white or colored race.

The judgment of the court below is, therefore, *Affirmed.*

7. PLESSY v. FERGUSON
Justice Harlan dissenting

By the Louisiana statute, the validity of which is here involved, all railway companies (other than street railroad companies) carrying passengers in that State are required to have separate but equal accommodations for white and colored persons, "by providing two or more passenger coaches for each passenger train, *or* by dividing the passenger coaches by a *partition* so as to secure separate accommodations." Under this statute, nor colored person is permitted to occupy a seat in a coach assigned to white persons; nor any white person, to occupy a seat in a coach assigned to colored persons. The managers of the railroad are not allowed to exercise any discretion in the premises, but are required to assign each passenger to some coach or compartment set apart for the exclusive use of his race. If a passenger insists upon going into a coach or compartment not set apart for persons of his race, he is subject to be fined, or to be imprisoned in the parish jail. Penalties are prescribed for the refusal or neglect of the officers, directors, conductors and employés of railroad companies to comply with the provisions of the act.

Only "nurses attending children of the other race" are excepted from the operation of the statute. No exception is made of colored attendants travelling with adults. A white man is not permitted to have his colored servant with him in the same coach, even if his condition of health requires the constant, personal assistance of such servant. If a colored maid insists upon riding in the same coach with a white woman whom she has been employed to serve, and who may need her personal attention while travelling, she is subject to be fined or imprisoned for such an exhibition of zeal in the discharge of duty.

While there may be in Louisiana persons of different races who are not citizens of the United States, the words in the act, "white and colored races," necessarily include all citizens of the United States of both races residing in that State. So that we have before us a state enactment that compels, under penalties, the separation of the two races in railroad passenger coahes, and makes it a crime for a citizen of either race to enter a coach that has been assigned to citizens of the other race.

Thus the State regulates the use of a public highway by citizens of the United States solely upon the basis of race.

. . .

Plessy *v.* Ferguson, 163 U.S. 537 (1895).

The Thirteenth Amendment does not permit the withholding or the deprivation of any right necessarily inhering in freedom. It not only struck down the institution of slavery as previously existing in the United States, but it prevents the imposition of any burdens or disabilities that constitute badges of slavery or servitude. It decreed universal civil freedom in this country. This court has so adjudged. But that amendment having been found inadequate to the protection of the rights of those who had been in slavery, it was followed by the Fourteenth Amendment, which added greatly to the dignity and glory of American citizenship, and to the security of personal liberty, by declaring that "all persons born or naturalized in the United States, and subject to the jurisdiction thereof, are citizens of the United States and of the State wherein they reside," and that "no State shall make or enforce any law which shall abridge the privileges or immunities of citizens of the United States; nor shall any State deprive any person of life, liberty or property without due process of law, nor deny to any person within its jurisdiction the equal protection of the laws." These two amendments, if enforced according to their true intent and meaning, will protect all the civil rights that pertain to freedom and citizenship. Finally, and to the end that no citizen should be denied, on account of his race, the privilege of participating in the political control of his country, it was declared by the Fifteenth Amendment that "the right of citizens of the United States to vote shall not be denied or abridged by the United States or by any State on account of race, color or previous condition of servitude."

These notable additions to the fundamental law were welcomed by the friends of liberty throughout the world. They removed the race line from our governmental systems. They had, as this court has said, a common purpose, namely, to secure "to a race recently emancipated, a race that through many generations have been held in slavery, all the civil rights that the superior race enjoy." They declared, in legal effect, this court has further said, "that the law in the States shall be the same for the black as for the white; that all persons, whether colored or white, shall stand equal before the laws of the States, and, in regard to the colored race, for whose protection the amendment was primarily designed, that no discrimination shall be made against them by law because of their color."

. . .

It was said in argument that the statute of Louisiana does not discriminate against either race, but prescribes a rule applicable alike to white and colored citizens. But this argument does not meet the difficulty. Every one knows that the statute in question had its origin in the purpose, not so much to exclude white persons from railroad cars occupied by blacks, as to exclude colored people from coaches occupied by or assigned to white persons. Railroad corporations of Louisiana did not make discrimination among whites in the matter of accommodation for travellers. The thing to accomplish was, under the guise of giving equal accommodation for whites and blacks, to compel the latter to keep to themselves while travelling in railroad passenger coaches. No one would be so wanting in candor as to assert the contrary. The fundamental objection, therefore, to the statute is that it interferes with the personal freedom of citizens. "Personal liberty," it has been well said, "consists in the power of locomotion, of changing situation, or removing one's person to whatsoever places one's own inclination may direct, without imprisonment or restraint, unless by due course of law." If a white man and a black man choose to occupy the same public conveyance on a public highway, it is their right to do so, and no government, proceeding alone on grounds of race, can prevent it without infringing the personal liberty of each.

· · ·

In my opinion, the judgment this day rendered will, in time, prove to be quite as pernicious as the decision made by this tribunal in the *Dred Scott case.* It was adjudged in that case that the descendants of Africans who were imported into this country and sold as slaves were not included nor intended to be included under the word "citizens" in the Constitution, and could not claim any of the rights and privileges which that instrument provided for and secured to citizens of the United States; that at the time of the adoption of the Constitution they were "considered as a subordinate and inferior class of beings, who had been subjugated by the dominant race, and, whether emancipated or not, yet remained subject to their authority, and had no rights or privileges but such as those who held the power and the government might choose to grant them." The recent amendments of the Constitution, it was supposed, had eradicated these principles from our institutions. But it seems that we have yet, in some of the States, a dominant race—a superior class of citizens, which assumes to regulate the enjoyment of civil rights, common to all citizens, upon the basis of race. . . .

The arbitrary separation of citizens, on the basis of race, while they are on a public highway, is a badge of servitude wholly inconsistent with the civil freedom and the equality before the law established by the Constitution. It cannot be justified upon any legal grounds.

· · ·

For the reasons stated, I am constrained to withhold my assent from the opinion and judgment of the majority.

8. COLLECTIVE NEGOTIATIONS
AND PROFESSIONALISM
Donald L. Conrad

In considering the applicability of traditional collective bargaining to the public school environment, a variety of important factors must be examined. My task will be to consider the educator apart from (as much as this is possible) other significant features in this environment. Insofar as negotiation is concerned, the teacher must be thought of as possessing three identities. Public school teachers are *employees*. They are *public* employees. And they are *professional* public employees. . . .

We will want to search out the effect of forms of joint participation on the objectives expressed by professional organizations and on the methods used by professions to achieve these objectives.

Professional Role Defined

. . . Though many traditional stereotypes fail to meaningfully define the professional role, there are some landmarks that can be located and described. Professor Barber, writing in *The Professions in America*,[1] said:

> Professional behavior may be defined in terms of four essential attributes: a high degree of generalized and systematic knowledge; primary orientation to the community interest rather than to individual self-interest; a high degree of self-control of behavior through codes of ethics internalized in the process of work socialization and through voluntary associations organized and operated by the work specialists themselves; and a system of rewards (monetary and honorary) that is primarily a set of symbols of work achievement and thus ends in themselves, not means to some end of individual self-interest. . . .

The difficulty (if not the impossibility) of the layman's evaluating the quality of professional expertness appears to be a particularly central

[1] Bernard Barber, "Some Problems in the Sociology of the Profession," in K. S. Lynn, *The Professions in America* (Boston, Mass.: Houghton-Mifflin Co., 1965).

characteristic. As a result of this, the client has little choice but to put himself in the hands of the practitioner. The necessary buyer trust is contrasted sharply with the more familiar *caveat emptor*. Actions that tend to interfere with the trust relationship tend also to limit severely any gains that might have accrued from the application of professional skill. The professional is obligated to exercise no less care in the client interest than in dealing with his own affairs. He must not only generally behave in an honest and upright manner; just as important, he must be believed to be scrupulous by clients, colleagues, and by the public. The professional practitioner is no special kind of paragon, but his code of ethics demands behavior from him that will generally support a trust relationship. A flagrant disregard for the mandates of the code could result in professional discipline from one's colleagues. . . .

The services of the physician, the lawyer, the teacher, the scientist, the engineer, the architect, the dentist, the accountant, the journalist, and the psychologist—to mention some—have never been more valued and valuable than they are today. Accommodation and variation are the key themes. In some cases the professional services go through a kind of selective modification, and in others variation occurs in the work environment. Both have shown themselves capable of change without damage to their basic operational requirements. Though the professions vary greatly (as do individual professionals) in terms of any absolute standard of professionhood, the qualities of colleague control and freedom to apply expertness are absolutely essential.

Creative Negotiation

Just as some would adopt unrealistic stereotypes of an absolute and unmodified professional, others would apply this same thinking approach to collective negotiation or collective bargaining. Some would insist that the negotiatory relationship must mean an adversary struggle, much name calling, a kind of count-down atmosphere, and an aggressive economic warfare between the manager and the managed. The mass media tend to focus our attention on the drama and sham of bargaining, of the strike and lockout, of the apparently unrestricted profit seeking of the major unions and associations in both private and public employment. But public attention has been called to observe the "freak relationship" rather than the much less spectacular day-to-day relationships in our economy that are producing growing stability and increasing productivity. In the science of economics, negotiation has shown that it can be applied to a great variety of work environments with successful results and that it is not only a means for the reconciliation of differences between employer and employee but also a valuable method of advancing common objectives. For optimal results in agreement reaching, collective bargaining techiques must be freely adaptable as the work environment changes and as the techniques are introduced into wholly new and different environments.

In the private sector of the economy, where we see negotiation most fully utilized, the following important changes are being instituted: [1]

1. Much greater use of continuous negotiation rather than deadline bargaining.

2. Joint desire to seek answers to the needs of the industry and the needs of the organized employees through research and expert investigation, rather than through "out-of-this-world" demands, subterfuge, and a double set of books.

3. A mature and mutual realization that each is important to the other. The new manager doesn't see the employee organization as a threat to his management but as an irreplaceable asset.

4. Employees and unions are more disposed to agonize over peaceable solutions to a bargaining impasse rather than taking the "easy way" to the strike. They see this not only as mutually advantageous, but also essential (not just incidentally) in the public interest.

Resulting from Presidential Executive Order 10988, the federal government has introduced an additional set of innovations of interest to all professionals and particularly of interest to educator professionals.[2] Some of these social inventions will undergo further modification, while it is certain that others will be included into our general concepts of the body of collective negotiation. . . .

The creative forms that negotiation has incorporated in recent years makes it a more adaptable instrument in the environments that utilize its techniques. It also permits a reasonable assumption that it can be adapted to new employment environments in the coming years with greater growth in its versatility and with benefit to the new environment.

Professional Educators Negotiate

The local control of public schools presents at least one asset in terms of professional negotiation. It would appear that we are going to

---

[1] James J. Healy, Ed., *Creative Collective Bargaining* (Englewood Cliffs, N.J.: Prentice-Hall, Inc., 1965).

[2] U.S. Department of Labor, Report of the President's Task Force on Employee-Management Relations in the Federal Service, *A Policy for Employee-Management Cooperation in the Federal Service* (Washington, D.C.: Government Printing Office, 1961).

be able to observe the life cycle of a very large number of experimental animals. Each of the half-dozen or more states that has legislated in this area has incorporated many novel features. And in states with an absence of legislative formula, individual school districts are experimenting with still greater diversity.

What criteria should we advance in answer to the question, "Can professional educators negotiate with boards of education without loss or weakening of essential professionalization?" The usual criteria that are suggested in a general employment environment are: (1) strong community of interest; (2) common skills; (3) shared working conditions, supervision, and physical location; and (4) similarity of authority structure.

These must be supplemented with regard to the special demands of the professional environment. We would have to additionally ask: (1) Does the negotiation relationship limit the freedom of the professional to make decisions in the client's interest? (2) Does it distort the specialized expertness that the professional brings to his work? (3) Is bargaining incompatible with serving the public good—does it mean a selfish serving of collective egotism?

I feel that we can safely reject the assertion that the strike is an obligatory feature of collective bargaining. Other power alternatives are being utilized in federal service and in public schools to give us reason to believe that this means of resolving impasse, or more frequently this means of reserved deterrence, need be resorted to in only the most refractory circumstances and as a last resort.

Other critics of professional negotiation insist that the bargaining relationship is a union weapon and therefore incompatible with professionalism.[3] Without entering into the controversy of the ethical propriety of professionals joining unions affiliated with the AFL-CIO versus joining organizations of a clearly independent nature,[4] let it be stated that negotiation is a social invention that resides in the public domain. It is an ancient and noble technique for agreement-reaching used in diplomatic circles, in legislative activity, and of course widely in the marketplace.

Not only have teachers at all levels shown a marked reluctance to become involved in meaningful collective action,[5] many would take the position that collective action is patently unprofessional. Implied in this position is an unstated approval of individual bargaining but a rejection

[3] P. L. Alger, N. A. Christensen, and S. P. Olmsted, *Ethical Problems in Engineering* (New York: John Wiley and Sons, Inc., 1965).

[4] Office of Professional Development and Welfare, *Guidelines for Professional Negotiation* (Washington, D.C.: National Education Association, 1965).

[5] Myron Lieberman, *Education as a Profession* (Englewood Cliffs, N.J.: Prentice-Hall, Inc., 1956).

of collective negotiations. This opinion is just plain irrational. An individual can be a vegetarian, but an individual as an individual can not be a professional. He becomes a professional as he joins with others of similar disposition to form a collectivity that asserts: control over admission to practice, the direction of pre-professional education, and jurisdiction in the expulsion of the unscrupulous. A profession cannot hope to meet its role demands unless it is prepared, through strong internal organization and through public sanction, to assure the control of the profession over whom it shall count as a colleague.

Many educators are disturbed about solutions growing out of a bargaining relationship because this method of solution-seeking is so different from what might be the more familiar scientific method. To think of negotiating a person's body temperature, the distance to the moon, or the amount of mineral in a soil analysis is just ludicrous. But problems that the education profession faces cannot all be approached in a coldly scientific manner. We don't have objective answers to questions like: What is a teacher worth? How long should the school day be? What text supplements should be chosen? How much tax load should people properly assume? Questions of this sort require the utilization of the democratic processes of involvement and participation by those who can contribute meaningfully, and of accommodation and compromise with the purpose of discovering a consensus that can be successfully implemented.

Educators can enter into employment negotiation relationships without danger to their professional status. Negotiatory associations should properly be understood as a neutral operational feature in the functioning of employed professionals. To negotiate or not to negotiate is the wrong question. The question that must be asked and answered is, "How can negotiation techniques be best utilized to improve public education?"

PEDAGOGICAL MODEL:
The Teacher as Professional

1. "PUBLIC AND PROFESSIONAL DECISIONS"
Myron Lieberman

Professional Autonomy Is Not Undemocratic

Quite frequently, the supporters of professional autonomy in education are thought to be persons who have an authoritarian bent. Be this as it may, there is nothing undemocratic in the proposal that teachers and not school boards should decide the subjects to be taught. However, the reasons why people think the proposal is undemocratic are not difficult to understand. The relevant cliché here is that the public should determine what should be taught, and the teachers should determine how to teach whatever it is that the public wants taught. Like most educational clichés, this one has just enough plausibility to stay alive despite the abuses to which it leads.

The crux of the matter lies in the words "what" and "how." The public determines *what* to teach in the sense that it sets the broad purposes of education. The fallacy lies in regarding the *what* as a list of subjects instead of a set of purposes. "Teachers should teach students to communicate effectively" is one thing. "Teachers should teach penmanship one hour per day in the sixth grade" is something else again. The first statement is one of purpose, which should be made by the public; the second is a statement of the means to be employed and should never be legislated by a non-professional agency.

At any time, research may justify changes in the time devoted to a subject or the grade levels at which it is taught. This is why it is foolish for a state legislature to prescribe the curriculum. It is like legislating that drug X must always be employed to cure a certain illness. Imagine the predicament that doctors would be in if they had to have a

From Myron Lieberman, *The Future of Public Education* (Chicago, Ill.: The University of Chicago Press, 1960), pp. 62–70. Copyright © 1960, The University of Chicago Press. Reprinted by permission of Phoenix Books.

new law passed every time they wished to employ a new and better drug for this illness.

The other side of this coin is the confusion over *how* in "how to teach." If people were clear that the public should determine the broad purposes of education, then it would be understood that "how to teach" refers to subjects as well as teaching methods. When we say that a doctor knows how to cure, we do not mean to limit the *how* to a bedside manner. We mean it to include the substantive knowledge which the doctor applies to achieve a desired end.

The public expects the medical profession to prolong life and to reduce physical pain. No one in his right mind assumes that the public should decide what drugs should be used and that doctors should decide only how to apply them. Absurd as this would be, it is exactly analogous to the notion that the public should determine the subjects to be taught and teachers should decide how to teach them. "How to teach" should be interpreted to mean "how to achieve the goals set for the profession by the public." It would then be clear that non-professional determination of the curriculum is a threat, not a safeguard, to our democratic institutions.

How does one know what purposes the public has set for education? At the local level, the school board can state what they are. The state legislatures can do this at the state level. There is no inherent reason why Congress cannot and should not do this at the national level. In fact, we are likely to get a much better statement of purpose from Congress than we are from a local board.

Theoretically, it is possible for the American people to accord the schools a very narrow purpose. Instead of saying that one of the purposes of education is to develop an understanding and appreciation of our democratic heritage, they might say that the purpose of education is to insure that every student can recite the Bill of Rights from memory. We would regard such a statement of purpose as a mistake. Our thought would be that what the people specified as an end (memorizing the Bill of Rights) should have been regarded only as a means to a larger end. Whether memorizing the Bill of Rights is the best means to this end should be left up to the teachers to decide.

Still, it is logically possible that the American people could define the purposes of education in such a way that the curriculum would not be a matter for professional decision. I hope this will not happen, but it remains a possibility. No matter how often it is pointed out that memorizing the Bill of Rights should be regarded as only a means, and not a very effective one at that, people might insist that this is what they want their schools to accomplish above all else.

It should be clear, however, that the danger of having such narrow purposes decreases as we have a larger and larger community set the purpose. In particular localities, people might insist the purpose of education to be the rejection of the theory of evolution, or an understanding of the history of Oklahoma, or an appreciation of the importance of dairy products, to cite only a few things that have been prescribed by state laws. But, at the national level, such narrow purposes would be manifestly unfeasible.

In the abstract, practically everyone agrees that our schools should teach students to think critically in important areas of concern—politics, economics, international affairs, and so on. What subject matters and what teaching methods will develop such critical thinking? You cannot develop critical thinking if the students and teachers cannot criticize anything. Teachers who are serious about developing critical thinking must have the freedom to be critical of points of view learned at home, in the community, at church, and so on.

A teacher who wishes to develop critical thinking in the area of international relations must stimulate students to analyze the concept of sovereignty. I do not say the teacher should persuade students that national sovereignty is outmoded or even that what was good enough for McKinley's day is not good enough for ours. These are conclusions which a student might or might not reach after he has studied the matter. The point is that if the teacher does his job properly, some students may get the idea that national sovereignty is not the unmixed blessing that the local American Legion post makes it out to be.

The development of critical thinking, of an understanding and appreciation of our democratic heritage, of dedication to the truth wherever it may lead—these purposes take precedence over any particular political, economic, racial, religious, or social point of view. This means that in principle no point of view should be above analysis and criticism in the public schools. However, as things stand, teachers do not have the power to act on this principle.

In the long run, we must see to it that non-professional determination of the curriculum is as unthinkable as nonprofessional determination of the techniques of brain surgery. In the short run, the solution is to resist non-professional interference in every way possible while working toward a system in which such interference would be impossible. However, there is no thought that individual teachers should seek martyrdom. The problem is essentially one of institutionalizing professional autonomy rather than leaving it to heroic individual defenders to protect. And it should go without saying that there is a difference between non-professional interference with the curriculum and non-professional advice concerning it. My contention is that teachers should have the power to decide what subjects are to be taught. This does not mean that teachers would be justified in ignoring every suggestion from non-professional sources or in adopting a "To hell with the public" point of view.

If teachers should decide what subjects should be taught, then clearly they should decide what instructional materials should be used in teaching these subjects. The power to determine the choice of instructional materials is in fact the power to determine the subjects. Nevertheless, some people persist in the view that the school board should decide on teaching materials.

The absurdity of having school boards, parents, or citizens' committees evaluate and pass on the fitness of instructional tools is most clearly reflected in controversies over "subversive" materials. It is or ought to be obvious that instructional materials are neither subversive or non-subversive in isolation. The Constitution can be utilized for subversive purposes, just as the *Daily Worker* can be used to expose the nature of the Communist party. . . .

Fundamentally, the confusion between public and professional decisions in education is one aspect of our failure to clarify the role of the expert in a democratic society. As a result of this failure, we count noses to answer questions which should be settled by reference to experts, and we rely upon experts to answer questions which should be settled by counting noses. In education, the first type of mistake is the most prevalent. Public education developed in the United States in the absence of a teaching profession. Teachers simply accepted without question the idea that the community had the right to decide subjects, instructional materials, and methods as well as the broad purposes of education. Teachers often questioned whether the community was exercising its rights wisely, but they never questioned the legitimacy of these rights.

The precarious employment position of public school personnel, especially school administrators, is another important factor contributing to the absence of professional autonomy in education. Superintendents are often hired on a year-to-year basis. Few have contracts running for more than two or three years, and practically none has tenure. This being the case, few superintendents are going to insist upon their professional autonomy when they know that such a stand may cost them their jobs.

What is worse, the exposed position of superintendents inevitably weakens their support for the professional autonomy of teachers. Suppose a teacher uses a textbook which the school board regards as subversive. Since the superintendent has to please the board, not the teachers, to hold his own job, he is not likely to take the attitude that instructional materials are strictly a matter of professional autonomy. He is much more likely to tell the teacher to drop the textbook. This will, of course, be done in the name of democracy. The elected representatives of the people have the right to say what goes on in their schools; if they have said that *Robin Hood* tends to justify stealing from the rich to give to the poor, we must drop *Robin Hood*—or else.

The real tragedy in this situation is that superintendents and teachers accept it as the way things ought to be. Those who submit curriculum proposals to their school boards are not fuming inwardly at their lack of professional autonomy. In their own eyes, they are following the democratic process when they permit, even encourage, school boards to tell them what subjects to teach and what instructional materials to use. Thus a power structure and an ideology which antedates any serious thought of teaching as a profession is precisely what stands in the way of its becoming one today.

Schools of education, and especially their departments of educational administration, have propagated the notion that public school personnel should not make an important change in the curriculum without first securing community support. This counsel is typically labeled a "democratic theory" or a "democratic philosophy" of education. Advocated as it usually is without any conception of professional autonomy, its effect has been to make any insistence upon autonomy appear undemocratic to the teachers themselves. In all seriousness, the damage has been even worse. The concept of professional autonomy has been eliminated from the consciousness of teachers. In effect, the schools of education tell teachers they are "professionals" while simultaneously undermining the independence which is an essential ingredient of professional status.

Much of the opposition to determination of the curriculum by teachers is due to certain misconceptions about the rationale for professional autonomy. First, it should be emphasized that the justification for taking authority over the curriculum away from local boards and giving it to the teachers is not that the teachers are always right or that the school boards are always wrong, even on admittedly professional matters. Professional autonomy does not result in the absence of error but in the reduction of it.

Opponents of professional autonomy often point to particular instances wherein teachers have made indefensible curriculum decisions. Such instances are cited to justify the denial of teacher control over the curriculum. Such reasoning demolishes only the nonexistent position that perfection is the rationale for professional autonomy. It is like saying that laymen should perscribe drugs because doctors make mistakes.

This brings me to a related point. Professional autonomy does not mean the absence of any control over the professional workers. On the contrary, it means that controls requiring technical competence are exercised by persons who possess such competence. To be specific, if the issue is whether a teacher is choosing appropriate instructional materials, the issue should be settled by persons competent to judge this, not by irate parents or American Legion posts or even intelligent and responsible school boards. Professional autonomy, then, does not imply the absence of all controls. On the contrary, it logically calls for the development of a wide range of professional controls. These are often much more rigorous than those exercised by lay boards.

People tend to think that giving professional autonomy to public school teachers is tantamount to turning over public business to private interests. Actually, it amounts to turning over public business to the kind of public employees most likely to conduct it properly. It can safely be stated that more unwarranted inferences have been drawn from the fact that teachers are publicly employed than from any other single fact about public education. Teachers should not control entry to teaching, should not determine the subjects taught or the instructional materials to be used, should not be permitted to bargain collectively, should not have the right to strike, do not need to formulate and enforce a code of professional ethics—the list of *non sequiturs* that invariably follows the "point" that teachers are public employees constitutes a fairly complete catalogue of what's wrong with American education.

When the average citizen thinks of himself as an employer, he tends to think of public servants as a group that should be servile. The public (which is "I") puts up the money, so "I" have the right to tell teachers what to teach. But it is not an unqualified good for employers, public or private, to be able to coerce their employees. Surely, we can learn this much from what is going on in other parts of the world. When the private patient says to his physician: "Restore me to health, but I shall tell you what drugs to use and the dosage," the physician is ethically obligated to withdraw. The reason is that the physician cannot take responsibility for the health of his patient under such circumstances. The same reasoning would apply in the case of a publicly employed physician—he would be obligated to withdraw from employment wherein he had to submit to lay interference in professional matters.

This is the way teachers should regard the matter. If school boards prescribe subjects and teaching materials, the teachers should withdraw as employees on the grounds that it is not in the interest of their client, the public, to permit it to make professional decisions. Teachers cannot accept responsibility for educational outcomes under such circumstances, any more than physicians can accept responsibility for medical outcomes when laymen tell them how to diagnose and what to prescribe for the sick. It is not in the public's interest as an employer to insist upon lay control of professional matters. The teachers have no moral obligation to acquiesce in the actions of any employer, public or private, who violates their professional autonomy; on the contrary, their obligation to the public interest is to resist such action with all their might.

. . .